Essays from
Cradle to Couch

Essays from Cradle to Couch

Essays in Honor of the Psychoanalytic Developmental Psychology of Sylvia Brody

Edited by

Burton N. Seitler
Kim S. Kleinman

IPBOOKS.net
International Psychoanalytic Books

Cover Design by Ronald Seitler, MFA.
Interior book design by Maureen Cutajar, gopublished.com

ISBN: 978-0-9980833-3-9

Acknowledgements

Many people contributed to the making of this book, some in less visible, but nonetheless essential and invaluable ways. Initially, the idea for this book came out of the fertile mind of Dr. Arnold Richards, who rightly felt that the important work of Dr. Sylvia Brody, who is now over 100 years young, needed to be more widely recognized. The Editors are grateful to him for approaching us with his brainchild, for having faith that we could gather some of the top people in the field, and that we could assemble a body of work worthy of Dr. Brody's own amazing contributions spanning several decades to the field of infant, child, and adolescent psychoanalysis. We are grateful as well, to our publishers, *International Psychoanalysis Books* for supporting this project.

My wish—as I was going through various developmental phases of my own—was to make my parents, Irving and Shirley Seitler, proud of me. Even now, after all this time, I still miss you and hope that wherever you are, I have been able (however imperfectly) to live up to your unwavering belief in me.

On a further personal note, I wish to thank my wife, Jeanne, for her steadfast dedication to helping me achieve my dreams. She continues to be my inspirational muse, as well as my friend. My children, Kim Roma and Dana Seitler-Schmitt are reminders to me of how important it is to appreciate the crucial role of child development over the entire life cycle. I am so proud of how they turned out (whether because of, or in spite of me). They are caring, warm, sensitive human beings, and the wonderful parents of Gabrielle and Cassidy (Kim and Michael's) and Beckett and

Dylan, (Dana and Cannon's kids) respectively. Who could want for more?

My brother, Ron, has always been there for me. And, when I asked for his specialized help—in the form of artwork, he answered without hesitation. He created the wonderful cover design for this book, which has been getting a great deal of positive attention and accolades, even before the book has officially gone to press. Thank you Ron, once again.

My final word, I reserve for my Co-Editor, Kim S. Kleinman, who has been a wonderful partner-in-crime collaborator. She has struck the perfect balance of taking on things with which I struggle, and allowing me to step in and perform those tasks that are not her forte, all this in a sensitive, very intuitive and seamless way. Together, we have managed to assemble a volume of research about which we ourselves are very excited and which we believe our readers will enjoy as well. BNS

Children in each generation are obsessed with how *things* like newborn siblings come into being, and yet each generation of parents struggles to answer such questions. Describing how this book came about is easier. First is the inspiration of Sylvia Brody. Her clarity and intellectual rigor has been a beacon to us. Next is Arnold Richards and the people at IP Books whose generosity in asking Dr. Seitler and myself to edit this book has provided us the opportunity to collate the work of some of the brightest stars in the infant, child and adolescent professional universe. We of course have to thank the authors who contributed the chapters in this book. Each one walked across the invisible lines that divide the various points of view in psychoanalysis to contribute their unique voice and their brilliant perspectives.

I want to thank my husband Thomas Portzline, and my son, Alexander Kleinman. You both provide the wind in my sails that makes my work go and my life a pleasure.

I also have been delighted to work with my co-editor Burton Seitler. My apprehension about being a first time editor disappeared after our first conversation. Your appreciation of my contribution to this work has made the process a joy.

—Kim S. Kleinman

Table of Contents

Introduction

From Cradle to Couch: Essays in Honor of the Psychoanalytic Developmental Psychology of Sylvia Brody is a compilation of select papers written by distinguished authorities in the field that are specifically dedicated to the important and extensive body of work of Dr. Sylvia Brody with regard to the fields of infant, child, adolescent, developmental psychology and psychoanalysis.

So extensive and far-reaching have her longitudinal investigations been that more and more research studies are now being done with infants, children and adolescents. Moreover, as a result of her dedication over many decades, there is a greater awareness and emphasis *worldwide* of the critical importance of understanding normal child developmental processes and of recognizing the circumstances that interfere with a child's emotional and physical growth, as well as appreciating and fostering the intrapsychic, interpersonal, and social/cultural conditions necessary for children to thrive. But that is not where her contributions end. Dr. Brody has also supplied us with psychoanalytic and psychodynamic methods by which children whose early development was less than optimal, and where normal development was detoured or otherwise impeded, can be helped.

In the following pages, the editors have gathered together an anthology of fine papers which examine children from this country and abroad; manuscripts that in one way or another—either explicitly or implicitly—have been influenced by the trailblazing work of Dr. Sylvia Brody and the tradition she set for carrying out research and using her findings as her primary basis for many of the innovative therapeutic practices she helped to establish.

For the reader who is somehow unfamiliar with Dr. Brody's work, a cursory review of a mere smattering of her publications ought to be sufficient to provide at least a sense of her pioneering labors, and ultimately, what turns out to be, her prescience:

- Beginning to Grow: Five Studies.
- Patterns of Mother: A Study of Maternal Influence During Infancy
- Mothers, Fathers, and Children: Explorations in the Formation of Character in the First 7 Years
- The Component Instincts: Their Emergence in Infancy and Early Childhood
- The Evolution of Character: Birth to 18 Years
- The Development of Anorexia Nervosa
- Anxiety and Ego Formation in Infancy
- Determinants of Infant Behavior

In addition to the partial listing of the books cited above, she has written countless articles, all of which are as topical today as when they were first published. For example:

- Contributions to psychoanalysis.
- The son of a refugee.
- Some aspects of transference resistance in pre-puberty.
- The techniques of child analysis: Discussions with Anna Freud, Joseph Sandler, and Robert L. Tyson.
- Overcoming the odds: High-risk children from birth to adulthood.
- Psychoanalytic Theories of infant development and its disturbances: A Critical evaluation.
- Transitional objects: Idealization of a phenomenon.
- Early phases in the development of object relations
- Anxiety, socialization, and ego formation in infancy

- The concepts of attachment and bonding
- Self-rocking in infancy.
- And a host of other articles, lectures, interviews, and correspondence.

While it is most certainly true that knowledge mainly proceeds from qualitative to quantitative, that is—from curiosity and inquisitiveness, to detailed descriptions, to measurable magnitudes, to potentially generalizable predictions, Dr. Brody utilized a combination of both approaches to more fully understand the inner workings of humans, starting from infancy (or even earlier) on to adulthood. Accordingly, the chapters in this book reflect our respect for Dr. Sylvia Brody's long-standing commitment to quantitative materials, built as they were on top of detailed qualitative descriptions by which we too, as clinicians, can be guided in our work with infants, children, and adolescents. The chapters have been arranged in accordance with the following rationale: Since Dr. Brody emphasized the formative influences and thus importance of attitudes, unconscious feelings, and parental practices on children, we begin by tracing the history of theoretical formulations with regard to parenting. Following this schema, we then move to quantitative studies, descriptions of the use of psychoanalytic understandings and applications to community work, work with those who have been disadvantaged, dispossessed, or outright dismissed by society. We then harken back to a highly comprehensive, sometimes intensely personal, and consistently detailed examination of individual cases.

In Chapter 1, entitled, *Psychoanalysis and Child- Rearing*, Kerry Kelly Novick and Jack Novick provide an historical overview of early, single-track theoretical positions related to parenting, which they indicate, sharply contrasts with their dual track formulations. The Novick's have contributed a paper that synthesizes metapsychological questions regarding omnipotence and grandiosity, both of which are of great importance to psychoanalytic theory-building. They further trace the trajectory of using shame and fear as ubiquitous techniques in Freud's day, to the failed "liberation" philosophy that was based on misguided applications of early psychoanalytic theoretical understandings, and point out that children do not benefit from being raised in an indulgent "Eden." Rather, they fare much better from the pleasure derived from developing competency and inner sturdiness.

In 1945, Sylvia Brody was noted to have lamented, back then, that she barely had a glimmering amount of knowledge of the preeminence of infancy and expressed the wish to have observed infants at much more frequent intervals than she did. Our current cadre of baby watchers confirm Brody's conviction of the importance of infancy.

This is born out by Beatrice Beebe's extraordinary powers of observation in Chapter 2 entitled, *How Mother-Infant Research Informs Mother-Infant Treatment*, in which she used microanalysis to depict and put words to describing the difficulties, yet pivotal significance of observing babies up-close, in slow-motion, and over time. Beebe reviews our field's newly acquired understanding of the predominant roles and relationship of gaze, vocalization, and self-regulation in babies, and how these understandings have the potential to be used as scaffolding necessary for therapists who are trying to help mothers really see and interact with their babies.

In Chapter 3, *Playing in the Intersubjective Spaces*, Laurel Silber gives us the benefit of her profound insights and sensitive discussion of the importance of an attuned interactive relational reworking through play. She describes how the previous weight that had been afforded to verbal interpretation of repressed unconscious material has shifted away from that position and now emphasizes the co- (or even tri-) construction of an emergent intersubjective psychotherapy treatment space. This conceptualization says Silber, allows for unformulated or dissociated experience, associated with the transmission of intergenerational trauma, to become known and "thought about" through play and enactment in the safety of the therapy relationship.

Eva Rotenberg, contributes a compelling voice from Latin America in her Chapter 4 monograph, *The "True Self" Parental Function, the Basis of Ego Integration*. She offers us her conceptually rich recognition and elucidation of the singular significance of subjectivity—which Beebe and Silber also describe, both in terms of metapsychology and empirical observation. She brings up the function of the parent and the effect on the mind and body of the child if s/he does not receive recognition of his/her subjectivity.

Monisha Akhtar and Sumedha Ariely produced an exceptionally comprehensive Chapter 5, entitled, *Attachment and Context: Evolving Perspectives in a Clinical Realm*. They have produced research that demonstrates a high degree of scholarship as well deep sensitivity to and understanding of the children that they observed. They take us on an expedition into the exotic regions of South Asia, where, using the prism of attachment theory they view children who have been orphaned and wonder how this set of extraordinary conditions effects their level of attachment. They note that attachment theories are fairly robust and universal in many, but not all ways, and they stipulate some of the ways in which children raised away from primary caregivers, namely, their parents, are effected. The authors' careful research explores the needs of children who are in orphanages. This chapter is a crucial reminder that, as much we do know about attachment, there is a great deal more that is unknown. In fact, Akhtar and Ariely's work resulted in more than a few unexpected findings concerning who children chose as their primary attachment figures. Their extensive work cautions us that while we have discovered a considerable amount of knowledge about infant attachment, we cannot assume that we know everything about the fate of attachment as development proceeds, and that we need to be quite careful about making assumptions based upon applying our norms to other cultures.

Phyllis Ackman, in Chapter 6, brings to bear an important and often unaddressed consideration in her manuscript entitled, *Helping the Helpers: Consultation to Childcare Staff Using Psychoanalytically Informed Concepts*. Ackman explores the development of cross-cultural communication skills; Mexican culture, medical culture, class/education/ and language barriers. Her paper's main focus is on developing ways to foster and enrich the observational skills and subsequent practices of Child Care workers so that they, in turn, would be able to develop intervention strategies that are based upon sound psychodynamic principles, such as (but not limited to) an understanding of intersubjectivity, for mothers to utilize with their respective children. In short, as the Child Care workers became more astute in their observations of the mother-child dyad and were able to sensitively communicate what they had seen, taking into account the perspective of "the third or the other," the mother-child dynamic was notably enhanced and demonstrably improved.

In Chapter 7, we are greeted by the compassionate work of Ann Smolen's, *Mothering Without a Home: A Psychoanalytically-Informed Approach*. She observes the sad fact that, of the homeless population, mothers with young children comprise the fastest growing subdivision. This is particularly troubling because mothers without a home are unable to offer their children the normal requisites of being provider, comforter, and protector. And, because mothers in such a predicament are preoccupied with the ongoing rigors of daily survival, their children often feel overwhelmed by her (and now, their) plight. Dr. Smolen was able to form a strong therapeutic alliance with these mothers by learning about and attuning to their pain. In so doing, she was able to help them disentangle their own affects from their babies' which ultimately helped reduce, or even prevent their children from inheriting their mothers' traumatic projections and destructive projective identifications.

Joseph Schaller adds his own empathic component to working with and creating a heart-felt space for those individuals who easily could have been disenfranchised by society. In Chapter 8, entitled, *Relational Hope: Foster Care and a Home Within,* a program which was the early brain-child of San Franciscan, Toni Heineman, Dr. Schaller describes how he and his like-minded, similarly idealistic associates, adapted Heineman's Home Within program and created one of their own, one that was designed to fit in with and try to meet the emotional needs of foster children in the greater Philadelphia area. In poignant detail, he vividly portrays their trauma, and the deleterious effects of continuous interference with and disruption of close interpersonal bonds, and ways in which trust and essential human connections were effected. In this chapter, the reader is the beneficiary of the author's hard-fought, well-earned insights, which he derived from his roll-up-your-sleeves, into the trenches hard-work, which, as we can see was worth much more than the noble high-mindedness that may have been the initial motivation for actively engaging in such an important undertaking. We are indebted to Dr. Schaller both for his work as well for sharing with us what he learned from his experiences.

We continue the thread of the significance and importance of the mother-child dyad in Martin Silverman's Chapter 9, entitled, *Behavior Disorders Stemming from Disturbed Mother-Baby Experiences and their Repair through Joint Work with a Mother and Her Young Child.*

In this chapter, Dr. Silverman cites several clinical case examples of the emotional effect and behavioral reaction of children after having been separated from their mothers early on. In one extreme instance, a mother developed tuberculosis just after her son, Andy, was born and was not allowed to embrace or have direct contact with him in any way. Her only means of relating to him was through a glass window. The extent of Andy's mother's anguish is clearly seen in the following agonizing quote which pretty much says it all: "*I couldn't hold him.*" *I couldn't touch him. I couldn't kiss him. I couldn't smell him. We never bonded!*" Dr. Silverman recreates for us the path that he blazed that eventually led Andy and his mother to a position where they could engage with and ultimately relate to one another in a new and reparative way.

In another instance, he describes his work with an adopted child, named David. Quite often, adopted children are at high risk for emotional problems. Therefore, it is not unusual for children who have been adopted, even when it was right at the time of birth, to "act out" in some fashion. With girls, we often see signs of depression while in boys, its typical overt manifestation is in the form of aggression. And that certainly was the case with David, who was highly sensitive and reactive to even the slightest potential threat of loss (remote as it might have been in reality). Because of this, secure attachment, so vital for a child to experience in order to thrive, was simultaneously dangerous because of the prospect of abandonment. Dr. Silverman describes how he utilized his skills and knowledge of child development and psychoanalysis, as well as his own personal sensitivity and warmth, to help this youngster overcome anxiety, sadness, and angry eruptions whenever he perceived the specter of abandonment on the horizon.

In Chapter 10, Corinne Masur enlarges upon the age and maturationally-linked scope and focus of this book in her discussion of *The Effect on Children when the Attachment to the Mother is Broken: A Developmental Overview.* Her chapter represents a comprehensive consideration of questions regarding what happens when children suffer a loss of their mothers at specific developmental stages. Common belief has long held that the younger the child is the less s/he will be effected by events, such as the loss of the mother, that would typically be considered to be traumatic for older individuals. After all, it has been suggested that children are too young to remember such adverse events. While that question is still being debated, Dr. Masur provides us with an extensive review of the psychoanalytic literature (including her own research contributions) which casts considerable doubt on the previous assumption. Not only does her writing indicate that children are deeply effected by the loss of such an important figure, but she points out that the extent of the impact of loss of the mother is directly related to several central factors—the phase of the child's development at the time of the loss, the ability of adults to find ways to help the child learn to grieve and mourn, how the father and/or other significant caretakers tend to the child who has undergone the loss, as well as number of other important circumstances.

In Chapter 11, Rosa Spagnolo, has contributed an important examination of the arts (specifically, music), an often neglected subject area, in relation to expanding the repertoire of psychodynamic approaches to treatment, as well as theory-building. Her piece is entitled, *An Unexpected Pathway for Interpsychic Exchange: Music in the Analysis of a Young Adult*. In this chapter, Dr. Spagnolo resorted to an extraordinarily creative solution to working with a 20-year old whose mind was closed-off to "therapy (and relationships) as usual." Her approach to this young man, who was rapidly descending down the path of renunciation of and departure from reality leading to a psychotic withdrawal, was a veritable synesthesia of music, melody, the rhythms inherent in the musicality of speech and relating, which she observed to be generated by the interpsychic, emerging out of the context of a deep psychoanalytic psychotherapeutic working relationship with this particularly unique patient. By recognizing that music can speak for the self by acting as an auxiliary ego, she insightfully observed that typically incomprehensible, and thus, overwhelming feelings may be better tolerated. Accordingly, she was able to act as her patient's interlocutor, container, and holder of unbearable affect. He, in turn, through the medium—and safety—

afforded him by her employment of the musical meme that they eventually came to share, was now able to speak the unspeakable, and confront the previously unopposable feelings of despair and his dreaded, much anticipated obliteration of the self. Much like the attuned (interesting word) mother, who is caringly attentive to her infant's unverbalized needs, Dr. Spagnolo adjusted her approach to her patient's intra-psychic rhythms, both unspoken and subsequently acknowledged through the mutuality of their inter-psychic exchange.

The title of Chapter 12 is *The Emergence of the Speaking Subject: Child Therapy and the Subject of Desire.* It features the clinical work of Michael O'Loughlin, who allows the reader into his home, his head, and his heart in a very personal set of disclosures, which are nonetheless unquestionably professionally presented. We see that Dr. O'Loughlin has come a long way from his childhood privation and physically imperiled roots, yet he neither forgets his humble beginnings nor ignores the lessons that he gleaned from them, lessons of empathic attunement, tenderness and using oneself to understand the subjective state(s) of the other by relating in a gentle and partially indirect manner, that he refers to as *working obliquely* with children.

Otto Kernberg once wrote that if we truly want to master our craft as clinicians, it is best to learn how to work with primitive states like those seen in psychosis and/or children, which Dr. O'Loughlin does quite effectively. Dr. O'Loughlin raises and answers the question, *"Is it possible to create a tone in maternal emotional communication that invites the child to experience separateness and being in ways that are not potentially annihilatory and do not foreclose symbolization?"*

No stranger to suffering, Dr. O'Loughlin had to develop the capacity to metabolize emotions and fearlessly confront his own demons. As a consequence, he has learned what it takes to assist his young charges to face the fiends that beset them, as well. With resolute kindness, openness, honesty, and compassion, he loans them his resilient sense of self so that they too can meet head on, speak up (what Lacan refers to as "parletre," speaking into being) and eventually conquer their ghosts, much as he has done (and continues to do) in his life. We are grateful that he saw fit to describe these lessons for us in, ***From Cradle to Couch***.

The final chapter, by Burton Norman Seitler, is called *Sophistry and ADHD: The Dual Myths of Organicity and Biochemical Imbalance and the Ensuing Medication Tidal Wave*. It could just as easily have been entitled "ADHD: An Idealization of a Phenomenon," to echo Brody's careful unpacking of the myths and misperceptions that are the components of sloppy thinking about Transitional Objects. Dr. Seitler invokes the philosophical and scientific methods that are our bulwarks against simplistic sophistry. He reviews for us the body of knowledge that suggests that the current understanding of ADHD is not only misguided, but harmful physiologically and socio-culturally. Dr. Seitler implies that there are a number of experts who, in effect, think that ADHD diagnoses excuse both parents and teachers, while simultaneously creating an atmosphere where so-called ADHD children are seen and treated as "the other."

Influenced by the extensive writings of Dr. Sylvia Brody, whose work spans many decades, this book reflects a compilation of ideas, research, and psychoanalytically-informed approaches. Contained in the following pages are illustrations of the collective dedication and years of experience of our contributing authors, all whom have taken the time to express in great detail a host of developmental/psychoanalytic reasons why a child, for example, may become disorganized and agitated in response to loss, insecure attachment, or trauma.

The Editors believe that the efforts of our contributing authors have been worthwhile and hope that you, the reader, agree with this assessment, enjoy the contents, and obtain something of value from the perspectives represented in, ***From Cradle to Couch***.

—Burton N. Seitler & Kim S. Kleinman

CHAPTER 1

Psychoanalysis and Child Rearing

Kerry Kelly Novick and Jack Novick, Ph.D.

Psychoanalysis and Child Rearing

Kerry Kelly Novick and Jack Novick, Ph.D.[1,2]

In this chapter we suggest that current controversies around the psycho-analytic concepts of narcissism, omnipotence, specialness and so forth derive from reliance on a single-track developmental model. A single-track model, used implicitly or explicitly by almost all psychoanalytic theorists, posits that normal infants and children function in ways that would be considered pathological in later life. This way of thinking is contradicted by modern infant and developmental research. Additionally, it contra-dicts common-sense experience and is therefore not a useful model for parenting.

On the other hand, Freud and many other writers also posited a du-al-track model, which simultaneously allows for both healthy and pathological choices throughout life. In this paper, we describe some of the ways in which a dual-track model, which we have elaborated as "two systems of self-regulation," can be usefully applied to theory, technique, and applications with all those involved with children.

The editors of this book asked us to write about psychoanalytic de-velopmental theories of narcissism, grandiosity, and omnipotence and their relevance to parental dilemmas over discipline and indulgence through time as both psychoanalysis and the world have changed. This

---

[1] Kerry Kelly Novick and Jack Novick are both child and adult psychoanalysts, trained at the Hampstead Clinic (Anna Freud Centre), the British Psychoanalytic Institute, and the Contemporary Freudian Society. They are Training Analysts of the IPA, and founders of Allen Creek Preschool, Ann Arbor, Michigan, where they are in private practice.

[2] 2 Novick, K.K. and Novick, J. (2014). Psychoanalysis and child rearing. Psa. Inq. 34, 5: 440-451.

is an important question in general and it also provides a microcosm in which to examine some basic premises. This issue is devoted to weighty topics like narcissism, grandiosity, exceptions and entitlement. These terms and concepts have long histories, with overlapping and evolving meanings. They have profound implications for theory and technique of clinical work; there are questions about their meaning for models of development. We understand the continuing confusion and dispute around narcissism and omnipotence as a result of historical analytic adherence to a prevalent single-track model of psychic development. In contrast, we have found it useful to follow the alternative psychoanalytic tradition of a dual-track developmental model in devising a model of two systems of self-regulation. In addition to solving some theoretical puzzles and offering profound technical implications, the two-systems model clarifies ideas and makes them more accessible and useful for clinicians, parents, and all who have an interest in child development. In this chapter we will contrast different conceptualizations of the development of omnipotence. A crucial measure of a developmental theory, however, is how helpful, accessible and relevant it is to parents and clinicians of all kinds.

TRANSLATIONAL RESEARCH

Freud's work is a model of what has recently been called "translational research" (Toth and Cicchetti 2011). Translational research looks at the transfer of knowledge to a) diagnosis, prevention and treatment, and b) the application of results from clinical trials into everyday clinical practice. But it can be hard to predict what aspect of a theory may be taken up into general parlance and it is bound to be changed, simplified, and even distorted in the process. This depends not only on the nature of the theory, but surely also on many other factors of history, the current zeitgeist, the challenges of the moment, and more.

Freud emerged from and hastened the passing of a nineteenth-century society in which parents wielded autocratic power. When Freud first published his ideas at the beginning of the twentieth century, psychoanalysis almost immediately had a direct and liberating impact on culture. One of the new freedoms was permission to focus on the self and look inward. The language of psychoanalysis was, in its original form, direct, evocative, forceful, and carried radical ideas that could be grasped and reacted to by a wide range of people, including Marxists, Zionists, Socialists, artists, teachers, feminists, young people seeking sexual liberation, and parents looking for guidance. Early psychoanalytic language had the power and adaptive force to engage with and change large segments of the community. Both the theory and the language that described it came at a pivotal historical and cultural moment of change.

In Freud's description of little Hans (1909), a number of important issues emerged that conveyed a psychoanalytic concept of child rearing, even though that was not Freud's explicit agenda. Even in Hans' enlightened, middle-class family, it was so ordinary for a child to be threatened with castration if he didn't stop masturbating that Freud doesn't even remark on it. The prevalent image of children at the time was that they were little wild animals who had to be controlled from the outside by threats, punishments, shame, and the possibility of eternal damnation. Little Hans' "irrational" thoughts were being contradicted by his mother and his father, and it was Freud who insisted that Hans be taken seriously, that his inner life had meaning. This is what constituted the revolutionary contribution of psychoanalytic ideas to child rearing at the beginning of the twentieth century. Instead of seeing children as savages to be tamed (see, for example, the case of Schreber, whose father promulgated a popular system of controlling children by tying them up (Freud 1911a]), parents were encouraged by psychoanalysts to respect and listen to their children, liberating them from the yoke of repression.

Psychoanalytic theory informed parents that their children were not beasts, but only being children, with all kinds of urges to feel good. As shocking as the idea of infantile sexuality may have been, it was clear that it issued from wishes to be close to one's mother and father. Those were positive, loving feelings. Aggressive and murderous wishes could be accepted by adults since they were just little children who couldn't implement them. The "Oedipus complex" carried the authority of classical mythology and literature, as well as deep resonances in those who allowed themselves a degree of self-knowledge. Coercion and punishment for all these natural impulses were said to lead to repression, later neurosis and low self-esteem due to injured narcissism. Parents who wanted to prevent that fate embraced psychoanalytic ideas.

In this volume we are all talking about modes of thinking that Freud, Ferenczi and others called "omnipotent." The theory that evolved at that time is clearly explicated in Freud's "Two Principles of Mental Functioning" (1911b). The way Freud described babies in that paper defined the field for years to come. Building on Freud's description, Ferenczi (1913) elaborated a schema of the stages of omnipotence from unconditional omnipotence in the womb, to magical hallucinatory omnipotence in the newborn, the omnipotence of magical gestures in the preverbal child, the omnipotence of animistic thinking of the older toddler, and then magic thoughts and magic words, where the function of speech is imbued with omnipotence validated by an adoring entourage of adults.

These stages were said to define the baby's relation to inner and outer reality. They also were described as the fixation points for serious adult pathology, such as psychosis, hysteria, obsessional neurosis and so forth. Despite the ominous future potential of such pathological fixations, it is striking how Ferenczi, like Freud, describes these early infantile states in loving, joyful, sympathetic terms. Ferenczi summed up his developmental model, saying "All children live in the happy delusion of omnipotence, which at some time or other - even if only in the womb - they really partook of" (1913 p. 232).

This was the model presented to parents, with the charming picture of "His Majesty the Baby" that Freud described in 1914. The child was imagined as omnipotent, regulated by the pleasure principle well into late adolescence. Child rearing was reconfigured with the aim of liberating this happy self to promote creative flowering and healthy relationships. A reality principle applied too soon would lead to repression and neurosis. So the avoidance of repression in child rearing, just like the lifting of repression in treatment, was the take-home message of early psychoanalysis to the public.

Everyone was caught up in the excitement of those heady early days of psychoanalysis, including the analysts. Peter Heller was a 9-year-old when he entered analysis with Anna Freud in 1929. Sixty years later, as a history professor, he wrote a memoir of his analysis in which he also vividly described the fervid Viennese cultural milieu between the two World Wars. The avant-garde Socialist circles of arts, letters and politics overlapped with the left-wing radical psychoanalysts, creating an atmosphere of liberated experimentation in all areas, including sexuality. He observed that "these people [analysts] acted out and dramatized their sexuality, and let themselves go in order to parade their opposition to convention..." (Heller 1990, p.340).

This was the psychoanalysis that captured people's imaginations and spread also through American culture during and after World War II, reaching its zenith in the 1960's and 70's. Psychoanalytic ideas were so integrated culturally that films, books, cartoons and common parlance included casual references to, for instance, the Oedipus complex, anal character, Freudian slips, repression and so forth. Psychoanalysis was the treatment of choice for adults and children struggling with emotional troubles. Parents sought and used psychoanalytic guidance in child-rearing, particularly with books like Benjamin Spock's well-rounded 1945 "Common-sense Book of Baby and Child Care." What people took from it was a fairly unitary thrust toward feeding on demand, acceptance, permissiveness – basically not to quell the child's natural omnipotence too harshly or too soon.

In the mid-twentieth century, several analysts, such as Anna Freud, Erik Erikson (1950), Winnicott (1964 [1949]), Bowlby (1969, 1973, 1980), and Selma Fraiberg (1959), had a big impact on general child development theories and practices. Anna Freud, with her experiments in nurseries before, during and after the Second World War, demonstrated the importance of the child's attachment to the mother. Her work led to radical changes in medical practice and to Bowlby's focus on the study of attachment.

She went on to build on Ferenczi's and Freud's emphasis on empathy (Einfuhlung) to write her ground-breaking legal volumes on the "best interests of the child" (1973).

Winnicott explicitly built on Sigmund Freud's statement that looking at a child's development has to include the ministrations of the mothering person when he made the famous pronouncement that there is "no such thing as a baby, there is only a mother and a baby" ([1949] 1964). His work led to an increased focus on the real interactions between mothers and children. In his public talks and on the radio he presented a model of translational research, using an effective delivery system to help parents understand complex psychoanalytic ideas. In this he was much influenced by Anna Freud, who introduced psychoanalytic ideas to pediatricians, psychiatrists, judges, teachers and parents.

Kohut and Anna Freud were colleagues from the early Vienna days. We imagine that some of his emphasis on parent-child interactions as critical to psychic development and mental health came from his close involvement with the active outreach work of the Viennese analysts to daycare centers, nurseries and schools. His assertion of the centrality of what parents "are" to the development of the "nuclear" self and its subsequent crystallization and maturation places the parent-child relationship at the center of development (1981).

Anna Freud and Winnicott saw their contributions as explicit extensions of Freud's developmental ideas, while Kohut increasingly contrasted his ideas with Freud's. All three, however, retained the original Freud/Ferenczi theory of normal infantile omnipotence only gradually given up under the impact of reality. Simplified, in a sense over-simplified, yet justified by this persistent psychoanalytic description of the happy omnipotent infant, the style of child rearing understood to derive from psychoanalysis continued the 'liberation philosophy' that had swept Europe in art, politics and sexual mores throughout the first half of the twentieth century.

But twentieth-century parents were thereby also left uncertain as to when or how they should set limits, impose frustration, punish misbehavior. At the beginning of the century children were afraid to lose their parents' love; by the end of the century, at least in the United States, it was parents who seemed afraid they would lose their children's love. Parents not only feared the neurotic consequences of repressing their children; even more they feared loss and angry reproach from their children if they set standards, made demands, or invoked any consequences of behavior. Like all revolutions that contain the seeds of their own destruction, there was bound to be a backlash to the extreme and simplistic psychoanalytic influence on child rearing.

Child therapists began to report different presenting complaints in children and parents. Instead of classical neurotic symptoms, an increasing number of child patients came with difficulties in self-regulation of behavior, feelings or attention. Teachers complained of defiant, disruptive students; parents reported feeling completely helpless in relation to ordinary daily situations, like meals, bedtime, dressing and more. In the popular view, psychoanalysis did not seem to offer anything useful; indeed, it seemed to have created a monster.

Within the theory there seemed at this point little alternative to the old emphasis on the happy omnipotent child, whose more modern description has often been couched in terms of attachment/attunement. From an original psychoanalytic conceptualization of the importance of the mother-infant bond, bolstered by studies of animal development, a whole field has arisen of clinical theory and techniques, and spin-off philosophies of child rearing, like "attachment parenting," which may include ideas like the "family bed," breastfeeding to advanced ages, and so forth. Building on an extreme and over-simplified understanding of attachment research, latter-day parents may set themselves the impossible task of total attunement and availability in the effort to prevent neurosis and low self-esteem in their children. This approach is based on a fantasy that the child should live in a Garden of Eden where no effort or work is required. This tends to backfire with the outcome of over-anxious, out-of-control, and incompetent children. These are often the indulged, grandiose, "special" children.

In the face of the demonstrated failure of the liberation philosophy of the psychoanalytic model to produce civilized children, helpless parents and teachers were presented by some academics and professionals with a reactive, repressive model of external controls, almost a reversion to nineteenth-century modes of domination. These take the form of behavior modification techniques and now, more pervasively and perniciously, medication in order to control children. ADHD and bipolar diagnoses and their accompanying prescriptions have increased exponentially in the past twenty years. 2.5 million American children are medicated for ADHD (10% of *all* 10-year-old boys); between 1994 and 2003 the number of children diagnosed with bipolar disorder increased 40-fold, from 25 to 1003 per 100,000 children under 19 (Carlat 2010). This is not only the result of concentrated biased research and marketing by drug companies and some psychiatrists, but also represents a failure of psychoanalysis to develop and promulgate effective, accessible developmental models and applications of them. What different kind of model could return psychoanalysis to relevance in the wider world and also offer greater congruence with the findings of modern developmental research?

DEVELOPMENT OF OMNIPOTENCE

All psychoanalytic theories implicitly or explicitly include a theory of development. Each one carries a particular image of how babies and children experience themselves and the world. There is a Freudian baby, a Jungian baby, a Kleinian baby, a Bowlby baby, a Mahlerian baby, a Kohutian baby and so forth. But, as we noted above, all these babies are thought to be omnipotent by nature.

The concept of normal infantile omnipotence is part of a single-track developmental model. In a single-track model normal children are routinely described as "autistic," "omnipotent," "paranoid-schizoid," "depressive," "polymorphously perverse," "anal-sadistic," "narcissistic," and so forth, all examples of descriptors of severe pathology in adults. Adult pathology is explained as fixation or regression to, or persistence or arrest of what was normal in childhood. Adult normality and even creativity are explained as sublimations or compromise formations on the basis of infantile "perverse" impulses.

The classical psychoanalytic description is that the child is born feeling omnipotent and gradually and reluctantly, only under the impact of failure of the magical omnipotent system, turns to and accepts reality. This is where we part company with the mainstream traditional, single-track psychoanalytic models of development. In our model, it is the failure of reality that impels the child to turn to omnipotent solutions (Novick and Novick 1991, 1996a, 2007 [1996b]). To us omnipotence is not normal. Rather it is a defensive, compensatory belief, generated as a sometimes necessary response to the trauma of the failure of reality,

20

including real people, to meet what Lichtenberg (1989) described as the five basic needs embodied in his model of five motivational systems.

Many others have also criticized this single-track model; Frances Tustin, an eminent Kleinian pioneer in the field of autism, wrote a moving paper called "The perpetuation of an error" in an effort to correct what she saw as an untenable clinging to single-track theory (1994). It leads to neglect of the individual's strengths, capacities, and push toward progressive development, with underestimation of the opportunities provided by reality experience, including treatment, and the role of parent-child interactions and relationships in healthy and pathological development. The single-track model with its emphasis on pathology does not speak to modern parents of the children they know or meet their needs for guidance in ordinary life challenges.

In contrast to this single-track model we have suggested in a series of writings that a dual-track model can revive the relevance of psychoanalytic theory to child rearing and move analysts again into a central position for parents (Novick and Novick 2001b, 2005, 2010, 2011). There are also implications for theory and clinical technique that improves outcomes (Novick, K.K. and Novick, J. 2005). In a dual-track model we assume that conflict and conflict-resolution are universal but neurosis is not. Neurosis is one of numerous possible solutions to conflict and ways to regulate oneself. It follows then that the normal mother-infant bond is not necessarily symbiotic, the anal phase is not in itself sadistic, the oedipal period need not be experienced as a trauma, latency is not a period of arid repression, masochism may be pervasive but it is not normal, and normal adolescence is not a period of emotional turbulence akin to a severe mental disorder.

Our formulation assumes a developmental path in which, from the very beginning, "healthy" or "adaptive" solutions to conflict may be achieved throughout life. We suggest that omnipotence, or its corollaries grandiosity, exceptionalism, entitlement, does not play a significant role in normal development, beyond an occasional appearance as a pleasurable accompaniment to daydreams, where the distinction between real and pretend is secure.

Rather, the presence of omnipotent functioning and beliefs is a sign of pathological solution to conflict. Parental over-indulgence is an omnipotent attempt to force a child to love and not hate them, and validates for the child his omnipotent power to control others' feelings and actions, rather than staying in charge of himself. Since complete indulgence is an impossibility, children are left constantly dissatisfied and disappointed. The omnipotent beliefs on both sides are divorced from realistic limitations and capacities; this can lead to character distortions that are based on a feeling of frustrated grievance or victimization that entitles the child to be a special case who does not have to live by the ordinary rules that bind society together (Freud, 1916).

There is a long history in psychoanalytic theory of alternatives to the single-track model of early pathological functioning issuing in normal development. From Freud's "original reality ego" (1915, p.136) that preceded the "purified pleasure ego" (ibid p.136), through Anna Freud's (1965) focus on progressive development as the hallmark of health, to the present, there are elements of description of a potential dual-track model scattered in the analytic literature (for detailed discussion of the history see Novick, J. and Novick, K.K. 2001, 2003, 2005). But it has never been fully realized.[3] This is partly because analysts have always generalized to development from their work with disturbed individuals, and thus their developmental models always revert to the single- track, leaving no room for the inclusion of creativity, love, work, collaboration, hope, mutuality, and cooperation in relationships and development.

Infantile omnipotence as described by Freud and Ferenczi represents an omnipotent fantasy of easy solutions to life's challenges. There is no work or change demanded in such a model. Many modern psychoanalytic approaches focus primarily on the very early mother-child relationship, with no attention to preschool, latency or adolescent transformations (Novick, J. and Novick, K.K. 2007 [1996b]). These theories often neglect the crucial role of work on the part of the child, in partnership with adults. The hallmark of latency is pleasure in work; healthy adolescent development includes working to create pleasurable engagement with new realities.

---

[3] Lichtenberg's work, grounded as it is in infant research on normal populations, is a notable exception (1989).

The late twentieth-century explosion of developmental research in infancy and childhood all zeroes in on self-regulation as central. The new body of knowledge also definitively contradicts the assumptions of the omnipotent baby lost in hallucinatory reverie of the single-track developmental model. A dual-track model allows us to retain the clinical insights of analysts from Freud through Mahler, Winnicott, and others into pathological development while integrating the findings of modern infant research that describes the competent baby grounded in the reality of his world and his relationships (Novick, K.K. and Novick, J. 2011 in press).

From our clinical work on sadomasochistic power relationships and the defensive omnipotent beliefs and fantasies that organize them we have built on the dual-track model to postulate two systems of self-regulation and conflict resolution. One system, the "open system," is attuned to reality and characterized by joy, love, competence, and creativity. The other, the "closed system," avoids reality and is characterized by power dynamics, sadomasochism, omnipotence and stasis. Children operating in the closed system feel like entitled exceptions to the parameters of reality. With a two-systems model we have developed a different understanding of the role of omnipotence in mental life. Rather than the classical view that the failure of omnipotence forces the child to turn to reality, we suggest that it is the failure of reality that can force a child, at any point in development, to turn to closed-system omnipotent solutions, resulting in self-centered, entitled functioning.

The aim of self-regulation is the same in both systems. In the open system, the maximum use of one's genuine mental and physical capacities to be realistically effective and competent is the method of mastering inner and outer forces and conflicts. This is the way a child develops positive self-esteem. In the closed system, the basis for mastery is omnipotent belief in the power and necessity to be a perpetrator or victim in order to survive. This too leads to self-esteem, but it is based on pathological, omnipotent manoeuvers. The closed and open systems do not differentiate people, that is, they are not diagnostic categories. Rather, the constructs describe potential choices of adaptation *within each individual at **any** challenging point in development.*

23

Adaptations involve a person in what is going on inside and outside in his world. Reality is what babies and children have to adapt to. Parents are the major reality of children's lives. They construct the context of the child's experience, define what's real, interpret what happens, and set goals. Engaging with this reality is thus central to the therapeutic endeavor.

With the failure of his seduction hypothesis Freud (1897) made a decisive turn away from external reality, which would include the effect of parents, to intrapsychic wishes and desires as the prime determinants of neuroses. The shift to the internal world was reinforced by a theory of development that emphasized endogenous unfolding of psychosexual phases independent of environmental influences. Influenced by this change in psychoanalytic theory, the past and current impact of parents was denied. Close reading of Freud's writings reveals that his practice was to integrate theoretical changes, rather than reject earlier formulations and replace them with newer ideas. But that complexity did not lend itself to easy translation into popular applications. Many of Freud's followers were more likely to embrace new theories to the exclusion of previous ones. They tended to use the changes in theory to justify ignoring the role of parents in the development and treatment of children, forgetting that, in the very paper where Freud sets forth a single-track transformation from infantile omnipotence to the reality principle at the end of adolescence, he also says that development in a child can only take place "...provided one includes the care it receives from its mother" (1911b, p.220).

Although child observation and the developmental point of view were at the core of psychoanalysis from the very beginning, psychoanalysis as a method of treatment for children did not start until the 1920's with the work of Anna Freud, Melanie Klein, Hug-Hellmuth and the Bornsteins (A. Freud, 1966). These pioneers were very eager to demonstrate that child analysis followed the same principles as the most recent models of adult work, and thus they further reinforced denial of the pathogenic or constructive impact of the family. This was especially true of Melanie Klein, whose theory and technique ignored environmental effects and presented child analysis as equivalent in all respects to adult work. Modern Kleinians continue this style, as described, for instance, by Elmhirst (1988), Baruch (1997), and Pick and Segal (1978).

The inherent limitations of a single-track theory of development also inhibited child analysts from grappling with and formulating a theory and technique that integrates the central reality of the relationship between children and parents throughout life. The two-system model expands the possibilities of understanding the infinite variations in development and offers a wider range of techniques in treatment (Novick, K.K. and Novick, J. 2005). The open system allows us to reclaim a complete metapsychological view of the child, his parents, and their relationship over the life span, which encompasses both normality and pathology. The way is then open for psychoanalytic theory once again to become relevant to parents and child rearing. But what is the delivery system? How can parents access and make use of these new ideas? It takes an active effort on the part of analysts to communicate and apply these concepts.

Child analysts have always stepped out of the consulting room, from the early free clinics in Vienna and Berlin (Danto, 1998, 1999) to Anna Freud's war nurseries, to the establishment of psychoanalytic schools, first at Hampstead, then in Cleveland, Houston, Cary, Birmingham, Ann Arbor, and Detroit, among others (Novick, K.K. and Novick, J. 2011, in press). These schools are the interface between modern psychoanalytic developmental ideas and parents. They constitute an actualization of a dual-track model of development, as they work both with closed-system pathology resistant to change and the open-system strengths that parents and children bring and develop further.

Such work assumes that psychoanalysis is a general psychology, applicable to the full range of human experience. It pushes us to abandon the pseudoscientific jargon of Strachey's translation of Freud and find a language that is immediate, relevant, and encompasses the whole child, strengths and positive capacities as well as conflict and potential for pathology. A mother at a psychoanalytic school described how she could make use of what child psychoanalysts had to offer her as she struggled with the usual challenges of parenting in the regular twice-monthly evening meetings of the parents in her child's classroom with two child analysts: "The things I learned in these Wednesday evenings I brought home to my children. Supported by her teacher and classmates, my daughter is growing emotional muscle. Her joy, mastery, confidence and self esteem shine from her face. Children can easily grow up without developing their emotional muscles which can result in lives led in sadness and anger and a kind of emotional isolation" (quoted in Novick, K.K. and Novick, J. 2011).

"Emotional muscle" is one of the terms that have emerged from both our clinical and school work. It translates concepts such as ego strength, general characteristics of the ego, ego instincts, frustration tolerance, mentalization, and resilience, among others, into language that is experience-near and vivid to parents and teachers. "Emotional muscle" rests on assumptions about the centrality of open-system work in development. Similarly, we talk accessibly at the psychoanalytic schools of an "inside helper" rather than the superego, "two-way feelings" rather than ambivalence, "toilet mastery" rather than toilet training, "keeping people in mind" rather than object constancy, and so forth (Novick, K.K. and Novick J. 2010).

Here are some examples, taken from our book on Emotional Muscle (Novick, K.K. and Novick, J. 2010), of further work in relation to the open system with a group of toddler parents.

Nora, nearly 3, was ordering everyone around about what she wanted to do and what she wanted them to do. She seemed desperately invested in being the boss. Her parents were frustrated and felt helpless and angry. They didn't want to squash her assertion or initiative, but her exasperated parents likened her to a dictator. In the context of the continuing discussion about who is in charge of what, the family consultant devised an activity for them to do with Nora and her older sister Katie.

They set up three buckets and threw balls of paper into them. One bucket was for what Nora and Katie were in charge of, one was for what their parents or teachers were in charge of, and the last was for what no one can be in charge of. Each person called something out in turn and decided, with the help of the others, which bucket to toss the ball into.

For instance, when Nora shouted bedtime, her parents said, "Bedtime goes into our bucket, but sleep time goes into your bucket because you are in charge of your own body." When Katie shouted, "Sunshine," Nora, nearly three, said, "No one is in charge of that. It has to go in the last bucket." Everyone cheered. Their daddy shouted, "Rain! I'm in charge of the rain!" The children laughed and contradicted him, insisting that his ball go in the last bucket. They also were learning from his joke that everyone may sometimes wish to be in charge of everything. And so it went.

This activity could be repeated over time since, as the children grew, there were changes in what they could be in charge of. One day, Nora said, "Let's play the buckets. I want to put in there that I'm in charge of riding my trike and using the potty." "Hurray" said everyone and they all enjoyed throwing in the balls for the new skills.

The buckets became a shorthand way of thinking and talking for all the parents and children in this group. Through the active teaching of who is in charge of what the children had gained a sense of mastery through knowledge, not only of what they could now actually control, but also of the things they did not have to be responsible for (pp, 110, 111).

When 3-year-old Nicky's grandmother was ill, his mother felt very sad one day. Nicky saw her crying and looked worried. Then he began acting silly, trying to make his mother laugh. She understood his need and reassured him, "It's all right that I am sad. It's because I'm worried about Grandma. You don't have to take care of my feelings, that's my job. But thank you for noticing. I'm still sad, but it also feels good when you give me a hug."

When his grandmother died a few months later, Nicky became very anxious. He eventually confided to his mother that he was scared because Grandma died after he had been angry with her. Nicky's mom could tell him that sometimes she too had been angry with Grandma, but that her feelings and Nicky's had not caused Grandma's death. No one was in charge of when that happened. Grandma was very old and ready to die. "Feelings are important to talk about, but they are just feelings and they don't make things happen. Remember the three buckets? Grandma's death would go into the bucket of what no one is in charge of."

The toddler Nicky was helpless in the face of his mother's sadness and the incomprehensibility of his grandmother's death. He fell back on a magical idea that he had caused it with his anger. Without his mother's helpful understanding and intervention, he might have carried this feeling of omnipotent responsibility and guilt forward to color his later development. Nicky's mother gave him an additional important lesson. She did not convey her experience of the grandmother's death as one of awful helplessness; rather, she presented it as a fact that can be encompassed. Acceptance of something that cannot be changed or affected is not the same as passive submission or resignation (pp. 112).

The two-systems model offers additional tools also when working with the more familiar omnipotent pathology that we would characterize as "closed-system functioning." A 19-year-old college student was sent to treatment by his mother because he was failing school, in a rage at everyone, especially his parents, and was constantly complaining about being let down by everyone in his life. When he first came, he said he had no wish for treatment, as he was fine. He claimed his parents and his fraternity were to blame for all his troubles. His rage was palpable and he felt he had a perfect right to be angry.

He was a well-built young man who spent considerable time at the gym. Early in our first meeting I said to him that he was letting his anger control him. Alternatively, he could learn to use his emotional muscles to make his feelings just the right size to be useful. A first goal could be to turn his feelings into signals rather than experiencing them as overwhelming, potentially traumatic, states that needed strong medications. Appealing to his capacities and his wish to be in charge of himself created a beginning therapeutic alliance and the groundwork for a conflict between closed, omnipotent solutions and a more realistic, open-system competence. He responded immediately to the idea of increasing strength by gaining self-control and mastery. In subsequent sessions we then explored the pathological parent-child dynamic where he dominated them with his distress. His parents felt so guilty and anxious that they could not refuse him anything.

Concurrent work with his parents throughout his analysis illustrated the general point that working with a two-systems model facilitates the transformation of the parent-child relationship. His parents moved from being collusive enablers of his omnipotent functioning to active engagement with the reality of their and his strengths and weaknesses. It became clear that he had idealized his father; then a business failure so shattered his image that the boy had to create an omnipotent self who controlled everyone and needed no one. Once he and his parents began to enjoy the multi-faceted reality of each other's personalities, the idealization and the attendant defenses faded away. Good-enough parents and good-enough children do not need to idealize each other. Emphasis on the reality pleasure of work, persistence, trying and so forth (all important emotional muscles) meant that he did not have to keep searching for mirroring self- objects, but could enjoy his own competence.

Before Freud and Ferenzci wrote the papers that described and codified a single- track model of "normal omnipotence," Freud responded to little Hans in a very different way. When five-year-old Hans stands up to his father's moralizing and insists that thinking is not the same as doing, Freud exclaims in a footnote, "Well done, little Hans! I could wish for no better understanding of psychoanalysis from any grownup" (1909, p. 72). The distinction between wishes and actions, between pretend and real, between magic and effective action, between grandiosity and ambition, between specialness and individuality, between indulgence and responsiveness, between omnipotence and competence, is a fundamental assumption and contribution of psychoanalysis. A two- system model can reclaim that insight and offer parents in the twenty-first century usable and helpful psychoanalytic ideas to solve their dilemmas.

REFERENCES

Baruch, (1997). The impact of parental interventions on the analysis of a 5-year-old boy. Int. J. Psycho-anal. 78: 913-26.

Bowlby, J. (1969). Attachment and Loss, Vol. 1 Attachment. New York: Hogarth Press.

——— (1973). Attachment and Loss, Vol. 2 Separation: Anxiety and Anger. New York: Basic Books.

——— (1980). Attachment and Loss, Vol 3 Sadness and Depression. London: Hogarth Press.

Carlat, D. (2010). Unhinged: The Trouble with Psychiatry – A Doctor's Revelations About A Profession In Crisis. New York: Free Press.

Danto, E.A. (1998). The Ambulatorium: Freud's free clinic in Vienna. Int. J. Psycho-Anal. 79: 287-300.

——— (1999). The Berlin Polyklinik: psychoanalytic innovation in Weimar Germany. J. Amer. Psychoanal. Assn. 47: 1269-1292.

Elmhirst, S.I. (1988). The Kleinian setting for child analysis. Int. Rev. Psycho-anal. 15: 5-12.

Erikson, E. (1950). Childhood and Society. New York: Norton

Ferenczi, S. (1913). Stages in the development of the sense of reality. In: First Contributions to Psycho-Analysis (1952). The International Psycho-Analytical Library, 45:1-331. London: The Hogarth Press and the Institute of Psycho- Analysis. pp. 213-239.

Fraiberg, S. (1959). The Magic Years: Understanding and Handling the Problems of Early Childhood. New York: Simon and Schuster.

Freud, A. (1965). Normality and Pathology in Childhood. Writings 6:3-273. New York: International Universities Press.

——— (1966). A short history of child analysis. W 7: 48-58.

Freud, S. (1897). Letter to Fliess [December 12]. In: The Origins of Psychoanalysis, p.237. New York: Basic Books (1954).

——— (1909). Analysis of a Phobia in a Five-Year-Old Boy. S.E. 10: 1-150.

——— (1911a). Psycho-analytic notes on an autobiographical account of a case of paranoia (Dementia Paranoides). S.E. 12: 3-82.

——— (1911b). Formulations on the two principles of mental function-ing. S.E. 12: 215-226.

——— (1914). On narcissism: an introduction. S.E. 14: 69-102.

——— (1915). Instincts and their vicissitudes. S.E.14: 117-140.

——— (1916). Some Character-Types Met with in Psycho-Analytic Work. S.E. 14: 311-336.

Heller, P. (1990). A Child Analysis with Anna Freud. Madison, CT: International Universities Press.

Kohut, H. (1981). Analysis of the Self: A Systematic Approach to Treat-ment of Narcissistic Personality Disorders. Madison, CT: International Universities Press.

Lichtenberg, J. (1989). Psychoanalysis and Motivation. Hillsdale, NJ: Analytic Press.

Novick, J. and Novick, K.K. (1991). Some comments on masochism and the delusion of omnipotence from a developmental perspective. JAPA 39: 307-321.

——— (1996a). A developmental perspective on omnipotence. J. Clinical Psychoanalysis 5: 129-173.

——— (2000). Love in the therapeutic alliance. JAPA 48: 189-218.

——— (2001a). Trauma and deferred action in adolescence. American J. of Psa. 61: 43-61.

——— (2001b). Two systems of self-regulation. Psychoanalytic Social Work, vol. 8, 3/4: 95-122.

——— (2003). Two systems and the differential application of psycho-analytic technique. Amer. J. of Psychoanal. 63: 1-19.

——— (2005). The superego and the two-systems model. Psychoanal. Inq. 24: 232-56.

——— (2006). Good Goodbyes: Knowing How to End in Psychoanalysis and Psychotherapy. New York: Jason Aronson.

——— (2007 [1996]). Fearful Symmetry: The Development and Treatment of Sadomasochism. Northvale, NJ: Jason Aronson

——— (2011). Altruistic analysis. in press. Novick, K.K. and Novick, J. (1987). The essence of masochism. Psychoanal. Study Child 42: 353-384. New Haven: Yale University Press.

——— (1998). The application of the concept of the therapeutic alliance to sadomasochism. JAPA 46: 813-846.

——— (2002). Reclaiming the land. Psychoanal. Psychology 19: 348-377.

——— (2005). Working With Parents Makes Therapy Work. New York: Jason Aronson.

——— (2010). Emotional Muscle: Strong Parents, Strong Children. Indiana: XLibris.

——— (2011). Building emotional muscle in children and parents. PSC, in press.

Pick, I. and Segal, H. (1978). Melanie Klein's contribution to child analysis: Theory and Technique. In: J. Glenn (Ed.), Child Analysis and Therapy. Northvale, NJ: Jason Aronson.

Spock, B. (1945). The Common-sense Book of Baby and Child Care. New York, NY: Simon and Schuster.

Toth, S.L. and Cicchetti, D. (2011). Frontiers of translational research on trauma. Development and Psychopathology 23, issue 2, pp.353-355.

Tustin, F. (1994). The perpetuation of an error. J. of Child Psychotherapy 20: 3-23.

Winnicott, D.W. (1949). The ordinary devoted mother and her baby. In: The Child, the Family, and the Outside World. Middlesex, England: Penguin Books (1964), pp. 15-24.

BRIEF BIOS.

KERRY KELLY NOVICK AND JACK NOVICK are both child and adult psycho-analysts, trained at the Hampstead Clinic (Anna Freud Centre), the British Psychoanalytic Institute, and the Contemporary Freudian Society. They are Training Analysts of the IPA, and founders of Allen Creek Preschool, Ann Arbor, Michigan, where they are in private practice.

617 Stratford Drive Ann Arbor, MI, 48104, USA
+1-734-665-6745
kerrynovick@gmail.com

CHAPTER 2

Mother-Infant Research
Informs Mother-Infant Treatment

Beatrice Beebe, Ph.D.

Mother-Infant Research Informs Mother-Infant Treatment[1]

Beatrice Beebe, Ph.D.

A brief mother-infant treatment approach using "video feedback" is described. This approach is informed both by psychoanalysis and by research on mother-infant face-to-face interaction using video microanalysis. Two cases are presented. In the first, descriptions of the videotaped interactions which informed the interventions are presented. In the second, knowledge of mother-infant microanalysis research informed the treatment, even though videotaping was not an option. The respective "stories" of the presenting complaints, the video interaction, and the parent's own upbringing are linked.

Specific representations of the baby that may interfere with the parent's ability to observe and process her nonverbal interaction with her infant are identified. The mother has a powerful experience during the video feedback of watching herself and her baby interact. Our attempts together to translate the action-sequences into words facilitates the mother's ability to "see" and to "remember," fostering a rapid integration of implicit and explicit modes of processing.

INTRODUCTION

More than two decades of research on maternal distress, mother-infant interaction, and infant and child developmental outcomes have shown that infants suffer when a parent is distressed. At times parental distress

---

[1] The original citation of this work was: Beebe, B. (2005). Mother-infant research informs mother-infant treatment. *The Psychoanalytic study of the child*, 60(1), 7-46. Reprinted with permission.

stems from longstanding character psychopathology. Research on depressed mothers and their infants shows that these infants are at risk for insecure attachments and compromised cognitive outcomes (Murray & Cooper, 1997). Maternal prenatal anxiety has been shown to predict behavior problems in the children at age 4 years (O'Connor, Heron, Golding, Beveridge, & Glover, 2002). Maternal unresolved mourning has been specifically linked to infant and childhood disorganized attachment, a form of insecure attachment that predicts childhood psychopathology (Lyons-Ruth, 1998). But even highly competent parents can become destabilized under the impact of illness, loss, or other traumas, such as the loss of the husbands of 100 pregnant women from the 9/11 World Trade Center tragedy (Beebe, Cohen, & Jaffe, 2002). In addition to maternal contributions, infants may also bring their own difficulties to the relationship, based on constitutional or developmental factors.

In this paper I describe a brief mother-infant treatment approach using "video feedback." This approach is informed both by psychoanalysis and by research on mother-infant face-to-face interaction using video microanalysis. Two cases are presented. In the first, Cecil, descriptions of the videotaped interactions which informed the interventions are included. In the second, Nicole, I show how knowledge of mother-infant microanalysis research can inform a treatment even when videotaping is not an option. Whereas the implicit, procedural mode of exchange addresses behavioral transactions which are usually out of awareness, the explicit, declarative mode refers to our symbolic, verbalized narrative. In the discussion, I suggest that the mother's experience during the video feedback of watching herself and her baby interact, and our joint attempts to translate the action-sequences into words, facilitates the mother's ability to "see" and to "remember," stimulating a rapid integration of procedural and declarative modes of processing (see Beebe, 2003). Some mothers, however, require more extensive treatment (see Cohen & Beebe, 2002).

Psychoanalytic pioneers such as Anna Freud, Melanie Klein, Margaret Mahler, Fred Pine, Anni Bergman, and Paulina Kernberg understood the importance of intervention in the first years of life. Parent-infant therapy specifically has been known for several decades, spearheaded by Adelson and Shapiro (1975); Call (1963); Ferholt and Provence (1976); Fraiberg (1971, 1980); Greenacre (1971); Greenspan (1981); Lebovici (1983); Spitz (1965), Lieberman & Pawl (1993); and Weil (1970), among others. Although therapeutic interventions are widely available for young children, mother-infant treatment remains less available.

The last decade has shown great progress in conceptualizing methods of intervention with parents and infants. Both psychodynamic approaches aimed at the mother's representations and interactional approaches attempting to intervene into specific behavioral transactions are effective (see for example Brazelton, 1994; Fraiberg, 1980; Field et al., 1996; Hofacker & Papousek, 1998; Hopkins, 1992; McDonough, 1993; Marvin, Cooper, Hoffman, & Powell, 2002; Malphurs, et al., 1996; Murray & Cooper, 1997; Seligman, 1994; Stern, 1995; van den Boom, 1995). Many different kinds of mother-infant therapies have been shown to predict positive outcomes (Cramer et al., 1990).

Nevertheless, even in current approaches to mother-infant treatment, the infant is in danger of being the "forgotten patient" (see Lojkasek, Cohen & Muir, 1994; Weinberg & Tronick, 1998). Weinberg and Tronick (1998) documented by video microanalysis that the infants of mothers with panic disorder, obsessive- compulsive disorder, and major depression were still in distress, even though the mothers reported improvement of their own symptoms with medication and individual psychotherapy.

Our approach to mother-infant treatment integrates psychodynamic and interactional approaches within the context of feedback on videotaped interactions. We address the mother's representations of and transferences to the infant as well as mother-infant interaction patterns visible on videotape.

Microanalytic research describing face-to-face patterns has been extensively reviewed (see Beebe 2003, 2000; Beebe & Lachmann, 2002; Stern, 1985,1995). Two treatment cases informed by mircoanalytic research have previously been presented in Beebe (2003) and Cohen and Beebe (2002); see also Freeman (2001).

FACE-TO-FACE INTERACTION RESEARCH

The video feedback treatment method attends to specific patterns of mother and infant self- and interactive regulation which have been documented by three decades of video microanalysis research. This work focuses on face-to-face interaction rather than the regulation of feeding and sleep (but see as an exception Sander, 1977) and is most relevant for infants 3 to 12 months. The importance of mother-infant face-to-face interaction for social and cognitive development is extensively documented (see Belsky, Rovine, & Taylor, 1984; Cohn & Tronick, 1988; Cohn, Campbell, Matias, & Hopkins, 1990; Field, 1995; Lewis & Feiring, 1989; Leyendecker, Lamb, Fracasso, Scholmerich, & Larson, 1997; Martin, 1981; Malatesta et al., 1989; Lester, Hoffman, & Brazelton, 1985; Stern, 1985; Tronick, 1989). This research provides a rich resource for the parent-infant clinician, but has nevertheless remained strikingly under-utilized.

A "dyadic systems view" of face-to-face communication informs our approach to this research (Beebe, Jaffe, & Lachmann, 1992; Beebe & Lachmann, 2002). Because each person must both monitor the partner and regulate inner state, in this view all interactions are a simultaneous product of self- and interactive regulation, and each form of regulation affects the other (Gianino & Tronick, 1988; Sander, 1977; Thomas & Malone, 1979). Both the individual and the dyad contribute to the organization of behavior and experience.

Interactive regulation is defined as bi-directional contingencies in which each partner's behavioral stream can be predicted from that of the other. It is a "co-constructed" process in which each partner makes moment-by- moment adjustments to the other's shifts in behaviors, such as gaze, facial expression, orientation, touch, vocal quality, and body and vocal rhythms. Although the mother has the greater capacity and range of resources, the infant is a very active participant in this exchange, bringing remarkable capacities to seek and avoid engagement (Beebe & Lachmann, 2002; Beebe & Stern, 1977; Stern, 1971, 1985; Tronick, 1989). This emphasis on the contribution of both partners to the organization of the exchange avoids the temptation to locate the source of difficulty in only one partner or the other, for example, in maternal intrusiveness or in infant temperament difficulty.

From birth and even in utero, infants perceive durations of events and temporal sequences (DeCasper & Carstens, 1980). By the time infants are 3 to 4 months, when most of this research is conducted, infants perceive the existence and magnitude of contingencies and can anticipate when events will occur (Haith, Hazan, & Goodman, 1988; Jaffe et al., 2001; Watson, 1985). These capacities enable the infant to anticipate how each partner changes predictably in relation to the other's changes, organizing "expectancies" of "how I affect you," and "how you affect me." These infant capacities for the perception of sequence, contingency detection, and the anticipation of events underlie the generation of procedural, presymbolic representations of interactive sequences (Beebe & Stern, 1977; Beebe, Lachmann, & Jaffe, 1997; Gergeley & Watson, 1997; Stern, 1985; Tronick, 1989).

Although the terms "mutual influence" or "mutual regulation" are often used to describe the co-construction of interactive regulation, we no longer use these terms because neither "mutuality" nor "influence" in their usual meanings is accurate. Mutuality usually connotes a positive interchange, but aversive interactions such as "chase and dodge" are also co-constructed, in the sense that each partner's behavioral stream can be predicted from that of the other (Beebe & Stern, 1977). The term "influence" can also be misleading because no conscious intention to influence the behavior of the partner is implied in these contingency analyses (although obviously the parent has many conscious intentions to influence the infant). It is not a causal process but rather a probabilistic one. The interactions we study are extremely rapid, with individual behaviors lasting on the average 1/4 to 1/3 of a second; lag times between the onset of one individual's behavior and the onset of the partner's behavior are generally within 1/2 second (Beebe, 1982; Cohn & Beebe, 1990; Stern, 1971). Thus many aspects of these interactions occur out of awareness, often subliminally; they are "nonconscious," rather than dynamically "unconscious" (see Lyons-Ruth, 1998), although again, the parent has many dynamically unconscious motivations as well. Thus we prefer the more neutral terms "bi-directional regulation" or "coordination" to describe these contingency analyses.

Self-regulation is just as important as interactive regulation. While participating in the interactive exchange, each partner must simultaneously regulate his or her inner state. Both infant and parent bring constitutional proclivities such as temperamental dispositions and arousal regulation styles which affect self-regulation. Each partner's self-regulation capacity and style affects the nature of the interactive regulation, and vice-versa. Whereas one meaning of "co-construction" is that each partner contributes to the interactive regulation, a second meaning is that inner and relational processes are co-constructed (see Beebe & Lachmann, 1998). Thus both partners come to expect particular interactive patterns, associated with particular self-regulation processes. Infant expectancies of different patterns of self- and interactive regulation provide one process by which parental distress can be transmitted to the infant and alter the trajectory of development.

In applying this research to treatment, it is important to recognize that ranges of "normal" interactions are more ambiguous than extremes of difficulty, and there is no one optimal mode of interaction. Despite extensive research predicting developmental outcomes from face-to-face interaction patterns, there are no official "norms," and this research is still in progress. All dyads use problematic patterns at some moments, as adaptive modes of coping and defense in the context of specific interactive dilemmas.

THE INFANT'S NONVERBAL LANGUAGE

The use of "video feedback" as part of parent-infant psychotherapy still constitutes a new approach to mother- infant treatment, despite the fact that Stern (1995; Cramer & Stern, 1988), McDonough (1993), Tutors (1991), and Downing (2004), among others, have been using variations of this technique for over a decade (for current work see for example Bakermans-Kranenberg, Juffer, & van Ijzendoorn, 1998; Hofacker & Papousek, 1998; Malphurs, et al., 1996; Marvin, Cooper, Hoffman, & Powell, 2002; van den Boom, 1995). Video feedback is introduced to the parent as a way of learning about the infant's "nonverbal language," and of becoming aware of the ways the parent may respond. Video feedback is a remarkable clinical tool in the hands of an experienced "baby watcher" who is also a sensitive clinician. Videotape played in slowed time, or frame-by-frame, acts like a "social microscope," revealing subtleties and subliminal details of interactions which are too rapid and complex to grasp with the naked eye in ongoing time. It is difficult for anyone to be aware of his or her nonverbal behavior. If the video feedback is handled with great care to protect the parent's self-esteem, it helps the parent to see how both infant and parent affect each other, moment-by-moment. Video feedback provides an opportunity for the parent to process and reflect on the difficult moments in the interaction, as well as the successful ones (Fonagy, Gergely, Jurist, & Target, 2002).

MICROANALYSIS TEACHES US TO OBSERVE

Video microanalysis can teach us to observe the subtle, fleeting details of the mother-infant action language. The infant's repertoire during a face-to-face exchange is complex. There is a remarkable range of behaviors at the infant's disposal to initiate, maintain, disrupt, or avoid a face-to-face encounter (Stern, 1971, 1985). The mother is instructed to play with the infant as she would at home. Until 9 to 12 months, we do not provide toys. The infant is placed in an infant seat opposite the mother, who is seated in the same plane. Two cameras, one on each partner's face and upper torso, generate a split-screen view of the pair interacting.

GAZE

We begin by observing gaze. Mothers tend to look at the infant's face most of the time, and it is the infant who typically engages in a look-look away cycle, looking at mother's face for a period of time, looking away, and then looking back (Stern, 1971, 1974). As the ethologists note, looking into the face of a partner can be very stimulating; most animals do not sustain long periods of such looking unless they are about to fight or make love (Chance & Larsen, 1996; Eibl-Eibesfeldt, 1970). Field (1981) verified that infants organize their look-look away cycle to regulate degree of arousal. She monitored infant heart rate during face-to-face play and showed that the moment that the infant looks away is preceded by a burst of arousal in the previous 5 seconds; following the infant's gaze aversion, heart rate decreases back down to baseline within the next 5 seconds, and then the infant returns to gazing at mother's face. Thus infant gaze aversion is an important aspect of infant self-regulation. Brazelton, Kozlowski, and Main (1974) first showed that mothers typically pace the amount of stimulation according to this gaze cycle, stimulating more as the infant looks, and decreasing stimulation as the infant looks away. Although these are typical patterns, we have also noted a pattern of mutual "eye love" (Beebe, 1973; Beebe & Stern, 1977) in which mothers and infants can sustain prolonged mutual gaze for up to 100 seconds during periods of positive affect. These are the moments, of course, that every parent loves.

Maternal difficulty in tolerating momentary infant gaze aversion is one of the most common pictures observed in mothers and infants who present for treatment. If the mother feels that her infant does not like her or is not interested in her, she may pursue the infant, increasing rather than decreasing the amount of stimulation. In her pursuit or "chase," mother may call the infant's name, pull the infant's hand, or in rare instances actually attempt to force the infant's head to get the infant to look. Maternal "chase" behavior is counterproductive; the infant then requires more time to regulate arousal down sufficiently to return to gazing at mother. Instead, if the mother can be helped to give the baby a "time-out" to re-regulate, "cooling it" when the infant looks away, trusting her infant to return to her, the infant will rapidly re-engage.

HEAD ORIENTATION

We next observe infant head orientation to the mother: is the head oriented vis-à-vis, or displaced in the horizontal plane approximately 30, 60, or 90 degrees away? In the 90-degree aversion, first described by Stern (1971), the infant's head is tucked into the chin, which takes considerable energy. Are head aversion movements in the horizontal plane complicated by oblique angles of the head down (or up) as well? These increasing degrees of head aversion are described by ethologists as degrees of severity of "cut-off" acts (Chance, 1962; McGrew, 1972).

They are "read" by the partner as active initiations of disengagement. As the infant turns away up to about 60 degrees, he can still monitor the mother with his peripheral vision (tracking presence, direction, and intensity of movement); by 90 degrees away, or arching, however, he may lose peripheral visual monitoring of her movements. More usual gaze aversions retain head orientation within an approximately 30-degree angle from the vis-à-vis, retaining access to rapid visual re-engagement with minimal effort.

In relation to the maternal "chase" behaviors above, the infant may "dodge" with increasing degrees of head aversion, as well as arching back, freezing (described by Fraiberg, 1982), or going limp and giving up tonus. Beebe and Stern (1977) described split-second sequences of "chase and dodge" in which maternal chase movements predicted infant dodges, as the infant monitored her every movement through peripheral vision; but infant dodges also predicted maternal chase behaviors, a reciprocal, bi-lateral interactive regulation. Through increasing head aversions, arching, or going limp, this infant had a remarkable "veto power" over the possibility of a sustained, mutual gaze encounter.

FACE

If mother and infant together manage the infant's look-look away cycle so that the infant can comfortably regulate arousal, periods of sustained mutual gaze with infant vis-à-vis orientation can be enjoyed. During these periods, facial and vocal communication take center stage. By 3 to 4 months there is a flowering of the infant's social capacity. Although the innervation of the facial musculature is myelinated before the infant is born, the full display of facial expression emerges only gradually from 2 to 4 months.

The infant's opening and closing of the mouth is a powerful and continuous form of communication. Even without any hint of widening or smiling, a fully opened mouth ("neutral gape") is highly evocative (Beebe, 1973; Bennett, 1971). A fully widened smile by itself, with closed lips, is only moderately positive. As increasing degrees of mouth opening are added to a smile, positive affect increases up and up into the fully opened "gape smile," hugely exciting for both partners. Mothers intuitively roughly match the infant's increments, so that both build to a peak of positive facial excitement. Often both partners excitedly vocalize at such moments, further increasing the intensity (see Beebe, 1973; Beebe & Lachmann, 2002; Stern, 1985; Tronick, 1989). In general, mothers and infants tend to match the direction of the other's positive-to-negative affective change, increasing and decreasing together (Beebe et al., 2004). Rarely is there an exact match of expression. Elaboration (Fogel, 1993), echo, or comple-menting (Trevarthen, 1977) are better metaphors than matching or imitation (Stern, 1985). Instead of the more romanticized notion that mothers and infants exactly match, or are in exact "synch," Tronick and Cohn (1989) have shown that a more flexible process of match, mismatch, and re-match (disruption and repair) characterizes the exchange. Fur-thermore, a greater likelihood of rapid rematch (within 2 seconds) predicts secure attachment at one year. It is unusual for mothers to display no facial matching at all, particularly when infants are distressed. Malatesta et al. (1989) showed that unusual responses such as maternal joy or surprise to infant anger or sadness predict toddler preoccupation with attempts to dampen negative affect (compressed lips, frowning, sadness). We construe these patterns as "failures of facial empathy."

VOCALIZATION

A key feature of the vocal exchange is a turn-taking structure. Both partners contribute to turn-taking by matching the brief "switching pause" as turns are exchanged. Mothers contribute by slowing their speech rhythms, providing a great deal of repetition, and matching the intonation of the infant's sounds. Vocal contours refer to the "shape" of the sound. Across cultures, a sinusoidal shape indicates approval and a rightward falling shape disapproval (Fernald, 1993). Mothers also opti-mally pause sufficiently to give the infant a turn. On the one hand, mothers who prattle continuously do not permit this; on the other hand, mothers who are silent partners can disturb the development of vocal turn-taking, an essential building block of language. When infants present for treatment with difficulty in sustaining mutual gaze and the face-to-face encounter, matching the infant's vocal contours and rhythms can be an effective way to make contact with the infant. Because the infant does not have to orient or to look, approximately matching the infant's rhythms (vocal or motoric) is a non-intrusive way of helping the infant feel sensed: someone is on his "wavelength."

VOCAL RHYTHM AND THE PREDICTION OF ATTACHMENT: THE MIDRANGE MODEL

Security of attachment as assessed at 12 to 18 months is a key milestone in the infant's development. In the Ainsworth "Strange Situation" attachment test, mother and infant go through periods of free play, separations, and reunions (Ainsworth, Blehar, Waters, & Wall, 1978). Based on the infant's reactions, individual infants can be classified as having a secure, insecure-avoidant, insecure-anxious-resistant, or disorganized attachment style.

The secure infant can easily be comforted by mother and return to play, using mother as a secure base while being able to explore the environment. The insecure-avoidant infant shows little distress at separation, avoids mother at reunion, and continues to play on his own. The insecure-anxious-resistant infant is very distressed at separation, but cannot be comforted by mother's return and does not easily return to play (Ainsworth et al., 1978). The insecure-disorganized infant simultaneously approaches and avoids the mother, such as opening the door for her but then sharply ignoring her. The mother herself acts frightened or frightening, and typically has a history of unresolved loss, mourning, or abuse (Lyons-Ruth et al., 1999; Main & Hesse, 1990).

In contrast, secure attachment at 1 year is associated with better peer relations, school performance, and capacity to regulate emotions, as well as less psychopathology in childhood and adolescence (Sroufe, 1983).

Disorganized attachment at 1 to 2 years is associated with oppositional, hostile-aggressive, fearful and disorganized behavior, low self-esteem, and cognitive difficulties in childhood (Lyons-Ruth, Bronfman & Parsons, 1999; Jacobson, Edelstein, & Hofmann, 1994).

Over 50 studies have shown that the security of the child's attachment to the parent is dependent on the emotional availability of the parent, using global assessments and clinical ratings (see van Ijzendorn, 1997 for a review). Nevertheless, we still lack a full understanding of the origins of attachment, its modes of transmission, and the role of the infant (and infant temperament) in this process. Fewer than a dozen studies have used microanalysis of videotape to predict attachment outcomes.

Although infants typically vocalize only about 10% of the time at 4 months, vocalization is such a central means of communication that the way mothers and infants coordinate their vocal rhythms predicts infant attachment. Jaffe, Beebe, Feldstein, Crown, and Jasnow (2001; Beebe et al., 2000) predicted 12-month attachment outcomes from 4-month vocal rhythm coordination, assessed with a technique that samples behavior every quarter of a second. As each individual shortens or elongates the durations of sounds and silences, how tightly or loosely does the partner coordinate with adjustments in his or her own sound and silence durations? Midrange degrees of mother-infant and stranger-infant coordination at 4 months predicted secure attachment; very high and very low degrees of coordination predicted insecure attachment classifications.

This work led us to conceptualize interactive regulation on a continuum, with an optimal midrange, and two poles defined by very high (excessive) or very low (withdrawn) monitoring of the partner. High coordination increases the predictability of the interaction, construed as a coping strategy elicited by the uncertainty or threat experienced by both mother and infant. At the very low pole of coordination, both partners are behaving relatively independently of the other, interpreted as a withdrawal or inhibition of interpersonal monitoring. Although much research literature concentrates on the concept that lowered interactive coordination is a risk condition for infant development, a substantial body of work examining both high and low poles is now converging on an "optimum midrange model" as well (see Belsky et al., 1984; Cohn & Elmore, 1988; Lewis & Feiring, 1989; Malatesta et al., 1989; Sander, 1995; Roe, Roe, Drivas, & Bronstein, 1990; Leyendecker et al., 1997).

In our vocal rhythm study, very high mother-infant bi-directional coordination predicted insecure-disorganized attachment, the most problematic of attachment classifications. We interpreted the high coordination on the part of both partners as vigilance, arousal, or hyper-reactivity. Our research film of Clara at 4 months dramatically illustrates a very disturbing mother-infant pair with very high vocal rhythm coordination; subsequently, at one year, Clara was classified as showing disorganized attachment. In the research film, Clara is crying and flailing as the interaction begins. Mother excitedly repeats her name. Clara's crying rhythm and mother's rhythmic repetition of her name synchronize. Mother flashes big smiles at Clara as she synchronizes with the cry rhythm, as if attempting to "ride" high negative arousal into a more positive state. Both escalate, Clara screaming more loudly, mother now frantically vocalizing and moving Clara's arms. Although most mothers would back off, this mother just keeps going, and each partner continues to "top" the other. By the end Clara has thrown up, sobbing and writhing. In addition to vigilant vocal rhythm coordination, this interaction illustrates "mutually escalating over- arousal," a disturbance of the ability of the dyad to manage the infant's distress.

The optimum midrange model has direct clinical relevance. Vocal rhythm coordination is an important means of attachment formation and transmission. Whereas the midrange dyad retains more variability and flexibility, the tightly coordinated dyad is less flexible and variable. Too much predictability in the system may compromise flexibility and openness to change; too little may index a loss of coherence (Beebe et al., 2000). These concepts can be used in mother-infant treatments as a framework with which to evaluate interactive difficulties and the process of change, in any modality (not just vocal rhythm), as we do in the first case described below.

THE KEY ROLE OF THE FACE-TO-FACE INTERACTION

An ongoing NIMH-funded study in our lab has examined maternal self-report depression and anxiety at 6 weeks and 4 months, mother infant face-to-face interaction at 4 months, and infant attachment at 12 months, in a community sample of 132 families (Beebe, Jaffe, Chen, Cohen, Buck, Feldstein, et al., 2003). Maternal depression and anxiety at infant age 6 weeks or 4 months did robustly affect patterns of self- and interactive regulation at 4 months, but did not predict infant attachment outcomes at 1 year. Instead, it was the quality of the 4-month mother-infant face-to-face interaction itself that predicted infant attachment outcomes. The implication is that, in a community sample, distressed maternal states of mind at 6 weeks or 4 months do not necessarily lead to insecure infant attachment outcomes unless there is also difficulty in the face-to-face interaction. This study provides a further rationale for therapeutically supporting the quality of the mother-infant face-to-face interaction when mothers are distressed, which may then prevent later insecure infant attachment outcomes. Such an effort is currently under-way with the 9/11 widowed mothers and their infants, using brief videotape-assisted clinical interventions (Beebe et al., 2002).

SELF-REGULATION

From birth onward, self-regulation refers to the management of arousal, the maintenance of alertness, the ability to dampen positive or negative arousal in the face of over-stimulation, and the capacity to inhibit be-havior (Beebe & Lachmann, 2002). Neonates differ in their ability to regulate state (see for example, Korner and Grobstein, 1977; Brazelton, 1994). Infant temperament patterns, including sleep, feeding, arousal difficulties, or special sensitivities to sound, smell, or touch, are an important area of inquiry in the treatment (see DeGangi, Di Pietro, Greenspan, & Porges, 1991; Greenspan, 1981; Korner & Grobstein, 1977; van den Boom, 1995). Disturbances of infant self-regulation can be noted in patterns of autonomic distress (hiccupping; vomiting) and disorganized visual scanning, as well as pulling the hair or ear, or a history of head-banging (Tronick, 1989). Although maternal touch is a primary means of soothing a distressed infant, and extra handling is associated with diminished irritability (Korner & Thoman, 1972), some infants with difficult temperaments do not tolerate a great deal of touch (see DiGangi et al., 1991).

48

By the time infants are assessed in the face-to-face situation, typically at 3 to 6 months of age, state regulation has stabilized and fluctuations in the management of an alert state have receded with maturation of the nervous system. At this point it is difficult to distinguish between infant constitutional processing difficulties that may have existed at birth from problematic interactive patterns. Infant temperament and self-regulation are already intertwined with interactive regulation difficulties (see also Hofacker & Papousek, 1998). For this reason, infant self-regulation is both a property of the individual and of the dyad.

A study from our lab using second-by-second microanalysis of videotaped face-to-face interactions showed that 4-month infants who would be classified as insecure-avoidant at 12 months were already distinctly different from infants who would be classified secure (Koulomzin, Beebe, Anderson, & Jaffe, 2002). These future "avoidant" 4-month infants showed: (1) more self touch; (2) the necessity to self-touch while looking at mother in order to look for durations comparable to those of secure infants; (3) decreased range of facial expression, with constriction toward a predominance of neutral; (4) a disruption of the capacity to coordinate gaze and head orientation into a stable posture while smiling, so that infant gaze at mother occurred while head was "cocked for escape"; and (5) more "labile" behaviors (lasting one second), in contrast to "stable" (lasting 2 seconds or more). This study describes infant self-regulation patterns that are directly useful for identifying infants who are at risk for avoidant attachment. An examination of the mother's contribution to the interactive process is planned.

DISTRESS REGULATION

Dyads show important differences in infant ability to manage moments of heightened distress, and maternal management of infant distress. Both partners bring capacities to soothe and dampen as opposed to escalate distress. Obviously the mother has greater range and resources in this process. The pattern of "mutually escalating over- arousal," where each ups the ante, was illustrated above. In contrast, an effective form of distress regulation is a partial or loosely coordinated "joining" or matching of the infant's fuss or cry rhythm, with "woe face" and associated vocal "woe" contours (vocal empathy). In this process, the rhythm (but not the volume or intensity) of the crying is matched, and then gradually slowed down (Beebe, 2000; Gergeley & Watson, 1997; Stern, 1985).

THE STRANGER AS PARTNER

Identical to our research lab assessment, in our treatment cases mother and infant first play face-to-face, followed by infant and stranger. The stranger-infant interaction has been shown to be a sensitive predictor of infant attachment outcomes (Jaffe et al., 2001) and to discriminate treatment and control dyads (Weinberg & Tronick, 1998). Before the end of the first year, when some infants develop "stranger anxiety," the stranger is both a novel challenge and at the same time an intensely interesting new partner. On the one hand, most 4-month infants are very sociable with the stranger, to the point where often the stranger has an initial advantage over the mother. On the other hand, some infants are wary with the stranger, for example the infants of the treatment dyads in Weinberg and Tronick's (1998) study. We assess the infant's capacity to engage the stranger and, if the interaction is stressful with the mother, the infant's ability to "repair" with the stranger. The degree to which the stranger feels at ease with the infant vs. feels "wary" or needs to be "careful" not to over-arouse the infant is also noted.

PSYCHOANALYTICALLY INFORMED VIDEO FEEDBACK

"Mother-infant treatment occurs at a unique intersection of implicit 'procedural' (repetitive action-sequences) and explicit 'declarative' (symbolic) modes of processing, and it fosters a greater integration between the two modes" (Beebe, 2003, p. 34). Three orienting questions organize our approach: (1) In the procedural bi-directional "action-dialogue," how does each individual's patterns of behavior affect those of the partner? (2) In the declarative mode, can the parent verbally describe any of the ways in which he or she affects the infant, and the ways in which the infant affects the parent? (3) Are there ways in which the parent's representation of the infant, and the parent's own childhood history, may interfere with the ability to perceive the action-dialogue and to put it into words?

In the initial contact I usually have a long telephone conversation with the parent. I explain my videotape approach and my preference that the first meeting be a lab visit, because I can "see" more with the aid of the videotaped interaction. However, if the parent prefers, I start with an office visit. In the lab, infant with mother, father, stranger, and possibly nanny, are videotaped in face-to-face interaction.

The format of the lab visit for a treatment pair is identical to that for a research pair. The parent is instructed to play with the infant as she or he would at home. Each lab visit is followed within a few weeks by a two-hour feedback session in my psychotherapy office. This treatment format is extremely flexible. If a brief treatment is indicated, two to four lab visits and accompanying feedback sessions may be adequate, as in the first case presented below (see also Beebe, 2003). If a longer treatment is indicated, the same basic method is applicable. Or, in the case of a more serious situation, two therapists may easily collaborate, one proceeding with a standard individual treatment, and one functioning in the role of the consultant for the video feedback consultations (see Cohen & Beebe, 2002). An Ainsworth attachment test, coded by someone blind to the infant's status, is usually included in each treatment, somewhere between 12 and 18 months.

A long session, usually two hours, greatly facilitates the work of the feedback session. I have reviewed the videotape in detail prior to the session, informed by the patterns of regulation documented by research microanalyses, described above. In the session I follow the parent's lead, attempting to construct with the parent the "stories" of the presenting complaints and the parent's own history. This initial psychoanalytically informed conversation is a critical background to our ability to understand the "story" that unfolds in the videotape. Other important aspects of the parent's history usually emerge during or after watching the videotape together. (It is extremely rare for a parent to refuse to view the videotape. In only two of approximately 50 cases that I have seen have a parent refused. In those cases, I understood the refusal as an index of the level of trauma, and I simply used my own microanalysis to inform the interventions.)

In viewing the videotape, I attempt to translate specific details of interaction patterns revealed by microanalytic research into terms that the parent can use, based on a psychoanalytically informed view of the meaning of the parent's complaints in relation to his or her own functioning and history, and based on my understanding of any temperament or arousal-regulation difficulties the infant may have. Viewing a small portion of videotape, often at the beginning of the interaction, usually is sufficient. Nonverbal interactions are highly repetitive, and similar patterns can be discerned over and over.

I consider that one of my most important functions is to admire the parent-infant pair wherever possible. Bringing into awareness the ways in which this dyad already "finds" each other, enjoys each other, copes with disruptions, and negotiates repairs, is itself a powerful therapeutic intervention. My first goal is to point out a successful moment, using this example as an entry into learning to observe the small micro-moments of the interaction. Together we view the videotape slowly, trying to see exactly when and how and in what sequence each partner oriented, looked, cooed, smiled, or increased a smile by opening the mouth or reaching the head forward. I try to help the parent identify the exact moments where the parent responds to the infant and the infant responds to the parent. My goal is to give the parent "new eyes" to see the infant's remarkable nonverbal language, and the infant's ability to respond to minute, but nevertheless identifiable, behaviors. Together we try to describe what we see, finding a "new language" for their exchange as well. I encourage the parent to put into words what he or she is feeling, and what the infant may be feeling. Very likely I will play this positive portion several times, at least once in slow-motion.

As we proceed I illustrate how evocative minute infant facial expressions can be, moments when the parent matches the infant's vocal contours, how the parent paces and pauses, facilitating the infant "taking a turn." I note infant self-regulation and self-soothing behaviors, and ways the pair manage moments of infant distress, as they occur in the interaction. Having studied the videotape in detail in advance, I will also have selected one or two central difficult interaction patterns that I would like the parent to be able to see. Together we try to observe the effects of each partner's behaviors on the other in these difficult moments. I again inquire into what the parent felt, what the parent thinks the infant felt, and the meaning these moments have for the parent. It is here that the parent is likely to have a spontaneous insight into the problem. Being confronted with the implicit "action-dialogue" in the videotape often triggers the parent's associations to aspects of his or her history that the parent always "knew" but could not productively use in the current context with the infant.

Wherever possible I like to use research findings, illustrating with a drawing, to help parents understand the infant's behavior, shifting attention away from "the right way to do it" to infants' remarkable capacities. I emphasize what this particular infant needs to stay optimally engaged. My role is often to give permission to do less, to slow down, to wait. For example, with an infant who easily becomes over-aroused and irritable, I suggest slower rhythms, more repetition, longer pauses, and more "waiting" when the infant looks away.

I attempt to link the "stories" of the presenting complaint, the video drama, and the parent's childhood history, in an effort to understand what may interfere with the parent's ability to "see" the infant and the interaction. When specific representations of the infant (or "transferences") seem to interfere with the parent's ability to "see" the infant and how each partner affects the other, they are identified. At the end of the session the parent is encouraged to trust what has been learned, and to try not to be too self-conscious. Another videotaped assessment is scheduled in another month or two.

THE CASE OF CECIL

May: First Contact

In my first contact with Mrs. C. over the phone she told me that she had an eight-year-old son and a 9-month- old baby boy, Cecil. The older son had always been easier and had seemed to match the mother's temperament. This second baby had been different from the beginning. "He is a friendly baby, but he is not focused on me when I play with him. Cecil looks past me, unless I energetically try to engage him. He seems happier by himself. He seems more connected to the babysitter than to me." Mrs. C. thought that perhaps Cecil needed a higher level of stimulation. Or perhaps she herself had disturbed the relationship initially, she wondered, by talking to her older son while nursing Cecil. Or maybe she had never given Cecil sufficient eye-contact and intimate engagement during nursing.

The first consultation occurred in my office. Mrs. C. was warm, friendly, and seemed quite relaxed. Cecil made very good eye contact with me, with excited positive affect, and even had moments of a "gape smile." The mother then took Cecil, tried to play with him face-to-face, and could not get Cecil to engage. Cecil never even looked at her. Mrs. C. said this was typical. Mrs. C. then tried a peek-a-boo game, putting the blanket over Cecil's head. As the blanket came off, there was a moment of brief eye contact, but Cecil emerged from the blanket momentarily dazed, with a sober look. He then smiled at his mother briefly, and looked away.

My suggestion in this initial meeting was that although the peek-a-boo game did have a moment of "built-in" eye contact, it did not seem to engage Cecil. Instead of trying to force more contact through high arousal games, I suspected she would have more success if she followed Cecil's lead for eye-contact, letting him go when he looked away, and waiting until he initiated gaze before trying to engage him. I explained that looking away is the baby's natural method of re-regulating his arousal when it has become a little too high. We agreed to do a split-screen lab videotaping, so that I could try to see more of the details of the interaction. From what I could observe in the office, I had difficulty understanding in more detail why the infant was so avoidant with his mother.

June: First Lab Videotaping, Cecil 10 Months

In the lab mother and infant were asked to sit face-to-face, with the infant in a high chair. The standard instructions to the mother are to play with the infant as she would at home. One camera is focused on the mother's face, and one on the infant's face, producing a split-screen view, in which both partners can be simultaneously observed. In my microanalysis of the face-to-face play interaction, I observed that the mother continuously gave Cecil toy after toy.

Microanalysis of First Two Minutes of Mother-Infant Interaction

In the opening moments of the interaction, mother shook the toy toward Cecil, with abrupt, rapid movements, each accompanied by a strong sound, "gheh!" At each maternal movement, Cecil blinked, with mild startles. Mother then moved into, "What's that!" showing the toy, making a series of "ooooh" sounds, and Cecil's face showed a hint of a smile. As mother continued with, "Say hello, dolly, hello, Cecil, hi, baby," Cecil's face showed a hint of a slight mouth opening, and then receded into his more characteristic neutral expression, as if the stimulation was just a bit too much for him.

After a brief interruption to get the seating and the camera angles right, Cecil briefly glanced at his mother with a neutral face, and then looked down. While he was still looking down, mother asked Cecil to look at the toy, but Cecil stayed with his head down. Then mother made an interesting noise, "gurooom!" and got Cecil's attention. Cecil responded with his own "ghum!"

There was then a repetition of the earlier series of mother's rapid movements shaking the toy toward Cecil, each accompanied by a strong sound. At each Cecil blinked. Cecil then looked down and away, then shifted his body and hung over the side of the chair, limp. We have come to view such loss of postural tonus as a coping strategy in the face of overstimulation.

While Cecil was still hanging over the side of the chair, not looking, mother found a new toy, and offered it with a "sinusoidal" shaped vocal contour (the contour of approval and flirtation): "Hello, Cecil; and do you know what else?" This vocal contour is usually reserved for greeting, once eye contact has already been made. It was successful in getting Cecil to look at mother, and to pay attention to the new toy, as mother continued, "Look what's here, the dolly, look at her, look at her."

However, just at this moment, Cecil's face took on a negative frown expression, and he looked down, moved his head down, then averted, moved his head farther down, and then uttered a fussy sound. Finally, he gave up body tonus and collapsed his head into his stomach. Simultaneously with the collapsing tonus mother said, "Hello, Cecil" and gently tapped Cecil on the head with the toy. Cecil's head collapsed further into his stomach.

This is a detailed description of approximately the first two minutes of the interaction. At a more global level of description, in the rest of the ten-minute session there were nice moments of mutual gaze, and some interest on Cecil's part in the toys mother offered. However, often without pausing in her movements, or sounds, mother offered Cecil another toy, and yet another. Periodically, Cecil continued to collapse, into his stomach, or over the side of the chair, and mother gently tapped him on the head with the toy. When the play was more successful, there were nice long strings of vocal exchanges, and the mother beautifully matched the contours of Cecil's sounds. Several times Cecil showed intense interest and vocal excitement in a toy, and mother joined the excited sounds. However, Cecil did not smile. When Cecil became fussy, started to cry and shake his body, mother offered more toys.

Overall, Cecil was low-key, with his face mostly neutral. Occasionally there were some moments of eye contact, and some nice low positive moments. Mother showed excellent capacity for vocal rhythm matching, facial mirroring, and following the infant's line of regard to an object of interest. But she did not give the baby a chance to respond, or to organize an interest in the toys on his own, and thus she disrupted the baby's initiative. She also disrupted the baby's arousal regulation, over-arousing the baby by never pausing, offering one toy after another, and then "chasing" the baby when he averted gaze. I understood Cecil's difficulty with eye contact and the restriction of his facial expressiveness toward neutral as the baby's attempt to reduce his arousal toward a more comfortable range, but at the expense of the social engagement.

Toward the end of the ten-minute interaction, Cecil began to get fussy. Mother took a rattle and began to shake it, further increasing the intensity of the stimulation. Cecil got even fussier, orienting away, averting gaze. Mother then called to Cecil in the "sinusoidal" vocal contour usually reserved for greeting. Cecil did not respond. By the end Cecil was openly protesting the level of stimulation, very fussy, throwing to the floor all the toys that mother handed him, while mother never paused.

STRANGER-INFANT INTERACTION

Following the interaction with mother, I played with Cecil for three minutes, while the mother watched the interaction over a TV monitor from another room. The infant's ability to engage with a trained novel partner is a critical aspect of the assessment. Those babies who can "repair" the engagement with a novel partner are generally more resilient, whereas those who generalize the difficulty to a novel partner are in more difficulty (see Field et al., 1988). In evaluating this interaction, I noted that my tempo was noticeably slower than that of the mother. I waited for Cecil to look at me before I attempted to engage him. When he did look, he quickly smiled broadly. But then Cecil became fussy. When I handed Cecil a toy, he quickly threw it on the floor, and this was repeated over and over. In the process, Cecil was very physically active, turning around in his chair a lot.

Eventually Cecil began to bang his own body gently against the seat, as if to both self-stimulate and self-soothe. There were then a few moments of eye contact with me, with midrange positive affect, but these were very brief. Each brief gaze encounter was followed by a sequence of immediate averting, mild negative facial expression, looking down on the floor at an object, and then hanging limp, sideways over the chair, body tonus collapsed. Each time I waited, and he came back into the engagement on his own. Once he looked, he became slightly excited, with a positive expression, and then immediately became negative and averted, looking down. My overall impression was that he easily over-aroused. On the other hand, he had the capacity to re-engage on his own when I waited.

July: Video-Assisted Intervention

A two-and-a-half-hour period was set aside to meet with the mother to discuss how things were going and to review the videotape. The mother had already watched the tape and she felt bad. She realized that she was "trying too hard" and it was not working. She saw me as smoother, quieter. I suggested that as we watched the tape, we could try to make quite specific just what she was doing when she felt she was "trying too hard." My own goal was to help the mother notice exactly what she did, and exactly what the infant did, as each responded to the other. In essence, I wanted to give her new "eyes," a new ability to observe the details of interaction.

In this process my goal was to help her confirm what she did quite beautifully, which elicited the response from the baby that she wanted, as well as to notice what did not work for her baby. I admired her facial empathy, her vocal responsiveness, and her well-modulated vocal con-touring (see McDonough, 1993). She was quite surprised when I pointed out the infant's blinks and startles at the beginning of the inter-action, in response to her abrupt movements with the toys. She was also surprised to see me point out very subtle facial expressions of slight mouth openings, hints of shifts in cheek tonus, which can be expressions of interest and involvement, even when the infant is not smiling.

We succeeded in defining the mother's "trying too hard" as lack of pausing in movement or voice, trying to get the infant's attention when he was turned away, and calling the infant in a "greeting" contour at moments when the infant was clearly not receptive. I told Mrs. C. my hypothesis that Cecil dampened his face, lowered his arousal, averted gaze, and turned away, as self-regulation strategies in the face of feeling over-stimulated. Mrs. C. then told me that her own mother was rigid, controlling, distant, and quite depressed, although she had managed to work. Her mother was never attuned, had never been able to sense Mrs. C.'s feeling state as a child, and never knew "where she was at." Mrs. C.'s mother had "set the pace," irrespective of where she was emotionally or what she needed. And now Mrs. C. could see that she was doing the same thing with Cecil—setting the pace, and setting it too fast for him.

We then discussed my description of Cecil's face as too neutral, and I showed her again a section of the videotape illustrating it. I reenacted for her the face I saw in the baby. Mrs. C. said that all of a sudden she saw Cecil's face as like that of her own mother, who had always appeared impassive, hard to read, hard to reach. She saw that she now felt the same way about Cecil—that Cecil was hard to read, hard to reach, like her mother. And she saw that she would become anxious, and try harder with Cecil, as she had when her own mother had been so difficult to read. In this interaction, the mother's ability to "see" Cecil's "too-neutral" face seemed to be facilitated by watching the videotape as well as watching my own entry into the baby's neutral face. Now "seeing" Cecil's neutral face seemed to trigger her procedural "motor memory" of her own mother's face.

Together we saw how understandable it was that she could be treating Cecil the way her own mother had treated her by setting the pace, and that she could be seeing Cecil as like her own difficult and removed mother. We both empathized with how hard it must have been for Mrs. C., as Cecil seemed to become more and more un-readable. How natural it was to keep trying harder, as a way of reaching him. And how counterintuitive it was to lower the stimulation, to "try less hard," to be slower and calmer, to wait, just when she was feeling more and more desperate to reach Cecil.

We both felt sad over Mrs. C.'s own difficult childhood, and the aspects of it that entered into her interactions with Cecil. But as we parted we both felt encouraged by understanding what the difficulty was. Mrs. C. felt very positive about the experience, and stated that she thought she could shift what she was doing with Cecil now. I suggested that she try to trust herself with what she had learned, without becoming overly self-conscious or self-critical. We agreed to do a follow-up split-screen videotaping and an Ainsworth "separation test" in a couple of months.

AUGUST: SECOND FILMING, 12 MONTHS

There had been a long wait in the lab, and technical difficulty delayed the beginning of the filming. Even without such delays, sitting in a high chair for ten minutes is hard for any active 12-month toddler. Once we got started, there was no sound track for a couple of minutes. In evaluating the interaction, I observed that the mother was slower and softer, and she paused in between her movements and her vocalizations. Cecil made more eye contact, and it was more sustained. The mother did not push toys at Cecil; instead Cecil himself took a toy and explored it, and mother was able to wait. There was clearly more room for Cecil's own initiative.

MICROANALYSIS OF FIRST TWO MINUTES OF MOTHER-INFANT INTERACTION

As the videotape began, Cecil was tired. He had been there a long time, waiting for us to get going. Without the sound in this section, we see Cecil rocking his body back and forth in the chair. Mother then rocked her own body a bit too, matching the rhythm. Mother then showed Cecil a doll. Cecil concentrated on it, while mother held it quietly. After a few minutes, Cecil lost interest, and mother showed him another toy. Cecil took the toy, held it close to his body, explored it, again while mother waited quietly. Then there was an interruption at the door. Mother was told that the sound was now working, and was asked if she wanted to continue the filming. We agreed to continue.

The interruption disturbed Cecil, and now he very much wanted to get out of the seat, holding his hand up in an appeal to be picked up. The mother was gentle, slow, and held him, but without taking him out of the chair. Mother made a "woe face," joining the infant's distress, and was very sorry that Cecil couldn't get out yet. Cecil collapsed into his stomach, fussing, and mother matched the distress sounds. Mother then tried some puppet play, moving the puppet very slowly, and Cecil briefly engaged. Then Cecil was distracted by the sound of the camera moving, and mother joined his line of regard, explaining the noise. Cecil then made another bid to get out, and mother joined Cecil's vocal distress with similar sounds, and held him close.

Describing the rest of the session, at a more global level: after a few minutes, mother did a peek-a-boo game, covering Cecil's face with her hands and saying, "where is Cecil?" This time the quality was totally different: slower and very successful. Cecil emerged smiling, and sustained the positive affect. Then Cecil was briefly quiet, and mother waited. Cecil then heard the noise of the camera again, and mother joined his line of regard, and waited. Now Cecil wanted to get out again, and this time I stopped the filming after seven minutes. There was nothing the mother did in this second filming that seemed to interfere with the infant's capacity to play and to respond.

STRANGER-INFANT INTERACTION

We then attempted a stranger-infant filming, but Cecil would have none of it. He cried loudly, angrily, and threw any toys on the floor. Three different attempts by me to play with Cecil had to be aborted, since he was crying hard. Finally, we organized a set-up in which Cecil sat in mother's lap, and mother was instructed to "be the chair," not to help or respond.

For the first five minutes of the interaction, Cecil was disengaged. He was silent, made no eye contact, and every toy that I tried to engage him with was immediately thrown on the floor. However, at some point he finally made a vocalization, a "spit" sound. Immediately I matched this sound. And right away he looked at me and made another, similar one. All of a sudden the whole tenor of the interaction had changed, and we were engaged in a fascinating vocal dialogue. As we continued to match and elaborate on each other's sounds, at some point Cecil began to move his tongue as he made the sounds, and it came out as "la-ler, la-ler." He was intensely visually engaged. I tried making the "la-ler" sound, and we both burst into big smiles, and giggled. Variations on this rich vocal dialogue continued for the next four minutes. Cecil had been enormously responsive to my matching his vocalization. Since this form of engagement does not require the child to be visually engaged, it can potentially provide a less intrusive or demanding means of making contact. His own willingness to elaborate on the jointly formed patterns was critical to the success of the dialogue.

Toward the end of the interaction Cecil began to be tired. Although he had been having a spirited, at times elated, turn taking dialogue with me (as he sat in his mother's lap), when he began to get tired, he arched away into his mother's body, and avoided me. But then he was able to keep coming back to me, and to continue the rhythm of the vocal exchange. These movements away from me were his own self-regulatory efforts to manage his arousal within a comfortable range. The success of his self-regulation efforts could be seen in his continuing ability to re-engage me, in cycles of vocal dialogue, disruption, and then repair (see Tronick, 1989; Beebe & Lachmann, 1994). This aspect of the interaction with me was used as part of the therapy. It was a demonstration of a way to make contact without forcing, intruding, or chasing. It also vividly showed the power of vocal rhythm matching in making contact, since the child does not have to make eye contact.

This laboratory filming ended with a brief discussion with the mother that her interaction with Cecil was going extremely well now. We made a decision not to pursue the attachment test since the visit had already been too long. Cecil was doing well, and all we needed to do was to watch to be sure he continued to be fine.

FOLLOW-UP CONTACTS

September

A telephone conversation: "Things are just great. We were on vacation for three weeks and we had a lot of time to spend ... I totally relaxed with Cecil. I got to know him better. I stopped my agendas, stopped comparing him to his brother. He is a delightful baby; we are just charmed by him; he is now so social. I had seen this side of him from time to time, but now it has really come out. He is more bonded with me too; he wants mommy only. He seems terrific. I'm enjoying how different he is from his brother.

November

A letter: "You have played an absolutely pivotal role in my life.... To begin with, Cecil; our connection is deep and easy and full of joy. He is an absolutely delicious, funny, charming, very loving little person.... you helped me relax and see him; I stopped focusing on who he was not and on how he and I were not.... So, having discovered Cecil, I fell in love with Cecil. No surprise.... In retrospect, my feeling of self-reproach was based on some accurately sensed stuff. I intuitively knew that I was not being with him or being emotionally responsive to him anywhere near as much as I can be. Now I am, and let me tell you, the difference is not minor."

DISCUSSION OF THE C. CASE

We return here to the theme that parent-infant treatment occurs at a unique intersection of implicit and explicit modes of processing and fosters a greater integration between the two.

Our three orienting questions provide a framework for conceptualizing the treatment: (1) In the implicit mode of action-sequences, how does each partner affect the other? (2) In the explicit narrative mode, can the parent verbalize the nature of either partner's effect on the other? (3) And does the parent's representation of the infant interfere with the ability to perceive the nonverbal action dialogue? From the presenting complaints it is clear that parents are aware of some aspect of the infant's behaviors, and particularly ways in which the infant affects the parent, such as, "my baby does not smile at me," or "my baby does not look at me." But it is harder to observe one's own behaviors which affect the infant. Often various representations of the infant disturb this process further.

Addressing the infant's impact on the mother, Mrs. C. could observe as well as verbalize that her infant often did not look at her, or smile at her. When asked how she would respond to this, however, Mrs. C. was vague: "I try harder," or "He needs more stimulation." Addressing the mother's impact on her infant, Mrs. C. had not been aware of the specific behaviors that we were able to describe together, for example, rapidly moving into the face, not pausing, continually offering toys. Identifying these specific behaviors enabled Mrs. C. to observe the moments in which they influenced the infant to disengage, for example, to startle, look away, collapse into the stomach, or inhibit initiation with toys.

We were able to identify some of the "transferences" to the infant that seemed to disturb Mrs. C.'s ability to observe and verbalize both sides of the bilateral effects of each partner on the other. She acted like her own mother, who had "set the pace," and her infant seemed to act like Mrs. C. had as a little girl, that is, to "withdraw." Her own "setting the pace" behaviors (not pausing, continually offering toys) were out of her awareness. Mrs. C. was aware that her infant was withdrawing from her, but she was not aware of how similar her infant's behavior was to that of her own in childhood. Thus she and her infant had "re-enacted" an aspect of her own history, the mother who sets the pace and the child who withdraws.

Similarly, the infant seemed to act like Mrs. C.'s own mother, since the infant had an "impassive" face, neutral, impossible to read, which reminded Mrs. C. vividly of her own mother's face. Mrs. C.'s response to her own infant's impassive face was very similar to her response to her mother's face when she had been a little girl, that is, to become anxious and to try harder. Presumably the similarity of this interaction with ones in her childhood interfered with Mrs. C.'s ability to see that her "trying harder" was just pushing her infant farther away from her.

These transferences were identified in the process of watching the videotape. Being presented with the procedural level of action sequences which are out of the mother's awareness, presumably because they are connected to painful childhood experiences, facilitates the mother's ability to see, and to remember. The mother is being asked to make a unique integration of procedural and declarative information, in an arena that has been out of awareness due to some kind of unresolved pain. This work allows the mother to shift her representation, for example, from the baby rejecting her, to the baby as over-stimulated and attempting to dampen his arousal.

The optimum midrange model of regulation described above is useful as a framework for evaluating the progress of the treatment. At the outset of the treatment, Cecil could be described as preoccupied with self-regulation (looking away, showing lowered level of arousal, constricting the range of the face), with lowered levels of contingent

64

coordination with mother's behaviors through facial, visual, and vocal behaviors, and with his initiative shut down, body collapsed. Mother could be described as a "high coordinator," very contingently responsive to the infant's every move, with excellent facial-mirroring and vocal rhythm matching, but interacting with levels of stimulation that were too high, with patterns that were spatially intrusive, that disturbed the infant's initiative.

Following the videotape intervention, the mother was able to move from high to more "midrange" coordination, less vigilantly responsive to every infant move. She was able to pause more, do less, wait, tolerate the infant's disengagement without "chasing," tolerate the infant's distress, and give the infant space to initiate play. Moments of matching were interspersed with "waiting" for the infant's own moves (of self-regulation, or initiative), so that they did not seem "excessive," or imposed. The infant for his part shifted from a "low-coordinator" and became more "midrange" in his level of contingent tracking of the mother, more midrange in facial responsivity with both positive and negative expressions rather than a predominance of neutral, more visually engaged, and much more active in initiating play with objects.

THE CASE OF NICOLE

The case of Nicole is a useful counterpoint to the Cecil case, which illustrates mild maternal intrusion coupled with some temperament and arousal regulation difficulty in the infant. Nicole, on the other hand, illustrates a maternal "absence of provision." Because this family was from a distant city, and I happened to be traveling nearby, the mother-infant pair was not evaluated in my lab, but rather in an office, and they were only seen in person for one extended three-hour evaluation, together with a number of follow-up telephone consultations. Since the problem turned out to be an absence of intimate engagement, rather than a complex misregulation of engagement between infant and mother, it was a case in which a detailed videotape evaluation was luckily not essential. In the Cecil case, I was not able to detect the problem without the videotape microanalysis. In the case of Nicole, knowledge of the microanalysis research was nevertheless essential to the treatment.

Mrs. N. was referred by her therapist, who described her as an anxious new mother, strongly involved in her hard-driving career. Mrs. N. had become worried that her five-month-old baby was not as responsive to her as she was to the Nanny, and she had requested a consultation with an infant "expert." The therapist suggested that Mrs. N. probably had difficulty giving focused attention to her daughter because she had never gotten much herself.

The first contact was a telephone session. Mrs. N. felt "disconnected" from her daughter. She described feeling crushed when she arrived home to see her daughter laughing and giggling with the Nanny, but Nicole would not even look at her. "I've been going 100 miles per hour all day, and Nicole has been with someone laid back with nothing to do but to be with her. I take Fridays off, and it takes her quite a while to warm up. My husband does not think it is anything to worry about. But what will it do to her in the long-term? I feel like she does not love me, that I'm not good as a mother, I'm not as natural as the Nanny. How much I need her love. I envisioned a different reaction to me. She smiles more to my husband and the Nanny than to me."

"I have never seen myself as a mother. I was little 'Miss Career.' My mother was domestic, but she resented it. We were toys and dolls to her. Now I want to pick back up the domestic side, but it does not come naturally." I commented that evidently she did not have a model of what it would be like to really enjoy one's child: her mother resented children and domesticity. It was very understandable that it would be hard for her to learn. "I don't measure up to the Nanny; she knows exactly what to do. I don't mind if she loves the Nanny, but I want her to love me more. It's my nature to be doing three things at once. Instead of being able to relax, and take the time to be with her, I'm on the phone. I tell myself, this is her time, don't pick up the phone." As she told me this, I sensed the rapid clip of her speech. I commented on how aware she was that she needed to try to relax and slow down to be with Nicole. "I don't like myself when I am with her. I feel like my mother when she's running around like crazy and can't get organized." I said that evidently she had learned to be like her mother in this, and perhaps it had been a way of being close to her own mother. But now she's not so happy about it, and she's trying to help herself change it. We then discussed exactly what happens when she comes home from work. She nurses Nicole when she comes in, but the infant will not look at her. "Maybe it's because I always had the phone in my ear when she was nursing. Have I hurt her now? Can it be fixed? Would I have had a better relationship with her if I had been different? She did not deserve a mother like me." And then she cried.

I empathized with her agony over feeling that she had disturbed her relationship with Nicole. I told her how important it was that she had taken the step of calling me, and that she was struggling to find a way to slow down to be with Nicole. She lamented that she did not do it right, and that she had been stupid. I said that we needed to find a way of re-righting this without blaming. She responded that I had a beautiful voice, and that she felt smart for trying to get help.

The second contact was a three-hour consultation with the mother and baby. Although the father came as well, he declined to be involved. This was the only contact in which I actually saw them in person because of the extremely long distance involved. Nicole at 5 1/2 months was a big girl, and heavy. Mrs. N. propped her up at one end of the couch with a toy. As she was settling Nicole in, the infant's body arched away from her. Mrs. N. then sat at the other end of the couch. I pulled up a footstool and sat halfway between the two of them. The baby played with the toy, putting each different part of it in her mouth, quite placid and self-sufficient. She never looked at her mother or at me, nor did she look around the room, while her mother talked to me about her work schedule and her dilemma of work vs. home life.

Nicole then needed her diaper changed. She had a large bowel movement. Mrs. N. was gentle, solicitous, and managed it well. Now Mother and Nicole were together on the couch, and Mrs. N. showed me a "pull-to-sit" game that she plays with Nicole, a game that her friend had taught her. The baby clearly knew the game, anticipating the moves with her body, but she did not look at her mother, her face showed no animation, and at the last moment before attaining the sitting position, her head oriented up and 30 degrees away from the vis-à-vis. Mrs. N. then held Nicole lying across her lap on the infant's back. This was the nicest connection they made, slow, both bodies relaxed, both looking at the other, but without smiling. Mrs. N. then began to talk about how terrible she felt: "Have I hurt her, what will be the effect, will she know her own mother, should I stop working?" She cried during most of this discussion.

After about an hour, I suggested that we start to see how we could help her engage Nicole more. I said that I did not think the issue was the amount of time that she worked, as much as finding a way to make a connection with Nicole. I explained that first I needed to play with her to try to see her range of responsiveness. Nicole chortled, with high positive affect, sustaining long gazes with me. She was marvelously socially engaged. From this interaction it was clear that the difficulty was not an incapacity on the part of the infant. Evidently, the social engagements with her Nanny and her father were going well.

I then set about trying to teach Mrs. N. how to engage Nicole. The first thing I taught her was vocal rhythm "matching," making sounds contingent on the baby's sounds, both matching and elaborating on the intonation, pitch, and rhythm. I chose this first because the child does not have to make eye contact in this mode of relating. Mrs. N.'s sounds were thin and squeaky. She did not give the sounds a robust prosody, she could not elaborate on them, and she did not put any words to the sounds. She did not seem to know how to play. I coached the sounds from the sidelines. Eventually the sounds she made were adequate to make some contact with the baby. Nicole oriented to her a bit more, and returned some of Mrs. N.'s sounds with her own, beginning a rudimentary vocal dialogue. But Nicole did not look at her mother.

Noting how flat her face was as she interacted with Nicole, I then tried to teach Mrs. N. facial mirroring, by having her roughly match some of my faces (gape smile, mock surprise). I tried to get her to move her face in ways similar to the ways I moved mine (small increments of open mouth, open a little more, then a little more; moving the upper lip in and out of a purse etc.). She was unable to play with her face; her face was tight, flat, and unvarying. I then had the idea of showing her how to unlock her jaw, and how to massage her face. I asked her if she would be interested in trying this. She agreed. In this process she had an association to her mother's angry, tight face, and she became a little teary. I suggested that her reaction to her mother's angry face was expressed in her own facial tightness and constriction. She was receptive and felt sobered by this idea. The attention to the behavioral details of the procedural level, particularly the constriction, seemed to trigger her representation, which we could then address and elaborate at the symbolic level.

We then moved to an attempt at face-to-face interaction between mother and baby. At first Nicole was very gaze avoidant and her whole body arched away from her mother. The infant made absolutely no eye contact. Gradually I taught Mrs. N. to slow down and to make some slow rhythmic sounds, and to do vocal rhythm matching if Nicole made any sound. When the infant would give her a darting glance, I taught her to give an exaggerated mock surprise greeting. The instant the infant looked away, I taught her to "cool it." Nicole began looking a bit more. We spent quite a while at this.

By the end of the three-hour session Nicole showed some brief partial smiles to her mother. The gazes were not sustained. But Mrs. N. had a direct, powerful experience of getting some more response from her baby. She could see that she was getting somewhere. She expressed relief and gratitude that I had validated that something was wrong. I reminded her of the many things that were right as well: she had a very gentle and affectionate capacity to hold Nicole and to feed her, she did have some games she played with the infant, and most of all, she wanted more contact with her.

Ten days later we had a telephone session. "Now I make it totally Nicole's time when I get home. If I can slow down, we can connect better. By the end of the week I feel totally disconnected from her. When the Nanny leaves, she is used to her. I have to be careful: I expect her to demonstrate affection and attachment. When I don't get it, I get worried. Sometimes she does not make any sounds, so I can't mimic her." I asked her if she could start it with occasional sounds of her own. "My husband can walk in the room and connect with her right away. He is like the Pied Piper. It is hard for me. I feel bad that I don't connect the way he does. If I don't get a lot of feedback, I feel unliked." I asked if there was then a danger that she would feel rejected and withdraw. She agreed, yes, very much. She then reported that Nicole is not as avoidant as she was: "She looks at me, she watches, though she does not smile. She can concentrate on my face though, that's new." She told me that Nicole was right there with her, looking at her face right now. I suggested she try a mock surprise expression right now, and she did. I waited a moment while Mrs. N. played with her. She reported that Nicole looks but she does not smile. "She will watch me now if I do interesting things with my face. But I noticed that if I'm tense I close my face up." I said that it was wonderful that she was trying to engage her child with her face, and that Nicole was clearly beginning to respond. I congratulated her on becoming so aware of her own face, and able to notice when she closes it up.

"When Nicole looks at my husband, she gets this glow; will it always be this way? In the morning I am terrible with her. I'm trying to get ready, I'm in a hurry, and I do a dancing conversation in front of her face, all speeded up." I commented on Mrs. N.'s increasing ability to notice what she does and to see if it is disturbing Nicole's ability to connect with her. She then asked, "Have I lost my chance? When I left you, I felt so bad, and angry; I missed my chance. I should have stayed home and not worked." Without waiting for me to respond, she immediately told me that Nicole was looking at her right now, and Mrs. N. began to make sounds. We practiced the "sinusoidal" shaped "hello," she and I saying it to each other, and she reported that Nicole was looking constantly at her while she made the sinusoidal sounds.

Then I asked her about feeling angry. She said that she was angry her husband wasn't encouraging her to quit work, and she was angry that no one had been agreeing with her that something was wrong. She felt that finally I had validated her. "I would be devastated if I do not have a good relationship with Nicole. She lights up for my husband. She is so responsive to the Nanny. But what you are saying to me is, it's not too late for me to connect. I've never felt so insecure in my life." I empathized with her fear and distress. Then I told her how terrific it was that she was holding on to her hope to connect with Nicole, and that she and I could both see progress.

A telephone message two weeks after the initial three-hour session in person: Mrs. N. was canceling our tentative appointment to see each other in person because she and Nicole were doing so well: "I am getting so much feedback from her, I am relaxing a little. She smiles more, looks more. I don't feel crazy anymore. All of a sudden she has started really vocalizing. The biggest thing you said was, focus on her. When I'm with her, I'm just giving her all my attention."

A telephone session one month after the initial three-hour session in person: "She's wonderful, she's happy, she's more vocal, more expressive, she's really relating to me. Occasionally we have a bad evening. But I'm more comfortable around her. I may be doing more of her language. I try to slow it down for her. If I'm rushing, I notice it. Then I just hand her to the Nanny, because I don't want her to sense it. I imitate her sounds, but not all the time. If she initiates, and I respond, and make it even bigger, then she laughs." I tell her how wonderful all this is, how thrilled I am that things are so much better. "I think we're doing a lot better. When I come home, I get a greeting. She looks, she smiles, she kicks." Then she asked me if it was a mistake not to come for a second consultation in person, and I said no, I didn't think so, because things were going so much better. We agreed that she would call me if she had any more concerns. She thanked me profusely. I told her that it was so remarkable how quickly she and Nicole were able to turn things around.

DISCUSSION OF THE N. CASE

This pair illustrates an absence of maternal provision of the usual "infantized" facial and vocal behaviors that engage infants in face-to-face play. Presumably the more adequate "provision" of the Nanny and the father had to this point safeguarded the overall social development of Nicole. The mother's frozen face and inhibition of maternal "play" behavior required me to figure out how to get the action sequences going, how to "prime the pump."

Mrs. N.'s immediate transference to me in the first telephone contact as having a beautiful voice set the stage for me to "provide" something that seemed to have been absent for her. By teaching her specific ways of engaging the infant, that is, vocal rhythm matching, vocal contouring, facial mirroring, and "cooling it" when the baby looked away, it is possible that she experienced a "provision" from me. I was also admiring of her willingness to try these new behaviors, and of her increasing ability to engage Nicole, as she tried it, over the phone.

The key to unlocking Mrs. N.'s capacity to mother Nicole was the discovery of her traumatic reaction to her own mother's face, which was then "carried" in a procedural form through her inhibition of her own face with Nicole. In retrospect, the vocal modality proved to be easier for Mrs. N. to develop with Nicole. Since the vocal modality did not require Nicole to look, it was initially easier to reach Nicole this way. But Mrs. N. had also been so responsive to my voice, from the very first contact, and she carried on most of her relationship with me over the telephone. It may be that the voice was a "non-traumatized" mode for Mrs. N., compared to the face (M.S. Moore, personal communication, August 18, 1999).

DISCUSSION

Many different approaches to mother-infant treatment yield dramatic progress (see for example Cramer et al.,1990; Fraiberg, 1980; Seligman, 1994; Stern, 1995) (but note that controlled clinical trials are rare). Although the use of video feedback is growing, three decades of micro-analysis research on the mother-infant face-to-face exchange is surprisingly under-utilized in current treatment approaches. Microanalysis of behavior allows us to perceive the details of interactions which are usually too rapid to grasp with the naked eye. These details provide the clinician with the ability to translate the parent's presenting complaints into specific behaviors which can then be understood as an unfolding "story" of the relationship. With the additional perspective of the dyadic systems view of communication (despite the mother's obviously greater ability and range of resources) the clinician can continually attempt to understand how each partner contributes to the exchange, how each affects the other. And the clinician can notice how the self-regulation strategies and styles of both partners affect and are affected by the nature of the interactive exchange. With this perspective, for example, negative interactions such as "chase and dodge" or "mutually escalating over-arousal" can be seen as reciprocally responsive co-constructed forms of engagement. This system's view helps us remain empathic to how each partner is affected by the other.

However, video microanalysis of the interaction from a systems view can only richly set the stage for the treatment. A clinician's sensitive ability to construct jointly with the parent a description of the exchange, to help the parent use the behavioral details of the video drama as a springboard for memories and associations, and to link the stories of the presenting complaints and the parent's own history to the video drama, form the core of the treatment. The clinician's careful attention to the parent's self-esteem, particularly feelings of shame and humiliation, is essential.

The video feedback method does not disturb the dyad while they interact. Later, when the parent and I view the videotape, it is simultaneously "immediate" and visually concrete, as well as somewhat "distant" and safer, in that it is not happening right now (Lefcourt, personal communication, July 7, 1998). In the video replay we can concentrate on a particular modality, and slow it down, whereas in the live interaction all modalities, as well as words, flood the senses. Since the visual information speaks on its own, the therapist is free to emphasize different aspects, to underscore the positive elements as well as identify derailments (Tabin, personal communication, September 10, 1998). Because the mother is usually so motivated to engage her infant, she can make an effort to overcome any natural awkwardness at seeing herself. We rarely know what we really look like as we interact. Seeing oneself on videotape may operate like a "shock" to the unconscious, "perturbing" the system (Milyentijevic, personal communication, June 26, 1998; Kohler, personal communication, October 23, 1998). This "shock" may be part of the emotional power of the video feedback method. The therapeutic viewing promotes a capacity to observe oneself in interaction, to think about the emotions seen in the video, and to reorganize representations (Beebe, 2003, p. 45).

Both parents in the two cases presented felt that the treatment validated their sense that "something was wrong." Mrs. N. was able to persist in trusting her discomfort even though her husband did not think there was a problem. This vague discomfort is the parent's ability to sense the impact of the implicit procedural mode and enables the parent to seek treatment. But the meaning of this discomfort is not usually recognizable without help (Tabin, personal communication, September 10,1998). Procedurally organized interactive memories that are unrecognized and unsymbolized often come to play a role in shaping the action-language of our intimate interactions as well as the representations of our intimate partners. The psychoanalytically oriented video feedback method goes directly to the core interactional dynamic that is out of awareness and provides a safe format in which this dynamic can be verbalized and reflected on. The parent can become more aware of the infant's "mind" as well as her own (Fonagy et al., 2002). In this process, implicit, procedural aspects of the parent's mode of relating to the infant, which have remained out of awareness, can be translated into explicit, narrative forms of understanding.

BIBLIOGRAPHY

AINSWORTH, M., BLEHAR, M., WATERS, E., & WALL, S. (1978). Patterns of attachment. Hillsdale, N.J.: Lawrence Erlbaum Press.

BAKERMANS-KRANENBURG, M., JUFFER, F., VAN IJZENDOORN, M. (1998). Interventions with video feedback and attachment discussions: Does type of maternal insecurity make a difference? Infant Mental Health Journal, 19 (2), 202-219.

BEEBE, B. (1973). Ontogeny of positive affect in the third and fourth months of the life of one infant. Dissertation Abstracts International, 35 (2), 1014B.

BEEBE, B. (1982). Micro-timing in mother-infant communication. In M. R. Key (Ed.), Nonverbal communication today. Series Edited by Joshua Fishman, Contributions to the sociology of language. Volume 33. New York: Mouton.

BEEBE, B. (2000). Co-constructing mother-infant distress. Psychoanal. Inq., 20, 421-440.

BEEBE, B. (2003). Brief mother-infant treatment using psychoanalytically informed video microanalysis. Infant Mental Health Journal, 24 (1), 24-52.

BEEBE, B., JAFFE, J. & COHEN, P. (2002). Support groups and video-bonding consultations for mothers and infants of 9-11. Manuscript, NYSPI, April, 2002. FEMA Liberty Fund; Robin Hood Foundation.

BEEBE, B., JAFFE, J., & LACHMANN, F. (1992). A dyadic systems view of communication. In Skolnick & S. Warshaw (Eds.), Relational perspectives in psychoanalysis (pp. 61-81). Hillsdale, N.J.: Analytic Press.

BEEBE, B., JAFFE, J., LACHMANN, F., FELDSTEIN, S., CROWN, C., & JASNOW, J. (2000). Systems models in development and psychoanalysis: The case of vocal rhythm coordination and attachment. Infant Mental Health Journal, 21, 99-122.

BEEBE, B., JAFFE, J., BUCK, K., CHEN, H., COHEN, P., FELDSTEIN, S., & ANDREWS. (in press). Maternal depression at 6 weeks postpartum and mother-infant 4-month selfand interactive regulation. Infant Mental Health Journal.

BEEBE, B., JAFFE, J., CHEN, H., COHEN, P., BUCK, K., & FELDSTEIN, S. (2004). Mother and infant self- and interactive regulation across modalities: A systems view. Manuscript submitted for publication, N.Y.S. Psychiatric Institute.

BEEBE, B., JAFFE, J., CHEN, H., COHEN, P., BUCK, K., FELDSTEIN, S., et al. (2003). Mother and infant self- and interactive regulation and distress: Maternal distressed states of mind, mother and infant behavioral distress patterns, and infant attachment. Report submitted to NIMH, R01MH41675, Nov. 1.

BEEBE, B., & LACHMANN, F. (1994). Representation and internalization in infancy: Three principles of salience. Psychoanal. Psychol., 11 (2), 127-165.

BEEBE, B., & LACHMANN, F. (2002). Infant research and adult treatment: Co-constructing interactions. Hillsdale, N.J.: Analytic Press.

BEEBE, B., LACHMANN, F., & JAFFE, J. (1997). Mother-infant interaction structures and presymbolic self and object representations. Psychoanal. Dial., 7 (2), 133-182.

BEEBE, B., & STERN, D. (1977). Engagement-disengagement and early object experiences. In N. Freedman & S. Grand (Eds.), Communicative structures and psychic structures (pp. 33-55). NY: Plenum.

BENNETT, S. L. (1971). Infant-caretaker interaction. J. Amer. Acad. Chld

Psychiat.10: 321-35.

BOWLBY, J. (1969). Attachment and loss (Vol. 1: Attachment). London: Hogarth Press.

BRAZELTON, T. B. (1994). Touchpoints: Opportunities for preventing problems in the parent-child relationship. Acta Paediatrica, 394 (Suppl.), 35-39.

BRAZELTON, T. B., KOSLOWSKI, B., & MAIN, M. (1974). The origins of reciprocity. In M. Lewis & L. Rosenblum (Eds.), The effect of the infant on its caregiver (pp. 49-70). New York: Wiley-Interscience.

CALL, J. (1963). Prevention of autism in a young infant in a well-child conference. J. Amer. Acad. Child Psychiat., 2, 451-459.

CHANCE, M. (1962). An interpretation of some agonistic postures. Symposium of the Zoological Society of London, 8, 71-89.

CHANCE, M. & LARSEN, R. (Eds.) (1996). The social structure of attention. New York: Wiley.

COHEN, P., & BEEBE, B. (2002). Video feedback with a depressed mother and her infant: A collaborative individual psychoanalytic and mother-infant treatment. Journal of Infant, Child & Adolescent Psychotherapy 2 (3), 1-55.

COHN, J., & BEEBE, B. (1990). Sampling interval affects time-series regression estimates of mother-infant influence. Abstracts, ICIS. Infant Behavior and Development [Abstracts], 13, 317.

CRAMER, B. (1995). Short-term dynamic psychotherapy for infants and their parents. Child and Adolescent Psychiatric Clinics of North America, 4, 649-659.

CRAMER, B. (1998). Mother-infant psychotherapies: A widening scope in technique. Infant Mental Health Journal, 19 (2), 151-167.

CRAMER, B., ROBERT-TISSOT, C., STERN, D., SERPA-RUSCONI, S., DE MURALT, M., BESSON, G., et al. (1990). Outcome evaluation in brief mother-infant psychotherapy: A preliminary report. Infant Mental Health Journal, 11 (3), 278-300.

CRAMER, B., & STERN, D. (1988). Evaluation of changes in mother-infant brief psychotherapy: A single case study. Infant Mental Health Journal, 9 (1), 20-45.

DEGANGI, G., DI PIETRO, J., GREENSPAN, S., & PORGES, S. (1991). Psychophysiological characteristics of the regulatory disordered infant. Infant Behavior and Development, 14, 37-50.

DOWNING, G. (2004). Emotion, body and parent-infant interaction. In: J. Nadel & Muir D, editors. Emotional development: Recent research advances. Oxford: Oxford University Press.

EIBL-EIBESFELDT, I. (1970). Ethology: The biology of behavior. New York: Holt, Rhinehart & Winston.

FERNALD, A. (1993). Approval and disapproval: Infant responsiveness to vocal affect in familiar and unfamiliar languages. Child Dev., 64 (3), 657-674.

FIELD, T. (1981). Infant gaze aversion and heart rate during face-to-face interactions. Infant Behavior and Development, 4, 307-315.

FIELD, T., HEALY, B., GOLDSTEIN, S., PERRY, D., BENDELL, D., SCHANBERG, S., et al. (1988). Infants of depressed mothers show "depressed" behavior even with nondepressed adults. Child Dev., 59, 1569-1579.

FOGEL, A. (1993). Two principles of communication: Co-Regulation and framing. In J. Nadel & L. Camaioni (Eds.), New perspectives in early communicative development (pp. 9-22). London: Routledge.

FONAGY, P., GERGELY, G., JURIST, E., & TARGET, M. (2002). Affect regulation, mentalization, and the development of self. New York: Other Press.

FRAIBERG, S. (1980). Clinical studies in infant mental health: The first year of life. NY: Basic Books.

GERGELY, G., & WATSON, J. (1997). The social biofeedback theory of parental affect-mirroring. Int. J. Psycho- Anal., 77, 1181-1212.

GOTTMAN, J. (1981). Time-series analysis. Cambridge: Cambridge University Press.

GREENACRE, P. (1971). Emotional growth. New York: International Universities Press.

GREENSPAN, S. (1981). Psychopathology and adaptation in infancy and early childhood: Principles of clinical diagnosis and preventive intervention. New York: International Universities Press.

HOFACKER, N., & PAPOUSEK, M. (1998). Disorders of excessive crying, feeding, and sleeping: The Munich interdisciplinary research and intervention program. Infant Mental Health Journal, 19 (2), 180-201.

HOPKINS, J. (1992). Infant and parent psychotherapy. Journal of Child Psychotherapy, 18 (1), 5-19.

ISABELLA, R., & BELSKY, J. (1991). Interactional synchrony and the origins of infant-mother attachment: A replication study. Child Dev., 62, 373-384.

JAFFE, J., BEEBE, B., FELDSTEIN, S., CROWN, C., & JASNOW, M. (2001). Rhythms of dialogue in infancy (pp. 1-132) Monographs of the Society for Research in Child Development, 66, (2, Serial No. 265).

KEENER, M., ZEANAH, C., & ANDERS, T. (1989). Infant temperament, sleep organization and nighttime parental interventions. Annual Progress Child Psychiatry & Child Development, 257-274.

KOULOMZIN, M., BEEBE, B., ANDERSON, S., JAFFE, J., FELDSTEIN, S., & CROWN, C. (2002). Infant gaze, head, face and self-touch at 4 months differentiate secure vs. avoidant attachment at 1 year: A microanalytic approach. *Attachment & Human Development*, 4(1), 3-24.

KORNER, A., & GROBSTEIN, R. (1977). Individual differences at birth. In E. Rexford, L. Sander, T. Shapiro (Eds.), Infant Psychiatry (pp. 69-78). New Haven: Yale University Press.

KORNER, A., & THOMAN, E. B. (1972). The relative efficacy of contact and vertibular-proprioceptive stimulation in soothing neonates. Child Dev., 43, 443-453.

LANDRY, S. (1996). Effects of maternal scaffolding during joint toy play with preterm and full-term infants. Merrill-Palmer-Quarterly, 42 (2), 177-199.

LEBOVICI, S. (1983). Le nourrison, la mere, et le psychoanalyste: Les interventions precoces. Paris: Le Centurion.

LESTER, B. M., HOFFMAN, J., & BRAZELTON, T. B. (1985). The rhythmic structure of mother-infant interaction in term and preterm infants. Child Dev., 56, 15-27.

LEWIS, M., & FEIRING, C. (1989). Infant, mother, and mother-infant behavior and subsequent attachment. Child Dev., 60, 831-837.

LIEBERMAN, A., & PAWL, J. (1993). Infant-parent psychotherapy. In C. Zeanah (Ed.), Handbook of infant mental health (pp. 427-442). New York: Guilford Press.

LOJKASEK, M., COHEN, N., & MUIR, E. (1994). Where is the infant in infant intervention? A review of the literature on changing troubled mother-infant relationships.Psychotherapy, 31, 208-220.

LYONS-RUTH, K. (1998). Attachment disorganization: Unresolved loss, relational violence, and lapses in behavioral and attentional strategies. In J. Cassidy & P. Shaver (Eds.), Handbook of attachment theory and research (pp. 520-554). New York: Guilford Press.

MAIN, M., & HESSE, E. (1990). Parents' unresolved traumatic experiences are related to infant disorganized attachment status: Is frightened and/or frightening parental behavior the linking mechanism? In M. Greenberg, D. Cicchetti, & E. Cummings (Eds.), Attachment in the preschool years: Theory, research, and intervention (pp. 161-182). Chicago: University of Chicago Press.

MALATESTA, C., CULVER, C., TESMAN, J., & SHEPARD, B. (1989). The development of emotion expression during the first two years of life. Monograph of the Social Research in Child Development, 54, (1-2, Serial No. 219).

MALPHURS, J., FIELD, T., LARRAINE, C., PICKENS, J., PELAEZ-NOGUERAS, M., YANDO, R., et al. (1996). Altering withdrawn and intrusive interaction behaviors of depressed mothers. Infant Mental Health Journal, 17 (2), 152-160.

MARVIN, R., COOPER, G., HOFFMAN, K., & POWELL, B. (2002). The Circle of Security project: Attachment- based intervention with caregiver-pre-school dyads. Attachment & Human Development, 4 (1), 107-124.

McDONOUGH, S. (1993). Interaction guidance. In C. Zeanah (Ed.), Handbook of infant mental health (pp. 414- 426). New York: Guilford.

McGREW, W. (1972). An ethological study of children's behavior. New York: Academic Press.

O'CONNOR, T. G., HERON, J., GOLDING, J., BEVERIDGE, M., & GLOVER, V. (2002). Maternal antenatal anxiety and children's behavioural/emotional problems at 4 years. British Journal of Psychiatry, 180, 502-508.

PROVENCE, S. (Ed.). (1983). Infants and parents: Clinical case reports. Clinical Infant Reports: The National Center for Clinical Infant Programs. New York: International Universities Press.

SAMEROFF, A. (1983). Developmental systems: Contexts and evolution. In W. Kessen (Ed.), Mussen's Handbook of Child Psychology, Vol. 1 (pp. 237-94). New York: Wiley.

SANDER, L. (1977). The regulation of exchange in the infant-caretaker system and some aspects of the context- content relationship. In M. Lewis & L. Rosenblum (Eds.), Interaction, conversation, and the development of language (pp. 133-156). New York: Wiley.

SELIGMAN, S. (1994). Applying psychoanalysis in an unconventional context: Adapting infant-parent psychotherapy to a changing population. Psychoanal. St. Child, 49, 481-510.

STERN, D. (1995). The motherhood constellation. New York: Basic Books.

STERN, D. (1971). A microanalysis of the mother-infant interaction. J. Amer. Acad. Child Psychiat., 10, 501-507.

STERN, D. (1974). Goal and structure of mother-infant play. J Amer. Acad. Ch Psychiat.13, 402-421.

STERN, D. (1985). The interpersonal world of the infant. New York: Basic Books.

STERN-BRUSCHWEILER, N., & STERN, D. (1989). A model for conceptualizing the role of the mother's representational world in various mother-infant therapies. Infant Mental Health Journal, 10, 142-56.

THOMAS, E. A. C., & MALONE, T. W. (1979). On the dynamics of two-person interactions. Psychological Review, 86, (4), 331-360.

TREVARTHEN, C. (1977). Descriptive analyses of infant communicative behavior. In H. R. Schaffer (Ed.), Studies in mother-infant interaction (pp. 227-270). London: Academic Press.

TRONICK, E. (1989). Emotions and emotional communication in infants. Am. Psychol., 44, (2), 112-119.

TRONICK, E., & COHN, J. (1989). Infant-mother face-to-face interaction: Age and gender differences in coordination and miscoordination. Child Dev., 59, 85-92.

TUTORS, E. (1991). Developments in infant-parent psychotherapy: Therapeutic technique, therapeutic action and current infant observation research. Infant Mental Health Journal.

VAN DEN BOOM, D. (1995). Do first-year intervention effects endure? Follow up during toddlerhood of a sample of Dutch irritable infants. Child Dev., 66, 1798-1816.

WEINBERG, K., & TRONICK, E. (1998). The impact of maternal psychiatric illness on infant development. Journal Clinical Psychiatry, 59, 53-61.

BIO

BEATRICE BEEBE, PH.D. is Clinical Professor of Medical Psychology (in Psychiatry) at the College of Physicians and Surgeons, of Columbia University, the Department of Child and Adolescent Psychiatry, New York State Psychiatric Institute. She directs a basic research lab on mother-infant communication. She is a faculty member at the Columbia Psychoanalytic Center, the Institute for the Psychoanalytic Study of Subjectivity, and the New York University Postdoctoral Program in Psychotherapy and Psychoanalysis; she is also an honorary member of the William Alanson White Institute and the American Psychoanalytic Association. She is co-author with Jaffe, Feldstein, et al. of Rhythms of Dialogue in Infancy (2001); author with Lachmann of Infant Research and Adult Treatment (2014) and Co-Constructing Interactions (2002), author with Knoblauch, Rustin and Sorter of Forms of Intersubjectivity in Infant Research and Adult Treatment (2005); author with Jaffe, Markese, et al. of The Origins of 12-Month attachment: A microanalysis of a 4-month mother-infant interaction (2010) and author with Lachmann of the Origins of Attachment: Infant Research and Adult Treatment (2013). Currently, she directs a primary prevention Project for mothers who were pregnant and widowed on 9-11. The project therapists have written a book, Beebe, Cohen, Sossin, and Markese [Eds.], Mothers, infants and young children of September 11, 2001: A primary prevention project (2012). She is author with Cohen and Lachmann of "The Mother-Infant Interaction Picture Book: Origins of Attachment" (Norton, 2016).

CHAPTER 3

Playing in the Intergenerational Space

Laurel M. Silber, Psy.D.

Playing in the Intergenerational Space

Laurel M. Silber, Psy.D.

"The most obvious difficulty in observing maternal behavior lies in determining which of the partners in the mother-infant interaction initiates, sustains, or completes an observable act...as far as direct observation could show, and never considered in isolation, who did what to whom was in many cases very difficult to discern" (Brody & Axelrad, 1978, 20).

THE SUBJECT OF INFLUENCE

The bold scientific move to expose messy intersubjectivity ('who did what to whom') of real parents and children advanced our theoretical understanding beyond earlier psychoanalytic considerations of child development, derived primarily from the reconstructed analysis of adults (Warshaw, 1992). Infancy research findings contributed to the paradigm shifting from a one-person to a two- person relational psychoanalytic model. Sylvia Brody boldly proclaimed, essentially, the 'Emperor has no clothes,' as she examined the subject of parental influence on the developing child. Or was it rather, to play with the metaphor a bit, she took the clothes off the emperor? In either case, as her work illustrates, it sometimes becomes critical to 'go outside,' or to zoom in from a different angle, to illuminate a subject and see what is right in front of us.

"Our work is outside the usual tradition of psychoanalytic studies..." Brody and Axelrad (1978, p.4) continue, "specifically, we have tried to determine the parents' psychological influence on the development of the young child, in the way acceptable to the general scientific community, and with reliance on as few metaphorical concepts as our present psychoanalytic knowledge allows." To be clear, the objective was to replace reliance on the Oedipal Complex as a conceptual basis of child development with scientific data. The one-person notion of the analyst as neutral or free of influence was further deconstructed in the act of fixing the lens on 'what is really happening' in development between a parent and a child. This kind of empirical research became important to shifting technique in the relational turn within psychoanalysis. As a result of our enhanced understanding of developmental phenomena, the change process itself became better understood.

The boundaries between mother and infant (and by extrapolation, self and other), as Brody and Axelrad observed, were difficult to discern. Further articulation of this interaction from infancy research has given us rich concepts such as dyadic systems view (Beebe & Lachmann, 2003), implicit relational knowing (Lyons-Ruth, 1998), reflective functioning and mentalization (Fonagy, 2002, Slade, 2008), negative maternal attributions (Lieberman, 1997), and dyadic expansion of consciousness model (Tronick, 2007), for highlighting co-created procedural level processes that are highly influential to the change process. This confluence of findings was further augmented by attachment research (Main & Hesse, 1999) with special emphasis on the findings from the Adult Attachment Interview (George, Kaplan, & Main, 1984, Steele & Steele, 2008). The Boston Change Process Study Group (2010) collaborated across this prodigious area of child developmental research for its new implications for psychoanalytic technique. Infancy research essentially created a foundation for a bottom up model of child development. The import of the findings for the change process was a technical shift away from the emphasis on verbal interpretation of repressed unconscious material to co-creating or tri-creating (therapist, parent and child) emergent experience in the intersubjective space of the treatment relationship. Unformulated experience becomes known and 'thought about' through play and enactment. Dissociated experience becomes, through shared knowing, less a haunting influence disorganizing the quality of attachment to earning greater security within and between self and others. Moreover, by opening up parental subjectivity in the two- person model, the child's subjectivity becomes better understood as well as legitimizing the use of the therapists' subjectivity, as a vector of influence in the bi or multi-directional treatment process.

Consider the following comments regarding opening up the domain of parental subjectivity in the introductory remarks of Brody and Axelrad's study, *Mothers, Fathers, and Children*: "A parent may be gladdened by the child's progress or fearful or guilt-ridden because of the child's troubles; a parent's defensiveness may be more of less reinforced; he or she may acquire insight, gain or lose control of ego functions temporarily, or identify the child with his or her own parents or siblings; superego pressures in the parent may be, and usually are intensified. New tasks, new sensations come into play, suggesting that inner changes which may have profound emotional impact, especially on the body ego, are taking place in the parent" (Brody & Axelrad, 1978, p.10). Development is contextualized as a relational event and parents change along with their children. The transformations that happen are different, however, each acts as an influence to the change in the other.

The 'parental mistake' (Jacobs and Wachs, 2002) becomes an opportunity for relational reworking. When and how does a 'parental mistake' become the subject of the child's treatment? How to repair ruptures in the parent-child relationship? There is no one portal of entry into the tangled knots of troubled parent-child relationships. Shame can be a formidable force potentially foreclosing an expansive process. In the two cases to be discussed, a port of entry was through the child's play communication. How the child played in therapy was a special communication about the nature of the implicit relational knowing between themselves and their parents. Children express through their symptoms and spontaneous gestures of play where they are stuck and unable to make sense of their interpersonal world. Opening up the clinical domain of playing in the intergenerational spaces is an outgrowth of pioneering infancy research such as the work of Sylvia Brody. Parental influence grew into a more nuanced study of parental subjectivity, part of a mutual, albeit asymmetrical process, and an implicit part of the child's play communication. How the child experiences the subjectivity of the parent and how the parent mentalizes the child's subjectivity becomes part of the tri-constructed work for the relational child therapist. The child therapist's use of self and play in the paradigm shift to relational child therapy has technically expanded and become more complex. The child is developing in a non-linear dynamic system and the meaning of the play is seen in this context.

In the shift to discuss two clinical cases some of these theoretical aspects will hopefully be clarified in the discussion. In the first case, the play constructions are transparent as to better illustrate the link between a child's play communications to the implicit affective intersubjective space of the child-in-relation-to-their-caretakers. In the second case, a parental mistake, transgenerationally transmitted trauma, emerged into more explicit focus in the clinical example. In the latter example, relational work between the parent and child transformed the quality of the attachment.

FIRST CLINICAL EXAMPLE: PLAY AS A PORTAL INTO THE PARENT-CHILD INTERSUBJECTIVE SPACE

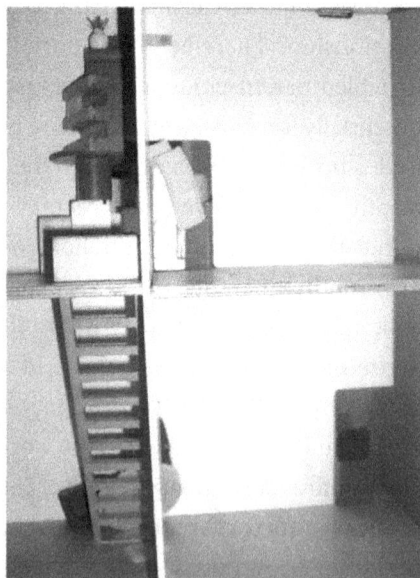

Figure A: Mary's construction of the dollhouse

The picture of a dollhouse shared above is the construction of a five-year old, whom I will call Mary, in her early play sessions. Ms. D brought Mary for a consultation due to a continuous troubling symptom of constipation, which stimulated a great deal of secondary shame and pain. Ms. D had taken Mary to her pediatrician who found no physical cause for her constipation and impacted colon and a psychotherapeutic consultation was recommended. Subsequent to her parents' messy and bitter divorce when Mary was two, she and her newly single mother and sister moved to a different city leaving their father behind. Mary couldn't tell me about her troubles, she was 5 years old, however she showed me.

I took pictures of the dollhouse Mary constructed after she left the session. If you will notice every entryway in the house is clogged. The doll furniture was used to stuff up the spaces between the rooms. The dollhouse is essentially constipated; every portal is blocked, nothing can get in or out; the house is in lock-down. The house was a representation of her embodied troubles. Mary giggled as my character attempted to move around the house and complained that she can't seem to get anywhere she needed to go. My character expressed fear as she tried to move unsuccessfully through blocked passageways: "Jeez, these chairs could fall down on me!" My character expressed feeling terribly alone: "is anyone there?" And, "Heh, I can't get out!" "Is no one going to come find me?" As a result of playing with a representation of her affective reality, and reflecting on the impact to her body's dysregulation, the following treatment strategy developed. With her in mind, we made a pivot to the intersubjective space of her family. Mary needed help to acknowledge and grieve her losses. In subsequent sessions her mother and sister joined us to talk together, sharing the process of the many transitions and losses the girls had sustained in their young lives. The girls moved around my consulting/playroom, playing, talking, drawing, sitting on their mother's lap (who was sitting on the floor, to be near them) and crying. They described a contemporary fear, how afraid they were when their mother and her new boyfriend went away on a vaca-tion. The mother newly registered, with my help, how that must have been scary to them. The girls had never been to the vacation spot the mother was going to and they had trouble imagining it. They wondered what was the fate of the new boyfriend? Would be become a stepfather, they wondered? The question, what about their father they didn't dare ask. The girls further elaborated what had been troubling and confusing to them by drawing pictures of a dog they had when they lived in their old house with their father. They explained to me how sad they felt when they dropped off the dog at a farm, as they prepared to move. As the mother was making her transition, packing up her girls to start their new life, there was an implicit relational request to dissociate the affect associated with these changes and Mary was having trouble conforming to the request. She was making a mess of it.

This illustration was a beginning to a therapeutic process that had a number of starts and stops. When Mary's father moved to the area while she was participating in therapy he joined her in sessions as well. We discussed her witnessing her parents in lock-down. When it was time to go to her father's (in the divorced landscape of alternating living locations) she was 'put outside' so the parents could remain in 'separate rooms' and not have to speak to each other, for example. The interpersonal field was formative for Mary: one she mapped out in her mind and body, disorganizing her regulatory mechanisms. What's outside is inside, what's inside influences what happens outside. This was 'the material' she drew from for her play, she was trying to make sense of the split off worlds of her parents, and she created a house with blocked access. It was the implicit field of her family and her self-development was vulnerable to the chaos.

Shining a light on the outside, the interaction, in a frame by millisecond frame of infancy research, has enhanced our ability to privilege the interaction and its effect on Mary's symptomatology. The psychic equivalence of her symptoms necessitated the scaffolding "a third" space, a therapeutic play space, not inside and not outside, but in the overlap of both, a pretend space to make explicit her feelings, and to move them out of her body. The mourning process was facilitated with support, and validating her experience within her family context, began the project of building an intermediate zone for representing her experience, and therefore her self-agency.

TRANSMITTED INTERGENERATIONAL TRAUMA IN THE IMPLICIT SPACE

"If you cannot get rid of the family skeleton, you may as well make it dance." George Bernard Shaw, Preface, Immaturity.

The mechanism of transmitted trauma to the next generation, or secondary generational effects (Main, 1999) is primarily in the procedural (Seligman, 1999), and implicit realm of experience. The play space is highly sensitive to registering the effects of intergenerational trauma. The parent's dissociative defenses, developed in relation to their primary trauma of the past, are co-creating an incoherent experience and fear in the child, which is a secondary trauma. The child in this intersubjective circumstance is frustrated in his/her attempts to understand the intentionality of their attachment figures, which serves as a developmental interference to mapping a theory of mind. The child wonders what is going on here and why the sense of danger? Mary embodied her fear; it was non-mentalizable. Added to the confusion, is the affective counterpart of parental dissociative defenses, for example, 'when I (the child) become helpless or scared and cry out it creates, 'crazy, mad dad' or 'withdrawn, gone mom.' This is the legacy to the next generation of the dissociated trauma on the part of the parent, it is felt and experienced, but the reasons for it are unknown and therefore incoherent to the child. Their compass to the social world is in need of repair. In the circumstance of transgenerationally transmitted trauma, the child's symptoms are incoherent to the parents, as well. The dilemma in the parent-child relationship describes what is inherent to disorganized attachment: "fright without solution" (Hesse & Main, 2000).

Locating the intergenerational vulnerability is an **opportunity** for the child in the present moment of his/her development and for the parent to re-represent the past experience. The child serves unwittingly as an evocative trigger to this aspect of the unresolved past in their parents (Coates, 2012). The adversity was defended against in the first generation (a parent's childhood trauma) and now in the next generation comes an opportunity for the parent to find meaning for the experience.

In addition to the trauma affecting their child, it is also happening at a distance from the parent; it is one step removed. These two factors (that are both different and the same) set up the conditions to potentially resolve the trauma within the parent- child relationship. The parent has new circumstances influencing the motivation and ability to grapple with the trauma. Dissociation was 'called in' to defend against the primary trauma, (an attempt to get rid of the skeleton, in line with the Shaw quote) however, in the secondary context of the next generation, new possibilities for therapeutic action emerge. Is there adequate distance, in adulthood, and concern/responsibility/love as a parent, to expand consciousness and see what had heretofore been felt as too scary? In the opportunity to recontextualize the trauma, the parents become instrumental in their own healing through recognizing their child. What had been a psychic equivalent mode of relating matures to a more differentiated mentalized ability within the parent to their child. Opening up dissociated trauma is experienced as dangerous and destabilizing, a vulnerability likely contributing to partial success or failed treatments. It is not always so easy to get the skeleton to dance.

SECOND CLINICAL EXAMPLE
THE NEXT GENERATION:
A FUTURE'S DANCE WITH THE PAST

In this next clinical piece, I will share a repetitive game Margaret invented during her play therapy when she was eight. I will then leap ahead and focus on family work when she was thirteen to illustrate the child's development of self agency in her relational context through the impasse of transmitted intergenerational trauma. I had seen the child when she was eight years of age because she was unhappy, and socially anxious. She had temper tantrums the night before a test at school, for example, fearing she would not be ready.

In her play therapy, when she was eight she made up a game. She instructed that I was to close my eyes, stand in the middle of the playroom and try and guess if, when and where light touches of a tissue were felt (it could have been my left arm, right shoulder, my head, and it may not have happened). This game was a unique variation on the popular game of hide and seek. I wondered what she was trying to tell me about her implicit affective experience? Could she be trying to tell me how confused she felt? She laughed as I shared my confusion and inability to be sure of what in fact happened with my eyes closed. The "other" in the game, is holding onto a secret that is having an influence on 'me'. I think I felt the tissue, but I am not sure I am right about that, did it really happen? I don't know if I can have confidence in my knowledge because while I felt it I don't know for sure. The experience of getting it wrong, repeatedly, without a way to "see" what is going on, was frustrating. This kind of affective experience brought forward in the play, is the kind of implicit field that is disorganizing to the developmental need for a social compass. Can I know what I know? It was interesting to me that Margaret would return to a next session and say, "let's play that game again!" The meaning of this sequence didn't fully make sense to me until she arrived back for some work when she was thirteen.

Margaret had made some progress during her play therapy and her parents discontinued the work after a year and a half, when she was ten. Sporadically, over the course of two years, her parents returned for consultation around parenting issues. A year following these sporadic parental consultations, the parents arrived back in a crisis. Margaret's distress had escalated and she was saying she wished she were dead. Margaret, who was now thirteen, was depressed, anxious, and irritable in the family. The intervention shifted to family sessions to respond to the crisis and due to the working alliance that had developed over the past few years. The session I am about to share is at the resumption of her direct participation in therapy. In the initial family session, as the parents began to talk, Margaret stormed out of the room and went to the bathroom down the hall, slamming the door. She was highly reactive to what they had to say. She returned to the session, explaining that she felt blamed for everything all the time. Her little brother was creating paper airplanes with misspelled words and from behind the couch he sent messages of doom, that we better get out of here, go home.

In a subsequent family session Margaret's mother called attention to an upsetting afternoon. She shared that her husband, Margaret's father had become very upset and shouted a long list of expletives about an adult concern – the garage door broke and now there are more bills to pay! What the mother was concerned about was that she saw Margaret, who witnessed the event nearby in the driveway, run and hide, shaking as she cried. As an aside, since extended family networks are not serving as a net for parents, children often feel the isolation and presume themselves into the spot of co-regulating parental anxiety. Margaret was overwhelmed and not sure how to regulate all that anger on the part of her father. Nor should she but there she is. Until this time in the family session, there had been no reflection on the child's reaction or state of mind, which now found an opportunity, introduced by her mother. Relevant to this moment in the work, was prior work with Margaret's mother to organize her thoughts to speak her mind, regarding parental and workplace concerns. She was now responsive to her daughter's need for support to speak her mind. Margaret had been sitting with her back turned at the drawing table, however her mother's brave move to begin to mentalize Margaret's experience turned a soft touch of a tissue into a represent-able feeling. That became the subject of the family work, helping the father to think about the impact of his moods on his children. We shifted to consider his influence in the here and now in relation to Margaret. In this discussion, his daughter turned in her chair to face her father directly and said that the way he acted scared her. Here is her repair, their repair and the way she came to find her self-agency, asking for her affective world to be made coherent. He began to see the situation from her point of view and this moved the dialogue further, by that, it is meant, both within himself and between them and within her.

This important recognition led to the father's request for some individual sessions. The individual work was in connection to the family work, and allowed him to elaborate now with a kind of immediate emotional urgency, a relevant important circumstance from his childhood. Mr. M (Margaret's father, who had participated in his own therapy and couples work independent of Margaret's therapy) was twelve when he lost his father in a shameful way; his father was arrested and incarcerated for two years. This trauma was kept as a formative secret. Mr. M's father (Margaret's grandfather) had experienced war trauma and was unable to find ways to resolve it. The secrets associated with his war trauma, we conjectured, had likely set the stage for his illegal activity, once returned to civilian life. The many challenges Mr. M faced in conjunction with this loss were discussed. The way he felt parentified to take care of his mother and younger brother, the shame he felt in the community and the doubts he carried about himself and sadness, confusion and anger toward his father. His fathering was deeply influenced by the feelings about his father from his childhood. We were able to draw connections between his experience as a child to what was happening to his daughter as she was becoming so depressed and anxious. He further began to see that he was burdening her with a sense of shame for any infraction. He would emphasize to her that as the oldest she was such an important influence to her younger siblings, saying things to her like, 'how could you do that?' 'What do you think your younger siblings will think?' 'You have to set an example.' We began to see his fear, in relation to his father, intensifying his reaction with projections to his children, most notably, Margaret. We thought about his anxieties and the burdens he carried and how his daughter unwittingly was sensitive to them. As he shifted his stance in relation to her and she became more supported to call him out on his incoherent behavior (too frightened and frightening) she was less anxious and more engaged socially. She was supported to know what she knew, which was that her father was misattributing to her aspects of his past trauma. He began to recontextualize his trauma, deescalate his fear, feel forgiving to his father, and then to himself. When the "skeleton was asked to dance," that is, reflect on what had been shrouded in pain and fear, Mr. M could see the present moment differently. He was a different father, and what happened to his father is not going to happen to him or his daughter. They will not have to experience abrupt departures. Margaret's father wrote a narrative of his childhood experience in conjunction with this work that he shared with me. In knowing what he knew, in a new way, he could trust in his own fathering at a time of heightened fears. The psychic equivalent aspects of the unresolved trauma were compromising the next generation's attempt at development. He felt more confidence regarding his fathering and appreciated his daughter more. The normative challenges of differentiating at her adolescence were triggering loss and trauma for which the system couldn't affectively regulate. The broken garage door wasn't the only thing needing repair. Margaret requested individual sessions of her own after the family work that spanned approximately six months. Her suicidal feelings were no longer in evidence and she was engaged in her academic and extra curricula projects. Her ability to reflect on her feelings took a major developmental leap.

DISCUSSION

The parental transmission of traumatic affect is simply translated; traumatic pain that the parent, when he/she was an overwhelmed child was unable to establish meaning for, and in the act of dissociating it they then became a latent carrier to the next generation. The adults relying on dissociation for the traumatic pain are very susceptible to triggers. That is the tricky aspect; one does not "get rid" of trauma. Parenting a child represents the most common evocative trigger (Coates, 2012). Children become mired in the confusing projections and the parents are mired in it as well. The relationship becomes out of whack and the child therapist is in a unique position to establish the links between them that honors the present capability – busting the past ghostly presences that are living in the present (Silber 2012).

That is what I found so uncanny about what Margaret's tissue game was symbolizing in the first phase of her work. The game was an ingenious metaphor for the "snags" and "chafings" (Stern, 2010) of affective discontinuities felt in her implicit relational world. Stern's reference to disjointed affective experiences as "snags" and "chafings," signifies, "Something feels inconsistent, countering an affective expectation we did not even know we had until that moment; it feels subtly 'wrong' or contradictory or just uncomfortable" (Stern, D.B., 2010, p.82). This description is to elaborate the experience for the adult relational analyst with their adult patient, suggesting an emergent moment in the work. Margaret had an ingenious way of 'telling' me of her experience of "snags" and "chafings"; incoherent affective experiences she was puzzled by in her intersubjective space with her parents. In her tissue game, she created a play sequence for me to understand how confusing it was for her. She didn't know what to believe, and that lonely, scary place in her childhood, was what was validated in her play. This play sequence foreshadowed her ability to assert a claim to make things right; her turn in her chair, to speak directly with eyes open. She was right to think something was wrong, in other words. She requested we play that game again and again. In reflecting back on her symptoms when she was eight, she was overwhelmed by a test at school, terrified that she was going to get something wrong. We did not yet discover the meaning to her perfectionistic attitude. She was overreacting and continuing to try to sort out her parents' overreaction. Her thought process suggested something like this, 'if my parents are this distressed about my behavior toward my younger siblings, for example, maybe that is who I am, someone who should fear it could go terribly wrong?' It was in the later phase, with her parents present in shared work that the tissues/ghostly presences of the affective relational world became more explicit.

As the boundaries of 'who is doing what to whom' while difficult to discern, as Dr. Brody, stated and quoted at the outset of the chapter, an additional layer was added of unpacking multi-generational influences informing the intersubjective space. This expanded space of inquiry led to Margaret and her parents moving out of a psychic equivalent mode to a more respectful renegotiating of real boundaries at her adolescence. Margaret's father was so worried about her, he felt fearful of being able to protect her, and that he could lose her (or she him), which we were able to recognize as transmitted trauma from his real experience of the abrupt shameful departure of his father at his adolescence. Her 'leaving,' part of a developmental passage, was shrouded in traumatic 'leaving,' and her anguished wish to die reflected the impasse. She was afraid and confused about what the incoherent affect meant and afraid of her father being afraid of her, in his many efforts to control her behavior. The escalating fear to the system is at the heart of the disorganized attachment dilemma. Margaret shifted to talking about anxieties in relation to her peers, in her request for individual sessions. The crisis had passed and she was in a new relational context. Remarkable for the physical differences, the prior stomping out of the room, slamming the door, refusing to participate, sitting with her back to the others in the room, to her shifting to sit upright and request sessions to discuss her concerns. Her parent's shift in relation to her, felt instrumental to this hopeful expression of her self- agency at her adolescence. Her mother felt less confused and anxious about her daughter and talked about being proud of her. Margaret's mother reflected on her own inability to confront her parents when she was a child.

Many parents were perplexed about their children state, "I was never able to speak that way to my parents!" This recognizes the frame of reference for parenting is the experience of having been parented. The current ambivalent wish to change that up, shared by the child as well, is in the present moment of their child's development. How to honor the ghost of the past with a known narrative, and convert the influence from an inhibiting secret that was dissipating to the system was the therapeutic challenge. In the course of the enactment in therapy, the dissociated experience and attendant pain gave way to relief that the present generational moment was different. Like waking from a nightmare, the fear was in relation to the past, not the reality of the present. The boost to Margaret's development, that she had instead the recognizable fears of adolescence, distinct from imagined, projected confusing heightened anxieties for which she was protesting, was a relational achievement. In empathizing with all of them, including mentalizing Margaret's paternal grandparents' troubles, I bore witness to the reorganizing of traumatic experience in the next generation. Kairos, quoted by Daniel Stern (2004, p.7), refers to an opening in the present to expand awareness of what is happening and demands action. New relational patterns have a chance to be formed, in both surviving the break to the old patterns and establishing the link between the evocative present moments to the past. The daughter did not die, though she felt like it and they feared it, it was the old patterns that were represented and mourned. The family moved on to a more complex relation to reality, with a better boundary between themselves and time.

CONCLUDING DISCUSSION

In reworking transgenerationally transmitted trauma, parents not only are influential to the child's development as Sylvia Brody set out to document, they can be a vital part of the corrective process. They transform themselves from functioning in a non-mentalizing, psychic equivalent mode of interaction, in relation to traumatic material, to a capacity for recognition in the expanded dyadic communication to their child. The research contributions of the Adult Attachment Interview (Hesse, 1999) are critical to scaffolding this clinical process. The strong connection between the parents' representational world to the quality of the attachment status in their child, established in this research, affirmed the therapeutic direction.

Child relational work involves a non-linear dynamic view of the open system of the family and therefore incorporates data from multiple parts of the system. Moreover, when working with the impact of intergenerational transmission of trauma within the system an important source of information comes from unformulated experience. The dynamic experience arrives in fragments and is a confluence of experiences across the system. As the system was destabilizing when Margaret was thirteen, from her distress and suicidal thoughts/feelings, her younger brother's missives, her father's parental anxieties and heightened affect and her mother's new assertiveness, there were multiple indicators of chaos in the shifting forces. In the parent's ability to take responsibility and recognize past trauma as interfering in their present relationship to their child, a newfound freedom to interact emerged. The interaction between Margaret and her siblings became less competitive and more playful subsequent to this work.

There are hazards to this kind of relational work. There have been other cases for which suicidal thoughts, comments, and even gestures on the part of the child and/or the parent have accompanied reworking of the intergenerational transmission process. The suicidal ideation became a 'thing of the past' as the change in the present relationship stabilized.

There are several ports of entry into the complex intersubjective space of the parent-child relationship. The child's play expresses their interpretation of events and therefore offers an opportunity to mentalize the child's perspective. Margaret and I played at the frustration she experienced in relation to her implicit relational space. The recognition of affective inconsistency (she knew I knew), represented in the play of the tissue game, further developed her resolve to authentically speak about her confusion with a direct gaze in her treatment context. The blindfold came off and she asked for reparation. The pivot to the parents was a clinically expansive shift and increased the complexity of the process.

Child relational therapists are in a unique position to continue to explore the clinical implications of infancy research for the purposes of linking generations in the shared pursuit of more complex knowing and being. Exposing the 'naked' vulnerability (in reference to the emperor) of the intergenerational relational space, in all it's vitality and blurred boundaries, errors, misattunements, distortions, and deletions, makes it real and creates the possibility of dance or repair into the next generation. Psychoanalysis has historically been reluctant to bring the implications of parental influence into direct focus for child treatment. Sylvia Brody was mindful of this resistance yet moved forward, as she stated, 'in the way acceptable to the general scientific community and with reliance on as few metaphorical concepts as our present psychoanalytic knowledge allows.' It is within the future of relational psychoanalysis to continue to develop clinical skills for working within this tri-created intersubjective space of mothers, fathers and their children.

REFERENCES

Beebe, B., Lachmann, F.M. (2003) The Relational Turn in Psychoanalysis: A Dyadic Systems View from Infant Research. Contem. Psychoanal., 39, 379-409.

Brody, S. Axelrad, S., (1978). Mothers, Fathers, and Children; Explorations in the Formation of Character in the First Seven Years. New York: International Universities Press, Inc.

Coates, S. (2012). The Child as Traumatic Trigger: Commentary on Paper by Laurel Moldawsky Silber. Psychoanalytic Dialogues, 22, (1) 123-128.

Fonagy, P. Gergeley, G., Jurist, E., & Target, M. (2002). Affect regulation, mentalization, and the development of the self. New York: Other Press.

George, C., Kaplan, N., & Main, M. (1984, 1985, 1996). Adult Attachment Interview [Unpublished protocol]. Berkeley: Department of Psychology, University of California, Berkeley.

Hesse, E. (1999), The Adult Attachment Interview: Historical and Current Perspectives. In Handbook of Attachment: Theory, Research, and Clinical Applications, (Eds.) Cassidy & Shaver. New York: Guilford Press. p.395-433.

Hesse, E., & Main, M. (1999). Second-generation effects of unresolved trauma as observed in non-maltreating parents: Dissociated, frightened, and threatening parental behavior. Psychoanalytic Inquiry, 19, 481–540.

Hesse, E., & Main, M. (2000). Disorganized infant, child, and adult attachment: Collapse in behavioral and attentional strategies. Journal of the American Psychoanalytic Association, 48, 1097–1127.

Jacobs, L. & Wachs, C., (2002). Parent Therapy; A Relational Alternative to Working with Children. Northvale, NJ: Jason Aronson, Inc.

Lieberman, A. (1997). Toddlers' internalization of maternal attributions as a factor in quality of attachment. In L. Atkinson & K. J. Zucker (Eds.), Attachment and psychopathology (pp. 277–291). New York, NY: Guilford.

Lyons-Ruth, K. (1998) Implicit Relational Knowing: Its Role in Development and Psychoanalytic Treatment. Infant Mental Health Journal, vol. 19(3), 282-289.

Seligman, S. (1999). Integrating Kleinian Theory and Intersubjective Infant Research: Observing Projective Identification. Psychoanalytic Dialogues, 9, 120-159.

Shaw, G.B. (1930) Immaturity, London: Constable and Company, Ltd.

Silber, L.M. (2012). Ghostbusting Transgenerational Processes. Psychoanalytic Dialogues, 22, (1), 106-122.

Slade, A. (2008) Mentalization as a Frame for Working with Parents in Child Psychotherapy, in Mind to Mind; Infant Research, Neuroscience and Psychoanalysis, (Ed) Jurist, Slade & Bergner, New York: Other Press, 307-334.

Steele, H. & Steele, M. (2008). Clinical Applications of the Adult Attachment Interview. New York: Guilford Press.

Stern, D. (2004). The Present Moment in Psychotherapy and Everyday Life. New York: W.W. Norton & Co.

Stern, D.B. (2010) Partners in Thought; Working with Unformulated Experience, Dissociation and Enactment. New York: Routledge.

Tronick, E., (2007). The Neurobehavioral and Social-Emotional Development of Infants and Children. New York: W.W. Norton & Co.

Warshaw, S. (1992) Mutative Factors in Child Psychoanalysis: A Comparison of Diverse Relational Perspectives, in (Eds., Warshaw, S. & Skolnick, N.) Relational Perspectives in Psychoanalysis, NJ: Analytic Press, 147-174.

BIO

LAUREL SILBER, PSY.D. is adjunct faculty with Widener University's Institute for Graduate Clinical Psychology, and is on faculty with the Institute for Relational Psychoanalysis of Philadelphia, where she teaches courses on child relational work. Her publications in Psychoanalytic Dialogues and the Journal of Infant, Child, and Adolescent Psychotherapy are on the subject of working clinically with intergenerational transmission of trauma and childism. She has also published a piece on the value of play with the International Play Association's online journal, and is one of the founders of the Philadelphia Declaration of Play, a child advocacy group, to promote play in childhood. In addition, Dr. Silber is the past president of the Philadelphia Society for Psychoanalytic Psychology and the Philadelphia Center for Psychoanalytic Education. She is in private practice with children, adolescents, and their parents. Her office is in Bryn Mawr, Pennsylvania.

CHAPTER 4

"The True Self" Parental Function, the Basis of Ego Integration

Lic. Eva Rotenberg

"The True Self" Parental Function, the Basis of Ego Integration

Lic. Eva Rotenberg

OBJECTIVES

In this chapter, I will elaborate the conceptualization of parenthood, and its importance as a function in the formation of the psyche of children, based on the idea of the process of formation of the ego. I consider the process of ego integration to be one of the primary tasks of the developing psyche.

I maintain that Ego integration is fundamental to the development of the psyche. I also maintain that there are certain mental processes that are not only of the baby, nor only of his parents, and these processes are constructed out of a mutual interdependence. Thus we acknowledge that the recognition of "the other in us" is always ready to be re-enacted as if it was an independent force.

INTRODUCTORY THOUGHTS

In the 21st century family configurations have changed a great deal. Previously there was a singular arrangement: father, mother and children. From the logical point of view, it is not the setting that has changed as agent, but the one that has suffered the change.

While there are important mechanisms of the parental function which have been connected to the concept of "family function" Alizade, *et al.* 2003), I think that there are differences that justify the conceptualization of the Parental function. One of them is that the "family function" includes the Fraternal Complex and in addition that all members are considered in the same way, including parents. While family membership and parenting are intertwined, as we (*can* or *shall*) see, there are also specific functions that would benefit from a more detailed exploration in order to tease out related complex mental processes.

In this chapter, I am going to focus on an elaboration of the concept of parenthood. There is no inherent parental quality. One becomes a parent through the daily reality of being a parent within the context of a society that encourages specific modes of relating. In addition, there is a blending of the parent as an individual and the influence of the societal and the material conditions of existence: income, educational level, work, play, societal norms and so on. Society has ethical and moral standards regarding parenting, and the parent's experience of him or herself within or outside of these standards play a part on how the parental function is constructed by the individual parent. Unconscious factors of the maternal function or holding (Brody, 1970), have effects on the methods of upbringing and on affective matches and mismatches.

What we call paternal function or the third provides the experience that the baby does not belong to the mother or the father, this third is the metaphor of symbolic castration. The Parental function lays the foundations of the self; it is essential for psychological development regardless of the conformation of each family due to the utter helplessness with which an infant is born. Evidence of this is that when there are failures, or deficit effects occur in children and if failures are early, they can affect his or her capacity as a desiring subject to varying degrees.

For years, I have been interested in articulating the fundamental importance of the Parental Function, which until now has been considered as maternal and paternal functions. Every adult has potentially maternal and paternal aspects in themselves, since as Freud said, we must take into account not only constitutional bisexuality, but also the expanded Oedipus, cross identifications and desire for both parents.

PARENTHOOD

Parenthood is a basic function, which includes the so-called maternal and paternal function. Typically, the father is thought of as the provider of a paternal function or thirdness, and the mother is thought of as providing support. In order to refrain from biological gender designations, I refer to these functions as support and thirdness, respectively (Rotenberg,2014, pp39). These functions can be staggered, shared or fixed. When Recamier started using the term "Parenthood" in 1961, he conceptualized both functions as joined.

The acquisition of subjectivity in the child is not only formed through the fact of generational difference or the difference of gender, but because the child has a connection with an adult who provides the scaffolding necessary for unfolding of the capacity to know and accept difference and because the adult also possesses this capacity as well. This is what I am calling the Parental Function.

Humans are born in a state of helplessness, with the potential to develop his or her self, but the actualization of a well constructed psyche requires affective exchange with an other. The other/others, is what constitutes the Parental function. Parenthood is a state of basic affective availability, available enough so that the infant finds "someone" with whom his/her need for attachment evolves, at the same time, the presence of the parent will make possible the achievement of separation/individuation.

Recamier (1992) called the paradoxical experience of the child being of the parents yet not of the parents' "original mourning" of the mother. This mourning begins before birth. Intrinsic to this concept is the assumption of both Oedipal and Pre-Oedipal castration, which is a form of renunciation that is symbolic and significant.

A good enough upbringing involves helping to build the emotional set-up so that the child is able to internalize emotional encounters. This is accomplished via the parental acknowledgement of his experience, as well as a parental acknowledgement of the child as a separate being. It is "a way of conceiving the internal set-up, the constitution of 'the psychical,' taking the encounter with the Other as a starting point" (…) "normogenic identifications structure the individual's Ego resources, while pathogenic identifications (…) constitute relationships that force the self to transform in order to satisfy the desire of the other" (Badaracco, 1985). I would add that in this way the true self becomes encapsulated.

THE MUTUAL CONSTRUCTION
(OR CO-CONSTRUCTION) OF THE INTRAPSYCHIC

Ego Integration occurs in the presence of specific mental processes that are not only of the baby, nor only of the baby's parents, but rather are constituted within a reciprocal interdependence. The capabilities and the difficulties of the parents have more of an impact on this process than the capabilities and difficulties of the baby.

The human paradox is that in order to become subject, first one must have felt subjectified by others that are imbued with meaning. I contend that in the development of the psyche, the second topography is organized in the first place and only once the ego has been formed as an agency can there be thoughts and the possibility of making the unconscious conscious. We must acknowledge from the beginning "the others in us" (Badaracco), and it can also be added that even in cases where pathogenic interdependence prevails, as in psychosis, there is still the capacity for the formation of a differentiated true ego.

Marcia, a 16-year old, consulted because of depression, and a four month period of mutism. She had been medicated with antipsychotic drugs. She was accompanied by her mother. When Marcia was asked for the reason for consultation, she answered: "I'm going to talk to you as my mom would talk, from her perspective."

I said: You are two different people, it would "be better if you could talk being you. You feel like you could talk like your mom, but you are not in her mind, nor she in yours!

The mother intruded on her daughter's narrative several times, describing what was happening with her daughter, with a certainty that prevented her from hearing that her daughter said — "you don't understand me, a lot of things have happened to me."

STRUCTURING FIRST PROCESSES

We know the importance of the mechanisms of primary identification that shape the child's early, primitive "I". Piera Aulagnier (2004) describes this as:

"The violence of anticipation," (an aspect of) "primary violence." The (parent) cannot avoid (being the voice of) her infant in all spheres of emotion and the infant has no choice but to swallow. In this encounter, there is a thin margin separating the necessary from the abusive, the structuring from the destructuring. The mother-voicing-the-child must address herself positively to every essential body zone in order to gradually induce body integration. The child may already reflect the neglect or the accentuation of some body parts via somatic dysfunction.

The mechanism of secondary identification is "the psychological process by which children actively assimilate features of the other's, movement, speech emotions, behavior in order to be like the significant adults in their environment." "Identification is a process which, in turn, rests on a series of underlying mechanisms: imitation, differentiation, affiliation, learning and the formation of cognitive schemes" (E. Bleichmar, *Homoparentalidades*, 2007).

Freud described the "operation of the psychic apparatus" to explain mental functioning. The father of psychoanalysis worked with adults, for this reason, according to the experience of those of us who work with infants and children, we consider that this explanation did not sufficiently explain early structuralization, nor early failures.

From the perspective of Ego formation in order for there to be an identification process there has to be a subject with his drives, with an Identification Function. But first, I would like to explain a series of previous psychic actions which at the same time are simultaneous to the identification process and make possible its internalization so that they form an integrated part of the ego in process. Otherwise they will not be experienced as part of the true self.

PSYCHIC ACTS INVOLVED IN EGO INTEGRATION

These psychic acts constituting subjectivity are not only developed in the mind of the baby, or not only in the minds of the parents, but in a mutual interdependence.

FIRST PSYCHIC ACTION

Freud says that a new psychic action must develop in addition to autoeroticism for the ego to develop. This Action consists of drives that are gathered into one unit. After the ego is taken as an object, and is libidinized by the drive, early narcissism is established. Freud doesn't explain how the ego becomes libidinized. Laplanche's conceptualization gives us the crucial component of this psychic action. According to Laplanche (1980), it is the mother who awakens and activates the drive of the baby. In my opinion, if this psychic action doesn't take place, the baby doesn't cathect it's own self (or ego) nor does it cathect the outer world.

SECOND PSYCHIC ACTION

The baby at birth has feelings and senses such as smell, touch, sight, taste; he can recognize rhythm and the sound of the voice. It is the other who appears in response to his signals, and either confirms or invalidates the infant's needs. The paradox is that the baby, at this stage, is still unable to distinguish between the internal and the external and this will establish aspects of his psychical reality.

The mother and/or the father decode the baby's needs from a very deep empathic identification. When the baby's need coincides with what the mother (or the father) understand, then the baby is able to start developing a logic of meaning, an experience of match, an encounter (ala Piera Aulagnier, 2004) and his/her Ego progressively develops in a coherent and integrated fashion: the internal feeling coincides with the external response. The baby is increasingly able to trust himself and others, because in the beginning he is still unable to differentiate the representations of the internal from those of the external worlds. If there is a response that confirms his feelings, he will then experience infantile omnipotence and his internal feeling of being safe will continue to develop. However, when the response of the parent is almost always distorting the baby grows up in a state of confusion, he is unable to [*reconcile and*] integrate his/her feelings and vital needs with the response s/he gets back from the environment.

Thus, when the mother does not give back to the baby an adequate confirmation of his/her perceptions and needs, she causes a distortion between the baby's awareness of a need, reality, and the desire of the mother. Or else, the mother's response could be mere discharge, no longer desire but something intrusive. An example: if the baby is hungry but the mother looks at him/her and says: 's/he is sleepy, just as I am, we didn't get enough sleep', her 'interpretation' disavows the acknowledgement of otherness, that is, the sensory experiences, the perception, and the reality of the baby and, in contrast, the negation of pleasure is configured according to the reality of the maternal desire: the desire to sleep rather than to acknowledge the other and his/her needs.

Perception is always supported by the pleasure it involves when it coincides with the need and the drive; we should bear in mind that the first Ego is a bodily Ego. Reality is [*thus*] configured in terms of pleasure-unpleasure, match-mismatch or traumatic encounter. If the significant other, who is an individual with his own drives and desires, fails to feed the infant when s/he is hungry, s/he feels unpleasure, feels there has been a mismatch, or else a traumatic encounter which, in turn, could cause a feeling of emptiness. However, if the infant lacks an incipient ego then he is unable to think and, in turn, unable to account for the confusion and the intrusion that he is feeling. If a child is fed when what s/he really feels is anxiety, he will eat not only out of hunger, but in order to 'fill an unthinkable anxiety' when he becomes an adult. This is a product of the distortion caused in the register of pleasure and of experiences: there is a distortion of meaning. The child needs to be held but gets food instead. This provokes in him/her a feeling of loss which will probably continue without his/her ever understanding why.

The desire or *jouissance* that comes from the other may remain encrypted within the Ego of the infant who, however, remains unable to 'realize' the causes for his feelings of 'perplexity, anxiety and/or confusion'. This confusion, in turn, can cause anxiety and then the child may be diagnosed as hyperactive and suffer insomnia or vomit and may therefore be prescribed medication; this is how mismatches are continually repeated. In this case, the perceptions of the other crush the infant's own perceptions and this intrusion causes an alteration of the infant's intrapsychic constitution.

THIRD PSYCHIC ACTION

The development that is product of a healthy interdependence depends on the ability of the mother (by which I refer to the parental function) to acknowledge her child as someone different from her. Paradoxically, from the very beginning of life, the baby cannot be considered as separate from the parental function, although an external observer might see different people. Also, it is important that the adults accept the difference between the generations, and also are capable of inhabiting the role of parental authority that they acknowledge the baby as a being that will increasingly manifest his own subjectivity.

As the auxiliary Ego of the parental function continues to be good enough, the process of Ego constitution and integration continues with, first, primary identifications, and then secondary ones. Thanks to this process the infant is increasingly capable of developing his Ego resources based on which he will be able to contain partial drives.

The parental function adjusts the baby's partial drives in order to allow ego integration. However, if this does not take place, the child becomes increasingly demanding, anxious and voracious and, while the parents believe that he is 'genetically' restless, what they fail to grasp is that they do not know how to contain their child.

From the perspective of Metapsychology, 'to contain' involves acknowledging that the other can feel pleasure of a different nature than the pleasure felt by the mother or the father. But when the parents do not acknowledge this and love the infant only as 'a part of themselves', that is, not as someone different, then they are unable to offer the singular pleasure that is expected by the child.

These are children who are restless, anxious, who are not easily soothed. The reason is that in the psyche there usually is a need 'to be oneself'; that is, to recognize reality in terms of pleasure and unpleasure. What is satisfactory to the infant begins in the inside and is 'real,' while what is not is outside or is intrusive.

FOURTH PSYCHIC ACTION

In the opinion of Winnicott (1960), the first year of life is essentially a period of ego development, and integration is the main feature of such development. He says: "In health the id becomes gathered into the service of the ego, and the ego masters the id, so that id satisfactions become ego- strengtheners."

In this aspect, Winnicott concurs with Freud's ideas regarding the experience of satisfaction, to which I would add that it should be 'stable enough.' Winnicott continues to say: "This, however, is an achievement of healthy development and in infancy there are many variants dependent on the relative failure of this achievement. In the ill health of infancy, achievements of this kind are minimally reached, or may be won and lost" (1960, p. 39, The theory of the parent-infant relationship, in *The maturational process and the facilitating environment*).

As I see it, the satisfactions of the id strengthen the Ego, which is in the process of integration, and constitute the 'genuine Ego resources' to which García Badaracco referred but which he failed to define.

Coming back to Winnicott, his position could be connected to Freud's concept of experience of satisfaction, which fits perfectly with the conceptual idea that the satisfaction of the id reinforces the Ego, in the same way as the mnemonic traces of the experience of satisfaction that constitute the Ego are, according to Freud, more connected to the pre-Oedipal aspects rather than with the Oedipus. In fact, Freud claims that: "I may point out that we are bound to suppose that a unity comparable to the ego cannot exist in the individual from the start; the ego has to be developed. The autoerotic instincts, however, are there from the very first; so there must be something added to auto-erotism—a new psychical action – in order to bring about narcissism" (1914, pp. 76-77, SE).

FIFTH PSYCHIC ACTION

Laplanche (1980) says that 'this new psychic action' is formed by the narcissistic exchanges between the mother and the baby. From my point of view he emphasizes the essential importance of the other.

SIXTH PSYCHIC ACTION

The need for safe attachment. The paradox and the metapsychological complexity in the process of the infant's 'humanization' is that the satisfaction of his needs is not enough; the provision of a safe attachment is also an element of the parental function that brings about the psychic action of a transition from primitivism to the capacity for subjectivity.

SEVENTH PSYCHIC ACTION

I believe that there are many founding psychic actions. The autoerotic drive searches the other and invests the Ego with libido. I consider that although the satisfaction of needs is important, there is one step more, a new psychic action that is no longer satisfaction alone, but the 'understanding' of the need: it's about offering back a gaze to the infant, offering a desire that will make him a subject of desire. In other words, if the infant is to feel real another action is needed, 'the mirror-role of mother', who gives him back a gaze stemming from her own desire and imaginary that in fact predate the baby. Indeed, this involves acknowledging the other as master of his own drives, needs and wishes. This is interesting because then the human subject not only is confirmed by the other, but also by the other 'with his others', as it were. I understand the experience of feeling real, as Winnicott puts it, as trusting one's own perceptions and experiences along with a significant other that gives them meaning.

The mirror role of mother is a metaphor that shows us that the ego is developed in an imaginary way and constitutes a narcissistic, libidinal projection involving both the infant's and the other's drives and their vicissitudes. For both Lacan and Winnicott, who picks it up again, in this metaphor the inevitability of the other with his libidinal compromise is implicit and opens up a structural course, although it will always be a distorting mirror. When Winnicott claims that what the baby sees when s/he looks at the mother's face is him or herself, it means that the baby sees in his/her mother how she sees him/her, and not what the baby projects.

114

Whereas for Freud ego constitution is intrapsychic, for Lacan it comes from the other. For Winnicott, it is developed within the transitional space. For Badaracco, in turn, it will be the effect of reciprocal interdependence that is not entirely the result of drives, nor of the influence of the other.

There is more, however: from my own point of view, interdependence. An example is the recognition on the part of the mother or father of the effects of their gaze on their infant, and the impact of this effect on them. This would be the reciprocal interdependence.

What does the mother see when she looks at her baby? Does she see the baby, herself, or another? The baby's condition offers back to his mother an imaginary gaze of herself as a mother. This is how interdependence is built.

Catalina, the mother of Cynthia, aged two, who was admitted into hospital several times due to atopic dermatitis, recalls that her own mother (Cynthia's grand- mother) used to tell her: 'I cannot look at you because in your face I see your father' (whom she hated). Catalina says that only now has she realized that the same happens to her with her daughter Cynthia: she looks at her face and can only see the atopic dermatitis, someone ill, not her child. And the face of her daughter, swelled with corticoids, reflects back an accusation: 'you are a bad mother'. That's how she experiences it. This is the pathogenic interdependence. 'When I was little, I felt that my mother rejected me, and now I see that the same happens to me!'.

It is essential to consider the kind of gaze offered back by the mother as mirror, as it will give rise to different qualities of identifications: those encouraging ego integration, the non-integration of the Ego, or else a failed ego constitution. We should remember that the infant also offers back a certain gaze to his parents.

If the child identifies with the maternal ideal, he will then identify with the Desire of the other. There might be a split off mark of detachment. A 'character' might be constituted in order to satisfy the maternal desire. Desire is in a quite different category from that of the drive; it's more passive than the drive, "to be the desire of the desire of the other" (Lacan). To exist in the desire of the other, where the infant's own drives are acknowledged, is a more 'active' desire, as it were. However, when the ego wishes to become the desire of the other without taking into account his own drives, a passive, alienating desire is constituted.

Nadia was born nine months after the death of her sister, aged four. For the mother her dead daughter was very present, and for Nadia her unknown dead sister was a rival because she, Nadia, had taken the place of her dead sister before her mother's eyes.

It is not the same to take the place of a dead person than that of a little princess in the parents' desire. This is connected to the *imaginary* of the parents, to their drives, that generate pathogenic interdependence. It is not the same to be cared for by an unsatisfied, traumatized mother than by a happy mother.

Nadia's parents were unable to understand their daughter's violence; while they merely tried to establish more limits for her, her problem, instead, was that 'she hadn't been seen' from the day she was born. Nadia's violence towards her younger brother and other children reflected back to them, like a distorting mirror, what had been split-off: 'the feelings of guilt for the death of a daughter and now the confirmation that they were bad parents, that's why their daughter was like this, and why they hadn't been able to save the other one'. This clinical example shows interdependence and the effects of the gaze as an imaginary mirror that returns from an unconscious confirmation from both sides.

TRUE SELF PARENTAL FUNCTION AND GENUINE EGO RESOURCES

This leads us once again to define the concept of 'genuine ego resources', which should not be confused with the so-called 'Ego functions,' described by Anna Freud. The development of genuine Ego resources is achieved when the 'emotional presence of the other' can be conceived, that is, when otherness can be acknowledged by discovering and respecting the pleasure of the baby, which will always be different from that of the 'imaginary baby' as well as from the one experienced by the adults. Adults need to face the difference between the imaginary baby, nearer to Narcissism and the Ego ideal, and the actual baby that not always responds in the way his parents expect.

If the parents are to succeed in achieving this 'primary empathic match,' and to tolerate the difference between the mythic baby and the real baby, they must have submitted to symbolic castration and they themselves should have their own genuine Ego resources. Only then will they tolerate the need to be available for their baby and refrain from considering that the difficulties intrinsic to the development of their children constitute failures that affect the parental narcissism. For this reason, we should establish a distinction between "as if" parents, "false-self parents" and the authentic parental functions that I call "true self parental function."

It is interesting to introduce Sylvia Brody (1970), who studied the maternal relationship according to unconscious experiences. She describes a kind of mother who, I in turn, have named the "false self mothers" (Rotenberg, 2014). Brody says that certain mothers "respond to their children in a highly 'mechanical' way. (...) they perform empty routines with a remarkable lack of perception towards their babies' feelings. They interact with their children with impatience, unwillingness, and tardiness. They ignore the visible affliction of their baby, speak to him in an improper tone and complain about him ..." (Translated for this edition, quoted in *Parentalidad*, 1970, p. 437).

The child's "coming into being" is facilitated by the parents' genuine Ego resources, who encourage the emergence of potential in their children, as Human infants cannot start to be except under certain conditions. In this phase, the ego changes over from an unintegrated state to a structured integration, and so the infant becomes able to experience anxiety associated with disintegration. The word disintegration begins to have a meaning which it did not possess before ego integration became a fact. (Disintegration is different from non-integration). The psyche indwelling in the soma, described by Winnicott, can only take place with the infant's new state of being a person. Therefore, ego-integration not only constitutes the integration of the preconscious ego that speaks, but is essentially the integration of the ego that was held, understood, satisfied from the perspective of drives by the parental function. Indeed, it is the interdependence with the other that allows the infant to have a body, to connect psyche and soma.

The unpleasurable experiences, if they are limited, and tolerable, will allow the ego to distinguish between him/herself and the other from the very beginning. Therefore, this process takes place not only when there has been fusion and attachment, but also when there has been differentiation: when the process of me-not me differentiation is encouraged, the child's autonomy, an important ego resource, is developed.

In my experience when children need to cover up for the lack of their parent's ego function they develop a false self. By so doing, they look after themselves and their parents as well. This is the aspect of reciprocal interdependence that Winnicott did not take into account.

INTERDEPENDENCE AND EGO RESOURCES

These early processes are part of the 'mesh' that constitutes healthy interdependence, which begins to be established within a net of meaning from the earliest infancy: an interdependence between the helplessness of the baby and the *imaginary* life of the parents. Following the ideas of G.J. Badaracco (1985), we understand that the interdependence that initiates the process of becoming a self includes the relationship with the other, the fantasy relationship with the other, the desire of the mother, the intergenerational desire, all of them interconnected with the drives.

This reciprocal interdependence can either be healthy, conflicted or a dilemma. The first two belong to the category of drives and subjectivity, while the third belongs to the category of the desire of the other: there is a struggle to get free from the alienation of the desire of the other, and as a consequence, different mental positions are mastered.

I wish to emphasize that only if there is Ego integration, only if there is continuity in the experience of satisfaction will ego resources develop and, in turn, the Ego will carry out the 'Ego functions' described by Anna Freud. We should bear this in mind when we are faced with behavior disorders and learning disabilities in children because a child whose ego is scarcely discriminated will not be able to carry out Ego functions. Therefore, when there is a failure of self-integration, Ego resources will fail to develop. The child will then have the added burden of the consequence of fragile or non-existent ego functions These failures manifest themselves in symptoms in the communication with others, in the acquisition of speech, in learning disabilities, in psychosomatic disorders. This is an important issue because, while child psychoanalysis has been mainly concerned with behavior disorders, learning disabilities and somatic disorders have been less of a focus for us. Many learning disabilities are the consequence of disturbed Ego integration and therefore, ought to be approached by a psychoanalyst rather than by an educational therapist.

INTEGRATION FAILURES

I would like to emphasize certain issues that I consider to be essential:

1-In psychoanalytic theory we know quite clearly that the failure of parental functions effects the capacity to symbolize and are the genesis of structural faults. However, if the parents feel criticized, this can activate a superego reaction on the part of the parents, making them feel even more guilty and this becomes an impingement on the process of change. However, what has not been explored sufficiently is how to help parents provide what the baby needs. If we simply state that 'the maternal or the paternal functions have failed' this does not provide sufficiently useful tools to create the possibility of psychic change.

2-The conceptualization of the paternal metaphor is another issue, because in psychoanalysis it was meant to signify someone of the male gender as the organizing agent of the child's psyche. The mother, on the other hand, has been thought of as the one encouraging, distorting, or else hindering the function of the father as facilitator of the process of separation-individuation. These hypotheses have been concretely connected to the masculine and feminine biological genders as if these gender assignments were inherent. Actually, it is culture that has influenced the assignment of parental roles based on biological gender. In my opinion, the notion of paternal metaphor as the organizer of the psyche has been overstated: in clinical practice we notice that functions can alternate. I believe that the maternal and the paternal functions exist as possibilities within each of us: there is a double function, a consequence of the broadened Oedipus complex.

119

3- In my view, it is essential to consider the effects that the parents' lack of genuine resources have on the upbringing of their children. These shortcomings prevent the function of *reverie* and, in my experience, are part of a vulnerability for postpartum depression; the 'false self parents' project their own insecurities and fears onto the 'failures' or the emotional demands of their children. These are some of the many difficulties that are frequently present when parents have limited capacity. It is one type of experience to be born into a family where parents feel that they have a true self, and the affective encounters are full of life, and another experience to be born to parents who operate with a false self and who lean on "mimetic identifications," and copy actions that supposedly constitute "what parents do."

Even though the concepts of false self, ego deficit, and trauma theory are the result of distinct theoretical frameworks, we can use all these ideas to understand the difficulties parents have in facilitating the development of genuine ego resources in the child.

When Melody comes to fetch her eight year old son John from his session, she is visibly angry and she scolds him: 'you took the sweets from home'. I ask her if she is angry because the boy has eaten too many sweets. No, she says, it's not that, it's the fact that he didn't ask for my permission.'

At another time she tells me: 'When I go to fetch him at school I see the other moms and I think that they are real mums, whereas I 'look like a mom but I'm not really one'. I offer her an interpretation: The time she berated her son because he hadn't asked for permission to have sweets, she was probably angry because she believed that 'being a mom' meant to be asked for permission. Yes! She replies, I hadn't thought about it, but I care more to be asked than to consider whether something is good for him or not. These parents have a feeling of "being trapped" in the urgent demands of the infant because they are incapable of feeling true empathy. They experience themselves as lacking genuine ego resources, as not having enough for the child.

Although the concepts of "oneself," "ego" and "self" have originated in different psychoanalytic theories, I consider that psychic constitution is so complex that establishing a connection between these concepts would be useful. When I treat the families I think of the Self as the part of my patient that is the focus of treatment. It is through the recognition of the self that the structure of the ego can expand to develop the capacity for healthy interdependence and the capacity for enjoyment.

In *Analysis, Terminable and Interminable,* Freud suggests that Ego distortions constitute an essential cause of psychopathology. Despite the fact that he does not actually work with the notion of "experience of being oneself," he nevertheless, develops it as a feeling of being out of one's wits. Something similar is felt in melancholia, in ego distortions, in the experience of the uncanny, but not as a time constitutive of the Ego.

The difference between the affective contact offered by the true self or the false self could be compared to Harry Harlow's experiment with "wire monkeys," in contact with whom baby monkeys risked depression and even death because they lacked the warmth and affection of their real mothers.

4. Another issue to consider is the 'transference from the minds of the adults to the mind of the child' of unbound contents: the trauma without word- representation. By means of passive primary identification within an emotional atmosphere that cannot be thought to correspond to the present, these traumatic contents are passed onto the mind of the child.

Freud says that: "We have decided to relate pleasure and unpleasure to the quantity of excitation that is present in the mind but is not in any way 'bound', and to relate them in such a manner that unpleasure corresponds to an increase in the quantity of excitation and pleasure to a diminution" (1920, pp. 7-8, SE).

In connection with the theoretical statements that I have so far developed we should ask ourselves what happens if an unconscious attempt at resolving the failed binding of excitation is made by means of projection and deposit of unthinkable anxiety onto the children. In other words, if on trying to bind overwhelming excitation parents project their own anxiety onto their child, what happens to the child? What happens to the adult? This is what could constitute what I have termed the "mute unconscious." I call it this because although there is lack of word-representation, its effects are indeed noticeable. In this way, the pathological parental function continues to develop and the child, as a depository, becomes the evacuative receptacle of the projections of his parents and his response is hatred. The child tries to cope with the anxiety and mental phenomena that he is incapable of understanding, but s/he feels more and more alienated in the voices and demands of the others, and then s/he becomes alienated. This is reciprocal pathological interdependence. Frequently, the child supports the evacuative role of his parents within the pathological interdependence until something dramatic happens that suggests the need for change. In extreme circumstances it may be a psychotic breakdown, which, from this perspective, could be considered an opportunity for change in as much as it shatters or denounces the pathological structure. Indeed, these kinds of structures or pathological kinds of dependence are frequently unmasked at the price of a psychotic crisis, which at the same time constitutes both a tragedy and the possibility for change.

Following the theoretical conceptualizations made by Norberto Marucco (1999) with regard to different psychic zones, splitting and structural disavowal, I wonder in which way we should consider the effects of parental disavowal and splitting in the structuring of the minds of their children, that is, the effects of these mechanisms on upbringing? We know of successful analyses of adult patients whose children were growing up while they completed their treatments. Could those "split off" zones of the mute unconscious, lacking word-representation, disavowed, produce the effect of emptiness?' The split off, disavowed contents can be seen to be passed onto the following generation, affecting the inner world. In what other way could we explain the prevalence of a sense of emptiness amongst the individuals in a family?

Adrián used to say that he did better at school when he could reason things out, but sometimes he had to study by memorizing. Despite all this, he failed all his exams. We discovered that when he studied by memorizing he was trying to face a situation in which his own Ego was not there, but where was he? He says he is a slacker, he follows routines but he isn't really there. His best attempt at describing the troubling experiences he could barely conceptualize was to say that the year was "gone." I wonder what kind of gaze can a mother that has disinvested her own Ego because of trauma or grief offer? This is a mother who is "somewhere else," as Green (2005). puts it.

The effects of these failures: I believe it is helpful to consider the notions of "integration" and "non-integration," which are broader than the notion of body-mind integration to which Winnicott referred. I consider that this perspective allows us to understand several cases of children who have been diagnosed with pervasive developmental disorder or infantile psychosis. We can understand the overwhelming anxiety suffered by these children who cannot enjoy inner peace because they have a failed ego integration, a failed constitution of the second topography, which prevents them from adjusting their own drives.

This is the therapeutic challenge that we are faced with, more so if the parents, who represent the external world, continue to 'be hostile' and the parental failures feed the superego of the child, which then becomes cruel. This could be attributed to the fact that the parental failure hinders the flow of the drives, Ego integration, and the path towards the acquisition of a subjective position. Parental failure is experienced as a hostile external world, which is not the projection of the cruel superego, but of "the others in us" (Badaracco), it is the failure of the parental world which continues to exercise influence from the others and from the incorporation of their voices.

Thus, when the subject is faced with scarce Ego resources he is unable to deal with the demands of the Id, and of the cruel super ego; as a result, the external reality becomes very hard to approach. Passive identifications and family imperatives can remain encrypted just like a polyphony of voices, to use an expression of Bakhtin (2008), which, Badaracco in turn, conceptualized as "the others in us." Those voices are characters that continue to act in the mind with a certain degree of detachment. The therapeutic task is for the patient to dis-identify from them.

In the psychoanalytic literature we have long studied the infant's dependence on his mother, but what I have confirmed in my own clinical practice is that adults frequently depend more subtly on their children. 'The child is aware of this dependence and uses it very early on' (Badaracco).

Juan, 29, a chronic patient who had been confined to the Borda Psychiatric Hospital, attended the Multi-family Group Therapy with his parents. After more than a year of treatment, changes in Juan became noticeable: he started to communicate with others after having been catatonic. His father, a very private man, was finally able to tell the Group that he had been in the war, fighting in the army under Mussolini and he had come back feeling extremely phobic and violent. He was terrified of going out. However, when Juan was born, he became able to go out when he took the baby for a ride in his pram. Thus, Juan was the "protective shield" of his father, the one who received the bullets, the deadly projections of his father.

This case illustrates how the father felt supported because his baby kept him company: this is the phenomenon I have termed "inverted holding." He had developed a fusional interdependence with his son and this had probably prevented Juan from being "himself." The son acted as a shield that protected his father from imaginary bullets, but 'the child received the bullets instead', therefore, the father could safely go for a walk because the one in front, in the pram, was his son: "the child was the Infantry."

When the parents unconsciously depend on the infant more than it would be expected this is usually due to the fact that the infant 'has an organizing function in the mind of his parents'. While the child might not be aware of this, it nevertheless encourages pathogenic interdependence.

At the School for parents, at the Dermatology Department in the Ricardo Gutiérrez Children's Hospital, a young mother of English nationality consulted with her fourteen-month old child who suffered atopic dermatitis. We saw the child irregularly because the mother interrupted his treatment at the hospital and then consulted somewhere else. The Paediatric dermatologist suspected this could be a case of Münchausen Syndrome, as the mother wandered from one hospital to the other, and her child had been admitted into different paediatric centres while his condition worsened more and more. When she came to the School for Parents, Susan, the mother, put up a charming smile which, in fact, attempted to conceal her strong rejection of the therapeutic group (Multifamily School for parents).

When the child, who was already two and a half years old, had been in the hospital for five months in 2012, the doctors considered changing corticoids for an immunosuppressant drug.

Faced with the seriousness of the situation, and as I had come to know the mother a little better, I inclined towards a more direct approach and asked her what was going on. On the one hand, she came and appeared to be very helpful but, then she disappeared and her child was getting worse. I have always taken into account Winnicott's interventions in London, where he sometimes considered that the possibility existed that there would only be one session. So he regarded the encounter as a unique opportunity for the family to leave with some understanding of what was happening. This was a difficult session because in the beginning Susan, far from welcoming my genuine concern and interest in helping them, felt attacked. I will now briefly describe the development of our meeting.

The mother, a highly cultured woman, spoke three languages and used to be an actress in London. However, the birth of her son coincided with an accident suffered by her husband, who remained an invalid. They came back to Argentina, where the family of origin of Susan's husband lived. But Susan didn't want to remain here with him and decided to file for divorce. Her husband, very upset, in turn refused to grant authorization for his child to leave the country [due to?] emotional demands of their children, among other factors. Anxiety, traumatic events and legal proceedings had prevented Susan from bonding with her child. Susan couldn't admit this until she was able to remember that, when she was sixteen, her parents had divorced. Her mother stayed in London and her father moved to Belgium. Both, however, considered her as their confidante. This stage, as well the previous rows between them had been very painful. At the time Susan promised herself that she would never do what her parents had done to her; she would never pass on her own anxieties to her children.

For Susan, establishing a connection between the atopic dermatitis and emotional aspects was intolerable because it meant she had done what she didn't want to do, and at a time when her own child was a lot younger. Her mechanism of disavowal caused her to reject her son, she went so far as to say: "sometimes I could throw him out of the window." When she could acknowledge, make conscious, what had been split off and disavowed she could come to the group. Her rejection of her son was remarkable, even though she tried to hide it.

A mother who doesn't gaze into the eyes of her baby, who doesn't invest in him even if she does not reject him, who is "somewhere else" (Green, A. 2005), does not play the mirror-role; she gives back emptiness rather than integration. In any case, it is the child, non-invested but socialized, who then becomes an inverted mirror that reflects the mother's difficulties, the maternal introversion that is experienced as rejection of the child, and the expression of her own shortcomings. In this pathogenic interdependence the guilt-ridden or cruel Superego becomes strengthened.

Coming back to the clinical material we were examining, Susan used to say:

When I go back home, at night, I have to take a deep breath in order to go in and face seeing him'. The following week Peter (the child) for the first time came in with a clear skin, without any rashes. There were only traces of disease on the corner of his mouth and on the neck.

They continued to come, but Peter not only suffered from atopic dermatitis, that was the 'visible' part; in fact, he presented a state of non-integration of the Ego. The other children in the group used to say he was a little animal. He would run all over the room while screaming. He didn't make eye contact with anyone, not even his mother. He did not communicate in a socially acceptable way, and he hurled anything within his reach. His mother didn't look at him in the eye either. She didn't talk to him, but rather, talked about him. Susan, who had previously so flatly refused to join the group, started to attend without missing any sessions and brought along her new partner, an Italian man. Peter began to draw and to acknowledge the presence of other children. He tried to play with some of them, his way of making contact was to throw pencils to them, so that they could throw the pencils back. Through playing, he was trying to discriminate me- not me possessions. The others did not always return the pencils, and this was a frustration that Peter still found intolerable.

The improvement in Peter's skin was very quick. Once I could understand the meaning of the maternal anxiety and her rejection of Peter, I began (first within myself) to transform the rejection we all felt towards Susan, due to her utter lack of maternal feeling, into an understanding that we were facing the inevitable compulsion to repeat infantile traumas that had not been worked though, that were unconscious and involuntary. I believe that in the group Peter felt that he was being looked at in a different way. Previously, he had been an "object with a skin disease" that had to be cured. There was no acknowledgement of Peter as an individual with desires. This was the first time that he blew us kisses with his little hands when he left. We were greatly surprised! Back from the holidays, both Susan and her partner noticed important changes in Peter's behavior and communication: before that he had been considered a "hyperactive little animal" However, someone unfamiliar with Peter's early state might still only notice his present serious condition. Susan's partner told us that it was very important for him to come to the therapeutic group and to see how I talked to Peter. Because when Peter screamed, he could only respond by screaming even louder, telling him not to scream! This is evidence that when the parental function started to change and Peter's early Ego slowly started to respond in a more human way, a process that can hardly be considered an easy one, given Peter's state of non-integration. In one of the sessions Peter started screaming and his little hand got rigid as if he were a robot, thus expressing his fury. His mother gave him a rice cake. Peter began to scratch himself, which in my opinion constitutes evidence of the discordant response of the mother. We should bear in mind the seriousness of his atopic dermatitis, due to which he had had to be admitted into hospital on several occasions. I went close to Susan and affectionately told her: It must be very hard for you. You are very lonely! But try to hold him as if he was a small baby. She did so and I held them both in mind. Peter calmed down.

We could explain Peter's improvement not only as the product of an analytic interpretation that brings back to the mother awareness of conflict that has been split off, by acknowledging repetition, but also as a kind of "betting on drives," as it were, on the part of the therapist, which allowed Peter and his mother to experience the containment of drives that diminishes the feelings of annihilation and madness. This also limits "the effects of the persecuting aspect of the maternal superego that had been projected onto the therapists."

RECIPROCAL INTERDEPENDENCE

I believe that the concept of "interdependence," coined by Badaracco, along with a number of others, is very useful as it not only includes the notions of relationship, and internal objects, but is even broader, and, as I have been trying to explain, it accounts for unconscious and conscious phenomena, character traits that are supported by the parents and their children.

The concept of interdependence includes a factor that has hardly been taken into account in the psychoanalytic conception of neuroses: the notion of dilemma. I understand interdependence as a psychic mesh that includes the trans-generational, the internal object, the inter-subjective, the trans-subjective, without leaving out the drives in each of the members. There is an original interdependence between 'the infant's helplessness, the parent's *imaginary* and the wish for a child (we must always consider what kind of wish it is). In the notion of "interdependence" the word dependence is included and, in fact, dependence is real for the infant and emotional for the parents.

From my point of view, the most interesting aspect is the paradox involved in the fact that these relationships can be at the same time indiscriminate and discriminate, narcissistic and oedipal, confusing. As they are supported by all those individuals included in the mesh, when they are pathological, they constitute a dilemma. Within pathogenic meshes, parents and their children cannot separate because they need each other in order to survive psychically.

When this traumatic overload intrudes upon primary interdependence the infant's mind is unable to develop ego integration for two reasons:

1- the excessive quantity of parental mental energy invades his/her mind

2- the imaginary gaze given back by the "mother as mirror" is distorting.

Illness could be a primitive unconscious attempt to calm down the adults, to ease endless anxious feelings of emptiness, as well as fantasies of persecution and death.

For some reason, the child who is to become a "seriously disturbed patie'" has constructed a false self in order to look after his parents and himself. We could also suppose that he has identified with the pathogenic structures imbued in the pre-psychotic self or the hidden psychosis of both, or at least one, of his parents. These identifications prevent him from developing libidinally according to his chronological age and what is more, they constitute the cause for the arrest in his psychological development. Drives are prevented from investing libido towards his objects of interest.

Badaracco gives new value to the observations made by Ferenczi (1952), when he says that intellectual disability is generated mainly between the id and the superego while the ego remains excluded. In this sense, Badaracco says that: "These relationships tend to structure following a perverse mode, and condition a kind of mental functioning that promotes permanent intra-psychic "acting out," which puts a stop to further development of "other ego resources" (1985, page).

In "Reparation in respect of mother's organized defense against depression" (1948), Winnicott describes "false reparation" as deriving from "the patient's identification with the mother and the dominating factor is not the patient's own guilt but the mother's organized defense against depression and unconscious guilt."

I think that this could be applied to both parents and we should add that the infant plays an active role in 'taking care of his parents' with his illness. I emphasize once again that these mechanisms are what we call pathogenic interdependence.

When the integration process fails, the child's ego is unable to contain his own drives (this is something relative and according to each life stage), and to face (with his incipient, unintegrated ego) what for other integrated egos could be a 'relative frustration' coming from the environment. When this failure takes place in the beginning of life it can be serious; the children who cannot contain the tolerable postponement of their drives because their egos have not incorporated satisfactory experiences are unable to make a synthesis of identifications and they become ill.

Those children that have been diagnosed as suffering from "pervasive developmental disorder," infantile psychosis, early psychosomatic disorder, in fact feel that they are invaded by the environment. The children whose egos have not yet been integrated are not in the slightest [way] capable of containing their drives, their anxieties. Their parents, on exercising a failed parental function, believe that 'establishing limits' is the answer. They lack the representation of what "comforting their baby or their child" really is.

When I speak of "failed parental function," I am not speaking of "bad parents" or bad people. In my clinical practice, I have seen many families, parents who love their children and yet have been unable to develop healthy parental functions, that is to say, they themselves lack ego resources to curb their own anxiety and avoid passing it on to their children. Some parents come with pitiful life histories; many disorders have a psycho-social nature. The essential task of the ego is that of articulation and elaboration for the constitution of subjectivity and the appearance of the person's own desire.

The difficulty in working through personal traumatic experiences, or else those of past generations, is a human trait that those of us who work in the field of mental health must understand. This is not about being "good or bad parents as persons' indeed, the quality of being "good or bad" is not attributed to individuals, but to their ability to transform, so that subjectivity is born in the infant. By subjectivity, I mean that the individual owns his own body, his own desire and is therefore able to plan a personal project.

Pathogenic interdependence starts to be transformed with therapeutic help, within healthy interdependence that allows both the structuring of the ego and the flow of the drives in search of adequate objects: we must remember that the ego can work through what he is able to feel, with the help from the parents' ego resources. The virtual potential of the infant can be either inhibited or developed according to the facilitating environment that is set in motion when the parental function has ego resources and therefore can transform, within the relationship, the catastrophic anxieties felt by the infant, anxieties that, if they fail to be thus transformed, directly affect his or her potential development.

FINAL THOUGHTS

In this chapter, I have tried to establish connections between concepts that serve as clinical tools in order to consider the complexity of psychic structuring. From my clinical experience with very young patients and their families, I have noticed that the 'non-integration of the ego' in some cases can explain emotional states that can be reversed with clinical practice. From this perspective, I wish for my paper to be considered as an invitation to carry on revisiting psychoanalytic theory, technique, and psychopathology during childhood and adolescence.

REFERENCES

Alizade, M. et al. (2003). Gender and family function: Theoretical and clinical contributions. Revista de Psicoanálisis., vol. 60, no. 3 (Julio-Septiembre). Buenos Aires, Asociación Psicoanalítica, pp. 727-739

Aulagnier, P. (2004). The Violence of Interpretation. NY: Brunner-Routledge.

Badaracco, G.J. (1985). Identification in Psychosis, Psychoanalytic Review, vol. XLII, May-June, pp. 214-242.

Badaracco, G.J. (2009). Alienating Identifications, The Future of Multifamily Psychoanalysis.

Bakhtin, M. (1980) The Esthetics of Verbal Creation. Ed. Nueva Vision, Spain.

Benjamín, J. (2006). Equal Subjects: Love Objects: Essays on Recognition and Sexual Difference. New Haven: Yale University Press.

Bleichmar, S. (1986). On the Origins of the Psychic Subject: From Myth to History.

D. Amorrortu Publishers.

Bleichmar, E. (2007). Same Sex Parents: New Families.

Sylvia Brody (1970). Sticking to a mother: an instinctive sapling and baby care. in, E.J. Anthony & T. Benedek, Parenting. Assapia, D. Amorrortu, pp.429-449.

Sylvia Brody and S. Axelrad, (1970). Eds. Anxiety and Ego Formation in infancy, New York: International Universities Press.

Judith Butler (1990). Gender Trouble: Feminism and The Subversion of Identity. NY: Routledge

Ferenczi, S. (1952). Transference and Introjection. In First Contributions to Psycho-Analysis (45:35-94). London: The Hogarth Press and the Institute of Psycho-Analysis Retrieved from http://www.pep-web.org/document.php?id=ipl.045.0001a#p0035

Freud, S. (1920-1922). The Id and the Ego. Vol. III Complete Standard Edition.

Freud, S. (1937). Analysis Terminable and Interminable. Complete Standard Edition.

Frisch, S. and Frisch-Desmarez, C. (2010). Some thoughts on the concept of the internal parental couple. The International Journal of Psychoanalysis, vol. 91 # 2, pp. 325-342.

Ginestet-Debreil, S. (2002). Trauma: Terror thinking about the Effects of Transgenerational Trauma. Publications Department of Investigations Psychoanalytic Research Family and APA, Pareja.

Glocer de Fiorini, L. (2001). The Feminine and the Complex Thought. — Buenos Aires: Lugar Editorial Place.

Glozman, M. (2012). Perspectives from Dialogs, Critical Spaces and Production. Published by the Faculty of Philosophy and Letters. Buenos Aires: UBA.

Green, A. (2005). Guidelines for Contemporary Psychoanalysis. Amorrortu.

Green, A. (1986). Narcissism of life, Narcissism of Death. NY: Routledge.

Laplanche, J. (1980). Castration- Symbolization Problems II. Amorrortu.

Laplanche, J. (1987). New Foundations for Psychoanalysis: The Original Seduction. Oxford: UK. John Wiley and Sons, Ltd. Press.

Lussier, A. (1989). La Violence De L'Interprétation: In, Piera Aulagnier. Paris: Presses Universitaires de France, 1975, 375, J. Amer. Psychoanal. Assn., 37: pp. 842-847

Levin de Said, A.D. (2004). The Support of Being: Contributions of Donald W. Winnicott and Piera Aulagnier. Cambridge: UK. Polity Press.

Marucco, N. C. Narcissism in the structuring of the couple and the family: Between family ideals and cultural ideals. Revista de Psicoanalisis, pp. 135-152.

Marucco, N. (1999). The Analytic Cure and Transference. Buenos Aires: Amorrortu, pp. 277-89

Mitre, M.E. (1998). The Voices of Madness. Buenos Aires: Emece.

Mitre, M.E. (2014). Fear of being Oneself as a result of Mutual Maddening Interdependencies. In, Parentalidades: Transforming Interdependencies Between Parents and Children. E. Rotenberg [Ed], pp. 95-108

Racamier, P.C. (1992). The Engineering of Origins. Paris: Payot Publishers.

Rotenberg E. (2014). [Ed.]. Transforming Interdependencies Between Parents and Children. Buenos Aires: Lugar Compilation.

Rotenberg, E. (2005). Processes of illness in the family context. Buenos Aires: Psychoanalytic Research Department for Families and Couples. APA Press.

Rotenberg, E. (2007). Difficult Children-Disoriented Parents, Difficult Parents-Disoriented Children. Lugar [Ed].

Rotenberg, E and Agrest, B. (2007). Same Sex Parents, New Families. Lugar [Ed].

Rotenberg, E. and Stenger, E. (2012). Therapy Consultation in a School for Multifamilies. Latin American Meeting on the Thought of Donald Winnicott: Dialogue with Winnicott in the 21 Cen.

Solis–Ponton, L. (2002). Parenthood. Challenge for the Third Millennium. An International Tribute to Serge Lebovici. The Red Collection.

Stenger, E. (2014). In, Rotenberg E. Ed.]. Transforming Interdependencies Between Parents and Children. Buenos Aires: Lugar Compilation.

Winnicott, D.O. (1958). Collected Papers: Through Paediatrics to Psychoanalysis. London: Tavistock.

D.W. Winnicott. (1965). Maturational Processes and the Facilitating Environment: Studies in the Theory of Emotional Development. London: Hogarth Press. Child: Studies

BIO

EVA ROTENBERG is a Licensed Psychologist in Buenos Aires, Argentina. She is the Coordinator for the FEPAL group (Investigation of Parenting in the Bund of Psychoanalysis of Latin America) and a full Member IPA and APA. She is the Founder and Director of the Multi-Family School for the Education of Parents—in Argentina, several other countries in Latin America, and Europe, which is dedicated to understanding and working with the pathology of children and adolescents and their scholastic problems. She was appointed consultant to the Ministry of Education in Argentina in order to use Psychoanalysis to address relationship problems between students, their parents and teachers in 2017. She specializes in cases of severe pathology in childhood and adolescence. She has imparted her expertise by providing courses on-line, for which she has received numerous awards for excellence by the Congress of Psychoanalysis of Latin America, and for her writings on Cognitive Neuroscience, and investigations of the effects of organ transplants in Children and adolescence. In addition, she is the author of numerous books and scientific works.

CHAPTER 5

Attachment and Context: Evolving Perspective in a Clinical Realm

Monisha Akhtar, Ph.D. and Sumedha Ariely, Ph.D.

Attachment and Context: Evolving Perspective in a Clinical Realm

Monisha Akhtar, Ph.D. and Sumedha Gupta Ariely, Ph.D.

INTRODUCTION TO ATTACHMENT

The role of attachment is central to the understanding of human development. The clear patterns of distress in seven to nine month old babies almost everywhere when separated from caregivers suggests there are universal features to the strong affectional and adaptive ties characterizing attachment. Building on Freud (1940/1964), Erikson (1963), Lorenz (1981) and others' emphasis on the importance of maternal-child bonds as the basis for adaptive survival and then later relationships, John Bowlby, conducted seminal studies of homeless and orphaned infants and their relationship to their caregivers, which served to fuel substantial research on attachment behavior and its patterns. Combining a variety of perspectives, from ethological, information- processing, systems control and psychoanalysis, these studies have contributed to a growing body of literature that examines how mothers and infants develop attachment bonds as well as the impact of these bonds on long-term social adjustment and interpersonal relationships. At the heart of this research is Bowlby's initial formulation of an infant's desire to be proximally close to its mother. Subsequent to Bowlby's initial findings, Mary Ainsworth and others (Ainsworth et al, 1978; Main, 2000) elaborated upon different patterns of attachment between mothers and infants. Ainsworth's observations conducted first on Ugandan Infants (Bowlby, 1969/1982), then predominantly on American children, led to the categorization of attachment into healthy (secure attachment) and unhealthy or maladjusted (insecure or disorganized attachment) patterns. The subsequent vast development of studies on attachment theory began to draw a link between vulnerable and marginalized children to insecure attachment (Spitz, 1945, 1946;) and long term impaired social adjustment. The infant's capacity to develop 'secure attachment' was increasingly seen as being quintessential to healthy development.

As might be expected, in addition to postulating normative attachment patterns, research on the devastating impact of institutionalization on orphaned and separated children (OSC) pushed for policy interventions, especially as global concerns regarding the fate of orphaned and neglected children continued to increase. Buttressed by a growing body of literature on attachment, longitudinal studies of orphaned institutionalized children, worldwide, began to emerge. Their findings painted a rather dismal picture of the long term adjustment of these children (Dozier, Zeanah, Wallin & Shauffer, 2011; Spitz, 1945, 1946, Zeanah, Smyke, Koga, & Carlson, 2005;). Significant distortions in affect regulation and affectional bonds with resulting impairments in exploration, learning, and psychological growth were reported. For the most part, this research was conducted on children of European heritage who had been institutionalized under severely neglected conditions. Guided by the overarching model of 'secure attachment' and its positive impact on long-term adjustment, these researchers advocated for and promoted more universal guidelines of healthy attachment behaviors (Dozier, Zeanah, Wallin, & Shauffer, 2011).

Researchers also examined the physiological effects of institutionalization as it pertained to the background of the children in the institutions (Dozier, Zeanah, Wallin, & Shauffer, 2011). Children coming from traumatized backgrounds including, disrupted attachment, sexual, physical and emotional abuse, and other grief and loss histories were often predisposed to impaired pituitary gland functioning which played an important role in their development (Dozier, Zeanah, Wallin, & Shauffer, 2011; The St. Petersburg-USA Orphanage Research Team, 2008). The emerging picture of attachment continues to illustrate the complexity of variables involved in the development of attachment bonds and later psychological impact. Within the global context, this picture became even more nuanced when sociocultural contexts were introduced into the clinical picture.

ATTACHMENT, PSYCHOANALYSIS AND SOCIOCULTURAL CONTEXT

Despite Bowlby's significant contributions, psychoanalysts for the most part remained rather distant from attachment theory and its findings for many years (Marrone, 2014). With advances in contemporary psycho-analytic theory and technique however, and growing recognition that trauma and early disruptions in attachment has a profound impact on the developing mind, (van IJzendoorn et al., 2011) analytic inquiry examining points of convergence and divergence between these two theories began to emerge (Fonagy, 1999; Levy & Blatt, 1999). Today, informed by both psychoanalytic case studies and developmental re-search, the nuance and complexity of the infant-caretaker relationship continues to expand to include the intergenerational transmission of attachment patterns (Fraiberg, Adelson, & Shapiro, 1975; Steele, 1990) lending further credence to earlier observations of the critical role of the caregiver's emotional attunement with the infant in the development of attachment patterns. The infant's relationship with a caregiver can be jeopardized for a variety of reasons (from neglect to abuse, to loss of caregiver, abandonment, parental mental illness, etc.). Parents' own working models of attachment should theoretically influence caretaking sensitivity and responsiveness, in turn effecting child attachment securi-ty. Research studying caretaker's state of mind and parental attunement (Slade et al., 2005; Steele et al., 2003; van IJzendoorn, 1995) has found general support for the intergenerational transmission of attachment, though the mechanisms through which that transmission occurs and the long-term repercussions are still uncertain (Slade, et al., 2005; Cassidy, Jones, & Shaver, 2013).

The implications of this type of research for child clinical work and OSC policy can be profound (Steele et al, 2003; Department of Health, 2002) and may have helped give momentum to the global push for de-institutionalization of OSCs. Undoubtedly, the variety of factors thought to be important to secure, insecure, and disorganized patterns of attachment such as stress in the rearing environment, adult sensitivity and responsiveness to child, and parenting styles within a group can be sub-optimal in orphanages and institutions. However, it is not clear that the other family care environments that OSCs worldwide have access to are systematically better (Whetten et al., 2014). The lack of empirical clarity on how predictive early ecological contexts are to later development or in what ways they lead to specific consequences have made policy prescriptions in the global context especially difficult. For example, while caregiver sensitivity to distress seems clearly important (e.g., Diener, Nievar & Wright, 2003; Kochanska & Kim, 2013; McElwain & Booth-LaForce, 2006), only modest relationships are often found between sensitivity or caregiving style and attachment security (De Wolff & van IJzendoorn, 1997; Madigan, et al., 2006). Likewise, if attachment is thought to be an internalized working model of life experience, it stands to reason that on-going changes in circumstance should influence internal attachment models and external behaviors.

Evidence that attachment styles can vary across time and situations (Baldwin et al., 1996; Gillath & Shaver, 2007) supports an ethological and constructivist approach to development and highlights the fact that many factors can link rearing environment to attachment security and long-term developmental outcomes. Furthermore, while categorization of mother-child attachment patterns as developed by Ainsworth show remarkable commonality across cultures (Behrens, Hesse, & Main, 2007; Posada et al., 1995; Posada, 2013), there are clearly important variations across and also within cultures (Rothbaum et al., 2000, 2001; van IJzendoorn & Kroonenberg, 1988; Keller, 2013;) that make the psychological significance of what interactions patterns imply or how they can be used to predict future functioning as yet indeterminate. The factors that lead to caregiving sensitivity or 'harmonious relationships' a la Ainsworth are also likely different depending on what values and socialization traits are idealized within a cultural or family group (Carlson & Harwood, 2003; Rothbaum et al., 2000; Valsiner, 1989). Thus, whether or how inter and intra group variations in the categories of secure/insecure/avoidant/ disorganized attachment behaviors across groups lead to mal-adaptation remains a central question for clinicians, policy makers, and researchers. Elaborating on this primary question, Harwood, Miller and Irizarry (1995) in their book "Culture and Attachment" write:

the mental health meanings of certain behaviors must be examined in the context of larger environmental demands, as well as differences in parental behaviors and socialization goals. Ontogenetic adaptations may have culturally specific relevance and the meanings of those adaptations can therefore be evaluated only in the context of their fit with the larger family and sociocultural settings. (p. 14)

These authors go on to identify two major approaches to a cross-cultural study of attachment behavior in the scientific community. The first approach focuses on "cultural adaptationism" (Keesing, 1981, as cited by Harwood, Miller, & Irizarry, 1995, p. 21) which emphasizes the socializing context of the child serving as the eco-system in which the "physical environment, modes of production, social organization and belief systems are all viewed as functionally interdependent and coexisting in an adaptive equilibrium" (p. 22). Expanding on this approach, Whiting and Edwards (1988) provided an extensive cross-cultural study of the child in which they examined maternal profiles in six cultures and noted differences in maternal control and training to accommodate varying sociological and ecological constraints. As argued above, this supports a general constructivist approach to development (Valsiner 1989; Vygotsky, 1978) in which children and their caregivers fashion a range of relationship types depending on environmental demands, life circumstances, and individual strengths, weaknesses, and histories, and those relationship types serve adaptive functions, leading to relatively defined positive or negative pathways and outcomes.

The second approach to the cross-cultural study of the child focuses on the "centrality of symbolic meaning systems for understanding and interpreting human behavior" (Harwood, Miller, & Irizarry, 1995, p. 24). This approach believes that meaning is constructed through a mutual cultural system, with language being a significant symbolic indicator. These two approaches to cross-cultural studies of attachment have important implications for investigating attachment behaviors in institutionalized children in a developing world. Investigative efforts can be directed to understand how children placed in institutions adapt and function in general (as in their attachment to key figures in their life) as well as understanding through qualitative explorations of case studies, the complex interplay of social and emotional cues and language in their attachment styles. Both approaches provide valid avenues for the exploration of context specific attachment styles in such children.

With this foundational basis, the ongoing longitudinal research on orphaned and separated children (OSC) in a low-middle income countries (LMICs) provides data to examine impact of context on the organization, function, and development of attachment patterns in a vulnerable population. Including the role of a variety of child care providers and significant others, such as mentor mothers, who serve as volunteers in the immediate environment, also continues to appropriately expand focused study of attachment from a primary attachment figure to configurations that involve multiple attachment figures.

Examining the complexity of attachment bonds in a social context involving multiple parenting models, Keller (2013) provides an alternative explanatory model to account for cross-cultural variations in attachment styles and its relation to later outcomes. According to Keller (2013), the original definition of attachment as an emotional bond between an infant and his or her caregiver(s) is "rooted in the conception of the self as a separate individual and a mental agent who 'owns' cognitions and emotions that are distinct from those of others" (p. 185). Keller (2013), along with others, stress that from both anthropological and cultural psychological accounts, there is considerable evidence that different cultural ecologies result in different views of the self with resulting consequences of perceptions and experiences of attachment relationships. Keller (2013) further stresses "mind-mindedness" (p. 185) as a quintessential recent phenomenon of the Western world. Expanding on this, she writes, "it is related to the 'inward turn,' which is seen as a consequence of the decline of fixed traditions and the loss of power of societal institutions. Thus, as a consequence of the 'disembedding' of society's ways of life, identities can no longer be defined to the same extent by social group membership" (p. 185).

Keller (2013) states that co-constructed, communal, and hierarchically organized relationship patterns may be more representative of

Non-western cultures where multiple caregiver arrangements are normative and culturally syntonic with child rearing.

While there seems to be stability across attachment categories cross-culturally, this does not mean that attachment insecurities as identified in some groups necessarily leads to negative outcomes or psychologically has the same meaning in different sociocultural contexts. Early attachment researchers have always acknowledged that children can use multiple attachment figures as a secure base (Ainsworth & Marvin, 1995; Bowlby 1969/1982), and that children can form selective attachments to multiple persons. One aspect of the current debate centers on whether the quality of attachment to a principle person (most often, but not always the mother) differs from that of other attachment figures. Likewise, questions persist as to how to measure and understand which relationships with multiple persons are meaningful attachment relationships going beyond superficial interactions, even if they are habitual, to create lasting psychological impact.

Conceptual questions also persist around the ways in which multiple attachment figures coordinate together in influencing on-going development and psychological outcomes. Examples of models include: monotropy or hierarchy of attachment, a la Bowlby, in which a primary figure is preferred and has more critical psychological influence, an integrated model of attachment across multiple figures in which all coalesce into a general representation with no one figure necessarily more important than another, and an independent model, in which different attachment figures can differentially influence outcomes (Bowlby, 1969/1982; Howes & Spieker, 2008; van IJzendoorn, Sagi, & Lambermon, 1992). Evidence for all three models is found in the literature depending on what outcomes are focused on and which care providers are included. There is also the possibility that combinations of these models are available to be employed.

Whether or how multiple attachment figures are organized to help construct on-going functioning could depend on the internal characteristics and ecological supports and challenges experienced by the individual child. Given the socio-ecological complexity and human systems' plasticity, it is not surprising there is difficulty in systematically predicting child and adult developmental outcomes (cognitive, emotional, and relational) from attachment classifications. Theoretical models helping to structure how and why different types of social relationships meaningfully influence immediate and later psychological functioning are still needed.

The tendency to give prescriptive policy recommendations, for example, on housing options for OSC, based on notions of the primacy of certain types of attachment structures and without careful formulation of positive or negative outcomes as they emerge in diverse global settings, makes building a literature on culturally sensitive formulations of what constitutes adaptive attachment in different social contexts a critical goal. This paper describes work on attachments in a vulnerable population. In examining the care and psychological needs of institutionalized children in a LMIC country, we see the continued need for ecologically sensitive discourse on the normative and prescriptive aspects of attachment theory as it relates to institutionalized children and vulnerable populations.

INSTITUTIONALIZED CHILDREN IN A SOUTH ASIAN CONTEXT

The picture of attachment in institutionalized children in the developing worlds is a complex one. It is generally believed that children raised in institutions suffer long term from a variety of social and behavioral problems, though level of negative consequences and ability to recover depends on the type of orphanage and pattern of immediate and later developmental experiences (Dennis, 1973; Hodges and Tizard, 1989; Wolff et al, 1995; Groark et al, 2005. The literature regarding these issues in the developing world, however, is still sparse. For the most part, findings from Western driven explorations of children raised in institutions have provided the foundational structures on which several non-Western countries have designed and implemented programs for the OSC population (Bailey, 2012). These studies attest to the increased incidence of psychological and psychiatric disturbances in institutionalized children (Beckett, Maughan, Rutter, Castle, Colvert, Groothues et al., 2006;

van IJzendoorn et al., 2011; van Londen, Juffer, & van IJzendoorn, 2007). From difficulties in developing intimacy, to cognitive difficulties, to problems in the child's social and emotional development, the list of psychological problems is extensive. Several research studies exploring the long-term impact of institutionalization on the developing child conclude for the most part that a home environment, whether it be through foster care or adoption remains the best alternative for vulnerable children (van Londen, Juffer, & van IJzendoorn, 2007). It is important to note that studies currently following OSCs in LMICs have begun to provide information suggesting that institutionalized OSCs in these settings do not necessarily differ from OSCs raised in families, when assessed on various measures of cognitive, emotional, and social functioning (see Whetten et al., 2014). However, these large, multi-country, longitudinal studies remain few, and more studies in the same vein are needed for comprehensive understanding of policy implications for the institutional world.

Unfortunately, the foster care and/or adoption models found in the West that are often presented as better options for institutionalized OSCs in LMICs, are far from ideal themselves, and are clearly not readily available or practical in resource constrained societies which have the largest and growing number of orphans in the world. More specifically, the number of orphaned children in India continues to grow at an alarming rate. In 2014, the "Institutionalized Children: Explorations and Beyond" journal was launched to publish articles pertinent to the care and management of vulnerable children in the core countries that form the South Asian Association for Regional Cooperation (Afghanistan, Bangladesh, Bhutan India, Nepal, Maldives, Pakistan, Sri Lanka). A disproportionate number of orphaned children and adolescents live in these countries, either in institutions or on the streets. They remain at risk for sex trafficking, for juvenile delinquency, and for other forms of abuse and neglect. When a form of disability enters the picture, the findings are even grimmer.

It is a growing imperative for the global psychological and psychoanalytic community to understand the care and management of these children within their cultural contexts so that best practices of care can be developed and implemented to ensure long-term adjustment and healthy functioning. Given the regional basis of this journal, the implications for cultural systems impacting attachment patterns is of significant concern as many of these countries are steeped in cultural practices with widely varying parenting and familial patterns and societal issues (Kakar, 1993, 1996) that may not necessarily be predictive of our commonly held assumptions for healthy attachment outcomes. It is imperative that an eco-centric discourse enters the psychoanalytic attachment field so that culturally sensitive patterns of care and management can be examined and explored.

CASE STUDY

The variables of culture, gender and caregiver take on different forms and become more complex in an institutionalized setting where girls and boys as orphans are raised in separate homes. The following case study illustrates how these variables interact and can be understood in an orphanage setting in New Delhi, which houses approximately two hundred boys and girls.

Udayan was established in 1994 to provide institutional care to girls and boys between the ages of five and eighteen. The orphanage, through Udayan Ghars Programmes and Aftercare Services, has evolved as a family-type regulated support system with long-term mentors, to help children transition from institutional care into independent living. Udayan Ghars operate on a Living in Family Environment (L.I.F.E.) model in which they create familial relationships, consistent living circumstances, and social/educational support systems necessary to move towards independent adulthood. This model developed out of a carefully researched model of group foster care. Its primary objective is to recreate the warmth and security of a home and family for orphaned children. Small groups of children, usually twelve in number and of the same gender, live in home like settings, which are located in community settings. Udayan's childcare model is based on the principles of familial relationships, consistent living circumstances, and a social/educational support system and care planning. Children separated by age and gender live in homes in the community and are nurtured by mentor mothers who as lifetime volunteers, serve as consistent attachment figures. In addition, each home has at least two caregivers who provide twenty-four-hour supervision and contact for each child. Udayan homes also have long-term leases and maintain a consistent standard of living. Education is also an important part of each child's life. Since the homes are established in middle class localities, the children attend the schools of their community. Educational achievement is viewed as an essential prerequisite to later social adjustment and prosperity in life.

Despite the orphanage's obvious intent to provide the best 'family like' environment for these abandoned and neglected children, a variety of problems were noted in the children, especially as they approached their adolescent years. These problems ranged from self-mutilating behaviors, to depression, excessive anxiety, running away, aggressive behaviors and a failure to adhere to group norms and requisites. In addition to a series of mental health workshops to address the educational needs of the social work staff, a research pilot project was also initiated in 2012 to examine the attachment bonds in these children. Attachment in about thirty children, ranging in age from 5 to 18, was examined using a variety of attachment measures in conjunction with measures of trauma, ego-resiliency, self-concept and psychopathology. One of the preliminary findings from this pilot study (Dyette & Nayar-Akhtar, 2015) suggests that institutionalized children develop stronger bonds of attachment to peers versus their attachment to mentor mothers and caregivers.

In 2014, a longitudinal study was initiated using a subset of measures from the pilot study, examining attachment, self-concept, trauma, depression, and psychopathology in a larger sample. The project was developed primarily to help Udayan Care better understand the psycho-social needs of the orphaned and separated children and young adults within their care and improve services (Ariely et al, 2015). The following describes a summary of some of the findings obtained during the 2014 and 2015 data collection period. By examining mental health profiles of children and caretakers over time, we highlight the need for understanding physical and mental health changes longitudinally and for considering the biopsychosocial forces that present strengths and challenges in vulnerable populations.

METHODS

PARTICIPANTS.

The summer 2014 and 2015 project focused on eleven of the thirteen Udayan homes spread across Delhi, excluding the two homes in Jaipur and Kurukshetra. After taking into account two subject characteristics, age and gender, a randomized subset of the 143 children living in these eleven homes was used to select a sample of 81 children. All children in the youngest age group (ages 5-8) were included in the sample. In addition, Udayan Care has almost double the numbers of girls than boys, but staff felt it important to have more comparable numbers represented across gender, therefore the sample recruited more boys proportionally to their total numbers. Approximately half of the children from each home were represented in the final sample. Of the eleven homes, four were boy's homes and seven were girl's homes. Depending on home size and resident capacity, each home had one to two caretakers who resided with the children, and one to two mentor mothers who were established members from the broader Delhi community and provided guidance, financial support, and motivational mentoring to the homes. More than one child usually shares a mentor mother, whom they see on a weekly basis, and whose role is to inspire Udayan Care children to see the opportunities that lie outside the residential care home, reflect on future hopes, and motivate them to aspire for achieving goals. The resident capacity of the homes varied, ranging from 7 - 20 children, with most serving approximately 12 children. Home assignments are determined by availability, location of a home closest to where a child was first brought for services, and accommodations needed given a child's educational and mental health background.

Table 1 provides general sample characteristics and numbers of children participating across 2014-2015 and those for whom longitudinal analysis across both years is possible.

Table 1:
Numbers of Participants A 14 Across Two-Years of Data Collection

Sample Descriptors	Total across 11 Delhi Homes	2014 Sample	2015 Sample	Two-year Longi-tudinal Data Presented Here
Number of Children	143	89	82	75
Females	99	52	51	46
Males	44	37	31	29
Age 5-8	14	12	14	8
Age 9-12	61	36	22	21
Age 13-17	68	41	46	46
Alumni and Aftercare young adults (Age 18- 29)	≈40	6	32	N/A

CONFIDENTIALITY

The project was approved by the IRB at Duke University and by the Udayan Care Board. All Udayan social workers and study staff were participants in developing and implementing confidentiality over the full duration of data collection. Information gathered during the interviews were recorded on paper copies of the measures, without audio or video recordings. Participant's responses to measures were only identifiable via randomized identification numbers. Physical survey data and consent forms were secured in approved locked cabinets. While data was being gathered and stored, interview sheets were kept separated from the consent forms and any other identifiable information to help maintain anonymity of participants. Once all data was entered, all response sheets were burned. Electronic data and master code sheets were stored on password protected encrypted computers. Informed consents were brought back to Duke University in Durham, North Carolina to keep on file.

MEASURES AND PROCEDURES

Data was collected between May and August in 2014 and 2015 in each of the eleven Delhi homes. Time for data collection at each home ranged from one to three days and an average of four participants were interviewed per day. Individual interviews with study participants were conducted in a private, secure room in each home. Udayan Care social workers helped schedule and oversee data collection. The team applied measures, used by Udayan Care and the 2013 pilot study, and supplemented additional constructs as resource and time constraints allowed. The selected questionnaires used in 2014 and 2015 were piloted, translated and back translated both in the United States and on the ground in India. Language and potential cultural and contextual issues with measures and constructs are of particular importance to this work and are of particular interest to the authors. The team spent considerable time consulting over wording and construct development of the instruments, noting areas where constructs may not transfer to the Udayan Care context. Discrepancies in translations and construct understanding were discussed and checked on an ongoing basis, and if possible resolved.

Table 2 lists the measures used across six mental health constructs, though our discussion here will focus on attachment in ages 9-17 via the Inventory of Parent and Peer Attachment.

Table 2:
Whole Sample Constructs and Measures Used in 2014 and 2015

Constructs	Measures
Self-concept	Piers Harris Self-Concept (age 4+)
Attachment	Randolph (age 4-8) Inventory of Parent and Peer Attachment, IPPA-R (age 9- 17)
Trauma	Trauma Symptoms Children's Checklist TSCYC (age 4-8); TSCC (age 9+)
Ego-resilience	Devereux Student Strength Assessment, DESSA (age 5-11) Ego Resilience Scale, ER-89 (age 12+)

Depression	Center of Epidemiological Studies Depression Scale for Children, CESD-C (age 6+)
Psychopathology	Childhood Psychopathology Measurement Schedule, CPMS (age 4+)

Resident caretakers filled out measures for children younger than nine, and those nine and above answered questionnaires for their age group in interview format. Children were invited to ask questions as they arose. If the interviewer felt that the child did not fully understand a question after further explanation, the social worker was brought in to clarify any mis-understandings. The measure employed for assessing attachment in children nine and above was the Inventory of Parent and Peer attachment revised (IPPA-R). The IPPA-R is a self-report measure of attachment (Armsden, 1986; Armsden & Greenberg, 1987; Armsden et al., 1991) developed to measure a child's attachment to their parents and close friends and designed to assess the cognitive and affective dimensions of how these social others support psychological security. Three attachment qualities are assessed: degree of mutual trust, communication quality, and degree of anger and alienation. The IPPA-R is comprised of 25 items on a 1-5 likert-scale, in each of the parent and peer sections yielding separate attachment scores. The IPPA-R is scored by reverse scoring negatively worded items and summing response values across each section to provide a global attachment security score, and separate subscale scores for the three dimensions. The IPPA-R is significantly correlated to well-being scores, such as life satisfaction, and has some predictive value in expected directions such as relations to depression, anxiety, and alienation (Armsden and Greenberg, 1987; Guarnieri, Ponti, & Tani, 2010). Just as a note, in our sample, Pearson correlations between our participants' IPPA-R guardian and peer scores and their scores on the above measures of Depression, Ego-resilience and Self-concept were all moderate to strong ($r > 0.4$), significance ($p < 0.01$), and in the expected directions (negative for depression and positive for ego-resilience and self-concept). There was no relationship between either guardian or peer attachment and trauma in our sample as measured by the TSCC.

Before filling out the IPPA-R for guardians, child participants were asked to pick the guardian (mentor mother or caregiver) they felt closest to in order to answer the guardian attachment questions. There were similar numbers of Mentor Mothers (MM) and Caregivers (CG) chosen by the participants each year (see Table 5 below) and for the most part across the eleven homes.

RESULTS

Table 3 shows the breakdown in sample by year, age and gender for the IPPA.

Table 3:
Numbers for IPPA Across Participant Characteristics

IPPA SAMPLE	2014 SAMPLE	2015 SAMPLE	LONGITUDINAL
# OF CHILDREN	71	68	60
FEMALES	40	42	36
MALES	31	26	24
Age group 2 (9-12)	28	22	17
Age Group 3 (13-17)	43	46	33

We focus our results here on three main areas of interest: Guardian/Peer, Age and Gender related trends in attachment across 2014 and 2015 for participants, aged 9 – 17. Results focus on descriptive trends, with means and standard deviations used to help describe some initial characteristics of attachment in this population. While significance testing is occasionally given via simple Students T-tests, just as a check on trends, meaningful inferences will require looking at long-term patterns, supplemented with qualitative measures to help illuminate the underlying quality of the relationships children in residential care are forming. Nevertheless, there are some current outcomes that are interesting across two years, which give us some basic insight into the current state of these children's attachment relationships.

GUARDIAN AND PEER ATTACHMENT

Overall, judging by range and distribution of scores, our sample total attachment scores showed moderate to high attachment levels to both guardians and peers.

Table 4:
IPPA Total Score Range Across Two Years

IPPA SUMMARY

Total-Scores	2015-Guardian	2015-Peer
MIN	57	61.96
Q1	82	84.78
MED	90.5	100
Q3	100.2	107.9
MAX	118	119.6
MEAN	91.21	96.29

IPPA-Guardian Data [bar graph]

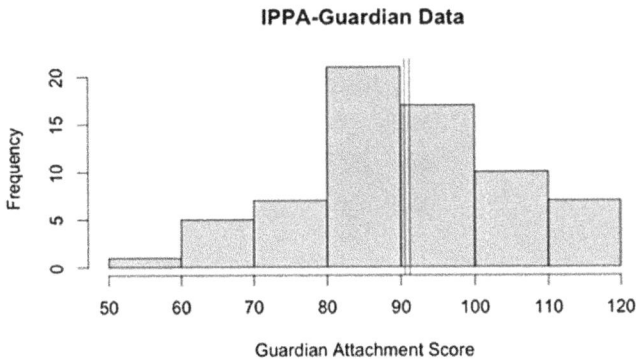

IPPA-Guardian Data

IPPA-Peer Data [bar graph]

IPPA-Peer Data

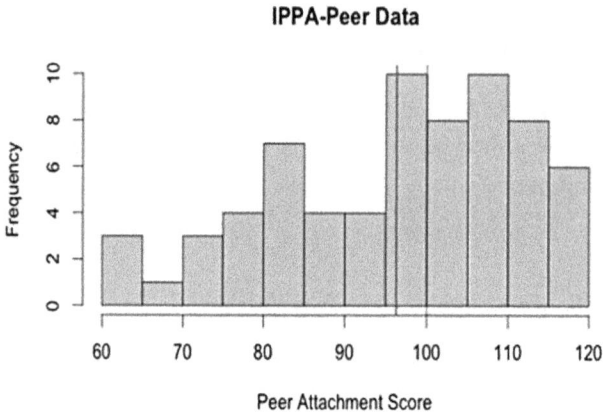

Peer Attachment Score

Ability to form and sustain attachment patterns to adult mentors and care providers are clearly key areas of concern to health care providers and attachment researchers, and the project team had various open-ended hypotheses about which type of adult the child residents could and would become closest to – those who may be of higher status, have more financial and mentoring experience, and a more middle-class caregiving style, but less availability on a day to day level (Mentor Mothers), vs. those who provide direct daily care, but without the same power or status within the broader Indian community or micro environment of the homes (Resident Caregivers). While participants had higher attachment scores to Mentor Mothers than Caregivers for both years, attachment scores were similar (see Table 5). In addition, attachment Means to both guardian types decreased between 2014 and 2015 (See Table 6 and Graph 1). Differences are not large or significant across either of these trends (between care-provider type or differences across year).

Table 5:
Mentor Mother and Caregiver IPPA-R Attachment Scores Across 2014 and 2015

Mentor Mother vs. Caregiver- Cross Sectional				
	2014 Means (st.d)	N=72	2015 Means (st.d)	N=68
Mentor Mother	97.5 (12.1)	N=39	93.6 (12.3)	N=35
Caregiver	91.6 (16.1)	N=33	88.7 (14.8)	N=33

Table 6:
Mentor Mother and Caregiver IPPA-R Longitudinal Trends

Mentor Mother vs. Caregiver- longitudinal			
	2014 Means	2015 Means	
Mentor Mother	96.7	92.4	N=33
Caregiver	92.3	88.1	N=28

Graph 1:
Caregiver and Mentor Mother Longitudinal Changes 2014-2015

CG vs. MM-longitudinal

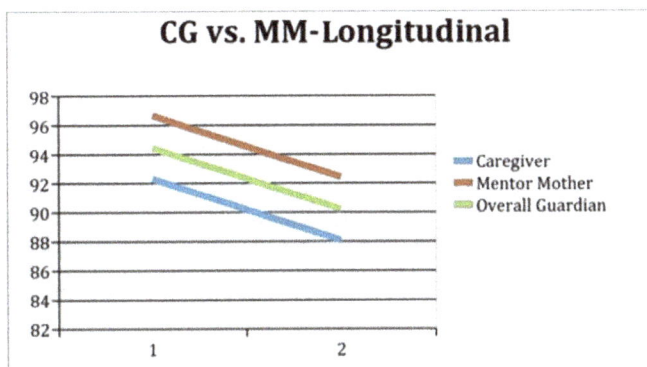

CAREGIVERMENTOR MOTHER OVERALL GUARDIAN

Peer attachment and its relative standing to adult attachment is a second important point of interest, especially in displaced and vulnerable populations. As seen in Table 7 and Graph 2, peer attachment was higher than guardian attachment across both years and significantly so $t(134) = 1.98$, $p=0.005$; $t(133) = 1.98$, $p=0.04$) respectively. Both peer and guardian attachment decreased from 2014 to 2015, and significantly so, [see Table 8 and Graph 2 ($p<0.01$)].

Table 7:

Peer vs. Guardian Attachment

	Peer vs. Guardian - Cross Sectional			
	2014 Means (SD)	N=142	2015 Means (SD)	N=136
Peer	100.8 (11.4)	N=71	96.3 (15.0)	N=68
Guardian	94.6 (14.3)	N=71	91.2 (13.7)	N=68

Table 8:

Changes in Peer and Guardian Attachment across Two Years

	Peer and Guardian - longitudinal		
	2014 Means (SD)	2015 Means (SD)	
Peer	100.3 (11.9)	95.7 (14.6)	N=60
Guardian	94.4 (13.8)	90.2 (13.8)	N=60

Graph 2:

Guardian and Peer Changes Across 2014 and 2015

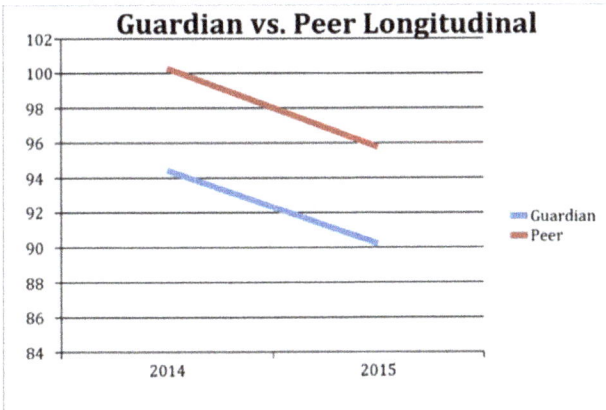

AGE BASED ATTACHMENT DIFFERENCES

We speculated that attachment quality would be different in younger vs. older age groups, especially for guardian attachment, and cross sectionally. This generally looks to be the case. Younger children (ages 9-12) had higher mean guardian attachment scores than the older 13-17 year old group across both years (see Table 9) with Mean differences approaching significance (p=0.056 and 0.071) respectively, across years. However, both younger and older groups had more similar peer attachment Means across both years (see Table 10).

Longitudinally, looking at children who stayed in the same age group across the two years, guardian attachment decreases across both younger and older age groups, but much more for the younger age group. Likewise, longitudinal analysis in peer attachment show interesting patterns, with peer attachment decreasing across the younger age group, but increasing over time in the older age group (see Graphs 3 and 4). Of course, longitudinal and time-point analysis across smaller age grouping and across each year, coupled with models that take into account length of time children have lived in each home, and quality of caregiving style and peer relations is needed to understand the changing dynamics of attachment patterns, and requires significantly more data. However, in as much as earlier peer and adult attachment relationships influence on-going and future social bonds, these results provide a starting base to monitor how peer and guardian attachment patterns may change over time, and especially as OSC children enter young adulthood.

Table 9:

Age 9-12 vs. Age 13-17 Guardian Attachment- Cross Sectional

	2014 Means (SD)	N=71	2015 Means (SD)	N=68
Age 9-12	98.2 (9.7)	N=28	95.1 (10.5)	N=22
Age 13-17	92.3 (16.3)	N=43	89.3 (14.7)	N=46

Table 10:

Age 9-12 vs. Age 13-17 Peer Attachment- Cross Sectional

	2014 Means (SD)	N=71	2015 Means (SD)	N=68
Age 9-12	99.5 (15.0)	N=28	94.9 (15.4)	N=22
Age 13-17	101.7 (9.4)	N=43	96.9 (15.0)	N=46

Graph 3:

Longitudinal Changes by Age group in Guardian Attachment

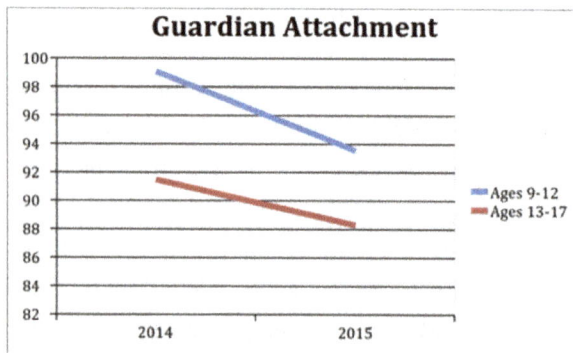

Guardian Attachment

Graph 4:

Longitudinal Changes by Age group in Peer Attachment

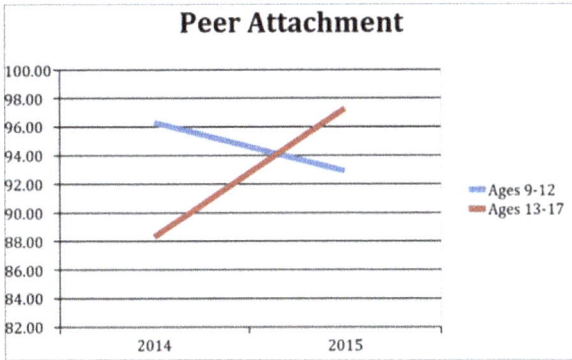

GENDER BASED ATTACHMENT DIFFERENCES

Across the whole sample, males have higher attachment Means than females for both guardian and peer attachment both years (see tables 11 and 12), but not by large margins, though in 2015 the Mean differences are getting larger. Longitudinally, across the two years, males (N=25) and females (N=36) decreased in guardian attachment significantly and females also decreased significantly in peer attachment (see Graph 5 and 6).

Table 11:

Males vs. Females Guardian - Cross Sectional

	2014 Means (SD)	N=71	2015 Means (SD)	N=68
Males	97.7 (13.3)	N=31	95.3 (15.2)	N=26
Females	92.3 (14.8)	N=40	88.6 (12.2)	N=42

Table 12:

Males vs. Females Peer - Cross Sectional

	2014 Means (SD)	N=71	2015 Means (SD)	N=68
Males	103.6 (13.3)	N=31	101.9 (12.5)	N=26
Females	98.7 (10.2)	N=40	92.8 (15.5)	N=42

Graph 5:

Longitudinal Changes by Gender in Guardian Attachment

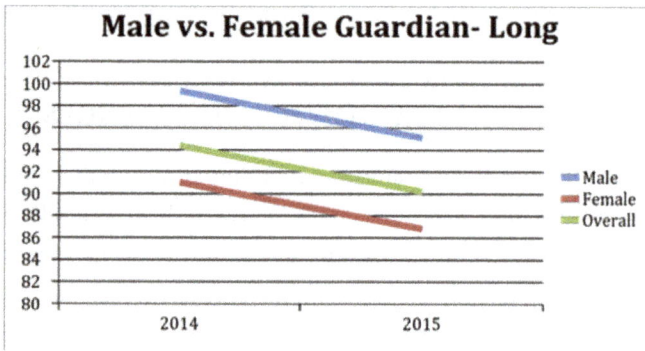

Graph 6:

Longitudinal Changes by Gender in Peer Attachment

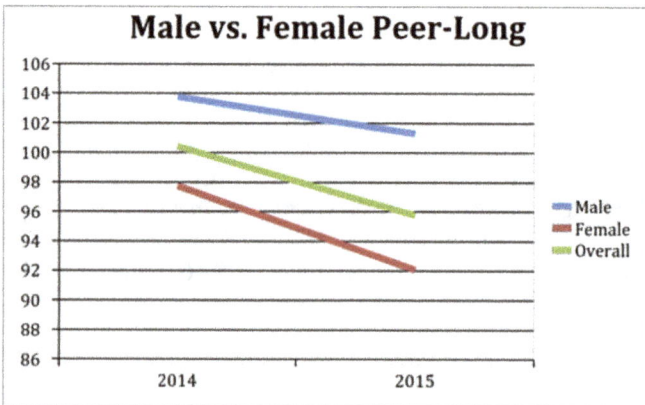

DISCUSSION

Taken together, these preliminary results provide some cause for hope and some hints for areas of intervention and support. First, on average, participants across gender and age seem to be able to form stable attachment relationships as measured by the IPPA-R. While there are differences between care-provider type (MM and CG), participants show similar levels of attachment to both across two years, giving some indication that OSC children can and are forming positive relations within the homes, feel connected, and feel reasonably secure in those connections.

The fact that almost half of the participants nominate MM, who they do not live with and see less frequently as their primary adult attachment figure, as opposed to the caregivers they do live with, is interesting. The fact that children nominating MM also present with similar levels of attachment to MM as those nominating caregivers present with, further emphasizes the need to understand whether the quality and level of attachment to the types of guardians OSC have access to endures over time and leads to internalized models of trust and self-worth.

Similarly, the finding that peer scores are higher than guardian scores may be surprising, troubling, or expected depending on one's theoretical perspectives on child and adolescent attachment development in OSCs. Given the group home environment, we believe it is expected that peers will play an important role in attachment quality, and it is encouraging that peer attachment scores are on the moderate to high end of the scales. As discussed earlier, while the attachment literature supports the general idea that adult-child attachment is protective for later well-being, and parental attachment, especially strong, sensitive maternal attachment, can mediate a variety of later positive psychological functioning, including development of close friendships, romantic connections, and life satisfaction, it is not clear that adult attachment is the only pathway through which transient and vulnerable populations find opportunities for developing functionally stable relationships.

Complex organisms can developmentally adjust, making continual on-course corrections to adapt to changing conditions and stressors.

Whether adult attachment disruptions, severe or not, constitute too great a deviation for what the human system has evolved to optimally adapt to is still much debated. It is clear, however, that socio-ecological context, parenting style, and preferences for how social interactions should be conducted and made sense of, vary greatly across societies and even within families in the same cultural group, making the meaning of attachment constructs less prescriptive than we may like. Likewise, potential for recovery in both human and non-human primates from physical and social trauma is remarkable (Harlow and Suomi, 1971; Suomi, Delizio, and Harlow, 1976), and speaks both to the malleability of sensitive periods in development and the complexity of the physical and semiotic material from which the psychological system can draw for recuperation.

The finding that peer and guardian scores are at similar levels and range speaks to the importance of understanding the influence peer relations have for OSC and residential home populations and of looking carefully into the ways peer and adult relationships can independently and together support positive psychological growth in vulnerable groups. Likewise, the observation of what looks like a possible decrease in attachment over time in this group, across age groups in both peer and guardian scores, and also across gender, could be either concerning or expected, especially as it comes in the middle childhood to young adult period, when negotiations towards independence and changing peer and guardian roles are already in developmental transition. These trends further highlight the importance of following OSC longitudinally and qualitatively to understand the developmental course of intimate relationships for transient groups and the potential support systems they have or do not have to make use of to construct positive outcomes.

Regarding the gender differences noted in this study, the trend which suggests decreasing peer related attachment in the second year of the study is interesting as is the finding that boys demonstrated a higher level of attachment then girls. Mary Ainsworth (Ainsworth et al., 1978) reported no gender differences and it is globally believed that attachment styles are neither gender specific nor culture specific (Pierrehumbert et al.; 2009; van IJzendoorn et al., 2011).

However, when age, socioeconomic status, and family configuration is introduced, research findings become more complex (van IJzendoorn et al., 2011). For example, current attachment literature on gender differences suggest little or no difference when examining two parent families. However, when the research was extended to single or divorced families, boys were found to be significantly less secure and more disorganized than boys from intact families (Carlson, Cicchetti, Barnett, & Braunwald, 1989). Using narratives to examine attachment styles, researchers also found girls demonstrating more caring behaviors than boys who depicted more violent themes in their enactments (Page & Bretherton, 2003). However, there are few explorations of culture-specific research on attachment styles and gender differences. It is possible that the developmental tasks of adolescence are far more complicated, especially in relationship with female caregiving figures, and in communities where gender based preferences can be explicit. Further exploration of this finding and its implications for care and long term adjustment, with institutionalized children and within a South Asian context is therefore warranted.

Longitudinal observations of normative development (Steele, 1990) are therefore fundamental to understanding developmental processes. Cross-cultural perspectives on normative developmental processes suggest considerable variance in child rearing and parenting patterns. Co-constructed communal hierarchically organized patterns (Keller, 2013) of definitions of self are more normative of the Non-western world. Investigating attachment patterns of boys and girls raised in institutions in the developing world provides us with data on how these complex attachment patterns vary, and impact internal psychological processes. It is now increasingly stated that attachment should be viewed through the perspectives of attachment, maturation and context (Crittenden, McKinsey, & Claussen, 2000). In the edited volume on this topic, Crittenden, McKinsey, & Claussen (2000) emphasize the need to examine the effects of maturation and experience on the organization of attachment beyond infancy. The socio-cultural context of this maturation and the capacity to develop attachment bonds beyond infancy is of central concern to developing countries in particular, who face the challenge of a growing orphaned population every year.

REFERENCES

Ainsworth, M.D.S., Blehar, M.C., Waters, E., & Wall, S. (1978). *Patterns of attachment: A psychological study of the strange situation.* Hillsdale, NJ: Lawrence Erlbaum.

Ainsworth. M.D.S., & Marvin, R.S. (1995). On the shaping of attachment theory and research:

An interview with Mary D.S. Ainsworth. *Monographs of the Society for Research in Child Development, 60(2-3),* 3-21. doi:10.1111/j.1540 -5834.1995.tb00200.x.

Ariely, S., Akhtar, M., Ahuja, C., Chodavadia, P., Kinger, K., Levy, J., & 2014 SRT team (2014-2015). Assessment of Mental and Physical Health of OVCs in Udayan Residential Care. Global Health Field Report, submitted to UdayanCare.

Armsden, G. (1986). Attachment to parents and peers in late adolescence: relationships to affective status, self-esteem, and coping with loss, threat and challenges. (Doctoral Dissertation). Retrieved from Dissertation Abstracts International, 47(4), University of Washington.

Armsden, G. C. & Greenberg, M. T. (1987). The Inventory of Parent and Peer Attachment: relationships to well-being in adolescence. *Journal of Youth and Adolescence, 16(5),* 427-454.

Armsden, G. C., McCauley, E., Greenberg, M.T., Burke, P., & Mitchell, J. (1991). Parent and peer attachment in early adolescence depression. *Journal of Youth and Adolescence, 18,* 683-692.

Baldwin, M.W., Keelan, J.P.R., Fehr, B., Enns, V., Koh-Rangarajoo, E. (1996). Social-cognitive conceptualization of attachment working models: Availability and accessibility effects. *Journal of Personality and Social Psychology, 71,* 94–109.

Bailey, J.D. (2012). *Orphan care: a comparative review.* Sterling, VA: Kumarian Press.

Beckett, C., Maughan, B., Rutter, M., Castle, J., Colvert, E., Groothues, C., Kreppner, J., Stevens, S., O'Connor, T., & Sonuga-Barke, E.J.S.. (2006). Do the effects of early severe deprivation on cognition persist into early adolescence? Findings from the English and Romanian

Adoptees Study. *Child Development, 77,* 696-771. doi:10.111/j.1467-8624.2006.00898.x.

Behrens, K.Y., Hesse, E., & Main, M. (2007). Mothers' attachment status as determined by the Adult Attachment Interview predicts their 6-year olds' reunion responses: a study conducted in Japan. *Developmental Psychology, 43(6),* 1553-1567.

Bowlby, J. (1969/1982). *Attachment and Loss: Vol. 1. Attachment* (2nd ed.). New York: Basic Books.

Carlson, V., Cicchetti, D., Barnett, D., & Braunwald, K. G. (1989). Finding order in disorganization: Lessons from research on maltreated infants' attachments to their caregivers. In

D. Cicchetti, V. Carlson (Eds.), Child maltreatment: Theory and research on the causes and consequences of child abuse and neglect (pp. 494-528).New York: Cambridge University Press.

Carlson, V.J., & Harwood, R.L. (2003). Attachment, culture, and the caregiving system: the cultural patterning of everyday experiences among Anglo and Puerto Rican mother-infant pairs. *Infant Mental Health Journal, 24(1),* 53-73.

Cassidy, J., Jones, J.D., & Shaver, P.R. (2013). Contributions of attachment theory and research: a framework for future research, translation and policy. *Developmental Psychopathology, 25,* 1415-1434. doi:10.1017/S0954579413000692.

Crittenden, P. McKinsey & Claussen A. H. (Ed. 2000). *The organization of attachment relationships: Maturation, culture and context.* New York, NY: Cambridge University Press.

De Wolff, M.S. & Van IJzendoorn, M.H. (1997). Sensitivity and attachment. A meta-analysis on parental antecedents of infant attachment. *Child Development, 68,* 571-591.

Dennis, W. (1973). *Children of the creche.* New York: Appleton-Century Crofts.

Diener, M., Nievar, M. A., & Wright, C. (2003). Attachment security among mothers and their young children living in poverty: associations with maternal, child, and contextual characteristics. *Merrill-Palmer Quarterly, 49,* 254-282.

Dozier, M., Zeanah, C.H., Wallin, A.R., & Shauffer, C. (2011). Institutional care for young children: review of literature and policy implications. *Social Issues and Policy Review, 6(1),* 1-25.

Dyette, K. & Nayar-Akhtar, M.C. (2015). Understanding institutionalized children in a developing country: exploration of trauma and attachment at an orphanage in India. *Journal of the American Psychoanalytic Association, 63(3),* NP14-NP19. doi: 101177/0003065115595218.

Erikson, E.H. (1963). *Childhood and society* (2nd ed.). New York: W.W. Norton.

Fonagy, P. (1999). Points of contact and divergence between psychoanalytic and attachment theories. *Psychoanalytic Inquiry, 19,* 448-480.

Fraiberg, S., Adelson, E. & Shapiro, V. (1975). Ghosts in the nursery: a psychoanalytic approach to the problems of impaired infant-mother relationships. In: *Clinical Studies in Infant Mental Health.* London, United Kingdom: Tavistock.

Freud, S. (1940/1964). An outline of psychoanalysis. In J. Strachey (Ed. And Trans.), *The Standard Edition of the Complete Psychological Works of Sigmund Freud (Vol 23).* London, United Kingdom: Hogarth Press.

Gillath, O., & Shaver, P. R. (2007). Effects of attachment style and relationship context on selection among relational strategies. *Journal of Research in Personality, 41,* 968-976.

Groark, C. J., Muhamedrahimov, R. J., Palmov, O. I., Nikiforova, N. V., & McCall, R. B. (2005). Improvements in early care in Russian orphanages and their relationship to observed behaviors. *Infant Mental Health Journal, 26*(2), 96–109.

Guarnieri, S., Ponti, L., & Tani, F. (2010). The Inventory of Parent and Peer Attachment (IPPA): a study on the validity of styles of adolescent attachment to parents and peers in an Italian sample. *TPM—Testing, Psychometrics, Methodology in Applied Psychology, 17(3),* 103–130.

Harlow, H.F. (1958). The nature of love. *American Psychologist, 13,* 673-685.

Harlow, H. F, & Suomi, S. J. (1971). Social Recovery by Isolation-Reared Monkeys. *Proceedings of the National Academy of Science of the United ed States of America, 68(7),* 1534-1538.

Harwood, R.L., Miller, J.G., & Irizarry, N.L. (1995) *Culture and attachment: perceptions of the child in context*. New York, NY: The Guilford Press.

Hodges, J. & Tizard, B. (1989) Social and family relationships of ex-institutional adolescents. *Journal of Child Psychology and Psychiatry*, 30, 77-97. doi: 10.1111/j.1469-7610.1989.tb00770.x

Howes, C., & Spieker, S., (2008). Attachment relationships in the context of multiple caregivers.

In J. Cassidy, J., & P.R. Shaver (Eds), *Handbook of attachment: Theory, research, and clinical applications* (2nd ed.) (317-332). New York: Guilford Press.

Kakar, S. (1993). In search of self in India and Japan. Toward a cross-cultural Psychology. *Psychoanalytic Quarterly, 62*, 305-309.

Kakar, S. (1996). *The Indian psyche*. Delhi, India: Oxford University Press.

Keller (2013). Attachment and culture. *Journal of Cross-Cultural Psychology, 44(2)*, p. 175-194. doi:10.1177/0022022112472253.

Kirkpatrick, L., & Davis, K.E. (1994). Attachment style, gender, and relationship stability: a longitudinal analysis. *Journal of Personality and Social Psychology, 66(3)*, 502-512.

Kochanska, G., & Kim, S. (2013). Early attachment Organization with both parents and future behavior problems: from infancy to middle childhood. *Child Development, 84*, 283–296.

Levy, K. & Blatt, S. (1999). Attachment theory and psychoanalysis. *Psychoanalytic Inquiry, 19*, 541-575.

Lorenz, K. (1981). *The foundations of ethology*. New York: Springer-Verlag New York.

Madigan, S., Bakermans-Kranenburg, M.J., van Ijzendoorn, M.H., G Moran., Pedersn, D.R., & Benoit, D. (2006). Unresolved states of mind, anomalous parental behavior, and disorganized attachment: a review and meta-analysis of a transmission gap. *Attachment & Human development, 8(2)*, 89-111.

Marrone, M. (2014). *Attachment and interaction: From Bowlby to current clinical theory and practice* (2nd ed.). London, United Kingdom: Jessica Kingsley Publishers

Main, M. (2000). The organized categories of infant, child and adult attachment. *Journal of the American Psychoanalytic Association, 48,* 1055-1095.

McElwain, N.L., Booth-LaForce, C. (2006). Maternal sensitivity to infant distress and non-distress as predictors of infant-mother attachment security. *Journal of Family Psychology, 20,* 247–255.

Page, T., & Bretherton, I. (2003). Gender differences in stories of violence and caring by preschool children in divorce families: Implications for social competence. *Child and Adolescent Social Work Journal,* 20, 485-508

Pierrehumbert, B., Santelices, M.P., Ibanez,M., Alberdi, M., Ongari, B., Roskam, I., Stievenart, M., Spencer, R., Rodriguez, A.F., & Borghini, A. (2009). Gender and Attachment Representations in the Preschool Years. *Journal of Cross-cultural Psychology, 40(4),* 543-566.

Posada, G. (2013). Piecing together the sensitivity construct: ethology and cross-cultural research. *Attachment and Human Development,* 15 (5-6), 637-656. http://dx.doi.org/10.1080/14616734.2013.842753

Posada, G., Gao, Y., Wu, F., Posada, R., Tascon, M., Schoelmerich, A., Sagi, A., Kondo-Ikemura, K., Ylaland, W., & Synnevaag, B. (1995). The secure-base phenomenon across cultures: children's behavior, mothers' preferences, and experts' concepts. In E. Waters, B. E. Vaughn, G. Posada, & K. Kondo-Ikemura (Eds.), Caregiving, Cultural, and Cognitive Perspectives on Secure-Base Behavior and Working Models: New Growing Points of Attachment Theory and Research. *Monographs of the Society for Research in Child Development,* 60(2–3), 27–48.

Rothbaum, F., Weisz, J., Pott, M., Miyake, K., and Morelli, G (2000). Attachment and culture: security in the United States and Japan. *American Psychologist, 55,* 1093-1104.

Rothbaum, F., Weisz, J., Pott, M., Miyake, K., & Morelli, G. (2001). Deeper into attachment and culture. American Psychologist, *56(10),* 827-829.

Slade, A., Grienenberger, J., Bernbach, E., Levy, D., & Locker, A. (2005). Maternal reflective functioning, attachment, and the transmission gap: A preliminary study. *Attachment and Human Development, 7,* 283–298.

Spitz, R. (1945). Hospitalism: An inquiry into the genesis of psychiatric conditions in early childhood. *Psychoanalytic Study of the Child, 1*, 53-74.

Spitz, R. (1946). Hospitalism: A follow-up report. *Psychoanalytic Study of the Child, 2*, 113-117.

Steele, M. (1990) Observations of an optimal fit between mother and baby: perspectives on normative development. *Bulletin of the Anna Freud Centre, 13*, 219-227.

Steele, M., Hodges, J., Kaniuk, J., Hillman, S., Henderson, K., (2003). Attachment representations and adoption: associations between maternal states of mind and emotion narratives in previously maltreated children. *Journal of Child Psychotherapy. 29*, 187-205.

St. Petersburg-USA Orphanage Research Team (2008). The effects of early social emotional and relationship experience on the development of young orphanage children. *Monographs of the Society for Research in Child Development, 73*, 1-262.

Suomi, S.J., Delizio, R., & Harlow, H. F. (1976). Social rehabilitation of separation-induced depressive disorders in monkeys. *American Journal of Psychiatry. 133(11)*, 1279-1285.

Valsiner, J. (1989). Human Development and Culture: The social nature of personality and its study. Lexington, MA & Toronto: Lexington Books.

van IJzendoorn, M.H. (1995). Adult attachment representations, parental responsiveness, and infant attachment. A meta-analysis on the predictive validity of the Adult Attachment Interview. *Psychological Bulletin, 117*, 387-403.

van IJzendoorn, M. H., & Kroonenberg, P. M. (1988). Cross-cultural patterns of attachment: A meta-analysis of the strange situation. *Child Development, 59*, 147-156.

van IJzendoorn, M.H., Palacios, J., Sonuga-Barke, E.J.S., Gunnar, M., Vorria, P., McCall, R.B., LeMare, L., Bakermans-Kranenburg, M.J., Dobrova-Krol, N.A., & Juffer, F. (2011). Children in institutional care: delayed development and resilience. *Monogr Soc Res Child Dev, 76(4)*, 8-30. doi:10.1111/j.1540-5834.2011.00626.x.

van IJzendoorn, M.H., Sagi, A., & Lambermon, M.W.E. (1992). The multiple caregiver paradox: Some Dutch and Israeli data. *New Directions for Child Development, 57*, 5-25.

van Londen, M.W., Juffer, F., & IJzendoor, M.H. (2007). Attachment, cognitive, and motor development in adopted children: short-term outcomes after international adoption. *Journal of Pediatric Psychology, 32(10),* 1249-1258.

Vygotsky, L. S. (1978). *Mind in society: The development of higher psychological processes.* Cambridge, MA: Harvard University Press.

Whetten, K., Osterman, J., Pence, B., Whetten, R.A., Messer, L.C., Ariely, S., O'Donnell, K.,

Wasonga, A.I., Vann. V., Itemba, D., Eticha, M., Madan, I., Thielman, N.M., & The POFO Research Team. (2014). Three-year change in the well-being of separated children in institutional and family-based care settings in low-and middle-income countries. *PLoS ONE, 9(8),* 1-10. doi:10.1371/journal.pone.0104872.

Whiting, B.B., & Edwards, C.P. (1988). *Children of different worlds: the formation of social behaviors.* Cambridge, MA: Harvard University Press.

Wolff, P. H., Tesfai, B., Egasso, H., & Aradom, T. (1995). The orphans of Eritrea: A comparison study. *Journal of Child Psychology and Psychiatry, 36,* 633–644.

Zeanah, C.H., Smyke, A.T., Koga, S.F., & Carlson, E. (2005). Attachment in institutionalized and community children in Romania. *Child Development, 76(5),* 1015-1028.

BIOS

MONISHA C. NAYAR-AKHTAR, PH.D., obtained her Masters and Ph.D. degrees in Clinical Psychology from Wayne State University. Later, she trained at the Michigan Psychoanalytic Institute in adult and child/adolecent analysis. After practicing for over 20 years in Southfield, Michigan, she relocated to suburban Philadelphia. Currently, she is affiliated with the Psychoanalytic Center of Philadephia, where she is a Training and Supervising Analyst and has taught courses on trauma, object relations and attachment. Dr. Akhtar has a keen interest in applying psychoanalytic principles to community issues. Moreover, she is actively involved in promoting psychoanalytic thinking in India, her country of origin. Dr. Akhtar has presented and published widely in the areas of trauma, cultural issues, attachment, and the impact of the internet on adolescent development. In addition, she has edited two books, entitled, *Play and Playfulness: Developmental, Cultural, and Clinical Aspects*; and *Identities in Transition: The Growth and Development of a Multicultural Therapist*. Currently, Dr. Akhtar practices full-time in Philadelphia as an adult and child/adolescent psychoanalyst. She is also an adjunct lecturer at Immaculata and Widener Universities.

SUMEDHA GUPTA ARIELY, Ph.D., is an Assistant Professor of Practices in Global Health and Ethics at Duke University. Her Ph.D. is in psychology with an emphasis on cognitive development and culture. She has been active in applied and basic research and has international experience in global and public health issues in a variety of contexts. Dr. Ariely lived in West Africa for two years, during which time she worked on maternal and child health care with communities at risk for HIV/AIDS exposure. As a developmental psychologist, she is interested in the inter-relations between cultural, social, and biological influences on development, health behaviors, and outcomes. Dr. Ariely has a passion for teaching and mentoring, directs the DGHI student research training sites in India, Ghana, and Uganda, and is involved in research examining the transition orphans and other vulnerable children make from institutions to communities in Africa and Asia. Before coming to Duke, she worked at MIT, where she taught classes in developmental psychology, seminars on research and assessment, and served as advisor to MBA students interning as social entrepreneur consultants for local and international NGOs.

CHAPTER 6

Helping the Helpers: Consultation to ChildCare Staff Using Psychoanalytically Informed Developmental Concepts

Phyllis Ackman, Ph.D.

Helping the Helpers: Consultation to ChildCare Staff Using Psychoanalytically Informed Developmental Concepts

Phyllis Ackman, Ph.D.[1]

This article reports on a consultation project with the early childhood staff at Little Sisters of the

Assumption (LSA) Health Center in East Harlem, New York City. LSA serves immigrant families, especially Mexican mothers and toddlers, currently unable to return to Mexico to visit those left behind, i.e., children, parents, etc. Because of their status, they cannot return to the United States if they leave.

The project had a dual purpose: to heighten staff members' observational skills and their ability to elicit accurate developmental information, so that they could use psychodynamic principles to design interventions that increase mother's reflective functioning in relation to her child. With mother being more mindful, most of the children were able to resume age-appropriate development. Once capable of sensitively observing these families, the staff's ability to conceptualize the mother–child dynamic markedly improved. Mothers, toddlers, and staff members benefited.

The project described in this article found a welcoming and accommodating home at the Little Sisters of the Assumption (LSA) Family

[1] Phyllis Ackman, Ph.D., is in private practice in New York City with adults, and does dyadic work with mothers and infants. She is a supervising and training analyst at the New York Freudian Society. She is a consultant to the Early Childhood Program at Little Sisters of the Assumption Health Center and on the core faculty of the Institute for Infant Child and Families of JBFCS. She was formerly coordinator of the Parent–Infant and Toddler Nursery Program at Pace University, where she was Adjunct Professor of Psychology.

Health Service, because LSA has always given top priority to helping the children of immigrant families. Our shared focus is the awareness of the long-term, enduring significance of the early mother–child relationship and its consequences. The LSA is a nonprofit community-based organization in East Harlem, New York City. From its inception in 1958, LSA has offered a range of home-based and center-based services to the changing immigrant population that passed through the neighborhood on its way to other parts of New York. Included in the basic survival services that LSA offers are food, clothing, medical services, at-home nursing, social work, English classes, sewing classes, computer classes, parent groups, and an extraordinary toddler nursery, which is described in this article.

In the1960s, the East Harlem population was mostly Black and Puerto Rican. The critical problems facing those mothers and babies were, as now, poverty and the stressors that adversity brings. In an effort to mitigate these problems, in those early days, nurses went to the apartments of those very poor Black and Puerto Rican families, treating their illnesses and, at the same time, encouraging mothers to play with their children.

By the early 1980s, the population of East Harlem had become predominantly Mexican. And at the time I started in 2006, LSA provided a diversity of services and classes to 280 adults and 205 children, offering English as a second language, Spanish as a second language for Mixteco Indian mothers, and computer classes. These classes represent a way out of poverty and, through the eyes of many of the mothers, the path to the realization of the American dream. Most of these families have come to America at great risk to escape extreme poverty and ensure a better life for themselves and their children, particularly the unborn children, who will be citizens, unlike their parents, who live with the specter of being discovered and deported.

For impoverished parents new to America and New York, living in an often hostile envi- ronment, immobilized by not having legitimate papers, and frequently frightened, providing adequate levels of responsiveness to their young children is a daunting task. Depression, particularly in mothers, has become a major problem, and a tremendous challenge to the helpers at the institutions committed to helping immigrant families. Providing essential and effective early intervention that may have consequences for several generations is the challenge that the LSA Health Center has taken on for many years.

Economic hardship can have dire consequences for parental conflict, maternal health, and child development. In fact, developmental problems are more than twice as common in some impoverished communities than in middle income neighborhoods. Multiple, cumulative risks have a greater than additive effect on prenatal outcome. Poor parents are frequently the least likely to participate in the medical resources that the system provides or to have easy access to supportive educational programs. Under conditions of economic hardship, parents are often less nurturing and more rejecting and inconsistent than better-off parents, because they are so troubled and preoccupied.

In the past, LSA tried to refer women presenting with depression to local mental health clinics. Most of the women referred did not follow through with appointments for a variety of reasons: They could not afford to pay; they were intimidated by the rules encountered; they did not have a support system that encouraged perseverance in the effort; and the clinic waiting list was so long that the moment of readiness had passed before an appointment could be scheduled. Most important, those who followed up found that the clinic personnel did not have the time or wherewithal to build a relation of trust with them.

My involvement with LSA came about during my consultations with the director of the toddler nursery, Lorraine Tierney. Early in the consultations it became clear that she had become increasingly puzzled about many of these Mexican children, who were not playing, not speaking, and not engaging with one another. The expensive toys were not used or even noticed by these children. Simultaneously, the toddlers were experiencing intense separation feelings; they could not bear being left by their mothers.

It is important to have a picture of how these Mexican families in East Harlem live. They are crowded into small apartments that are shared by several other families not related to them. They are one family to a single room. That small room has a mattress on the floor, perhaps one chair, and sometimes a TV set. The kitchen and bathroom are shared by the other Mexican families. If the families are a bit better off, there is a joint living room. These young children, until they come to the toddler nursery, have rarely, if ever, been out of eyeshot of their mothers. On Sunday, the father may take over for a short time. Nearly all these men work as kitchen help in restaurants as dishwashers, errand boys, and other low-level personnel.

The director and I set out to understand what we were observing, i.e., what was holding these toddlers back. What I saw were very quiet toddlers, who ate their snacks silently, rarely joining in the singing and games the staff tried to introduce, and again, were not interested in the toys. My first thought was that they were depressed and, if so, their mothers were also depressed. Together we put together an open-ended interview about a mother's relational history, particularly in the area of her play experiences as a child back in Puebla, Mexico, where most of these mothers had come from. It was no surprise to discover that many of these mothers had experienced a childhood with very little play. They reported that infants are held close to the mother's body and go everywhere in this position. Until the age of 7, many Mexican children run around freely in the bosom of the extended family, being cared for by aunts and cousins. After 7, childhood appears to end. The children start working in the fields with family members, making tortillas, selling them, cleaning house, taking care of younger siblings By contrast, here in New York, not only are the children not able to run around freely in the small space they live in, but mother's role is gone too. Mother is restricted, stuffed into a single room with her husband and children. All continuity with life as she had experienced it herself as a child, is gone. She now lives next to Mexicans who are not family, and she is deprived of the way she had formerly defined herself. Her children, who naturally engage in imitative play, so important for identification, face the same vacancy and emptiness that she does. Mexican soap operas on TV that accompany her in her daily life are important to many of these mothers, representing an idealized fantasy of a life left behind and lost.

The staff was startled by the open-ended interviews with these Mexican mothers, by the outpourings of grief about loss, exile, helplessness, their entrenched poverty, and confusing cultural differences that intensify longings for home and family, especially their own mothers. Since 9/11, many of these mothers can no longer consider returning to Puebla. Their plight has intensified with the immigration crackdown at the borders, and recent laws written in a way they cannot return here if they go home to visit. Many of these families have left older children with grandparents back in Mexico to try to give the babies born here, and thus American citizens, a better chance at life. Infant mortality is very high in Mexico's rural areas; in New York City, at the very least these immigrants have access to food stamps and medical aid for their children. Until their stories were revealed, these young women, often wearing freely donated stylish clothes, came and went silently, never sharing their painful and wrenching histories.

I quickly learned that many of the Mexican toddlers are developmentally delayed in a number of modalities. They are evaluated by early intervention specialists and are assigned to physical therapy, occupational therapy, speech therapy, etc. The developmental norms are, of course, based on American children of the same age. The pull toward pathologizing these delays, in lieu of seeing them as a result of a different developmental trajectory, is great.

After a few weeks observing in the nursery, I decided to meet regularly with the staff to try to understand what was going on in those children who were particularly troubled., i.e., very withdrawn, crying inconsolably, unable to let mother go, etc. At these meetings, every staff person who had had contact with any member of the family—nurse, home-based visitor, parenting class teacher, social work student, classroom teacher—contributed to the narrative concerning a particular child and his or her family. At first, I came twice a month for 2-hour sessions. I did this as a volunteer, which I learned later on, had great meaning to the staff members in charge of the toddler group. It highlighted for them the importance of what they were doing and how much I valued them and the children and their families After the first year, I was paid from a small grant, and I have continued for the last 6 years, adding a third session as a volunteer.

This was how the toddler nursery began a prevention and intervention program, evolving from a case-by-case study that was entirely compatible with the values of LSA.

The LSA staff members are the only people in the larger world with whom many of these

Mexican women have any contact. They find the larger world alien and dangerous. They are removed from their families, with no way to return to the United States if they go to visit their mothers and fathers and children left behind. Grandparents do not get to see grandchildren, but photos and videos pass back and forth. These East Harlem families have come from being exceedingly close to their families to permanently distant geographically, and the emotional toll is great. They feel alone, unknown, and often unknowable. We had to attempt to enter their world and get to know them, so they could feel they were seen and understood. By keeping them in mind, we believed, they would feel less lonely and lost, and it would help them to be more emotionally available to their own children so that they could keep them in mind.

Initially, the staff did not know how to introduce emotional help for the mothers, so that they might feel held and understood. This has been the challenge I have set for them and myself. These LSA helpers are helping these immigrant mothers to recover enough so they can connect to their children, a connection that had been seriously impeded. By being held in mind by a trusted person, a mother may begin to regain her sense of self and her own feelings. This parallel process passes from me to the helper, to the parent to the child.

The story I tell has two related but separate lines. The first concerns training a small diverse group of bilingual teachers (several of whom are paraprofessionals), occupational therapists, physical therapists, nurses, etc., the direct helpers of the toddlers and their families. The training involves my asking them to observe again and again, think about what they see, wonder about it, and go back and think further about how to find out more. I am trying to teach them how to reflect on what's going on in the interactions between child and mother, and to examine their own thoughts and feelings about what's going on in that interaction. When this process of reflection succeeds, what evolves is a narrative about the inner world of the child and his family. This talented staff has learned rapidly to connect the dots, the dots representing multiple observations from different observers on different days from multiple perspectives.

When a coherent pattern emerges, the second part of the work be-gins, creating an interven-tion that might help a troubled toddler and his mother. Fathers have been inaccessible until recently, because they generally work all night in the kitchens of restaurants and sleep during the day.

These exercises in observation resemble what Fonagy and Target (1997) are describing as mentalization. The caregiver's capacity to observe changes in the child's mental state is critical to the development of the capacity to mentalize in both mother and child (Slade, Sadler, and Mayes, 2005).

Recent compelling evidence suggests that the nature of maternal care received in infancy may determine aspects of the infant's response to stress later in life and have enduring consequences in his approach to the world. There are documented strong links between a mother's reflective capacity, i.e., her ability to think about her child's wishes, and the attachment security of her child. This is particularly the case for traumatized mothers. Deprived and traumatized women with high reflective capacity are more likely to have secure children, whereas deprived mothers with low reflective capacity almost always have inse-cure children. Effective intervention can alter the outcome for many of these children. The enduring and powerful impact of early deprivation does not stop with today's generation, but is transmitted from one generation to the next.

The model of reflective functioning, as described by Fonagy and Tar-get (1997), is not only cognitive, but also emotional, i.e., the capacity to hold, to regulate, and fully experience emotion, a non-defensive willing-ness to engage emotionally and to make meaning of feelings and internal experiences without becoming overwhelmed or shutting down. Fonagy (1998) demonstrates that increased knowledge about the devel-opmental pathways involved in many psychological disorders opens the door to important prevention initiatives. He argues that one of the strongest indicators for preventive early intervention is the recent discovery confirming sensitive periods in the development of the central nervous system. These include a number of areas involving emotional reactivity, self-organization, and regulation. Certain types of early sensory experience, particularly the overwhelming destructive effect of emotional stress does irreversible damage. Early maltreatment, lack of adequate stimulation, and maternal depression can have profound neuropsychological, as well as emotional, sequelae. Infants of mothers who are still depressed when their infants are 6 months old begin to show growth retardation and developmental delays as well as serious self-regulatory and emotional difficulties (Field et al., 1988). Our Mexican families are prime examples of many of these problems. Cultural issues multiply and aggravate the other adversities in their daily lives.

It is important to note that, as a non-Spanish speaker, I am dependent on the observations of the staff members; they are the source of data. I do some observing in the classroom, and in a number of cases I interview mothers with a translator.

For me, being an outsider was an anomalous position. At no point in my work as a psychoanalyst and clinical psychologist have I had to depend on others to provide me with the clinical data, except, of course, in supervision. I have always depended on my own observations, careful not to be persuaded by a direction suggested by someone else or dictated by theory. Early on in this LSA endeavor, my separation from direct encounter was a significant problem. The child and family narrative, related by inexperienced reporters, was fragmented and sometimes incoherent. The training component in my mission has been tremendously significant. How do you make sense of what you see? How do you ask the mother questions that do not hurt but provide important information? These have been the key educational elements. I am teaching basic psychoanalytic psychodynamics and developmental principles, always rooted in the real, the immediate, and the personal.

In other settings in which I teach prevention and intervention techniques, I have first-hand, face-to-face interaction with the young children and their parents. The students and I are looking together. The immediacy resulting from this hands-on approach, which clinicians depend on, has not been available to me in the LSA setting. Working with a good translator makes a great difference, but it is not the same as a first-hand interview. As a result, critical tasks in my work at LSA include training the helpers to see and understand the child and the mother, to find out information by asking affectively attuned questions, and to articulate that information in such a way that I can get an accurate picture of the troubled dyad. Only then can the staff members and

I tentatively form a representation that approximates the lives of these two people.

In the cases I present here, my effort was to help the staff member understand the mother, to start reflecting on what might be going on in mother's mind so that she, in turn, would start thinking about what was going on in her child's mind. Helping these mothers to understand that their children have wishes, feelings, and thoughts of their own was frequently a revelation to them because of their own life experience. Basic psychodynamic and psychoanalytic developmental information in each case presented a new perspective for the staff members, increasing their understanding of the dyad and helping them to stretch their thinking about the other mothers and children with whom they work.

CASE VIGNETTES

Esa and Donna—Mother's Guilt

One of the earliest cases presented to me was that of Esa and his mother, Donna. The family includes the father. All three of them live in one room in a crowded apartment with many children and adults sharing a common kitchen. Esa was 15 months old when an accident happened. Donna was worried and distracted when she went to answer the telephone in another room, asking the other women to watch Esa, because she was boiling water on the gas stove. Esa liked to use the broom to sweep the floor, and in his play spilled the pot of boiling water on himself. Panic reigned and by the time mother got back to the kitchen and the screaming child, the other women had pulled both his sock and his skin off one foot and left the other sock on. They called 911, and Esa was taken to a hospital with no burn unit and then finally to a burn unit at Harlem Hospital. Esa has had many surgeries and has needed continued treatments. Donna's job was to massage the scar tissue on Esa's foot twice a day. She repeatedly avoided doing this.

I surmised that Donna had become immensely guilty. The doctor was very angry with her and threatened to quit the case. I had to convey my understanding of the role of mother's guilt to the staff and how it was impeding her ability to touch Esa and do the urgently needed massage. How to teach this important psychodynamic to the well-intentioned staff? I talked about how guilty a mother feels when something like that happens to her child; and how that powerful self-blame can prevent the closeness and physical touch so necessary during this crucial time. Perhaps she was thinking that she might be even more harmful to him if she touched him at all. Each time she saw his angry scars, she was flooded with guilt and remorse—thinking she was a terrible person. The considerable scar tissue was impeding his progress and it was medically important for him to have this daily massage; otherwise the scar tissue would tighten further, leading to further crippling.

I encouraged the early intervention coordinator to work with the mother to persuade Donna to talk about her feelings and to share her horrible grief to reduce some of her crippling guilt. This dedicated young worker went with the mother to the hospital at the next appointment and explained to the doctor what Donna was experiencing. The doctor became much less blaming of the mother and, as a result of his changed attitude, much more gentle and helpful to her. Donna was able to slowly begin to massage her child. Esa, over time, has improved considerably and now walks almost normally.

Thus, using some basic psychodynamic principles, even without knowing very much about the mother's specific history, I helped the staff to understand and then encourage the mother to put into words her profound guilt. This developed into an intervention that freed the mother to do what was necessary for her child. The staff members caught on quickly. Among them are mothers, who understood this mother's agony. My discussion with the staff included some essential facts known to those who work clinically with mothers, i.e., how responsible and guilty mothers feel if their infants are born with any deformity

or are injured. Expanding their awareness of the dynamics of motherhood can only benefit all the other mothers and young children with
whom they are currently working.

HOW THE FATHER'S NEED FOR SAFETY AND SECURITY IMPEDED THE PSYCHOLOGICAL WELL-BEING OF THE FAMILY

Serafina and Alison—

Another family that the staff and I have talked about many times involves Serafina and her child, Alison. The father had been in New York
for 15 years, and for the past 8 they lived with his brother, his wife, their
children, and a number of their in-law families. Besides Serafina, her
husband, and Alison (aged 3), there is Henry (8), and a new baby born
after my contact with them had stopped. They have lived in the same
tiny room for the last 8 years. Serafina was very depressed. When Alison
was first presented, she was having sudden crying bouts, periods in
which she would rest her head on the table and withdraw from all play
activities. I learned from the staff that Serafina could no longer bear
living in this situation, made doubly dreadful by a hostile and combative
relationship with her sister-in-law, who seems to be the appointed
administrator of the apartment. Her husband works steadily at a menial,
but stable, restaurant job. Serafina begged him to move, but he gave
many excuses why they should not. She grew increasingly hopeless.
Miraculously, an apartment in a relatively safe area of the Bronx, at a
manageable rent, came their way and the father agreed to move. The
night they moved in, a street fracas broke out at about 11 p.m., with
neighborhood kids making a lot of noise. The father became panicked
and insisted that they pack up and move back that very night to their
old room at his brother's place.

I became increasingly convinced that the father had a profound separation problem and that, in living as he had all those years, he had
created a substitute secure base in this extremely uncomfortable apartment. Having left Puebla, Mexico, 15 years before, he had moved in with
his brother's family and seized on it as only the most terrified person

might, trying to feel safe away from his lost home. The reality of the problematic nature of this solution and his wife's profound distress was not an issue he could even begin to contemplate. Because of his profound anxiety, he could not make a move. All of this was probably out of his awareness.

One day, Serafina, late in her pregnancy, was later than the time she usually picked up Alison from the toddler group. The staff and I began our meeting while Alison got a box of blocks and started building a house, a large house with many rooms. One of the staff members phoned Serafina to find out what was keeping her, and Alison asked to talk to her, telling her in Spanish that she was building a house with a room for mother and father, another for Henry, and a large one for herself. She had to be reminded of the new baby. At the beginning of this play sequence, the assembled group did not recognize its striking theme. Only when I suggested what this play was about did they understand the significance of it.

I met with Serafina and a translator the following week, with Alison present. I told Serafina I knew how hard it was for her, and that I thought her husband needed some help, because he was probably not aware of how frightened he was to leave the one place that had provided a safe haven for him since his exile. She went on to tell me that in the 15 years here in New York, he had never left the neighborhood he lived in—not even to go to the other boroughs of the city.

It was arranged that Serafina and her husband would see an interim social worker together the following Saturday and then we would see if we could get him some longer term help. Taken with the beauty of her children, I told her that her children were very lovely, at which point she burst into tears. Until then, she had seemed depressed in a listless and hopeless way, but my mention of her lovely children, who were, indeed, wonderful in spite of the adversity, attesting to her motherliness, touched her a great deal. By talking to the staff members about the very likely underlying meanings behind father's seemingly peculiar behavior, I sparked their curiosity about what was going on in his mind. They began to wonder about it. What possibly could blind him to his wife and child's grief and depression? How can he be so callous? They know that he is not a monster, but they did not have any understanding of what meaning lay behind his irrational behavior. Nor could they speculate, as we have been trained to do. Earlier, not comprehending father's profound anxiety related to the trauma of exile, to which he reacted in a phobic and rigid manner, they were at a loss to understand his callous stance. By broadening their appreciation of unconscious factors at play, they became less judgmental, and more capable of thinking about how to help him.

The family did finally move, and although the children have been prospering, doing well in school, Serafina continues to struggle with depression. She gets some relief at LSA, taking relaxation and yoga classes, along with antidepressant medication.

INTENSE EMOTIONS THAT MAKE IT HARD TO HELP

Joseph—

A year before I started with the staff, Joseph began in the toddler group. He was so overwhelmed with anxiety, vomiting and crying inconsolably when mother left. This created so much disruption that the staff asked the mother to withdraw him. Months later she brought him back, but again he seemed barely able to tolerate her leaving. He glued himself onto one of the teachers, who was often angry with this adhesive behavior. Here was a helper who really needed help, but who was unaware of what made her so angry with this child.

In our staff discussion of this family, a traumatic situation for both mother and child came to light. The mother's first pregnancy ended in a late miscarriage, and Joseph, the replacement baby, was born 15 months later, with two club feet and other defects. He has suffered many painful procedures, surgeries, and separations from his mother. She was now pregnant for the third time, having some medical difficulties that reduced her focus on Joseph. Providing some understanding of how severely traumatized the child was helped the teacher establish a more empathic relationship with Joseph. It was important to encourage and enlist the child in activities that would enhance his competence.

Joseph was interested only in the grownups, and could rarely relax his watchful vigil so he could play. Halloween was coming shortly, and there were big boxes of candy on all the counter- tops. I suggested to the teacher that she might ask Joseph to help her fill the bags with candy and help her pass them to the children, a job that might help him feel more like everybody else. He loved doing it, and when his mother came to pick him up, he showed her the bags he had filled with great pride. This rather obvious action probably had not occurred to the teacher because of her irritation with him.

Joseph's mother ordinarily left him quickly in the morning, without an embrace. He struggled to keep the tears back and then glommed onto the teacher for the rest of the session. When mother came to pick him up, she was often impatient to get him dressed and out, even if he was drawing with crayons. This information caused me to speculate on whether Joseph's mother might be concerned about his inconsolable crying that had gotten them into trouble earlier. When she leaves him in the morning, she hurries away, knowing that if she does kiss him he will cry even more. After all, she had been asked to take him out of the group the year before because of his unendurable grief. I wondered whether that remained her nagging concern. The staff pondered this possibility. I suggested that the person she has the best relationship with meet with her and tell her that the toddler nursery can manage Joseph's crying; that is our specialty. I also suggested that when she comes at the end of the session she should linger, taking a few moments to appreciate his drawings and any other creative attempts to make a niche for himself. If she could build a bridge for him between herself and the toddler group, it might go very far in helping him calm down and feel at home. The staff thought this a very good plan, but no one felt confident enough to do it. So I did, with the same good translator. I was finding my way in this first year, and this seemed like a productive move.

We never lost sight of the child's experience and consistently introduced the child into the mother's frame of reference by describing to her how Joseph figured in her experience. We kept both of them in mind and worked to expand the mother's capacity to reflect not only on her feelings, but also on how that influenced Joseph.

This plan, so familiar who work within a psychoanalytic framework

with children and adults, is often unrecognized territory to the motivated and gifted people who are working in the trenches with parents and
children. The gap was very large at first, but shrank steadily, as the staff's
capacities to become increasingly reflective evolved.

When I met with Joseph's mother and the new baby brother, they all
were smiling and very happy. The baby brother is a perfectly normal
child, which is a great relief to the mother, and Joseph kisses him a lot.
Mother says that he doesn't want visitors to attend to the baby. In response, through the translator I tried to explain how displaced a young
child feels when, once the little prince in the family kingdom, he ac-
quires a real rival. She had some trouble under- standing this idea, but
did catch on when I suggested that Joseph be rewarded by being given
the status of the big brother. Giving him special jobs and responsibilities
that are realistically within his capacities, and praising him for how well
he does, could soften the blow. My speculation about her not kissing and
embracing him when she left him in the morning was corroborated. She
felt that she should leave as soon as possible or he would cry inconsolably. I told her that we were specialists in crying and would not be put off.
I asked her whether she could linger in the afternoon when she comes to
pick him up, appreciating his activity. She grasped quickly the idea of
being a bridge for him between herself and home, on the one hand, and
the toddler group on the other. She felt that this was going to be particularly important the following year, when he starts a new school. She was
very happy to hear that he had made a great deal of progress in the
group. He now plays with a very bossy little girl, who draws him out,
and with a very silent child, who rarely plays with anyone else.

COPING WITH LOSS

Arabella—

An unusual request for help came during a regular staff meeting.
Arabella, 2 years old, who had been attending the toddler nursery for a
number of months, brought by her elderly grandmother, began wearing
all her clothes in the classroom—her entire wardrobe, including hat,
mittens, scarf, coat and hood, boots, backpack, and umbrella. If grand-

mother or one of the teachers tried to remove any piece of clothing, she would have a major tantrum, crying without stop until the clothes were put back on. She tried to play with her clothes on but had a very difficult time moving about, getting so hot that sweat poured down her face. Still, she would not take off any of the clothes. The staff questioned whether to force her. Then they brought the case to me. There was no question that we were not to force Arabella to remove anything and that it was urgent that we meet with mother, Pearl, to find out what was going on. A few days later, the home-based worker came to tell us that Pearl had broken up with her partner, father to the new 3-month-old, and that he had taken all of the family's possessions out of the apartment. Pearl, her children, and her mother were forced to move because they could no longer afford the rent. They had no furniture and very few clothes. The remarkable show of strength that Arabella demonstrated by taking what was left of hers and securing it on her person astonished us. She was not going to be done in by this colossal loss, but instead rescued what remained. What an example of resiliency in a 2-year-old!

I met with Pearl, who brought bottles of soda for me and my excellent translator. In spite of her difficult life, she remained gracious and brought a gift, as her culture dictated. Pearl told us about the horrifying situation of being abandoned by her partner and robbed of her home. Then she began to talk about the child she had left behind in Mexico, now a teenager. We had not heard any of this before. This daughter lives with Pearl's brother, who is a doctor, and she is studying to be a nurse. Pearl told us about her guilt over leaving this child behind, describing how she called her frequently over the years, trying to stay in touch with her. She talked about how she was unable to be affectionate with her recently born American children, leaving the expression of affection to her mother. She leaves the apartment when Arabella has a tantrum, because she can't deal with it. Instead she works cleaning houses, buys the children things, and pays the bills. She said to us, "I know that Arabella is begging for my love, but I don't know how to show it." I feared that she was also telling us she couldn't feel love either. We were impressed with Pearl's ability to be so honest with herself in the midst of such sadness grief and guilt. Could Arabella's remarkable coping abilities be related to mother's capacity for self-reflection? The tremendous trauma that this child experienced can lead to a collapse in her understanding of herself and the people she cares about. Instead of disorientation and lack of continuity of her developing self, she found a way to regain her equilibrium by wearing everything that belonged to her on her little person.

Pearl found a new, smaller, apartment that she could afford and she slowly furnished it. She began to pay more attention to Arabella. The staff discussed at length how Pearl might connect to Arabella. Pearl was able to follow some of our suggestions about becoming more attuned to her child, spending more time with her, bringing her to school and staying with her for a while, thinking about what she would enjoy and what she was thinking about. She became more patient with her. Arabella continued to wear all her clothes for another 2 months. During the second month, she would let the teachers remove some clothing on some days. When Pearl brought her to school during the second month, she would allow mother to remove her clothing before leaving. Slowly, Arabella became comfortable in the new apartment. In the beginning, she missed her old apartment and would cry to go home. As Pearl spent more time with her and the new apartment felt more like home, the tantrums stopped. By the third month, she was doing well in the classroom, and she took off all the outer clothes. These were her best days.

Pearl brought home to us the tragic situation many of these parents' face, having left behind children with grandparents, sisters, and brothers when they came to the United States. They are unable to return to Mexico and then return here because of their legal status. They had not anticipated the tremendous emotional cost of their emigration on themselves, on the children left behind, and on the new children born in America. For many, the emigration has turned into exile. Pearl's grief, often unacknowledged even to herself, had clearly interfered with her ability to form an adequate relationship with her child born here in the United States.

Our encouragement, support, guidance, and concrete suggestions to Pearl that were so helpful to both mother and child certainly support the view that coaching mothers who are emotionally available for the coaching can help them not only to reflect and understand what is going on in their child's mind, but can substantially contribute to their child's ability to reflect and mentalize.

The LSA staff and I came up with an intervention that might help the mothers who had left children behind: a group so that they could do some grieving together. It failed very soon. The pain was too great. The women could not talk and cry with one another in this context, yet they also did not want to disband. They wanted to talk more about contemporary problems and wanted relaxation techniques, such as yoga, which we heartily endorsed and facilitated. These women wanted to feel better. Perhaps only a one-on-one, long-term psychotherapeutic relationship would be an intervention that had any chance of helping them to mourn effectively. This we could not offer. What they could not tolerate was retraumatization, and apparently the group context evoked the losses in unbearable ways.

The group continued and apparently, over time, they began talking about the children left behind, but very slowly. We could offer guidance and guidelines that Pearl was able to use. We referred them to a dyadic treatment center, but there was no space available. Still on her own, with her remarkable child, she took steps that made a difference, spending more pleasurable time with Arabella. Mother clearly got to know Arabella and made room in her mind for her. She did very much better with the new baby, as well.

Arabella is doing well in school and at home. Pearl is an attentive mother to Jose Manuel, who attends the LSA toddler nursery. We hope that the tide has turned in their relationship beyond the short term. The signs are encouraging, particularly given Pearl's capacity for reflective functioning and her increased awareness of her children's needs and wishes. We do not know enough about whether small and consistent changes in interaction can change preexisting patterns of interactions that have been internalized for children who have endured multiple losses, trauma, and deprivation.

STORIES OF SILENCE

I mentioned earlier that there are many Mixteco families living in East Harlem. Due to the out- reach of LSA, a number of these Indian mothers are now participating in some of the programs offered. I have heard a great deal about the mothers and toddlers who come to the toddler group, because they are so puzzling to the staff. The women rarely leave their homes, which are, as with other Mexican living places, crowded with many families living in tiny stall-like rooms, one to a family, in a larger apartment. They come as a group to the toddler nursery and seat themselves on the side of the room, silent and uncommunicative. One of the women who speaks Spanish, which many of them do not, also has some English. She has a 2-year relationship with LSA and is, herself, legal. It is to her apartment that these families come when they enter New York. She houses, feeds, advises, and bosses them around and threatens to turn them in if they do not listen to her. She has been described by one of the staff as the "foreman," with all the connotations of such a title. She makes moral judgments, intervenes, and intrudes on a regular basis. She is thought of as a witch and a fairy godmother, depending on the individual case. She always comes along with the group of women.

Picture the playroom: lots of toys and puzzles on the floor for the toddlers. However, the children only want to run and jump. Toys get in their way. The mothers sitting ramrod on the sidelines are encouraged to play with their children "as they do at home." That suggestion triggered a response that was a revelation to us. The mothers raced to the puzzles and toys and started playing by themselves. The behavior of both the children and mothers began to make sense to the staff after they got over their bewilderment. The children, so enclosed at home, in a tiny space, are thrilled to run and jump in a reasonably sized space. That is their first priority. Playing—as we think of it—with objects and toys is a later developmental luxury. These toddlers drop objects and never look for them. Out of sight, out of mind, even at 18 and 22 months. The mothers, never having played with toys in their lives, are thrilled with this exotica and have no concept yet of playing with their children and sharing these treasures They want the play all for themselves. As a result of our discussions, the staff began appreciating the developmental issues in the evolution of play for these people.

The Mixteco bossy lady is very unusual for the Indian group. She is upwardly mobile and her young son, Victor, is trilingual—Mixteco, Spanish, and English. She had made sure to bring him to the toddler group when he was very young, even when the weather was bad. She speaks Spanish to her children and her husband. Her wish for a better life for herself and her children is emblazoned on her face. Her younger brother came to her from Mexico. He is now a young man and speaks not a word of Mixteco, only Spanish and English. The other women speak only Mixteco with their children at home.

THE MANY USES OF PLAY

Emily—

Emily's case helped the staff to understand some important aspects of play that, until then, they were not aware of. Emily, another silent child, entered the toddler group because her mother had enrolled in the literacy education program and she needed a place for her child while she studied. Emily had a difficult adjustment to the nursery and became panic stricken, crying and screaming, whenever her mother tried to leave her. After a while, her mother decided to stay in the nursery classroom, giving up the idea of the literacy class. After a number of weeks, Emily began to be more comfortable in the classroom, relating to the teachers and playing with the other children. Still, Emily would not let her mother leave. The staff members worked hard but were unable to effect even a short separation.

When I met with the mother, we discovered that Emily had been hospitalized at 11 months old. The hospitalization had been very difficult for the child. She had blood drawn repeatedly, and there had been many painful procedures. Her mother had stayed in the hospital with her, but we believe that there were some times when Emily had to be left alone for short periods. The mother reported that, after this, Emily would not let her mother out of her sight. Now we were beginning to see why all efforts to help Emily were not working if we did not address the trauma that had so complicated her separation from mother. When I met with the staff, we discussed the issue of trauma and how the hospitalization, with its pain, terror, and probable absence of mother for short periods (when Emily had not yet developed a sense of time), had left her vulnerable to massive separation anxiety. We planned a play scenario, with a medical kit, stethoscope, make-believe taking of blood, giving injections to soft dolls, etc. Several of the other children were happy to join in, probably having had similar experiences. Over the next several weeks, Emily began to look happier, played in a more relaxed way, and eventually tolerated her mother leaving the room. After a year, Emily went on to Head Start and had no reported adjustment problems, relating well to the other children and trusting the adults. Emily's mother returned to the literacy basic education program. What the staff got from this clinical situation was an increased appreciation of the role of trauma in early childhood and how play can be crucial for the child to gain mastery over that trauma by slowly recontextualizing the experience. Although play was recognized as critical by the staff, until the case of Emily, play as necessary for helping a child master trauma had not been given full weight. Emily's mother had not connected her daughter's hospital experience with her separation difficulties in the nursery. We helped the mother to reflect on herself and her child and to think more about what might be going on in her child's mind, and to wonder what her distress was about. This kind of reflective thinking does not come naturally to many mothers, never having experienced it in a first-hand way themselves. We hope that this relatedness becomes part of their ongoing relationship and is generalized to the children who come later in the family. A mother's ability to be reflective and keep her child in mind, especially when trauma and separation occur, seems to act as an immunizing and protective agent for the young child, mitigating the worst effects of the trauma.

EDWARD: HISTORY ALMOST REPEATING ITSELF

Edward first came to our attention when his mother enrolled in an 8-week nutrition class. Child care is provided while the mothers attend class. Edward was not able to separate from his mother, and clung to her side all during the class. He would not play with the other children. Mother was obviously impatient with Edward and frequently angry, pushing him away, and, of course, the more he clung to her, the angrier she became. During one class, Edward was playing in the gym and when he saw his mother, he ran to her. She got so angry that she pushed him away so hard that he fell to the floor. She then walked away, leaving him crying. It was obvious we needed to intervene. We spoke to mother and asked her if she would participate in our toddler nursery program in addition to the nutrition class. Mother agreed, with mixed feelings, and he started a 2-mornings-a-week program. Mother sat on the couch and refused to play with Edward or interact with him in any way. Once again, he clung to her, not leaving her side. Only slowly did he begin to explore the classroom, showing very poor skills for his age, running from one activity to another in an unfocused, somewhat chaotic manner. We had begun a crafts program for the mothers staying with their children. It took place in the adjacent waiting room. As Edward became more comfortable with the teachers, his mother was able to go to the crafts class. She loved this class, and it gave her the opportunity to talk with other mothers. She took great pride in her crafts. Edward would look for her, and when he went to say hello, she would push him away and the clinging pushing away cycle would be repeated. The teacher would have to retrieve Edward. Of special concern during this time was that mother was pregnant. We felt that once the baby was born, there would be even less for Edward.

We learned that the mother and father had come from Ecuador. The mother had been a shepherd and was very accustomed to spending long periods of time alone with the sheep in the fields. She had married in Ecuador. She had a first child, a son. Her husband came to America and wanted her to join him as soon as he had gotten on his feet. Her son at this time was 4 years old. She could not bear to tell him that she was leaving him, so she told him nothing of her plans.

One day she left him with her sister, telling him that she was going to the store, and she never returned home. After a short time in New York, she called her sister, and much to her surprise, she found that her son had been inconsolable, crying for weeks. She felt very guilty about leaving him in this way, but she had desperately wanted to join her husband and start a new life away from the grinding poverty. So she consoled herself with many promises that she would make it up to her son.

She worked for a few years before having Edward. After his birth, she stayed home but she missed working. Caring for him was not fulfilling for her. Her husband worked long hours 6 days a week. She was lonely. Her years of herding sheep had a very different quality for her than caring for Eddie. Did the long days alone with the baby evoke grief about her older child left behind? We had no access to any of her thoughts at that time.

As mother's pregnancy progressed, she was having a harder time caring for Edward, and in

June of that year she told us she had decided to send Edward to Ecuador for the summer, placing him in the care of her sister and the son she had left behind, now about 16 years old. Here was history repeating itself. She said that her elder son wanted to meet his brother. An uncle whom Edward didn't know was going to Ecuador with his son, and he was asked to take Edward with him. We were very concerned about what effect this would have on Edward and tried to dissuade mother from sending him, but her mind was made up. The uncle, fortunately, decided that he needed to have some relationship with Edward before traveling with him, so he began to visit with Edward to prepare him for the trip. They left in early July.

When Edward returned in September, much to our surprise, he was in good spirits, He looked happy, and his mother was happy. He had no trouble separating from his mother. He walked into the classroom and was able to let her go. We wondered whether his brother and aunt in Ecuador had offered him the nurturance that mother had been incapable of. Had he experienced something different with these folks including the uncle who had cared to get to know him before they left for Ecuador? Had these different kinds of relatedness provided him with some inner sense of being seen and represented? Even mother seemed more patient with him on his return, perhaps reacting to a calmer, more self-contained child.

The baby girl was born in November. Edward stayed at home with his mother for the first month. He returned to the nursery with his dad, who we met for the first time. The father seemed attentive and nurturing. Edward was happy and smiling. After several weeks, mother and Edward started having difficulties again. The mother's attention was going to the baby, and they were cooped up in the apartment all day long. In early February, Edward started seeking out among the staff the affection he craved and missed. He became very cuddly with the nursery staff, relying on them for comfort. He would lean his head on a teacher's shoulder, not wanting to play. The staff, in turn, felt intensely angry at his mother for not providing more affection for Edward, and rescue fantasies surfaced and became a major source of conversation. Edward's mother became increasingly frustrated with him, describing that at home he was having tantrums when he did not get his way. He began talking like a baby again and would poke and push at his infant sister. The mother felt that she had to constantly protect the baby from Edward and began telling the teachers that she wanted to send Edward to live in Ecuador.

All compassion for mother from the staff was gone. The staff members met with me and talked very honestly about their countertransference feelings, wanting Edward to live with them. Unbounded sympathy for this hurt, frightened child was voiced by everyone present. Only the parent's harshness, and not any of the mother's adverse experiences, in these situations tends to be remembered. Helping the staff keep track of the parent's pain, while simultaneously keeping the child in mind, was an important accomplishment for this staff.

I arranged a meeting with the mother and the translator, but even before this meeting took place, the mother's state of mind took a serious depressive turn. She could not stop crying; she could not deal with Edward any longer. Her husband would not allow her to send him to Ecuador. She had no support from anyone when the children were sick. We were very concerned and further considered whether we had overlooked a postpartum depression. Luckily, one of our home-based social workers, Katya, usually overloaded with other cases, was able to see the mother, and this time she agreed. She was desperate to talk. She had been offered help earlier, but had rejected it. She started meeting with Katya regularly and joined the mothers' relaxation group. Edward increased his sessions at the nursery to 4 days a week.

I met with mother twice. She brought her baby girl and Edward, a beautiful child who has some artistic talent, as mother does. My acknowledgment of the splendidness of his art work and his physical beauty pleased the mother very much. I let her know that, despite all the troubles between them, she had done a good job raising him, and that he was beautiful and talented like she was. She responded with great pleasure. We went on to talk about the inevitable jealousy that arises with the birth of a sibling, particularly for the first-born. What astonished me was how little this mother understood sibling rivalry. Now that there was a new baby and a girl, Edward had to have a different role in the family. His mother, who had had so much difficulty seeing him as the unique child he was before the arrival of the new baby, was being asked to see him yet another way, as the big brother of a sister.

We encouraged Edward's mother to spend special time with him alone, engaging in an activity that they both enjoy, like going to the park together. This special one-to-one time together made him happy and probably provided some experience for him of being recognized and seen. He became her helper with the baby and was increasingly protective of her. The mother's meetings with Katya made a tremendous difference. Edward has moved into being the big brother and is enjoying it, particularly since mother appreciates him in a way she formerly had not.

The nursery opened a small library for parents to borrow books. Edward's mother attended a class about reading to your infant and toddler. She now borrows books and proudly tells us that she sits and reads to both children. The first books she chose were about mothers, fathers, and babies. Edward's father came to a session on his day off to talk about setting limits with Edward. He is eager to learn more about parenting and both he and the mother are reading books about child-rearing. The mother reads to the dad after supper.

Clearly, something important has shifted in this family. How enduring and generalized these changes will be remains to be seen, particularly given the mother's complicated and troubled history. So far, it has not been possible to do systematic follow-up on these families. Has mother become a more reflective person in relation to her son? The necessity for studying these efforts is obvious. At the very least, the LSA toddler staff is now addressing the subject of sibling rivalry with all pregnant mothers.

UNANSWERED QUESTIONS ABOUT SILENCE

The pervasive silence of these toddlers in the classroom that the staff members rarely mention in presenting a child to me because they have become so accustomed to it, was brought home to me several months ago once when I went into the classroom during snack time, and observed teachers trying to lead the toddlers in singing. The children were silent, expressionless, and mostly apathetic. Their demeanor indoors contrasts with their animation when they play out of doors, where they run, shout, and are deeply engaged, looking like typical toddlers. Their mothers, many of whom are in the classroom, also appear disengaged and apathetic, rarely playing with their children. The children in the older group that meets in the afternoon, are livelier and play more. This group is more ethnically diverse, from other parts of Latin America and Mexico.

The level of responsivity in most of these mothers is muted. Just as their movement in the places they live, cooped up in tiny crowded spaces, is restricted, so is their affect. A generalized dysphoria restricts their movement, both external in the world and internal in their emotional lives. The responsiveness we've come to think of as necessary to be an ordinary good enough mother, is not always available to these women, who suffer not only the inevitable clash of cultures but also the day-to-day loss of their loved ones left behind.

At parties around Christmas, when LSA offers bountiful feasts, the adults and children sit quietly and eat with little conversation. They are having a perfectly good time, but conversation is not part of the good time. The cultural issue of being in an American place, where "respect" is shown by keeping silent, both for the toddlers in the classroom and for their parents at these get-togethers, may be contributing to the silence we are unaccustomed to.

What has been reported is that many of these speech-delayed children going on to Head Start programs reach age level both in speech and language when they get to elementary school. What a striking change! We are faced with a major dilemma given these facts. How does this catching up happen? We are aware that many of these mothers speak very rarely to their children, and that they do not do much *interactive motherese* when these toddlers are infants. The babies are held against the mother's body in a shawl for many months and go everywhere with her. At home, they are confined to a small space so that when they come to the LSA nursery, they love to run around. Many children are required to be very quiet at home, in those tiny rooms, because the father is sleeping. Such conditions do not aid speech and vocal expression, and they do explain some of the silence. When the children are older and spend time with peers and adults who are talking, they become bilingual and the Mixteco children become trilingual. How does this transition occur? Again, we are faced with the lack of systematic study of these children. Vocal, face-to-face interaction between mother and infant is not typical for poor rural mothers even in Puebla, Mexico. The more urban and educated mothers in Mexico gaze and interact more with their babies.

What we do know about the shawl babies is that they are receiving and giving moment-to-moment kinesthetic and proprioceptive stimulation. Are these cues that are mutually regulatory to both baby and mother sufficient stimulation for the infant so that this information becomes cross-modally generalized for later speech and language development? What is the role of the mirror neurons? Is observing gesture sufficient substitute for being talked to for these infants?

We have come to think of those moment-to-moment interactions between infant and mother as being crucial for intersubjectivity from which optimal brain patterning emerges. Most of these poor mothers, in spite of their life circumstances and depression, offer some tender stimulation to their young babies. Gaze and verbal interactions do not seem to be part of mother's repertoire and many not be culturally normative and critical. How much weight can we place on the lack of face-to-face interaction to explain the speech and language delay we see with such regularity? Do toddlers back in Puebla, Mexico, show the same patterns including the recovery? What about genetics? Many questions are raised by these observations. Perhaps being a good enough mother from Puebla is accomplished by other kinds of caretaking than we have been considering necessary for all cultures. We do not have systematic follow-up of these children after they leave LSA. We do not know if or what they've missed in the way of brain development by not learning language at the same rate as their neighbor Americans. Do they truly catch up? Or are there crit- ical periods? Do we need to reexamine our certainties about early development for cultural short sightedness? Are there other sensory modalities that take over for speech and facial expressive communication that later become generalized to speech and language when these children's lives are different; when they are with peers and teachers who speak English and Spanish? Is it the inevitable clash of cultures both within and surrounding these dyads that restrict them in a way that is utterly different from what we have come to expect to be developmentally normative?

Finally, when considering the impact of mother's depression on children, there is impres-sive documentation as to how maternal depression compromises a mother's ability to read and respond to her infant's signals. Depressed mothers engage in less play and talk less motherese with their infants, who in turn have difficulties engaging in social inter-action, showing less ability to regulate affective states than infants of non-depressed mothers. So many of the mothers at LSA suffer from long-term and chronic depression. We know that infants are exquisitely sensitive to the emotional states of their mothers (Tronick, 1998.) In the developmental delays of the toddlers at the LSA nursery are we seeing what happens to those children, emotionally and cognitively, who have been exposed to prolonged periods of maternal social and emotional unavailability? Reflective function can play a protective function with regard to depression only when trauma is not overwhelming and de-pression is not severe.

STAFF REACTIONS AND CONCLUSIONS

This highly responsive staff reacted to their enhanced understanding and interviewing skills in a number of positive ways. I asked them to give me their evaluations at the end of the first year. Their former feelings of helplessness and powerlessness that had led to disengagement and depression that, if unchecked, led to burn-out, had diminished. Two teachers had returned to school, one to finish her bachelor's degree, the other to start a masters' program, in early childhood education. They spoke of gaining a new perspective on families that they had known every day. Another teacher spoke of how putting the child and mother and their story together reduced fragmentation: "We put the pieces together and got a whole picture. It was helpful to talk together and set goals to help the family." Another mentioned how unaware she had been of what was happening to the children behind the scenes: "It was such a benefit to them in the end. I look more carefully now; it broadened my view so I could find appropriate services." Another teacher said, *I am more aware, more conscious of the emotional needs of families. I was used to being engulfed in paperwork, and seeing the families on an ongoing basis without thinking too much about it. With Phyllis we can see families more clearly, to see signs that may need to be addressed. By talking together, we can have a clear picture of the family and problems that they are going through.*

A staff person from the home visiting program said, "It's amazing what I've learned. What questions to ask. You, Phyllis, are always in my mind when I see a mother. I ask about childhood, about relationships, more clinical questions. Before, I thought these questions were too private." And a teacher and translator said, "I was not comfortable before asking questions, but I have learned to be willing to listen and am more comfortable. It takes away having to guess. When you ask a question, they don't stop. They get an opportunity to talk. When given a chance to talk, they go on and on; they are all bottled up." Another worker said, "I always shied away from asking because I couldn't deliver. It's very hard. I do not have resources to help them on my own, but together we would find a way to help." A home visitor said, *When we are meeting, I go back afterwards and I apply this to myself. What do I need to change? How am I with some families? Try to analyze when I am with families. What is it that makes my heart break? I start to do free writing about my emotions of the day. The children have benefited dramatically.*

In this four-way parallel process, between myself, teacher, a mother, and her child, we all gained some benefits. The staff members learned ways of observing and talking in a comfortable way with the mothers. They had not been comfortable asking questions, fearful of intruding and causing pain. The staff members did not know how to listen, and when they did, they did not know what to do next. Learning some basic psychoanalytic developmental principles, and in modeling themselves after me, holding me in mind, their skill and competence increased. They were able to provide me with the clinical data that I could not get by myself because of my lack of Spanish. They also learned how to inquire on their own, to interview, opening doors to their own under-standing, and reducing their own powerlessness. These helpers learned to help these mothers and children in a way that had not been available to either of them before.

An important recent offshoot of the regular meetings with staff is a parent's meeting one afternoon and one morning a week. Parents drop in, and one of the teachers discusses whatever problem in development they raise, or the teacher brings up an issue like limit setting, father's role in child rearing, etc. We have been very impressed with how many fathers are participating.

The meetings are scheduled before or after work. They talk about the trouble they have being a father, wanting to be a better one. This is the first time in the staff's experience that fathers have participated. Throughout LSA, classes are made up almost entirely of mothers.

The parents and the children have benefited both in the short term, and we hope, in the long term from what started out as an exploratory clinical teaching exercise for a group of highly motivated teachers and staff. We wanted to understand why these toddlers were so lackluster and so disinterested in playing with wonderful toys. What evolved is a prevention and intervention program that the staff can do on its own. What started as a small investment in time and resources has yielded a large outcome, in significant ways in the lives of a number of mothers and their children.

REFERENCES

Field, T., Healy, B., Goldstein, S., Perry, S., Bendell, D., Schanberg, S., Zimmerman, E., &

Kuhn, S. (1988). Infants of depressed mothers show "depressed" behavior even with nondepressed adults. Child. Devel. Vol. 59, pp. 1569-1579.

Fonagy, P. (1998). Prevention, the appropriate target age of infant psychotherapy. Infant Mental Health, vol. 19, pp. 124-150.

Fonagy, P. Steele, H., Steele, M., & Holder, J. (1997). Attachment and theory of mind. Overlapping constructs? Assoc. Child Psych. Psychiatry Occasional Papers, pp. 31-40.

Fonagy, P. & Target, M. (1997). Attachment and reflective function: Their role in self-organization. Dev. Psychopathol., vol. 9, pp. 679-700.

Slade, A. (2005). Parental reflective functioning. An introduction. Attachment Human Devel., vol. 7, pp. 269-281.

Slade, A. Sadler, L., & Mayes, L.C. (2005). Minding the baby. Enhancing parental reflective functioning in a nursery/mental health home visiting program. In, Enhancing Early Attachments, Theory, Research, Intervention, and policy. [Eds.] Berlin, L., Ziv, Y., Amaga-Jackson, L. & Greenberg, M. New York: Guilford Publishers, pp. 152-177.

Target, M. & Fonagy, P. (1996). Playing with reality. II: The development of psychic reality from a theoretical perspective. Internat. J. Psychoanal. vol. 77, pp. 459-479.

Tronick, E. (1998). Dyadically expanded states of consciousness and the process of therapeutic change. Infant Mental Health J., vol. 19, pp. 290-299.

BIO

PHYLLIS ACKMAN, Ph.D., is a Clinical Psychologist, who practices Psychoanalysis in New York City with adults, and does dyadic work with mothers and infants. She is a Supervising and Training analyst at the Contemporary Freudian Society. She was a consultant to the Early Childhood Program at Little Sisters of the Assumption Health Center and was on the core faculty of the Institute for Infant, Child and Families of the Jewish Board of Family and Children's Services. Dr. Ackman was formerly the Coordinator of the Parent-Infant and Toddler Nursery Program at Pace University, where she also was an Adjunct Professor of Psychology. She has been involved with training the various professions that provide Early Intervention concerning the emotional impact of disability on the child and the family.

CHAPTER 7

Mothering Without A Home:
A Psychoanalytically-Informed Approach

Ann G. Smolen, Ph.D.

Psychoanalytically-Informed Approach

Ann G Smolen, Ph.D.

Mothers with young children are the fastest growing segment of the homeless population. When there is chronic stress as a result of extreme poverty and racism, how do families stay functional and cope? What happens when family structure breaks down, leaving young, single mothers alone to care for these children? What happens to parenting skills when the mother is poor, homeless, and isolated from family and community support? The combined stress of extreme poverty and homelessness can greatly impair the ability of single mothers to parent their children effectively. A history of poor attachments and abusive relationships added to the chronic stress of poverty and homelessness may cause the mother to feel powerless and inadequate. It has been documented that infants whose mothers are unable to provide comfort and protection, and who do not foster an interest in the world, form insecure attachments and are often unable to self-regulate. Greenspan states that these babies show increased tendencies toward muscle rigidity, gaze aversion, and disorganized sleep and eating patterns (Greenspan, 1990). Moreover, the homeless mother is preoccupied with daily, and sometimes hourly, survival. The homeless infant may be overwhelmed, and sleep, as a primitive defense, brings peace from an over-stimulating and abusive environment (Koplow, 1996). The mother without a home is unable to provide an intimate environment wherein the infant may experience her as provider and protector. This mother often feels helpless and inadequate in her ability to care for her child in terms of the most basic provision of shelter. Because she herself is totally dependent on others for survival she may defensively detach from her child's dependency needs (Koplow, 1996). Opening herself to her infant's emotional needs would require her to become reacquainted with painful experiences in the present and the past. If her experience was one of rejection and neglect it is much too painful and dangerous to feel in the absence of family and home.

Karen states: "when one becomes a parent, unresolved pain is shaken loose, the defensive wall is breached and new defensive efforts are required" (Karen 1998, pp.374). When a homeless mother gazes at her child, her own pain and sadness is mirrored back. Unable to bear her own painful feelings, the mother is also unable to feel empathy for her child's plight. Her new defense is to distance herself from her child. The mother's own depression and powerlessness become overwhelming.

Homeless women and their children, prior to residing in a transitional housing facility or long-term shelter, usually have experienced multiple traumas. These numerous, chronic traumas often result in disorganized patterns of attachment, which in turn affect all future development. There are few studies that explore the difficulties that homeless mothers experience in forming positive attachments with their babies. There are also a dearth of programs and interventions that address disturbed attachment patterns within this marginalized population.

The work I describe here was with five very special mothers and their six children. They met at a transitional housing facility or shelter for homeless women and children where they were able to live and receive multiple services for up to two years. When we think of the homeless we rarely think of a young mother pushing a baby stroller down the street with all of her essential belongings in tow. We cannot allow ourselves to think that a mother and baby have nowhere to sleep that night: it is too terrible a thought to allow ourselves to have.

Women with young children are rarely seen living on the street because they know that they will have their children taken from them. When a young woman has two or three little children under the age of four she will try to rely on different family members but quickly wears out her welcome. These mothers go from family member to family member, couch to couch, or even sleep on someone's floor with their children, never really knowing what to expect the next night. Other homeless mothers may even find themselves sleeping in abandoned buildings or cars, or seeking shelter in a public bathroom, their safety at stake.

How do you end up with a baby and no home? Each of the women in our group had their individual unique story, but there are many common background factors. Almost none of the women who come to live at homeless shelters come from stable families. Many have experienced abuse and neglect and never had a safe place to call home. Often their parents were not able to provide the basics of emotional security and a decent education. Abject poverty, oppressive racism, and dangerous living situations are traumas that get handed down from generation to generation.

As we are all aware, a good home is not just a physical structure but is where we build nurturing relationships that support us as we grow. Home is where we feel cared for, and where we learn to trust, to love, and to feel loved. What happens when our earliest relationships are laden with hurt, fear, and anger? Then home becomes a terrible place, a place to avoid.

Child psychoanalysts and infant researchers who study attachment patterns in infants and young children have much to tell us. Neglect and abuse early in life have long-term harmful effects. The infant brain is shaped by its early experience in the world of relationships. Children who are afraid of their caregivers, or cannot rely on them, cannot learn to trust. They often have grave difficulties in loving and accepting love. These children learn to protect themselves by avoiding or resisting others. As they grow, they may continue to distance themselves from others by violence or by drugs.

For some women, this shelter is their first good home. It is a place where they can feel safe and cared for, and for many a place where they come to know themselves and their babies for the first time. In our psychoanalytically informed mom/baby group the women were given a unique opportunity to share their stories with each other in an atmosphere that encouraged trust and hope. In the group the women were able to reflect on their own childhoods and I encouraged them to reflect on themselves as mothers. As they did this, they were able to connect the past with the present.

With the help of each other and the therapist, they began to explore new ways of being with their children, ways that promote more secure attachments and healthy emotional and physical development.

PURPOSE OF STUDY

The study that I undertook identified and described the attachment style of homeless mothers, and explored its effect on the resulting attachment style of their children. It incorporated psychoanalytically informed interventions with the goal of aiding the women in developing a deeper capacity to understand and be attuned to their babies' emotional needs. Within these interventions, the women began to learn to recognize attachment behaviors in their children and to see their children as separate individuals with minds of their own. Within the study, I made use of the Adult Attachment Interview (AAI), the Strange Situation, and the Bailey Infant Assessment Tool.

For this chapter, I will not describe my research methodology, research tools or results (Smolen, 2013), but instead will focus on the psychoanalytically informed interventions and the benefits to the women and children.

PSYCHOANALYTICALLY INFORMED GROUP INTERVENTION

The five women and their six children met twice per week for two-hour sessions with the therapist (myself) in a mom/baby group. Within this group the women, with the help of the therapist and of each other, came to know themselves and their babies, perhaps for the first time.

Within the group, the women had the opportunity to make photo journals of themselves with their children. They were also given cameras to take home. One purpose of the use of photographs was to help the mothers focus on and really see themselves and their babies. In addition, the mothers were encouraged to write in their journals and record hopes and wishes for the future as well as worries and concerns.

The women also participated in making a documentary where they were given the opportunity to tell their story and speak about how they came to be homeless. They were encouraged to speak about their hopes for the future for their families. The women also collaborated and wrote the script for, and acted in, a parenting film where they tell young women in situations like their own, what they wish someone had told them, and what they have learned from their experiences.

FIRST HOUR

In the first hour the women spoke about their children's current developmental issues and other relevant concerns with each other and the therapist as they made photo journals of themselves and their children. The photographs were taken during group-time when mothers and children played together. In these books the women wrote about hopes and wishes for their children. Some of the women included pictures, poems, and photos of their other children. In the early weeks, the women had difficulty finding words to describe their inner lives and the inner lives of their children.

Within the group they began to learn about themselves, and to think of their children as separate selves with complex emotions. Most of the women in the group had been abandoned emotionally or even betrayed by their own mothers when they were little. They grew-up in crisis amid a backdrop of trauma. "Knowing others and their minds had been fraught with terror, disappointment, and rage. And now they were faced with the enormous challenge of holding their own children in mind" (Slade et al., 2006, pp. 76).

SECOND HOUR

In the second hour the children joined their mothers in play. Ritualized structure was introduced at this time. All of the group meetings were videotaped, with the video footage used in several different ways. First, it was used in interventions with the mothers: making the films was an empowering experience for the women as they told their stories and offered advice to other young women in similar circumstances. It was also used by the mothers in making a documentary and a parenting film for use outside the study itself.

RITUALS

Structured activities were introduced in the mom/baby group. When I undertook an earlier exploratory study with homeless mothers and children it was evident that although the transitional housing facility provided stability and safety, and is an excellent "holding environment," many of the women continued to live chaotic lives. Perhaps because they lived with a background of violence and trauma as children, they never experienced what it is to have a bedtime or a goodnight story.

For many of the women, ritual was mostly absent from their childhood experiences. As described earlier, in the first hour of group the women met with the therapist without their children. In the second hour they joined the children, and were instructed to play with their children as they might do in their living units. After this period of undirected play, the therapist introduced structured activities that were repeated in every session. The group always ended with singing and movement and then a snack and a story.

The goal was for the mothers and children to find safety and comfort in the rituals as they

took on individual significance and meaning. The children might not understand the words of the story or the song, or they might not be capable of manipulating the symbols for communication, but I predicted that as the ritual took on meaning the baby would be able to respond to it.

Because the mothers participated with their children in the ritual activity, each learning their own part of it, the meaning became shared. However, for this shared meaning to occur the mother first had to be able to "accurately identify her infant's feelings" (Brinich 1982, pp. 6). Importantly, it is not the specific content of the ritual that is valuable, but the "sense of understanding and being understood: infant by mother and mother by infant" (Brinich 1982, pp. 6).

VIDEO INTERVENTION

The use of video feedback as an intervention is powerful, because it allows the mother to watch herself interact with her baby. As we watched mother's interactions with her child on videotape, I put words to the actions, addressing her "representations of her transferences to the infant" (Beebe 2007, pp. 9). This "translation" of the interaction helped the mother to learn to recognize the 8 baby's nonverbal language, to better comprehend her baby's communications, and to respond to them.

THE FAMILIES

All of the women in this study experienced multiple traumas which have been documented elsewhere (Smolen, 2013). For this paper I will not provide histories but instead will demonstrate the usefulness of the psychoanalytically informed mom/baby group for each family.

CHRISTA AND IRIS

Christa, a pretty 21year old African American woman with long reddish braids, was a single mother living in a homeless shelter with her two young children: a four year old son, and Iris, who was two-years old. Christa's large brown eyes, outlined by long thick eyelashes, were only out-done by her two young children, who had inherited the longest eyelashes I have ever seen. Christa's voluptuous body often became a soft climbing toy for her young daughter, as well as a perfect place for Iris to lay her head when in need of a hug.

Christa described how she had felt betrayed by her mother before she became homeless, and they had stopped speaking. Christa had been living with her mother when they were evicted and her mother moved into a tiny one room apartment, leaving Christa with nowhere to go with her two babies. "*I was just stuck. Um I just didn't have nowhere else to go. I was just stuck so it was going into a shelter or living on the street. I had no choice. It really hurt. I had to go to two shelters that were not safe. It was very very scary. I was very confused and it was depressing. Emotionally, physically, mentally. I was just depressed. And I thought the world was going to end. My world felt like it was going to fall apart.*"

When I first met Christa to speak with her about the project, she had been living at the transitional housing facility for thirteen months and was working hard to finish her GED, pay off her outstanding debts, and move forward toward her dream of becoming a chef and owning her own restaurant. She was eager to join our Mom/Baby group.

CHRISTA AND IRIS IN GROUP

In the "mother only" portion of our group, Christa was an active participant. She loved making pages for her photograph book and spoke about the journals she kept in her childhood and how important they were to her. Christa was engaged with the other group members, listening closely to what they had to say. She offered support and empathy when appropriate and was eager to give advice and share her own frustrations and concerns. She had creative advice for others and sought out their ideas when she was unsure of how to handle a certain situation. Christa seemed to integrate what I offered in the way of child development and parent education and was noticeably relieved when she became aware that it is normal to be frustrated and/or angry with your child at times. She also seemed open to figuring out better ways of expressing her frustrations and dealing with her own feelings of inadequacies as a mother. She spoke about wanting to be a better mother to her children and to be more available emotionally. It was most important to her that her children know that she loved them and that she would never abandon them.

Christa spoke candidly about how terrible it was for her when she was 15-years old and pregnant. She hid her pregnancy for fear of her mother's reaction; afraid she would be thrown out. She also spoke of the shame she felt when she had to go to the "pregnant" room in her high school. As she spoke her facial expression highlighted her words: "*I used to see those girls with their big bellies and think bad of them. Boy, now it was me. I couldn't believe it. I was one of them and everyone was thinking bad of me.*"

Iris was twenty-nine months old when the project began. She was tiny and appeared younger both physically, and behaviorally. Her speech was delayed, as she possessed just a few single words and these were difficult to understand. Iris was easily upset. If things did not go her way she quickly fell into tantrums. These moments were accompanied by piercing anguished crying. Christa had a difficult time comforting her daughter during tantrums and stated that her child was just being unreasonable and spiteful. What was most striking was that Christa felt that her little girl wanted to hurt her. She would often say: "She beats me up. She goes after me. She hates me."

It was interesting to watch Christa and Iris interact. Iris would approach her mother with excitement and vigor, jumping into her arms, kissing her face and playing with her hair. This lovely interaction would quickly turn "bad." Iris would begin to get over-stimulated as she climbed all over her mother using her as a jungle gym, and Christa would encourage this by holding her upside down or other exciting physical play. Iris would be so over-stimulated that she hit her mother or hurt her in some other way, and instead of explaining to her child that her play had crossed a boundary, and helping her to regulate, Christa would fake cry in an exaggerated way, saying that her daughter was "killing" her. These interactions would always end up with Iris crying and being rejected by her mother.

Iris and Christa both enjoyed the singing and movement portion of our group. Iris learned the words to many of the songs and sang and danced, imitating my movements and making her own creative additions. She loved being read to, and would bring me books asking me to start story-time. Iris also loved posing for the camera and was called "the little model'" by the other mothers.

Over the course of the group I felt that Christa was the participant who most benefited from the project as a whole. She seemed to gain a better understanding of her daughter's developmental and emotional needs and she became more capable of being a "secure base" for her child. In our final interview her words spoke for her accomplishments when she told the following story: "Iris was at her father's house for three days last week and I really missed her, I mean I needed the break, don't get me wrong and she does drive me crazy but I did miss her. So I go to get her and she runs and grabs my leg and she's so happy to see me..." *Mommy! Mommy! Mommy!" It was beautiful it really was. It was just beautiful."* This was an incredibly meaningful statement. It seemed as if Christa was now better able to accept her daughter's affection without turning it into a bad situation.

As our project came to an end, Christa and Iris were experiencing many more enjoyable interactions. Christa was better able to set limits and keep appropriate boundaries and Iris was less over stimulated. In addition, Iris's vocabulary increased by leaps and bounds as she was now speaking in sentences and making herself understood.

NINA AND KARL

Nina, an attractive, intelligent twenty-one year old African American woman, was openly emotional. It was easy to determine how she was feeling on any given day. When she was feeling well her eyes were bright and her features were soft. Her smile and laugh were infectious as she made excellent use of humor in her communications and interactions. However, when she was feeling depressed, her affect became flat and her sadness was palpable. Karl, her three-year old son, identified with his mother's moods.

When she was feeling badly, he also became depressed. When she was feeling well, Karl too seemed to come alive. Nina also had a one-year old son who lived with his father's family, and Nina hoped to one day regain custody of her youngest child.

NINA AND KARL IN GROUP

In our first interview, Nina spoke openly about the massive abuse she had endured throughout her childhood. Nina had a difficult time getting to group on time and would often arrive over a half hour late. Some mornings the effort to walk across the street from the residence to our group room was so taxing that when she arrived she appeared exhausted and depleted. There were many sessions in the early months when she would sit silently and contribute in monosyllables only when prodded by me. When she did speak, her words were barely audible. Nina seemed to like the idea of making the mom/baby books and requested that jewels be purchased so that she could decorate the cover of her book. When the jewels were purchased she painstakingly covered every inch of her cover in multicolored glass beads. While t he other mothers were making pages for their books with photos of their children, Nina was unable to do this. She was very critical of herself in the photographs and would refuse to enter them into her book.

As the weeks wore on, Nina's depression waned and she seemed to come alive. As this happened, her wonderful use of humor surfaced. At times she was just plain silly and reminded me of a little girl. She would sit close to me and want to "play." She began to participate in group conversations, sharing her own experiences. One morning the group was talking about what it is like when you are a single mother with nobody to help you and you have a new baby who is fussy and is unable to settle down and sleep. Nina shared how difficult these weeks were for her when Karl was a newborn.

She told her story: "*I didn't have nobody and I was so depressed, I had postpartum depression, and his father was abusive. I didn't have nobody. At night he cried and cried and nothing I did helped. I wanted to throw him out the window. I really did. So I went in the other room and turned my music on real loud and calmed myself. Then I went back and picked him up and sat myself down in the rocking chair and I tried all over again. I started out new. That's how I did it. I really wanted to throw him out the window, but I didn't.*"

However, Nina easily slipped back into depression. One particular morning she came in more depressed than I had seen her in the past. She shared with the group that over the weekend she had visited her grandmother's house for a party for her brother. The man who had sexually abused her as a child was invited to this party. She was enraged: "*I couldn't believe it! There he was. That's the thing they never believed me. He was always there. I stared at him and wanted to kill him. He just laughed at me. My cousin held me back. She said don't go to jail for him he isn't worth it. I couldn't believe they let him come there. It was terrible terrible just terrible!*"

The other women silently listened and commiserated by shaking their heads in agreement with her pain. There was nothing to say. We sat with her and listened to her despair.

The first time I met three-year old Karl was when I went to his day-care room to take him for his Bayley testing a week before group began. I knew him immediately; he looked just like his mother. His sadness was palpable as he was unable to engage with me and he performed poorly on the test. In group he would lean against his mother as she remained on the couch. The other mothers would get down on the quilt to play with their children. Nina was unable to do this. Karl was unable to leave his mother's side to explore with the other children. One page in their Photo book described their participation in the early weeks of group. It is a picture of Karl standing close to his mother as she sits on the couch. Her caption reads: *"Me and Karl look on."*

KARL'S FACIAL EXPRESSION MIRRORS HIS MOTHER'S DEPRESSION

As Nina came out of her depression, so did Karl. A lively, sweet, intelligent verbal little boy emerged. Karl began to play with the other children, joined in the singing and movement, and especially loved snack and reading time. His anger also emerged as he had an occasional temper tantrum when something did not go his way. Nina handled her son's anger by remaining calm. When he was extremely upset (which happened only once) she took him out of the room to help him to calm down and then rejoined the group. Karl made up creative games and Nina was able to participate with him and encourage his creativity and accomplishments.

There was one session when Nina and Karl were the only group members who attended that day (this happened only twice, once with Nina and Karl and once with Fannie and her sons). A fort with chairs and the quilt was constructed. At first, I helped Karl to build his fort but Nina quickly joined in as they both moved into their fort/home together. All had great fun as they made up a puppet show and played together. It was hard to tell who enjoyed this morning more!

It was extremely gratifying to once again retrieve Karl from his day-care room for his Bayley posttest a few weeks after the group had ended. He was engaged and animated as he sailed through the various activities.

As I took him out to the playground to rejoin his class, he asked when the group time would resume.

LENA AND NOEL

I met Lena for the first time in her living unit in the shelter. I was holding an open meeting for the eligible women to explain my research project and encourage them to participate. Lena's little girl Noel was sick in bed that evening, but Lena was interested in hearing more about the mother/child project and asked if I would speak with her privately in her rooms. Lena seemed exhausted from taking care of her sick two-year old as she cleared a spot at her table to sit and talk. Lena appeared older then her twenty-five years both in appearance and behavior. She felt she had lived a lot and wanted to impart her wisdom to the other, younger mothers. She expressed her shyness around cameras and was reluctant to be filmed, but she quickly became comfortable and was one of the more articulate members of the group.

LENA AND NOEL IN GROUP

From the beginning Lena loved to talk. She was the most vocal member of the group. Lena gave the impression of possessing a tough, rough exterior but she was capable of a softness that came out when she interacted with her two-year old daughter. Lena was extremely helpful to the other women on various topics, such as what to do when your baby is learning to crawl and you live in an unsafe environment, toilet training, and fathers.

On one particular day I asked the mothers about what to do if your baby is learning to crawl and you live in an undesirable place for your baby to explore his surroundings. Lena described an unsafe home where the floorboards were coming up and mice droppings as well as other garbage were on the floor. Lena told what she did: "*Well, what I did for my daughter was I made my own safe place. I cleaned up a space on the floor and I put blankets down and I surrounded it in pillows and put toys down for her and she could crawl there.*" This was a helpful story for Christa to hear, who also experienced unsuitable living arrangements when her child was crawling but kept her from crawling. She thought that if she were ever in that situation in the future she would now know what to do.

Lena also was able to tell the group about her toilet training experience with Noel. Early on in group Lena was frustrated but patient, stating that Noel must not be ready and she will just have to wait. When another mother said she beat her son so he would use the toilet, Lena became silent and pensive. Finally, after a long pause she said to the woman who had just confessed beating her son: "*Well my brother was beat to go to the toilet and he is in jail now so...*" This led to an intense discussion of beating and its ill effects on children as they all remembered their own beatings as children.

Lena was eloquent and made use of humor as she spoke about her children's fathers. She often had the group laughing about a difficult and sensitive subject. Lena was not going to take any nonsense from these men. She demanded that they pay attention to their respective children and she insisted that they deal with each other. Lena told the story of how the two men hated each other and were fighting in front of the children: "*I told them they better get along for the sake of my children and where my children are concerned they better not mess with me. I don't care if they hate each other but they better not take it out on my children. I told them they can just go ahead and kill each other and I will take their bodies and cremate them and put their ashes together in a bottle and sit it up on my mantle and they can fight for all eternity and I'll just sit there and look at that bottle and laugh!*"

When the project began, Noel, an adorable two-year old little girl, stayed close to her mother, bringing her toys one by one from the toy container. She was an observer, and seemed shy around me and the other women. It was obvious that Lena took great pride in her daughter's appearance, as Noel's hair was always neatly done with barrettes to match her outfit. By the end of our project, Noel was actively engaged with others and was speaking in full sentences and was toilet trained.

Lena and Noel both enjoyed the singing and movement part of the group. One of our songs was "*If you're happy and you know it...*" One verse is "*If you're scared and you know it give a scream!*" Noel loved this song, especially the screaming. Lena would encourage her daughter: "*You go girl! You scream it out!*" It was all great fun.

ZOE AND MELODY

Zoe was in her ninth month of pregnancy with her fourth child when we first met. She had two sons, ages nine and seven, and a four-year old daughter. Her appointment for her AAI was on her due date; that night she gave birth to a beautiful daughter. Zoe's radiant beauty was striking. She had large brown eyes that sparkled when she laughed and shot sparks of fire when angry. Zoe told her story with frank honesty and seemed to possess the wisdom of an older woman. She accepted the hardships of her childhood and her parent's shortcomings with compassion. She had a clear understanding that she had to take responsibility for her own future.

ZOE AND MELODY IN GROUP

Zoe was a dedicated member of the group. She was always the first to arrive, usually on time, and loyally attended until she was forced to enter the welfare-to-work program toward the latter half of the project. After her baby was placed in childcare, her attendance became sporadic.

Zoe had much to offer the group because Melody was her fourth child. She often spoke about her older children, especially around toilet training experiences and relationships with the children's fathers. Zoe demonstrated her understanding and empathy for her second son when the women were sharing how they arranged for their children to visit with their fathers. Zoe explained: "*Well, my oldest son, he sees his father. His father is in his life, he buys him some things and takes him places. He don't stay there much, if at all. I mean I never get a break, but he in his life. Now my second son, his father is just not there at all for him. I feel some kind of way about it but what can I do. He says: "My father must not love me" and this, that and a third. I'm not going to lie to him. It's just how it is. But I give him extra time alone with me. I might do something special just for him. The others understand that. They have fathers, he doesn't. It's good because my older son's father will include him. That's nice and I appreciate it. But I do feel some kind of way about it all!"*

Zoe was wonderful with infant, Melody. She was unrelenting about insisting that *"meat spoils, not babies."* Zoe felt that babies should be held, which she demonstrated by keeping Melody in her arms for most of group time. She was attuned to her baby and would pick her up out of her infant seat before Melody became uncomfortably upset. I was impressed with how quickly Zoe began to take some of my words as her own and incorporated the idea of thinking about what your baby was thinking into her interactions with her infant. This is beautifully illustrated in her photo book on several pages. For example, at times Zoe had a tendency to be over-intrusive, kissing Melody all over her face many times. On a page where the photo shows Zoe very much in Melody's face, Zoe writes: *"Too many kisses, Melody is thinking: Too many kisses."* And on another page there is a beautiful photograph depicting Zoe and Melody gazing into each other's eyes and Zoe writes: *"I wonder what Melody is thinking about? I wonder what is on her mind?"*

It was difficult for Zoe to put Melody in daycare; however, she was threatened with losing her welfare if she did not comply. Zoe spoke about finding appropriate daycare and how she needed to be nearby so she could just drop in at lunchtime and visit her baby. She also wanted to be able to make sure that her infant was being properly cared for. In the end, Zoe did not have to use a daycare but instead Melody's paternal grandmother took over her care. There were pros and cons to this situation. The good thing was that Melody was with a family member who loved and adored her and she got one-on-one attention. The unfortunate problem was that Zoe began to go several days at a time without seeing her baby. Zoe would come to group, stay until the children joined us and then she would go to her work program.

Several weeks later, Zoe brought Melody to group and there was a striking difference in her appearance. Melody seemed depressed, as it was difficult to get her to engage and to respond. Melody did not smile at all that week. I was concerned and wondered with Zoe how she thought her baby was feeling about this separation. This was very difficult for Zoe to allow herself to even think about, and she cut off the conversation with insisting that her baby did not miss her, and that she was absolutely fine. I certainly understood her anxiety, which caused her to become defensive. However, as the weeks progressed Zoe had her baby with her more often.

In the last weeks of group, I observed six-month old Melody, who was developmentally advanced, bright eyed, happily verbalizing and engaged.

FANNIE AND TOM AND ROB

Fannie moved into the shelter the week the mom/baby group began, missing the first two sessions. She appeared years older than twenty-three as she attempted to navigate her way through the system. Overwhelmed by her two little boys, ages one- and two-years old, it seemed as if she was unable to take care of herself as she was disheveled, while her living unit was immaculate and her boys were dressed in matching outfits down to the socks and shoes. It was not clear if Fannie understood the purpose of the group as she had significant cognitive limitations, but she was lonely and there was no room in daycare for her boys so she consented to join the group.

FANNIE AND TOM AND ROB IN GROUP

Fannie felt ill at ease when she first came into our group. She had just moved into the transitional housing facility, having come from a Women Against Abuse shelter, and was still adjusting to living in a shelter. She did not know any of the other women and did not try to engage with them. She was silent. I found it difficult to engage her and involve her in the group conversation. For the first few months she would silently work on her photo book, only speaking when spoken to.

As Fannie became more comfortable she began to share her own experiences with the group. She explained that nobody had taught her about how to care for a baby. When her first son was born she had to learn everything on her own. The other women in the group all seemed to have lots of experience caring for younger siblings or cousins as they were growing up, but not Fannie. She had an isolated childhood.

An uncomfortable situation arose as Fannie spoke to her children using an extremely mean tone. For the most part, all of her interactions were inappropriate to the situation. Her voice became very loud and she used a commanding rough manner. It became evident that she had no other way of being with her children in her repertoire. When this occurred, the mood was disrupted in the group and the other children became tense, looking on with concern. The other mothers did not interfere with Fannie's mothering. At first I tried modeling appropriate responses to setting limits and other interactions with her children. I hoped Fannie would follow my lead. However, a few weeks went by and when her behavior was not altered at all it became evident that a more direct intervention was needed. The quandary was how to do this without inflicting a narcissistic wound and embarrassing her in front of the other women. As it turned out, as I was wrestling with this problem, a day came when only Fannie and her boys came to group. It was the perfect opportunity to speak with Fannie alone and then to work one-on-one with Fannie with her boys during our playtime. This seemed to be a pivotal point, as Fannie became more aware of her own behavior and feelings. She would catch herself and change her tone and approach to her boys. She later shared that she struggled with her angry outbursts and knew she needed to have more patience.

Both two-year old Tom and one-year old Rob enjoyed the group. For several weeks they stayed very close to their mother, bringing her toys and sharing her lap. They watched the other children and soon felt comfortable enough to venture away from their mother. Tom became attached to an intern who was observing the group and began to sit on her lap and bring her toys. Rob began to walk backward and fall into my lap. Both children participated in the singing and movement, and snack time became a favorite.

As Tom adjusted to both his new living arrangements and participating in the group, he also exhibited angry episodes. His facial expression would darken as his eyebrows knitted together and he would kick and pinch not only other children, but me as well. When I spoke with Fannie about her angry tone, she was able to connect it to Tom's angry behaviors, which were meaningful to Fannie.

There were incidents when Fannie would tease Tom by holding him down with one hand and holding a toy just out of his reach. Tom would become enraged, crying and frustrated, while Fannie seemed to sadistically enjoy his pain. I made use of the video tape to help Fannie see how teasing her child caused him to not only feel pain but to then attack back in a violent way. The group experience was valuable to Fannie and her children; however, Fannie needed ongoing interventions to help her understand the emotional and developmental needs of her boys.

CULTURAL DIFFERENCES

The following vignette is an example of subtle differences in child rearing in this population, which may serve as an explanation of attachment scores. This interaction occurred in one of our last mom/baby group sessions:

All of the mothers were sitting on the floor on our quilt while the children played with the toys. The children occasionally interacted with one another, frequently returning to their mothers to show them a toy or sit on their lap. Lena was chatting with another mother when Noel threw a toy across the room, perhaps to regain her mother's undivided attention, and the toy accidentally hit another little girl on the back of her head. The other child was not hurt and hardly even noticed the offence other than to turn around to see what hit her. Noel made a beeline across the room, keeping her back turned toward her mother. Lena became harsh and in a somewhat loud and mean-sounding tone insisted that her daughter apologize to the other little girl. Noel continued to completely ignore her mother, refusing to acknowledge her demand, pretending that she did not even hear her mother calling to her.

I was sitting next to Lena and had observed the whole thing. I suggested to Lena that Noel had not meant to hurt the other child and the whole incident had been an accident. In my mind, I was thinking that Noel need not be disciplined since she obviously had hit the other child inadvertently. Lena turned to me and explained: "*I know she didn't do it on purpose and it doesn't matter that Iris wasn't hurt, but out there she could get killed. People don't care if you didn't mean it. She has to say she's sorry."* At that moment I knew that Lena's harsh tone demanding that her child apologize was not mean, but was urgently teaching her child how to survive in their world. Five minutes later Noel came skipping over to her mother, sat on her lap with her nose touching her mother's nose and exclaimed in the most innocent of voices: "Were you calling me? Did you call me?" Lena just laughed exclaiming: *"Yes I called you! I called you five minutes ago! I sure did call you!"* And the incident was forgotten.

To my ear, Lena sounded overly harsh, unnecessarily mean. Perhaps what I misinterpreted was an alarming urgency to teach her child to keep herself safe in a very hard, harsh world. I would further speculate that Noel interpreted her mother's words as loving even though she was somewhat afraid of getting into trouble, which is probably why she avoided her mother's demand to apologize. However, she knew that she would be accepted lovingly back into her mother's arms, which is exactly what happened.

DISCUSSION

The famous African proverb "It takes a village to raise a child" has significant meaning within the African American culture. In the African American community, child rearing is often viewed as a communal process. Extended families are valued, and often children grow up in multi-generational homes where disciplining and the socialization of children are distributed among all the adult members of the household.

Chronic stress due to abject poverty and homelessness may cause the young single mother to feel overwhelmed by anger, resentment, and frustration, all of which combine to make her feel powerless and inadequate. Studies have shown that mothers who have more peers in their support network are more competent parents. Mothers who receive greater support from family and friends "tend to be more emotionally responsive to their children" (MacPhee et al., 1996, pp.3279). Most of the women in shelters experience multiple forms of racism and oppression. As African American women they face racism on a daily basis. As poor, homeless women they experience chronic stress due to their marginalized status in society. Many of the women also live with the deeply personal wound of being rejected by their own families, left to care for their children alone and without support. Many homeless women with children expend all of their energy trying to meet their own and their children's basic needs. If a woman is worried about food and shelter she will often not have the energy (or the wherewithal) to interact with her children in a loving way, or be able to provide interesting activities for her children. The majority of homeless women have not had their own emotional needs met (in the past or present) and thus are more likely to be critical and irritable with their own children (MacPhee et al., 1996).

It seems obvious that homelessness would impair a mother's ability to parent her children effectively, yet there is little empirical research on the parenting and attachment styles of the homeless. By capitalizing on the strengths of the African American family, and providing interventions that assist the homeless mother in providing greater support and control and nurturing, agencies can help high-risk families function more efficiently in society. Mental health practitioners must appreciate ethnic and racial differences so they may facilitate ethnic pride within the families with whom they work. This in turn will help families be more receptive to formal supports with more positive outcomes.

PRACTICE IMPLICATIONS AND FUTURE RESEARCH

The stories of the women and children illustrate several areas where mental health workers need to focus. Professionals working with children who have experienced chronic trauma such as homelessness, profound poverty, physical and sexual abuses, and physical and emotional neglect often become overwhelmed. Many times only a specific maladaptive behavior is focused on and treatment is analogous to a bandage on a hemorrhage.

In our future work with these families, early attachment relationships must come into clear focus, and a combined treatment with both the child and the parent may be optimal. The parent's own attachment past must be acknowledged and dealt with. Psychoanalytic leaders such as Anna Freud, Mahler et al., Parens, Greenspan and others, valued the vital importance of intervention in the first years of life. Mother-infant therapy has been spearheaded by Fraiberg, Adelson & Shapiro (1975); Call (1963); Fraiberg (1971, 1980); Greenacre (1971); Greenspan (1981); Spitz (1965); and Liberman & Pawl (1993). The last decade "has shown great progress in conceptualizing methods of intervention with parents and infants. Both psychodynamic approaches aimed at the mother's representations and interactional approaches attempting to intervene into specific behavioral transactions are effective (see for example Brazelton, 1994; Fraiberg 1980; Field et al., 1996; Hofacker & Papousek, 1998; Hopkins, 1992; McDonough, 1993; Marvin, Cooper, Hoffman, & Powell, 2002; Malphurs et al., 1996; Seligman, 1994; Stern, 1995; Van den Boom, 1995)" (Beebe 2007, pp. 9). Several mother-infant interventions have demonstrated positive outcomes and improvements in the mother-infant relationship (Cramer et al., 1990). However, it is important to note that mother-infant intervention and treatment continues to be unavailable to underserved populations such as homeless mothers and children.

Another important area that needs to be addressed is providing culturally appropriate parenting classes and properly facilitated mom/baby groups that teach child development and help young mothers begin to recognize attachment behaviors in their babies. Those of us who have had the opportunity to work with parent/child dyads have observed how exquisitely sensitive these relationships are. A small change in the parent can make all the difference. As Daniel Stern describes in his book The Motherhood Constellation, the ultimate goal of parent/child therapy is to "free infants from the distortions and displaced affects engulfing them in parental conflict and to change the parent's internal representations of himself or herself and of the child" (Stern, 1995).

In my earlier exploratory work conducting parenting groups for homeless women, I searched for parenting films to show in class. Most studies examining parenting (and videos that teach parenting) have been conducted with Caucasian and African American middle-class families. Several of the films depicted single mothers who experienced poverty; however, all of the families shown in these films had a home to go to after their baby was born. These teaching materials proved to be ineffective and even detrimental to the very poor families I worked with. Not only are the women unable to relate to the families shown on the films, but these films added to the sense of worthlessness and poor self-esteem that these families already bear.

This project has produced a parenting video that homeless women and teenage single mothers will be able to identify with and learn from. The parenting video may be used in inner-city high school programs, foster care agencies, and the Department of Human Services as an aid in working with young girls/women who become pregnant. The documentary film gives voice to the otherwise silenced homeless women. In this film, the women raise their voices and speak out. These five courageous women have chosen to no longer remain silently invisible to a society that would like them to disappear.

CONCLUSION

Because of the work of Selma Fraiberg (1980) and her colleagues, psychoanalytically informed clinicians have been working with mothers and babies for over forty years. Within the psychoanalytic community, working with the mother-infant dyad is highly valued. In our work with high-risk mothers and children who have experienced trauma, the environment is not easily controlled or modified. While these circumstances may be viewed as unconventional and challenging, it is also becoming clear that these difficult populations benefit from psychoanalytically informed interventions.

We know that in mother-infant dyads that are troubled, the mother's "representation of the baby has been distorted by unmetabolized and undifferentiated affects stemming from her own early and usually traumatic relationship experiences. The goal of infant-parent psychotherapy is to disentangle these affects from the relationship with the baby" (Slade et al., 2006, pp. 79). It is in the relationship between the mother and the therapist that change occurs and representations begin to shift. The ultimate goal is that the child will no longer be the recipient of the mother's traumatic projections (Slade et al., 2006).

All of us who participated in this project benefited. The families' stories unfolded in the matrix of the trusting, caring relationships that developed between myself and the women and their children. I provided an essential transforming substitute to the women's earlier relationships with their mothers. Most valuable was the experience of being heard and seen and feeling valued by me. This in itself can be instrumental in freeing the mother and baby from earlier neglectful and harmful relationships (Slade et al., 2006).

However, it is not always easy to gain the trust and respect of women who have been abandoned and abused their whole lives. I feel the alliances that I was able to develop with the women were often disrupted by "transferential reactions on the part of mothers who had been betrayed and hurt by those who cared for them" (Slade et al., 2006, pp. 83). This was acted out by the women missing sessions or making me pursue them. I often found myself coaxing a mother to attend and giving frequent reminders of when we met. While this was frustrating and exhausting, I understood the multitude of internal conflicts that were stirred up as our relationship deepened. Becoming close was frightening to most of these women, and the fear and resulting defenses needed to be respected and understood.

Change and growth could be observed as the women gathered around the table where they worked on their Photo books and shared glorious and painful experiences of what it means to be homeless and to be a mother. It was rare that all five women attended a given session; yet they always knew I would be there, session after session, week after week. I was consistent and dependable, something they had never experienced before in an important relationship. As we spoke they sensed my appreciation of what they could teach me, and developed a powerful sense of pride that I was giving them the opportunity to help others.

As they came to see me as dependable and caring they began to integrate bits and pieces of information I offered them. A couple of the women identified with me and took my words as their own when making the films and writing in their photo books. Because I showed them that I appreciated and valued their minds (their thoughts and feelings) they in turn, began to notice and value the minds of their children.

I demonstrated a commitment and dedication to their well being that they, as a group, came to value. Over the course of this six-month project we weathered many storms, both intrapsychic and environmental. We cried together and listened to painful stories but we also laughed and played. I became their playmate, a playful, loving mother, bringing glitter and shiny stones, singing songs and dancing to childhood lyrics. I read them bedtime stories while I fed them cookies and juice. Our group provided a safe "holding environment," a place and time that was always the same. Within this sameness trust developed and healing could begin. They shared childhood memories and disappointments and began to ask for certain childhood stories and songs.

As I demonstrated flexibility and creative processes they too were able to become more flexible and creative. In the beginning, all five of the women had difficulties playing with their children. As the months wore on, all of the participants were more comfortable playing, not only with me, but also with their own children. The stories of the women and children may demonstrate weaknesses in our society and in our social service systems, but these stories also show the remarkable strength and resiliency that so many of these vulnerable families possess.

I am honored to have had the opportunity to work with and get to know all of the families. I leave them humbled by their strength and courage and proud of their ability to continue to dream for a better future for themselves and their children.

REFERENCES

Ainsworth, M., Blehar, M., Waters, E., & Wall, S. (1978). Patterns of Attachment. Hillsdale, NJ: Lawrence Erlbaum Press.

Bayley, N. (1993). Bayley Scales of Infant Development-II. New York: Psychological Corp.

Beebe, B. (2007). Mother-infant research informs mother-infant treatment. Psychoanal. Study of the Child. Vol. 60, pp. 7-46.

Brazelton, T.B. (1994). Touchpoints: Opportunities for preventing problems in the parent-child relationship. Acta Paediatrica, 394

(Suppl), pp. 35-39.

Brinich, P.M. (1982). Rituals and meanings—the emergence of mother-child communication. Psychoanal. Stud. Child, vol. 37, pp. 3-14.

Brisch, K.H. (2002). Treating attachment disorders from theory to therapy. London: Guildford.

Call, J. (1963). Prevention of autism in a young infant in a well-child conference. J. Am. Acad. Child Psychiatry, vol. 2, 451-459.

Cramer, B., Robert-Tissot, C., Stern, D, Serpa-Rusconi, S., De Muralt, M., and Besson, G. (1990). Outcome evaluation in bvrief mother-infant psychotherapy: A preliminary report. Inf. Mental Health J., vol. 11 (3), 278-300.

Field, T., B. Healy, S. Goldstein, S. Perry, D. Bendell, S. Schanberg, E. Zimmerman, S. Kuhn. (1988). Infants of depressed mothers show "depressed" behavior even with nondepressed adults. Child Dev., 59: 1569-1579.

Fraiberg, S. (1959). The Magic Years. New York: Simon and Schuster.

——— (1971). Intervention in infancy: A program for blind infants. J. Amer. Psychoanal. Assn, vol. 10 (3), pp. 381-405.

——— (1980). Clinical studies in infant mental health: The first year of life. NY: Basic Bks.

——— (1982). Pathological defenses in infancy. Psychoanal. Quart. Vol. LI, pp. 612-635.

Fraiberg, S., Adelson, E., & Shapiro, V. (1975). Ghosts in the nursery: A psychoanalytic approach to the problem of impaired infant-mother relationships, J. Acad. Of Child Psychiatry, vol. 14 (3), pp. 387-421.

Greenacre, P. (1971). Emotional Growth. New York: International Universities Press.

Greenspan, S. (1981). Psychopathology and adaptation in infancy and early childhood: Principals of clinical diagnosis and preventive intervention. New York: International Universities Press.

Hofacker, N., & Papousek, M. (1998). Disorders of excessive crying, feeding, and sleeping: The Munich interdisciplinary research and intervention program. Inf. Mental Health J. vol. 19 (2), 180-201.

Hopkins, J. (1992). Infant and parent psychotherapy. J. Child Psychother. vol. 18 (1), pp. 5-19.

Karen, R. (1998). Becoming attached: First relationships and how they shape our capacity to love. New York Warner Books.

Koplow, L. (1996). [Ed.] Unsmiling Faces. New York: Teachers College Press.

Lieberman, A., & Pawl, J. (1993). Infant-parent psychotherapy: In, Zeanah, C.H. [Ed.]. Handbook of Infant Mental Health. NY: Guildford Press. pp. 427-42.

Lieberman, A.F., Silverman, R., & Pawl, J. (1999). Infant-parent psychotherapy: Core concepts and current practices. In, Zeanah, C.H. [Ed.]. Handbook of Infant Mental Health. NY: Guildford Press. pp. 472-485.

Marvin, R.S., & Whelan, W.F. (2003). Discovered attachments: Toward evidence-based clinical practice. Attach. Human Development, vol. 5, pp. 283-288.

Marvin, R., Cooper, G., Hoffman, K., & Powell, B. (2002). The circle of security project: Attachment-based intervention with caregiver-preschool dyads. Attach. Human Development, vol. 4 (1), pp. 107-124.

MacPhee, D., Fritz, J., & Miller-Heyl, J. (1996). Ethnic variations in personal social networks and parenting. Child. Develop. Vol. 67, pp. 3278-3295.

McDonough, S. (1993). Interaction guidance. In, C. Zeanah [Ed.] Handbook of Infant Mental Health. New York: Guildford Press, pp. 414-426.

Parens, H. (1979). The Development of Aggression in Early Childhood. Northvale, NJ: Jason Aronson.

Parens, H., Pollock, L., Stern, J. & Kramer, S. (1976). On the girl's entry into the Oedipus complex. J. Amer. Psychoanal. Assn. vol. 24 (Suppl), pp. 79-107.

Paret, I.H. & Shapiro, V.B. (1998). The splintered holding environment and the vulnerable ego. Psychoanal. Study of the Child. Vol. 53, pp. 300-324.

Pinderhughes, E. (1995). Empowering diverse populations: Family practice in the 21st century. Fam. Soc. Vol. 76 (3), pp. 131-140.

Seligman, S. (1994). Applying psychoanalysis in an unconventional context: Adapting infant-parent psychotherapy to a changing population. Psychoanal. Study. Child. vol. 49, pp. 481-510.

Slade, A., Sadler, L., De Dios-Kenn, C. Webb, D., Currier-Ezepchick, J. &

Mayes, L. (2005),

Minding the baby: A reflective parenting program. Psychoanal Study of Child. 60, pp. 74-100.

Smolen, A. (2013). Mothering Without A Home: Attachment Representations and Behaviors in Homeless Mothers and Children. New York: Jason Aronson.

Spitz, R.A. (1965). The First Year of Life. A Psychoanalytic Study of Normal and Deviant Development of Object Relations. New York: International Universities Press.

Stern, D. (1985). The Interpersonal World of the Infant. New York: Basic Books.

——— (1995). The Motherhood Constellation: A Unified View of Parent-Infant Psychotherapy. New York: Basic Books.

Tronick, E. Z., Als, H., Adamson, L., Wise, S., & Brazelton, T.B. (1978). The infant's response to entrapment between contradictory messages in faced-to-face interaction. J. A. Acad. Child Psychiatry, vol. 17, pp. 1-13.

Tronick, E. (1989). Emotions and emotional communications in infants. Amer. Psychologist, vol. 44, pp. 112-119.

Tronick, E. Z. & Weinberg, M.K. (1997). Depressed mothers and infants: Failure to form dyadic states of consciousness. In, L. Murray and P.J Cooper [Eds.] Postpartum Depression and Child Development. New York: Guilford Press, pp. 54-81.

Van Den Boom, D. (1995). Do first-year intervention effects endure? Follow-up during toddlerhood of a sample of Dutch irritable infants. Child Devel. Vol. 66, pp. 2798-1816.

Winnicott, D. W. (1960). The theory of the parent infant relationship. Int. J. Psychoanal. vol. 41, pp. 585-595.

——— (1971). Playing and Reality. New York: Basic Books.

——— (1974). Fear of breakdown. Int. J. Psychoanal. vol. 1, pp. 103-107.

——— (1987). Babies and Their Mothers. New York: Addison-Wesley Publishers.

——— (1996). Thinking About Children. Reading, Massachusetts: Addison-Wesley.

Bio

ANN SMOLEN, PH.D. is a training and supervising analyst in child, adolescent, and adult psychoanalysis at the Psychoanalytic Center of Philadelphia. Dr. Smolen graduated Summa Cum Laude from Bryn Mawr College and received a Master's degree in Social Work from Bryn Mawr College School of Social Work and Social Research. She received her Doctorate in Philosophy from the Clinical Social Work Institute in Washington, DC. Her first profession was as a member of the New York City Ballet. Dr. Smolen has won several national awards for her clinical work, which she has presented both nationally and internationally. Dr. Smolen is the 2016-2017 recipient of the Helen Meyers Traveling Psychoanalytic Scholar Award. Dr. Smolen has published several articles including *Boys Only! No Mothers Allowed*, published in The International Journal of Psychoanalysis and translated into three languages. Dr. Smolen is the author of *Mothering Without a Home: Representations of Attachments Behaviors in Homeless Mothers and Children* (Aronson, 2013). Dr. Smolen has a new book: *Six Children: The Spectrum of Child Psychopathology and Its Treatment* (Karnac, 2015). She maintains a private practice in child, adolescent, and adult psychotherapy and psychoanalysis in Ardmore, PA

CHAPTER 8

Relational Hope:
Foster Care and *A Home Within*

Joseph Schaller, Psy.D.

Relational Hope: Foster Care and *A Home Within*

Joseph Schaller, Psy.D.

Psychoanalytic work with children began in the second generation of Freud's legacy, through the pioneering work of Anna Freud and Melanie Klein. Each in her own way realized the need to adapt the psychoanalytic technique to the special needs of children, including their level of development and their (real) dependency on parents. In the ensuing decades there would come a variety of techniques adapted to children, whose most comfortable means of expression was often in the form of play with the symbolic overtones which play contains. If Freud and his loyal followers privileged the role of insight in ushering growth, change and "cure," child therapists more and more appreciated the power of allowing children to express something of their experience and their inner world in non-verbal material, as well as the importance of a creation of a literal "holding" environment, which promoted a sense of safety.

Child analysis or psychotherapy—like adult psychoanalysis—was also cultivated within the reality of trauma. Anna Freud's and Donald Winnicott's work with children in London at the time of the Second World War provoked adaptations required for children who had been traumatized by loss of parents, existence in orphanages, and the terror and chaos which characterized the times. As a result, we cannot think of "child analysis" as a technique employed merely to resolve neurotic conflicts of children who were otherwise safe and well-cared for.

Rather, psychoanalysis was seen as an effective intervention in the face of the direst circumstances. Perhaps it is even useful to recall the controversy surrounding Freud's oscillation in his beliefs about the nature of childhood sexual abuse and his formulation of his seduction theory. Children (and adults) who come to work with a psychoanalyst or psychodynamic therapist are more likely than not to have been the victims of some significant trauma or the accumulation of traumatic experiences.

These remarks serve to place the following ideas in a certain context. From its inception, psychoanalysis has had to adapt to particular social and interpersonal circumstances that have allowed it to develop as a distinctively responsive method. Although stereotypes have developed about what it means to be "doing psychoanalysis"—often as a result of rigid orthodoxies which have been in place at various times in the history of the profession—in its essence, psychoanalysis understands behavior as determined and limited by a variety of internal and external factors. Even if Freud emphasized only a few factors as primarily implicated in psychic development, he certainly appreciated the culture which served to create and sustain human psychological interaction. His own vision of psychoanalysis as a tool which could be helpfully available to the widest possible population of people, resulting in an early establishment of free clinics providing psychoanalysis to the general population (Danto, 2005), suggests an appreciation for the capacity of psychoanalysis to be flexible enough to exist in a variety of circumstances.

A HOME WITHIN

A Home Within is a national organization, which was founded in San Francisco almost twenty years ago, and established as a not-for-profit organization for the past fifteen years. Its mission is to recruit and support trained and licensed therapists who are willing to volunteer to see a child or youth who is in foster care or who was once in foster care on a pro-bono basis. There are currently over forty local chapters of A Home Within throughout the country.

As with all organizations, there is a story about how it was founded. In this case, it's about a group of clinicians in training who had been involved with foster youth in the San Francisco Bay area. They found themselves of like minds with regard to the needs of this population of youth, lamenting the dilemma of their clients: kids who had been through a succession of short-term therapeutic relationships unable to attain what then seemed to so badly need—a sustained relationship with a concerned and responsible adult. Eventually, they decided to do something about this dilemma. As recalled by founder and current Executive Director of A Home Within Toni Heineman:

> We met together every few weeks for about a year over soup and salad at my dining room table, The conversations were lively, as they often are among people with divergent opinions who respect each other. Over the years, (typical) comments from those conversations stand out for me. From my left, 'There is so much to do; we need to move faster.' And from my right, 'We don't actually know what we are doing; we need to slow down.' This tension continues to inform the way the staff and board of A Home Within think about the organization as we grow and change (Heineman, 2015, p.6).

And so the project was born. This original core group became determined not only to carry on their individual efforts, but to band together as an ongoing "consultation group" in order to provide peer support in this difficult work. Because they were trained in a psychoanalytic framework, each had a deep understanding of the complexities of the children they worked with, as well as the importance and the challenge of building relationships with their clients. Others were inspired by this project, and within a few years A Home Within was established as a charitable organization.

The story is important for a couple of reasons. First of all, it represents a kind of idealism and determination indicative of many individuals who become therapists, particularly those who commit themselves to the rigor of psychoanalytic/psychodynamic training. Secondly, these founding members had a vision that more was needed for foster youth than simply providing case management or short-term behavioral intervention. Many children in foster care experience continual disruption and trauma in their lives, both in the circumstances which precipitated their removal from their families, but also in the sequence of foster placements, interaction with case workers and courts, and disconnection from their schools, families and friends. The one thing usually missing in the foster situation is a safe relationship with someone who is committed to the child beyond being paid to perform a service. Psychoanalytic orientations recognize that real change is most often only accomplished over a certain period of time in relationship with a therapist who can competently navigate the complexities of interpersonal experience and also communicate a form of dedication, which helps to rebuild trust. The final point about the founding story is that the intention of these first clinicians, though noble, can also seem naive. Pairing a volunteer clinician with a foster youth may sound simple, but it is far from easy. There are many obstacles to this well-intentioned effort, many of which were in the minds of that group of clinicians who sat around the dining room table; others which only became evident over time. The following is an attempt to delve into the complexities as well as the potential hope, which springs from a commitment to bringing a psychoanalytic sensibility to the challenging world of Foster Care.

THE TRAUMA OF FOSTER CARE

There is a sad irony at the heart of our current system of caring for children who cannot be cared for by their parents or families: There is probably no point in the history of Western Civilization where as many resources have been available to assist these children, yet it is a system which fails to live up to its promise. More often, the very structure of foster care almost inevitably guarantees that its participants will be traumatized many times over. We have come a long way from a time when children were left to fend for themselves if they were abandoned or neglected by their families. In Western cultures, we have largely moved beyond the institution of large orphanages which often warehoused children, perhaps providing for basic needs of food and shelter but offering little in the form of human contact and nurturing which are essential for psychological and emotional health of the individual. Yet those in foster care are sometimes considered to be "orphans of the living" who are subject to horrific violations of children's basic human rights (Toth, 1998).

According to the United States Department of Health and Human Services, there were over 400,000 children and youth in foster care as of 2011. As of 2012, there were 679,000 instances of confirmed child maltreatment (www.childwelfare.gov). In this country, a combination of civic and private agencies provide an array of services ranging from recruitment and supervision of foster parents to the myriad of support services including mental health treatments and various forms of case management. The need to assist older children in the process of "aging out" and moving toward independent living has also become an increasing focus of available services of late. The first legislation providing for specific services in recognition of the need for assistance for youth transitioning out of the system did not occur until 1986. In the 1990's, additional legislation extended benefits and services to cover youth between eighteen and twenty-one (Smith, 2011). As might be expected, our largest urban centers face the greatest need/demand and also are frequently overwhelmed with the budgetary restrictions and other systemic obstacles, which characterize sprawling social service networks. Rural communities face their own set of difficulties, particularly where resources are limited and where geographical distance poses a greater challenge to provide services and regular contact for the foster child and his or her family resources. Because foster children routinely move from one foster placement to another, or may move back and forth between their biological families and foster care, it becomes very difficult for them to maintain any real continuity with regard to their schools, friends, siblings, case workers and therapists.

Consider the story of Patty, whose experience is detailed in a collection of stories about children aging out of foster care (Shirk & Stangler, 2004). Although the story ends with a successful transition to college, which Patty considers "the perfect transition between living in a foster home and living on your own," Patty's experience is somewhat rare. "Children in foster care are half as likely as other children to be enrolled in college preparatory classes in high school, and frequent moves and school changes make it hard to compile the academic record necessary for admission to many four-year schools" (p.45). Remarkably—though not atypically— Patty had lived in seven different homes and attended five different schools during her high school years.

Patty was born as the second child to her mother when her mother was seventeen, who was one of a dozen children born to an alcoholic mother. Everyone in this generation ended up in foster care. Patty's mother left her abusive husband when Patty was eighteen months old. In spite of this, Patty's earliest memories of her mother were largely happy ones, and there is evidence of a strong attachment bond between mother and daughter. But by the time Patty was in second grade, her mother was drinking daily, taking her children to the bar with her, and using hard drugs. Patty and her older sister were removed by the Department of Social Services in Boston in third grade, and placed in the temporary care of experienced and caring foster parents. Patty actually loved her life with this family, and her mother's inability to complete her rehabilitation program meant that the temporary placement became long-term. At two-and-a-half years, the court changed the goal from reunification with Patty's mother to long-term foster care. By sixth grade Patty was blossoming in school and happy with her foster family. But a change in the goal meant a change in the supervising agency, meaning that Patty would need to move to a different family within the jurisdiction of the new agency. A few months later, a new home was found for her sister, which actually proved beneficial to Patty by calming the environment and allowing her to become both closer to her foster mom and more independent. Seven months later, Patty moved to a new family, which seemed promising initially. However, the move proved to be even more traumatic than the initial removal from her mother. The first night in the new home, she cried all night long. "The very first night is the worst night you spend in a new home, because all you want is to be in your previous home" (p. 54).

Several weeks later, Patty still wasn't happy. She talked a lot about wanting to visit her previous foster family, which her new foster parents resisted. But there were good experiences too, and her new family did a lot to encourage and support her musical talent. Now into her adolescence, conflict in the new home became more frequent. Ultimately, her foster parents decided she would have to be moved. She ended up being sent to another foster home which included several other foster children, many with special needs. Six months later, she was moved again. She became so distressed that she cut herself and ran away from home, ending up in the emergency room of a local hospital.

Patty's internal resourcefulness began to show itself. In spite of continual upheaval in her life, the comings and goings of adults who were sometimes helpful—and sometimes not, and all the challenges of adolescence, Patty continued to develop ways to cope as she changed schools, and lived for a time in a more structured group home, which proved to be beneficial. She then made a "decision to change," and began to improve academically and develop a happy social life (p. 62). Ironically, her behavioral and social improvements prompted an agency decision to move her out of the group home and seek to reunite her with one of her previous foster families. But she was now well established in a private Catholic school and didn't want to change. All of the available families lived a great distance away. By her senior year, she won the right to move back with her mother, working a part time job in order to pay rent for her room. Although her senior year was extremely busy and stressful, she won admission and scholarship support to a college in her hometown of Boston, moving to campus at the beginning of her freshman year.

Patty's story illustrates how difficult the journey through foster can be even when many conditions are favorable. Patty was herself a strong and resourceful individual; able to adapt to many situations and thrive when the circumstances were right. She was under the care of case workers and agencies who really were dedicated to trying to help her, and ad experiences with foster families which were often very positive. Yet in spite of all this, she was buffeted by the trauma of frequent dislocations in her life and the ultimate powerlessness of having so many aspects of her life determined by external forces. And though her life was difficult, she was not physically abused, subject to extreme poverty or prejudice, and had an intellectual capacity that made her capable of achieving a good education.

Patty's eventual success was undoubtedly influenced by her capacity to form stable relationships with several adults through her early life, including her first set of foster parents and a compassionate case worker who tracked her from the age of twelve. What Patty did not have was a sustained relationship with a therapist who might have served as an additional buffer against the continual challenges of late childhood and adolescence.

With regard to mental health services for foster youth, a number of problems emerge. Although the majority of adults involved in care of foster youth may recognize the need for therapeutic support, and though there are a myriad of service agencies that may be available for therapeutic intervention, the focus of treatment is quite limited. Children (including foster children) are generally only referred for therapy if there is an observable behavioral "problem" such as oppositional behavior, school difficulties or threats to run away or commit suicide. Given limited funding resources and the prevalence of reliance on short-term "evidence-based" therapies, intervention usually addresses only the specific behavioral concern with the goal of resolving the problem as soon as possible. Even so-called "trauma informed" treatments seem more inclined to fit a person to a protocol rather than provide the space and flexibility which treatment of trauma often requires. Frequently the therapists who are assigned to these children are at the early stage of their own training, and may often lack the experience to deal with complex issues and resistant clients. Though usually well intentioned and caring, their training or agency positions are often of short duration. So it is quite possible for a single child to see a dozen or more therapists in the course of his or her foster placement.

RELATIONSHIP DISRUPTIONS

From all that has been discussed to this point, one clear conclusion is that children who enter foster care are forced to experience chronic, traumatic disruption in relationships. These ruptures often occur quite early in the child's development, usually at the hands of caregivers who themselves may have been compromised and traumatized. These children are often victims of what has come to be called the intergenerational transmission of trauma.

A number of years ago, in a seminal paper entitled, "Ghosts in the

Nursery," Selma Fraiberg and her colleagues described their experience of mothers who were often prevented from providing anything near an adequate response to the emotional needs of their children (Fraiberg et al., 1975). Even if mothers were capable of providing a minimum of physical support, they often resembled the "wire monkey mothers" made famous in the experiments of Harry Harlow, which demonstrated that infant mothers who had to rely on nourishment from a bottle attached to a wire mother surrogate ultimately failed to thrive due to the lack of contact comfort with a warm and responsive human caregiver (Ottaviani & Meconia, 2007). Fraiberg and her associates found that providing psychoeducational and therapeutic support to the mothers of these children often provided a way to break the chain of the intergenerational transmission. These findings have been demonstrated again and again in experimental observations and clinical practice. The contemporary work of researchers such as Beatrice Beebe and others have robustly demonstrated how early attunement between infant and primary caregiver is essential in the formation of healthy attachments (Beebe & Lachman, 2013).

Attachment research and the theoretical and clinical considerations that flow from it demonstrate the variations of relationship patterns that can occur in the absence of secure attachment. By the time they are removed from their homes, many—if not most—of foster care manifest some form of insecure attachment style. Children may become avoidant—keeping a wary distance from others who might attempt to offer help or concern. Children who are anxiously preoccupied may seem to readily and indiscriminately attach to strangers and others who enter their lives, but without a sustained capacity to build trust. These children may also demonstrate an excessive need to be surrounded by certain peers or, as they age, become un- healthily attached to romantic partners, who often perpetuate the cycle of abuse. Or, children may manifest an ambivalent style of relating, desperately seeking help at one point, and then angrily rejecting support the next. These insecure styles can result in a considerable degree of disorganization in the capacity to remain attached to others, as well as produce continual emotional dysregulation. As difficult as these conditions are for ongoing development, "we must also remember that an 'insecure attachment' in and of itself, does not constitute a mental illness or psychiatric disorder. It simply describes a characteristic way of relating to others, particularly caregivers" (Heinemann, 2015). Yet, it is also clear that those children who are removed from their homes and taken into care—and who are already compromised in their attachment/rela-tionship style—will have the most difficulty adapting to even the most optimal foster parent, the most empathetic case worker, or the most dedicated therapist. The continual re-traumatizing disruption that typically charac-terizes the journey through the foster care system, serves to do little to heal and everything to reinforcing the child's lack of basic trust and the conviction that adults cannot be relied upon. Such children often become adept at survival, often becoming street smart, but have very poor capacity to engage in mutually supportive human relationships.

At some point in their development they seem to "hit a wall" in their maturation, making it very hard to survive as adults in a complex world.

THE EVOLUTION OF A MODEL

As was indicated in the earlier description of the founding of A Home Within, the parents of the organization were perhaps as idealistic as they were dedicated. One of the earliest taglines to describe the organization's intent was "One child, one therapist, for as long as it takes." The goal was to provide a person in foster care with a relationship with a skilled therapist who would not be constrained by an artificial limit on the length of the therapy or dependent on external funding. Among the most challenging obstacles to this good-intentioned approach was the fact of the geographic instability of the foster child. Since the plan was for the therapist to see the child in his or her private office, the therapy depended on the willingness and ability of others in the child's life to get that individual to the appointment on a regular basis. As the children grew older, they often developed a greater capacity to use public trans-portation and other means to reach the therapist. But as the youth's capacity for independent action increased, other obstacles became apparent. Younger children—whether in foster care or not—are often brought to therapy without much willingness to be there. Parents or caregivers have a good deal of authority over even their more dysregulated, oppositional children. When it goes well, the child may develop a positive relationship with the therapist or the therapy, and the level of resistance decreases. Most foster children, especially those who have been in the system for any length of time, are constantly being told to do things without any freedom of their own. These include fundamental decisions about where they will live and where they will go to school. Therefore, once they get to a point where they have any freedom at all, they are likely to utilize their power of choice in any way they can. This freedom includes the "choice" of whether or not they entrust themselves to a therapist. These choices are not always conscious, but are imbedded in all the dynamics imposed by their early relationship and attachment patterns as well as the fall-out of additional traumatic abuse.

When many therapists hear of the mission of *A Home Within*, they may think, "What a wonderful opportunity and privilege for these youth to have a therapist willing to meet with them each week for an undetermined length of time!" Perhaps comments like these reflect the benign narcissism many of us hold as therapists, who struggle against the injury caused by those who tend to dismiss our work as trivial. Nevertheless, the last kind of relationship the typical foster youth wants to form is with a therapist! And so, as *A Home Within* has expanded and matured, we have also needed to confront the complexities of both the internal landscapes and the systemic context of the individuals we seek to serve.

Those who founded and have sustained *A Home Within* were trained and have practiced as psychoanalytically oriented psychotherapists or as analysts. Clearly, those who became clients of these therapists were not going to be recruited into a traditional psychoanalytic modality. Yet just as psychoanalytic work with children has had to evolve through its history to meet the particular needs and constraints of those who would not be expected to enter into a full-blown adult "analysis," therapists engaged with *A Home Within* would need to adapt elements of theory and practice in a way which would cull the most critical aspects of psychoanalytic thinking and apply them to the situation at hand. Toward this end, Toni Heineman, along with her colleagues, has articulated eight key elements of what has been termed Relationship Based Therapy (RBT). (Heineman et al, 2013; Heineman, 2015). There is a paradox in this schematic theoretical outline which is "at the same time straightforward, drawing heavily on common sense, and also incredibly complex and nuanced." The eight essential of RBT are (1) Engagement: being fully present in the relationship; (2) Environment: appreciating the context surrounding the relationship; (3) Empathy: imagining the feelings of the other; (4) Egocentrism: recognizing the unique make-up of every individual; (5) Enthusiasm: bringing optimism to difficult realities; (6) Evidence: relying on demonstrably effective approaches; (7) Endurance: remaining open and available: and (8) Extending: appreciating the continuity of relationships (Heineman, 2013). I would also define "extending" to describe the inevitable pull of the therapist to be engaged in aspects of the client's life that exist beyond the 50-minute hour.

Even though volunteer clinicians with *A Home Within* are asked only to commit themselves to an hour with the client each week in addition to a commitment to a consultation group, the work often takes on an element of "case management" involving contact with other significant players in the client's life, such as Social Workers, Foster Parents, Attorneys. CASA (Court Appointed Special Advocates) volunteers, etc. Time in the therapy might often be spent assisting the older youth with transportation needs, discussing obstacles to maintaining a commitment to therapy, and other matters which are not prima face therapeutic. Yet the "case management" activities, though sometimes time consuming and frustrating, are not at the core of the work. The intention is not to "manage" a case but to build a relationship.

While the eight principles of RBT may not seem like the parameters of classical psychoanalysis, they do have a strong affinity to the Relational Movement within contemporary psychoanalysis, particularly work with children (Altman et al., 2010). Moreover, the Relational emphasis on attention to the mutual influence of the therapeutic process and the relevance of the therapist's subjective experience of the therapy, as well as the need to adjust the "frame" to fit the reality, all help in the understanding of what transpires in the clinical encounter (Bass, 2007).

Successful work with foster youth often demands a considerable degree of personal investment from the therapist, far beyond the cool, clinical detachment typified in the analytic caricature. At the same time, there is the need for continual analytic scrutiny of the therapeutic process. Aided with an appreciation for the complex conscious and unconscious dynamics of the individual as well as the dyad, analytically oriented therapists may have an advantage in maintaining a degree of equilibrium in the face of the difficult terrain.

It is not only the model of *A Home Within* that continues to evolve, but the very model of psychoanalytic practice itself. As had been argued by Relational Analysts such as Neil Altman and Lew Aron, psychoanalysis has been evolving in a way which not only recaptures much of Freud's earliest innovation and aspiration—along with the early experimentation and adaptation characteristic of the first generation of psychoanalysts—but also is responsive to the needs of a more diverse and often more traumatized population (Altman, 2009; Aron & Starr, 2013). Throughout the years, many AHW therapists have maintained continuous relationships with their clients, many of whom might "disappear" for a while, only to re-establish contact with their therapist when the need and the opportunity arise. At the same time, AHW therapists—largely through the help of their Consultation Groups—have learned to be more flexible, creative, and capable of recognizing when a treatment might be "good enough."

MOLLY

To illustrate the wide array of challenges and possibilities inherent in work with foster youth, we might consider the treatment of "Molly," in an extended case discussion included in a sampling of clinical experiences from several current A Home Within volunteer clinicians (Heineman, et al., 2013).

The first time eight-year-old Molly walked into my office, I was nervous. Although she was in third grade, Molly's diminutive size made her look more like a kindergartener. And small though she was, this little girl had such a history! Feeding disorder, sleep difficulty, extreme acting out behavior both at home and at school...I was not sure I was up for the task of addressing all these. There were also questions about underlying neurological issues. I was new to private practice. Based on the information I had received about this child, I felt her therapy would need to occur over a long period of time, a frame more likely to be measured in years rather than months. Molly lived some distance from my office and I was worried about the toll the weekly drive would take on the family (p. 5).

Molly had been adopted into a family of two gay fathers and two additional adopted children. The couple took her in at age four as part of a "foster-to-adopt" program. Molly entered foster care about two years previously when she was found "wandering the streets with an older sibling and an inebriated father" (p.9). From the start, she needed to compete with two younger foster siblings and tended to be impulsive and difficult to control. The therapist noted that "Dave," who played the role of the primary parent, seemed particularly anxious about maintaining order in the home and was also ambivalent about therapy. Nevertheless, the work proceeded as Molly demonstrated her need to maintain "control" of the therapeutic situation and would often come, open a book and begin reading to herself, with little regard for the therapist. For her part, she seemed willing to be there, and as time went on, she became more curious about the various play objects in the office. In this way she seemed to "settle in" for several months. Toward the end of the first year, some "breakthroughs" began to occur. Molly's behavior at home often continued to be out of control. Pushed by Molly's adoptive father to engage her in a discussion about her behavior, a subject which Molly skillfully avoided, the therapist decided to take a risk. After asking about her behavior...

Molly finally commented that it really didn't matter what she did. I considered this for a moment and I then exclaimed, 'Are you doing all this misbehaving so that your parents will hurry up and throw you out of this family in the same way that it feels your first family did?' Her eyes widened and she met my gaze—a phenomenon which, I was sure, I was not imagining, was happening more and more often. She looked astonished as she responded with, 'How'd you know?' I was finally feeling comfortable in our interactions. I held her gaze and solemnly responded, 'It makes perfect sense.' Again, the knowing look (pp 15-16).

Although there was a sense of progress in the therapy, school and home behavior remained disruptive. Dave had reached the point where he felt the therapy was making little difference and that it was time to bring it to an end. Perhaps out of a feeling of desperation, the therapist decided to read Molly the "riot act."

'You know I try to talk in here sometimes about your misbehaving, and you usually don't really want to talk about it. But today we have to talk about it. Your Dad is pretty upset that he is driving so far to bring you here, with the idea that you will start behaving better because of all this work. He is doing is part...(and) I am doing my part by making this time available for us to spend together so we can meet each week. We need you to do your part by cleaning up your act a bit—do you know what that means? It means you have to start working on behaving better so that you can still keep coming here, if that's what you want to do.' Molly nodded and said, 'I do still want to come here.' I asked, 'so does that mean we can count on seeing some improvement?' She did not answer and though she was somewhat more subdued for the rest of the hour, she played as usual and we did not talk about further difficulties in her behavior (p. 16).

The therapist worried about the wisdom of her intervention. She noted that she had largely been following a less directive, psychodynamic approach previously, but then decided to try something which seemed like a more traditional "social work move." Even her consultation group was unsure about what she had done, though they did help her to acknowledge that she had brought an authentic part of herself into the room in choosing to move from a stance of therapeutic holding to one of more direct confrontation.

The next week, Molly came skipping into her therapist's office, proudly presenting a behavioral chart from school, which noted a week of exceptional behavior. Her behavior at home also improved, though the therapist felt frustrated in her dad's reluctance to implement changes which she had suggested. After a summer when sessions became less frequent, Dave made the decision to transfer to a family therapist located closer to the family home. While family therapy had been a suggestion from the therapist, she was not prepared for the decision to stop the treatment with Molly. It was a sad, but also hopeful ending, since Molly seemed happy with the thought of working with someone who could also help her dads. Reflecting on the course of the therapy, the therapist is aware of much that has been accomplished as well as what more could be done. Still, though this is a true ending, she wonders if it might be "at least for now" (p. 18).

This case serves as a good illustration of what is often encountered in most cases with foster children. In fact, all who work with children therapeutically will recognize the challenges, frustrations and occasional risk-taking typical of working with children and their families in less than perfect circumstances. But the complexity is increased in the case of Molly. Though her attachment style was not discussed, she seems somewhat ambivalent. While it is clear that Molly adopts a strong connection to the weekly therapy sessions, it is not clear how attached she is to her therapist. The relative ease with which she seemed to entertain the transfer to another therapist suggests her capacity to distance herself from her emotions when necessary, perhaps in favor of responding to the needs of the adults in her life. Nevertheless, the therapist's risk in her confrontation of Molly seemed to turn a corner and allowed the therapy to have more of an impact. It was a good beginning. But like so many experiences with foster youth, it feels very incomplete.

WEAVING WITHOUT A LOOM

Perhaps the biggest challenge to those in foster care—and to clinicians seeking to treat individuals with these kind of experiences—is the extreme level of chaos in the child's internal world that does not yield to a quick or easy repair. As noted by Heineman:

We know from theory, research, and common sense that stability and consistency in relationships promote children's healthy development. Unfortunately, the foster care system often fails to provide reliable, sustaining relationships. The propensity of the system to look to the external world for explanations and solutions to problems too often overlooks the child's internal distress. When we suggest to unhappy or anxious children that their feelings can be relieved by a change in the environment, we insidiously undermine and disavow the fundamental importance of the child's internal world as a source of pleasure, pain, upheaval and regulation (Heineman, 2015, p.81).

Noting how we "watch children grow from tiny, helpless beings into young adults who carry within them a sense of self that is cohesive and reflects the multifaceted nature of personality," Heineman points to the impact of traumatic relational disruption on identity formation in those who "greet us without a coherent history and no cohesive story to explain who she is and how she came to be that person" (p.81). Ironically, children in foster care often accumulate a much more detailed log of the external circumstances of their lives than those who come of age in non-disrupted homes. Even when details of early abuse remains sketchy, their movement through the foster care system brings with it an ever-thinking dossier of case management notes, medical records and psychological reports. Yet this external "traumatic biography" belies the truth of the child's inner world, which remains disjointed, dissociated and often distant from any coherent narrative. Utilizing the metaphor of a weaver's loom, Heineman asks:

How does a child weave a history for herself out of random events and unrelated people? How does she do this without a loom—without the solid structure of home and community? How does she do this without the warp of parents, relatives and teachers in the background to hold the rules, history and values of family and community with just the right amount of tension? How does the child understand the self that is reflected in the eyes and words and touch of another if the reflecting other changes repeatedly? What does the child do with the threads of her life when there is no home—no loom to hold the warp? (pp. 82-83).

We are all "creatures of habit." Children, in particular, thrive on routines of regularity and predictability, as much as older children may complain of boredom, or seek to distance themselves from family routines in favor of an immersion into a world of peers. It is long standing clinical wisdom that understands that even when teenagers seem to abandon their primary dependency on their families or are "launched" as proto-adults by going away to college to obtaining a full-time job, they are much more successful at achieving true psychic independence if their "home base" of family remains relatively secure and unscathed. One needs such a "secure base" in order to achieve genuine differentiation. But children who are thrust into the world without a sense of a familial "place" or true sense of really belonging to someone else can continue in a state of internal isolation and turmoil.

All of this is not to say that dramatic intervention isn't necessary in the case of childhood abuse or severe neglect. Children who remain powerless at the hands of abusive adults do not fare well either. Yet this helps to explain the powerful pull of" invisible loyalties" which tie children to their biological parents, often causing them to continually seek to return to their families even in spite of repeated patterns of abuse (Boszormenyi-Nagy, I. & Spark, G.,1984).

In spite of placements with alternative families where they may have experienced genuine kindness and substantially improved material opportunity, they still feel they only "belong" to the families of their birth. This is a tremendous challenge to children even after they have been adopted out of foster care, as evidenced in the case of Molly discussed above.

At the very least, those concerned with the welfare of children in the foster care system must keep in mind that, in spite of the best efforts and presence of unavoidable circumstances, almost everything that happens to a child once he or she is removed from their biological parents constitutes a loss and a retraumatization. "I want to emphasize that every 'placement' involves a 'replacement' and every 'move' requires a 'removal.' Every time a child says 'Hello' to one family, he says 'Goodbye' to another. The warp is severed and the pattern of his life is left dangling again until he can reattach it" (p. 84).

Of course, continual disruptions in therapeutic relationships mimic this pattern of instability and loss. Foster children usually go through a succession of therapists, some who may be more competent and caring than others. But no matter how caring, foster children come to expect that any relationship with an apparently reliable adult "is only for now." This phenomenon also poses one of the greatest challenges to those therapists who, thorough *A Home Within*, offer to make themselves available to the child without a limitation of time. The fact that these therapists operate apparently outside of the "system" also presents a somewhat confounding factor for the foster child. In many cases, the AHW therapist may be the first person in the child's experience since entering foster care who has not been paid to taken interest in them.

From an adult perspective, such availability would seem to offer a strong antidote to the pattern of comings and goings in the child's life. The offer of a therapist who is somewhat unconditionally dedicated to the child may seem like a great thing. Yet it is not surprising that even older children would have trouble overcoming their guardedness and self-protective relational distancing which reflects the chaos of their internal world. As Piaget noted many years ago, "we are far more inclined to assimilate new information into previously developed schemata than to develop new theories or solutions to accommodate data that cannot be assimilated" (Heineman, p.84). To put it more simply, it makes little sense for a traumatized child to believe that future outcomes will be any different from what has happened in the past, in spite of promises, good intentions and new experiences.

While the challenges are formidable for building sustained relationships with foster youth, the potential benefits are well worth the effort. But it takes time and continuity to be able to explore old relational patterns and establish new ones. This is a key element of therapeutic interventions such as psychoanalysis, which recognize the necessity of longer-term commitments between a therapist and a client. Yet even when circumstances dictate shorter- term treatments, a therapist's understanding of the complicated interior landscape of the foster child, along with an ability to explore that landscape though a combination of verbal and non- verbal, symbolic expression, can lead to better outcomes and help establish the possibility of future growth.

A LOCAL CHAPTER'S STORY

A Home Within has existed and has been growing in the San Francisco Bay area and around the country for almost twenty years. Approximately six years ago, a local chapter was formed in Philadelphia. Two of the biggest structural challenges involved the recruitment of volunteer therapists along with the establishment of ongoing consultation groups, as well as the identification and connection to potential referral sources among the myriad of agencies and governmental agencies involved with the foster care system.

The most immediate challenge was to make contact with potentially interested therapists. This was accomplished through several personal conversations, presentations, and utilization of the list-serve capacities for groups such as the Philadelphia Society for Psychoanalytic Psychology (PSPP), (a local chapter of the American Psychological Association's Division 39 (Psychoanalysis) and the Philadelphia Society for Clinical Social Workers (PSCSW). Criteria for inclusion in this project required the therapists to have a certain level of experience with children and youth involved in the Child Welfare system, as well as the capacity to see clients at their private practice location and under the provision of their clinical license and liability insurance. In addition to a commitment to take on a potentially complicated client, therapists are also asked to commit to an ongoing consultation group, which meets regularly throughout the year. Eventually, a number of clinicians expressed interest throughout the Philadelphia region. Currently, over a dozen therapists—primarily Clinical Social Workers and Psychologists—constitute two ongoing consultation groups.

The second challenge was to establish relationships with referral sources. Because of the large number of agencies involved in the management and care of those in foster care, these contacts were made slowly through recommendations generated by the volunteer AHW clinicians. Among the difficulties encountered at the earliest stages was the fact that specific agencies operate under contracts with city or state entities, and so are reluctant to "refer out" to external clinicians. The other problem encountered was that often when a referral was made, a clinician would not be available within geographic proximity of the individual.

Nevertheless, referrals came from other sources. Our first Philadelphia clients came through the private practice of one of our first volunteers. These were two siblings who were adopted and had been in foster care, but did not have insurance to cover outpatient psychotherapy. Another AHW clinician received a referral through her Mosque, while another client came from a group with specializes in programs for grieving children.

As time went on, it became apparent that there was a significant need to address the needs of youth who were close to "aging out" of the foster care system (presently at age twenty-one). At one point, a liaison was established with a Charter High School in the City of Philadelphia, which was established solely for teenagers in foster care. Unfortunately, that Charter School closed, but some contact was sustained with youth who went on to attend the Community College of Philadelphia. Additional referrals were made through a department within the Division of Human Services for the City of Philadelphia, which specializes in assisting foster youth in their attainment of "independence" as defined by their ability to attain housing, education and work opportunities.

This cohort of "aging-out youth" or "emerging adults" has proved to be the most difficult to serve. Typically, a young person would be identified by a caseworker or mentor, as someone who was both in need of and motivated to participate in individual therapy. It is here where the lessons learned about the complications of work with foster youths had to be re-learned on a local level. From the viewpoint of the adult who made the referral, the value of having an AHW therapist for these individuals was obvious. There were largely urban youth who had been in the foster system for years, frequently from families with few resources and with a history typical of most youth in the foster system.

Moreover, these were usually youths who had already seemed to gain an external degree of success. In one situation, a very personable young man had been able to have a job after high school as part of his school's alumni organization. He was attending college and was very eager to meet with a therapist. Although his initial meetings with his therapist seemed to go well and suggested he had formed a preliminary "connection" with his therapist, his life soon became more chaotic as he was forced to move several times. This young man was articulate about his past history as well as his aspirations for his future, but soon he stopped coming to therapy, in spite of a continual effort to reach out to him and accommodate his schedule. Although he initially seemed to "have his act together" and was seemingly somewhat more mature than his peers, both the external chaos of his life in the city as well as the internal chaos of his disrupted development overcame him.

Many of these young people seem to recognize their need for therapy and initially agree to participate. In some cases, they are suspicious of the motivation of the therapist, and may need to overcome a good deal of history, including encounters with a previous therapist, which did not go so well. The idea that a therapist would be interested in them and not simply their behavior seemed foreign. One young man wondered, in his initial meeting with his therapist, "who is paying for this?" Others come because of a crisis and then leave once the crisis has passed or express their reluctance to talk about painful experiences in their past—a phenomenon similar to the way many people in the general population approach (and/or avoid) therapy. Ultimately, the notion that one might be "fortunate" to have a therapist of one's own is a hard sell.

In the face of the daunting challenge of engaging foster youths in some kind of therapeutic support, the Philadelphian Chapter of A Home Within is embarking on a new collaboration with a unique local project that is also designed to assist in the transition to adulthood and independence. The Monkey and the Elephant is a recently established Coffee shop that exclusively employs young adults who are transitioning out of foster care. The founder and owner of this enterprise is keenly aware of the needs of foster youths, and has created an environment which both challenges and supports her employees. In additional to making individual therapists available for these transitioning youth, AHW is exploring ways to provide further opportunities to learn more about the specific need of these individuals as well as provide psychoeducation in small informal groups. There has been a growing movement within the foster care community to allow these children and youth to tell their own story (Krebs & Pitcoff, 2006). The hope is to be able to discover new ways to provide the resource of our volunteer clinicians to a particular cohort of foster youth.

Meanwhile, there are a number of other on-going cases within the Philadelphia Chapter that continue to provide support to children in desperate circumstances. The following are representative of those cases:

"Jamil," a twelve-year-old boy who comes to his therapist's office by bus, spent most of his first year taking naps on his therapist's couch, but now has begun to talk about the death of both of his parents, a favorite aunt, and his worries about the aunt who currently takes care of him in kinship-foster care.

"Dora," an eight-year-old girl who was adopted at age three, only to experience her adopted mom declining more and more into the grip of a severe bipolar disorder and occasional separation from her husband. In her play, Dora has been able to gradually relinquish some control to her therapist as she becomes more comfortable allowing a
new person to care about her.

"Rebecca," Dora's sixteen-year old biological sister, is often silent with her therapist, particularly if there is any attempt to engage her in conversation about the problems she is experiencing at home. She has been able to begin to talk with her therapist a bit about fashion, music and other aspects of being a teenager, as the door continues to open.

"Ramon" is an eleven-year-old boy who just recently was adopted out of foster care by a young, eager but inexperienced couple. He had managed to "sabotage" previous adoption attempts through extreme oppositional behavior, but managed not to do so in this latest adoption attempt. He likes to draw pictures for his therapist and has begun to excitedly engage in sand play. He recently drew a picture of his memories of the murder of his biological mother, which he witnessed, having refused to talk about the subject previously.

"Katrina" is a ten-year old girl who has already been through five foster placements and a variety of caseworkers. Her current caseworker learned about A Home Within and drives Katrina for several miles to her session, in the hope of sustaining a long term, more permanent therapeutic relationship for her. Initially resistant, she reports she's starting to like her therapist.

Conclusion: Holding Hope

Toni Heineman has described one dimension of the over-all purpose of A Home Within as being a network of individuals who "hold the hope" for children in foster care (Heineman, et al, 2013). Those who enter into this effort understand the deep challenges to work with foster youth, as well as concede that the efforts of a couple of hundred therapists throughout the United States offer only drops in the ocean in face of the needs of thousands of children.

There is really no available research that demonstrates longitudinal outcomes for children who are engaged in therapy. Even when children are discharged from relatively long- term therapy with evidence of positive behavioral change, we really can't know the true difference, which the intervention will make in the course of the child's future life. Occasionally, we do get a call from a family or a child we have treated and hear about successes. Often, we become aware of failures as well. But by in large, we exist in a state of not really knowing the ultimate effects of our commitment and our hard work. Nonetheless, we are guided by a set of beliefs in the value of positive relationships in the formative years of each individual.

Foster children are usually among the most deprived with regard to positive, formative relationships. Frequently, they are unable to receive even the most sincere offers of help because of their own attachment and trauma history. Yet we continue to hold a "relational" hope in work with these children and young adults, realizing that beyond behavior change and adaptation to difficult circumstances, the foundation of psychological health is the capacity to establish and appreciate good relationships. Toni Heineman has also described this project as a long conversation between the aspirations of those engaged in A Home Within and the reality of the world of foster care. Even when engagement with foster youth is brief or ends without optimal outcomes, the work is set against the horizon of the importance of insistence on the right and importance of those in foster care to be held in mind by those who understand their pain and who seek to understand them.

REFERENCES

Altman, N (2009). The analyst in the inner city, Second edition: Race, class, and culture through a psychoanalytic lens. Hillsdale, NJ: The Analytic Press.

Altman, N., Briggs, R., Frankel, J., Gensler, D. & Pantone, P. (2010). Relational child psychotherapy. New York: Other Press.

Aron, L. & Starr, K. (2013). A psychotherapy for the people: Toward a progressive psychoanalysis. Hillsdale, NJ: The Analytic Press.

Bass, A. (2007). When the Frame Doesn't Fit the Picture. Psychoanalytic Dialogues, 17:1-27.

Beebe, B. & Lachmann, F. (2013). The origins of attachment: Infant research and adult treatment. Hillsdale, NJ: The Analytic Press.

Boszormenyi-Nagy, I. & Spark, G. (1984). Invisible loyalties: Reciprocity in intergenerational Family Therapy. New York: Brunner/Mazel.

Danto, E. (2005). Freud's free clinics: Psychoanalysis and social justice, 1918-1938. New York: Columbia University Press.

Fraiberg S, Adelson E, Shapiro V. (1975). Ghosts in the nursery. A psychoanalytic approach to the problems of impaired infant-mother relationships. J Am Acad Child Psychiatry.Summer;14(3):387-421.

Heineman, T, Clausen, J. & Ruff, S. (Eds.), (2013). Treating trauma:

Relationship-based psychotherapy with children, adolescents and young adults. Lanham, MD: Jason Aronson.

Heineman, T. (2015). Relational treatment of trauma: Stories of loss and hope. Hillsdale, NJ: The Analytic Press.

Krebs, B. & Pitcoff, P, (2006). Beyond the foster care system: The future for teens. New Brunswick, NJ: Rutgers University Press.

Ottaviani J. & Meconis, D. (2007). Wire mothers: Harry Harlow and the science of love. Ann Arbor, MI: G.T. Labs.

Shirk, W. & Stangler, (2006). On their own: What happens to kids when they age out of the foster care system. Cambridge, MA: Basic Books.

Smith, W. (2011). Youth leaving foster care: A developmental, relationship-based approach to practice. New York: Oxford University Press.

Toth, J. (1998) Orphans of the living: Stories of America's children in foster care. New York: Touchtone Press.

Bio

JOSEPH SCHALLER, Psy.D., is a Clinical Psychologist in private practice in Philadelphia and Wayne, PA, working with adults, children, and families. In addition to his general training as a psychologist, he has also trained and specialized as a family therapist and play therapist working with children as young as three. He is also on the adjunct faculty of the Institute for Graduate Clinical Psychology at Widener University, where he received his Psy.D, degree. Dr. Schaller is a graduate of the Institute for Relational Psychoanalysis, in Philadelphia. He is the Past President of the Philadelphia Society of Psychoanalytic Psychologists. In additional, Dr. Schaller is the Founder and current Clinical Co-Director of the Philadelphia chapter for *A Home Within*, the national organization which seeks to make volunteer therapists available for individuals who are now, or have been in foster care.

CHAPTER 9

Behavior Disorders Stemming from Disturbed Mother-Baby Experience And Their Repair through Joint Work with the Mother and Her Young Child

Martin Silverman, M.D.

Behavior Disorders Stemming from Disturbed Mother-Baby Experience and their Repair through Joint Work with the Mother and Her Young Child

Martin Silverman

Andy's first grade teachers were worried. He hardly participated in classroom activities and he barely interacted with the teachers or with other students. He preferred to look out the window and daydream. He came for evaluation quite readily, although he insisted that nothing was wrong with him. I shared his teachers' distress about his sitting and daydreaming instead of joining in with his classmates in the wonderful activities the teachers provided for them. He replied that he didn't want to cause trouble. It was just that he liked to sit and think about things. I told Andy that I was interested in hearing what he thought about while he was sitting in school and looking out the window. "I think about my mother," he said. "What's wrong with that?" "What about your mother?" I asked. "Oh," he said, "I wonder what she's doing at work. And I think about what we're going do together after school—whether we'll go to the park or play a game, what kind of snack she'll have for me—things like that."

Although he thought I could make better use of my time if I were to help children who *really* needed my assistance, he agreed to come regularly to talk and play with me. We had very pleasant times together, and I found it somewhat puzzling that (on the surface) there didn't seem to be anything wrong with the very bright, charming youngster whose company I enjoyed on a couple of occasions each week. On the other hand, his teachers' consternation over Andy's disinclination to involve himself with them and the curriculum they provided for him deserved respect. His willingness to come for treatment sessions, furthermore, suggested that, despite his seeming equanimity, there might actually be something troubling him.

Since his parents were mathematicians and scientists, it was not surprising that Andy's play tended to drift in the direction of what struck me as scientific experiments. One day, we were at the kitchen sink that was available to us where, at that time, I had my office. Andy and I were engaged together in trying to find out which of the paper boats we designed were likely to stay afloat longer than others before they became water logged and sank. We chatted as we worked. He said something to me, about an activity in which his family had engaged, that puzzled me. "That's odd," I said. "Your parents told me something different from what you just said." He replied to me in a casual, matter-of-fact tone of voice: "Those aren't my parents. My parents died. Those people who say they're my parents came from Mars and took their place. Now let's try making this type of boat a little wider. It might float better that way."

Andy agreed to my seeking further clarification from his parents. When Andy's mother and I met together a week or so later, I gingerly brought up what Andy had said to me. She had always been very calm and composed when she spoke with me, but this time she dissolved in tears. After sobbing for a while, she pulled herself together and said: "There's something I didn't tell you. I see that I should have. When Andy was born, I developed a hot, red swelling in one breast. It turned out to be tuberculosis. For the first six months after his birth, we could only relate to each other through a glass *window*. I couldn't hold him. I couldn't touch him. I couldn't kiss him. I couldn't smell him. *We never bonded!*" I worked with Andy and his mother, separately and together, to address the impact of the early interference with togetherness and attunement which they had experienced. It had prevented the development of the kind of bonding and secure attachment for which they both yearned but which had been denied to them. I helped them bond with one another, albeit years after it *should have* happened. He became a healthy, happy, academically successful youngster who no longer needed to stare out through a window searching for his mother!

This is an unusually extreme example of disturbance in the development of solidly secure attachment between a mother and her baby. Six months is a very long time for a mother and her newborn baby to be separated from one another by a glass window! Can a much briefer, albeit dramatic, disruption of mother-baby togetherness lead to significant emotional difficulties?

Ten-year-old Bobby came to me so that I might help him overcome the terror he was experiencing at the prospect of going away to camp for the first time. His fear was extremely puzzling not only to Bobby but to his parents as well. Except for a tendency to be irritable with his parents, especially his mother, when they didn't seem to him to understand his needs and wants, he appeared to be a pretty well-balanced, well-functioning, reasonably independent young man.

Bobby and I searched together to uncover the roots of the anxiety he was feeling about leaving home to go away to camp. He very much wanted to go, but he was terrified even to think about it. The key to solving the mystery turned out to be a recurrent nightmare which Bobby had been having for some time. In the dream, his mother approached him, waving her arms menacingly, with a wild look on her face and a large number of thick wires sticking out of her head that made her look like the Medusa of Ancient Greek mythology. It took a good deal of work, but we finally figured it out. When Bobby summoned up the courage to look at the dream image of his mother more closely, it became apparent that at least some of the "wires" were tubes. With assistance from his mother, we learned that when Bobby was about eight months of age, he developed pneumonia, together with severe dehydration, and had to be hospitalized for a number of weeks. The hospital at that time allowed parental visitation only once a day and for a very limited period of time. Each time his mother visited him, she found that he was tied to his bed and totally immobilized to restrict his range of motion, in order to prevent the intravenous tube through which he was being hydrated and given antibiotics from being pulled out from a vein in his arm or head. Sometimes, there were multiple tubes sticking out of him and he was covered with black and blue marks from all the needles that had been stuck into him.

She was so horrified by the dazed, horrible look she saw on his face each time she visited him that, after a while, she refused to leave. She insisted on being allowed to stay with him, twenty-four hours a day, until he was able to return home. The hue and cry Bobby's parents put up, in fact, played a significant role in getting the hospital to change its policy about parental visitation with children who were hospitalized there. It took Bobby a very long time to get over the effect upon him of his hospitalization, his parents told me. He was irritable, jumpy, and easily angered for a very long time before he seemed to settle down again.

Bobby reacted to what we had learned from his recurrent nightmare by feeling as though he had been released from bondage. He became able to assert himself in a way that had not been possible before. He also became extremely impatient with, angry at, and hostile toward his mother. As we worked together to understand what was going on, Bobby increasingly zeroed in on the rage he harbored at his mother for allowing him to be subjected to all the painful and terrifying things he had experienced during his hospitalization, as a helpless infant who was unable to protect himself. With my encouragement, Bobby's mother expressed deep regret and sorrow to him for not having helped him more effectively and for its having taken as long as it did before she *insisted* on being allowed to stay with him all the time while he was in the hospital. In her own defense, she did point out that there was no way hospitalization could have been avoided and that battling with the hospital administration had been no easy task. She reminded Bobby that she did succeed in staying with him twenty-four hours a day for the remainder of his stay there.

Bobby's fury at his mother gradually subsided, and his relationship with her improved steadily. He was able to go to camp when school ended for the year—and he sent me a wonderful letter from camp! In it, he told me how much he was enjoying camp, and he thanked me warmly for helping him become able to leave home to attend it. His newly acquired strength and feistiness were epitomized in the way he ended the letter: "But don't you take too much of the credit! I did most of the work!"

This too is a rather dramatic example of the effects of an unfortunate experience of traumatic interference with optimal mother-child interaction early in life. Those of us who work with young children and their families more often encounter seemingly ordinary, relatively garden variety interferences with optimal interaction—but at times they can exert an equally or even more severely damaging impact on the child's emotional functioning and on the relationship between the child and its parents. I have worked with a good number of families who have had to contend with such experiences. A treatment modality which has emerged out of that experience involves working simultaneously with a young child and his or her mother (and often with the father as well). I should like to share my experience with three such families in some detail. In each case, the children's parents were so pleased with what treatment accomplished that they gladly agreed to my sharing my experience working with them and their children with other people who might benefit from hearing about it.

JOINT TREATMENT OF A MOTHER AND A CHILD WHO HAVE HAD A TROUBLED EARLY RELATIONSHIP

Charlie's parents looked drained and beleaguered. They were at the end of their rope. Could I *possibly* help them, they asked? Charlie was only four years old, but he already was more than his thoroughly exhausted mother could handle. There was no way she could cope with the constant, unrelenting demands he made upon her and with the explosive rages into which he flew when she couldn't satisfy his needs. It drained her energies, and she was worried. She couldn't devote herself exclusively to him. His twin sister and almost eleven month old baby brother *also* required her attention. It pained her sorely that she could not calm him down and that she found herself getting angry at him instead of helping him. He was beginning to get angry at himself as well. "You don't love me!" he would cry out—and he was beginning to hit not only her but *himself* as well! He was beating on himself with his fists! He had started to call himself "bad" and to say that he did not want to live. It broke her heart!

His twin sister Allison was as easy as Charlie was difficult. It had *always* been that way, in fact. Thank goodness *one* of them was easy! They were born after a prolonged, difficult labor that left their mother feeling wiped out, totally drained, and completely overwhelmed. A lengthy, stress-filled fertility struggle had preceded the pregnancy. During most of the third trimester Charlie's mother had been confined to bed because of premature dilatation of the cervix at twenty-one weeks of gestation. This was extremely difficult for such a very active person. She went into labor at thirty-two weeks, and the babies were born at weights so low that Charlie had to spend three weeks in the NICU and Allison had to spend an additional week there before they could go home. There also was a terrifying instance when they stopped breathing—apnea—because of which they were sent home wearing heart monitors. As his mother put it to me: "It was very frightening and *horrific*—a very difficult, rough start, after a difficult fertility issue and then a difficult pregnancy!"

The two babies were as different from one another as they could be. Unlike his sister, who was relatively quiet and undemanding, although she did have esophageal reflux, Charlie was a very needy baby who screamed and thrashed when he was hungry and was an extremely vigorous sucker during his feedings. He also was restless, fretful, and in need of much more attention than his beleaguered mother could provide for him. She was not the kind of person, furthermore, who does well with loud demandingness, his mother said to me—"so it was a tough fit." In fact, it was a nightmare—for both of them!

Charlie was very competitive with his sister: "*She has more!*" Paradoxically, at least on the surface, he also worried about and protected Allison. If Mommy told her that she couldn't have dessert because she hadn't finished her dinner, for example, Charlie would cry out plaintively: "Give her dessert! She ate enough! She'll be unhappy!" For a while, beginning after he started nursery school, at the age of three, and gave up napping every afternoon, Charlie also would have night terrors whenever he hadn't napped that day. He also went through considerable separation anxiety after the birth of his baby brother ten months before I met Charlie (and he had missed his mother terribly while he was at school while she was pregnant). His reaction to his brother's birth was first to irritably ignore him, then to dislike him, then to fake being nice to him, and finally to truly adore him and be wonderful with him. It did not surprise me to hear this, as Charlie was described to me as very affectionate and loving with his parents—and vice versa.

Charlie anxiously ignored me during his first session in the play-room, although he listened as I told him about his parents informing me about his unhappiness. I offered to help him and his family. He leaned against and into his mother's body while I spoke with Charlie and his Mommy. He clung to her, and he rejected her encouragement to him to play with the toys. When she persisted in urging him to do so, he effect-ed a clever compromise between his need to be in contact with his mother and her desire that he leave her side and "play in the playroom." He looking at the toys on the shelves and then opened the cabinet that was next to them to see what was in it. He took out a ball he found in it, and he played catch with his mommy for the remainder of the session.

After a while, he allowed me to be of help to them, by retrieving an errantly tossed ball now and then. He even was able to exchange a few words with me. I called his mother a bit later in the day. She expressed disappointment and anxiousness about Charlie's not having engaged with me in playing with the toys. How could I help him if he wouldn't play with me? She was relieved when I indicated that it was a sign of emotional strength that Charlie was cautious about interacting with a grownup whom he had met for only the very first time. She was even more relieved when I noted that, after I had been patient, he did let me "help" and he did speak with me. I also pointed out that he had not thrown the ball *at her* the way he threw things at her at home but tossed it back and forth *with her.* I reminded her that, at home, they had happy times as well as difficult ones. She seemed to get my point, namely, that Charlie seemed to understand and subscribe to therapy to assist him and his mother to be "in control and happy together rather than being out of control and unhappy together."

What occurred during our second session in the playroom was dra-matic indeed! Charlie's mother brought some of *his* toys, and she encouraged him to play with them. He did so, but only after returning to the game of tossing a ball back and forth with his mother which had filled most of his first session with me. I put into words how much Charlie seemed to like bashing his Ninja Turtles with a weapon and what a good job he did when he fought with the Transformer. He re-sponded by (hesitantly) shooting his mother with a plastic gun he'd seen lying on one of the shelves. I nodded to her, and she restrained herself from voicing an objection. Charlie reacted to her tacit acceptance of his expression of aggression toward her by picking up a toy "sword" and *erupting into a full scale attack upon her*! He cut off her head! He stabbed her all over her body, including "in the butt!" He gave her "poison jelly" to eat. His mother said that Charlie doesn't like it when she puts "gel" in his hair to control wisps sticking up in the air when he wakes up in the morning. I wondered out loud if he might be getting back at her for that. I also made it clear to Charlie that he could think, feel, say, and pretend anything in my playroom but that there *could be no hurting for real!*

Charlie had us make it "dark" in the room. He went out, and returned quickly, as a "doctor" who promptly chopped Mommy in half! "Charlie," I said, "If you cut Mommy in two, then *she'll* know what it's like to be a twin—and to have to share Mommy." Mommy nodded understandingly. He smiled, stuck the knife (gently) under her blouse, and then shot her with the gun (but this time with a smile on his face). I said: "Charlie seems to be saying that he likes and loves Mommy but gets sad and mad at her sometimes." He responded by going into a corner of the room and doing "magic." He put a little plastic plate behind his rear end and asked me to guess where it was. "In your butt?" I asked. "No," he replied. He indicated that it was a "mystery." A little later, I said to Mommy, "I'm realizing that a big mystery to a four-year- old is what kind of magic makes a baby." "And we have one at home!" she replied.

For some time thereafter, Charlie would start out each session by attacking his Mommy with swords, to "cut her butt off," to "cut her boob off," and to "cut her in half." He then would switch to playing catch with her with a ball, pleasurably but also very competitively, and under his control so that he always would win. He expanded the play to include a dodge-ball-like game in which he *asked* his mother to try to hit him. I wondered out loud whether he was afraid of getting punished for his behavior. At times, he set soldiers up in front of each of them, at first to shoot their weapons but then to be members of the soccer teams. I noted his changing things "from battle to play," and I said that he didn't seem to like fighting with Mommy, even though he felt like he *had to* do that to get what he needed. I wondered out loud from time to time whether fighting with Mommy might be the *only* way he knew of getting to her. We were to return to this repeatedly as time went on.

Charlie threw himself into the treatment process with vim and vigor. He played out his ambivalent feelings toward his mother and siblings; his need to figure out and control the baby- making process that took his mother away from him, on top of his having had to share her from birth with a twin sister; and, especially, the dilemma in which he found himself in which he *had to* fight to connect with and gain possession of his mother, in competition with three family member rivals, to obtain her love and attention, but was doing it so intensely that he was alienating her and pushing her away. In the playroom, we worked together at promoting mutual understanding between Charlie and his mother of these issues as well as at facilitating increasing self-control and expression of his feelings in words rather than in action. Over the telephone, during Charlie's bathroom breaks (which after a while he became able to take by himself rather than requiring Mommy to accompany him), and briefly toward the end of some of the sessions, Charlie's mother and I were able to think together—about how *she* could restrain herself from becoming anxious, frantic, and angry when Charlie swooped in on her, like the Barbarians invading Rome, to sack it of its wonderful treasures, and instead *calmly* help him *say* what he wanted and needed. She was an understanding and eager learner, and she and I rapidly became effective co-workers in the therapeutic enterprise. Increasingly, it was Mommy who perceptively put into words what Charlie was expressing in action, and she joined with me in helping Charlie to stop, think, and control himself instead of erupting in volcanic behavior outbursts. It was *she* who came up with the idea that it might be good to meet more often.

Charlie's father made a major contribution in two ways. He helped Mommy gain perspective about boys being different from girls behaviorally, and he helped her appreciate the fact that she and Charlie were *two* strong-willed, *determined* people who butted heads together. When Mommy and I thought that the time was ripe, Daddy began to come in with Charlie for some of his new, Saturday sessions. At first, Charlie was unable to bear being away from his Mommy while she was lavishing love and attention upon his two sibling rivals. He screamed, kicked, threw things, and insisted on going back home! Daddy sensitively tolerated it up to a point and then, with back-up assistance from me, physically restrained Charlie when he needed to do so and sternly spoke sense to him. Charlie eventually pulled himself out of his fight-and-flight terror. He quieted down, and then politely requested a drink of water. I obtained some for him, and then I congratulated him on the "victory" he had achieved over his terror and over his loss of self-control. During subsequent Saturday visits to which his father accompanied him, we were able to *talk* about his yearning to be with his Mommy and about his distress over not having access to her when he felt he needed it. Charlie began to play out triangular, pre-oedipal and oedipal themes in board games, not only with Daddy and me but also, in other sessions, with Mommy and me. Charlie's struggles over the "rules" afforded an opportunity to put into words his *need* to win, his *fear of* losing, and his *need* to be in control (both in competing with rivals for his Mommy's love and over his anxious eruptions of anger when he couldn't win the battle). Both parents were perceptive and sensitive in their understanding of and in their appreciation of Charlie's (increasingly healthy, appropriate, and better controlled) macho competitiveness.

When his baby brother's first birthday arrived, it was *Mommy* who skillfully connected the growing irritation and anger Charlie was expressing toward her in the playroom with his recollection of her pregnancy and the birth of his baby brother (she reminded him that she had been unable to be a witch for Halloween, the previous year, as he had wanted her to do, *because she had a baby in her tummy*). I was able to work together with her toward increasingly transforming Charlie's expression of his feelings through action into verbal expression in its place. I translated *into words* his throwing a little ball *at her*, excitedly playing at pushing a penis-shaped baby bottle "into her butt" and pushing pretend food into her mouth, and then filling a large truck with little, plastic animals: "Mommy has one baby; you have lots of them! I think *you* want to be the one having babies with Mommy, so *you* can control the baby-making!" He verbally confirmed it, and he calmed down. I set firm rules against his hurting me or Mommy and against breaking things or putting his feet on the walls. Mommy in turn firmly stopped him from throwing the ball so hard that it hurt her. She made it clear to him that, although he enjoyed the privilege of being able to say anything he wanted in my playroom, he could not say "bad words" at school and should not have showed his teacher *how big* his daddy's "tush" and his daddy's penis were. (Charlie's mother was very pleased by our ability to collaborate effectively in helping him not only to learn to speak rather than act but also to regulate what he says when it is socially appropriate for him to do that.)

After a while, Charlie brought his struggles directly into his relationship with me. When we were prevented from meeting during one week, he punished *me* for not being there for him. He cut *me* in half with a sword, so that there would be two of me, and he put *me* in jail for being bad, as he had done with Mommy in previous sessions. He provided verbal confirmation when I interpreted these expressions as reflecting distress and anger at my not being there for him when he needed me and the guilty fear that I had not seen him because I was punishing him for being demanding, rude ("bad words"), and aggressive with me. In subsequent sessions, we were able to talk together about his feeling those same things toward his mother. (Young children do develop transference reactions to their therapists!) At another time, when I made Charlie feel a bit uncomfortable by verbalizing something which it turned out he had not been quite ready to hear, he expressed negative feelings about coming to see me. This worried his mother, but she was relieved to hear me say that Charlie *truly* needed to be able to express all sorts of feelings in relation to me, including negative ones. She sounded even more relieved when she called me the next day. After she had put Charlie to bed the previous night, he suddenly said, "I forgot to tell something!" "To me?" she asked. "No," he replied, "to Martin! I forgot to tell Martin he's a very good friend!"

As the therapy has continued, Charlie's parents and I have continued to work together to help him contain his behavioral expression of fear, worry, anger, and guilt and to become self-observant enough to recognize those feelings as signals for him to take more *effective* action— including using his growing skill with words (he began to proudly share things he was learning at school during treatment sessions and to display his growing mastery of the ability to write and spell words). Charlie began to turn the Candyland figures into "Power Rangers," and to show me and Mommy, as well as Daddy on the occasions on which he brought him for his sessions, that he could do special things with them with the aid of rubber bands. This provided the opportunity to speak with Charlie about his increasing, *big boy* powers, in contrast with the relative powerlessness he had experienced as a baby and then as a *little boy*, who couldn't always know how to get what he needed, was forced to wear casts on his feet for a while to correct his toeing in, and had a couple of experiences when he fell off things and injured himself.

Rome, of course, was not built in a day, as the saying goes. Charlie has continued to have tantrums and meltdowns in my playroom and at home when he feels lost or threatened. They have become far less frequent, however, and to last for a shorter period of time—and he has completely stopped hitting himself and saying that he is bad and that no one loves him.

A SECOND CLINICAL ILLUSTRATION OF JOINT MOTHER-CHILD THERAPY

David was the four-and-a-half year old son of a loving but exasperated couple who had adopted him after a frustrating, very unpleasant, unsuccessful attempt at fertility treatments. He was born six or seven weeks early and had to spend a week and a half in a NICU before he was able to leave the hospital. The doctors had predicted a stay *of several weeks* in the NICU, which worried his parents very much, especially since he was born two thousand miles from where they lived! The adoption agency strongly urged that his parents speak and sing to David, repeatedly and often, how wonderful it is to be adopted, and that they do so right from the very beginning—and David's parents trustingly followed their well-meaning but misguided advice.

The first year was unremarkable. David seemed to be a healthy, happy, active, and assertive baby, and his developmental milestones were well within normal limits, although, as a premie, he had to catch up with himself a bit in walking and talking. At the time David's pediatricians referred the family to me for assistance, David was an affectionate and affection- loving youngster, but who was a lot like the little nursery rhyme girl who had a curl right in the middle of her forehead. When he was good, he was a wonderfully likeable and loveable, bright and creative, cheerful child who was a delight to be around (although he squirmed and wriggled anxiously when he was very hungry or very tired). When he was bad, on the other hand, he could be a handful. When he was placed in day care, beginning when he was between one and one-and-a-half years of age, he was a biter. His parents were told that he would outgrow it, but he was still a biter when he was enrolled in the summer program that would prepare him for pre-school. He also was defiantly disrespectful to the teachers, and he hit and kicked them. Soon he began to act that way with his parents as well—pushing, hitting, kicking, and biting them after even minor disappointments and frustrations. Guidance from a behavioral therapist seemed to help somewhat, especially with regard to his behavior in school, but it clearly was not enough.

Another bit of relevant historical information was that when he was transitioned from a crib to a bed, at about twenty months of age, it went well. A few days later, however, a huge storm swept through the area. They lost electrical power and had to relocate for a while. When they returned home, David would not stay in his bed at night but *fought* to stay with his parents in their room. They had to put a lock on his door to keep him in his room.

He was enrolled in a summer camp session at his pre-school, following his first year there, and things seemed to be going well. Two weeks before David's parents came to me for assistance, however, it was as though a volcano had erupted. He began to hit, kick, spit at, and bite other children at camp—and he pushed one of them into the swimming pool. Then he began acting that way with his parents as well, including pushing his parents out of his room and barricading the door so that they couldn't come in. They were nonplussed and dumbfounded by what was going on. When we explored the circumstances in which all this misbehavior had broken out, it became evident that two things had happened that triggered this wild behavior. One was that his best friend left camp after the first session, after which some new children joined the program for the second session. The other was that, the day before the outbreak of the "terrible reign of terror" which he launched against his parents, his father, continuing to follow the advice given by the adoption agency, read a book to David, the title of which was "Place in My Heart." It was about a family of squirrels that adopted a chipmunk, who then became worried whether there would be enough room in his heart to love his adopted parents as well as his birth parents. The squirrel parents *insisted* that there was—but I had to wonder whether *David* was convinced!

David went right into my "toy room" after I introduced myself as someone his parents had engaged to help him with the apparent unhappiness he was going through. He said "yes" when his mother asked him if she could stay, but then he started playing with toys (airplanes, and then cars, trucks, and soldiers) *with his back to her and to me*. I exchanged a few words with his mother about how bright and inquisitive he was, and about how capable he was in figuring out how to do things. Suddenly, he asked his mother to leave. She asked me if that would be okay and, in response to my "Maybe," she left and returned to the waiting room. David explained his asking his mother to leave by saying that he could not talk and play at the same time—but that is precisely what he then did with me! I wondered to myself if he had sent her away the way he had been sent away—by his birth mother. We chatted back and forth about the toys and other playthings in my "toy room" and at his camp. He asked for my assistance in connecting things to one another (e.g., a cannon to a jeep and a tow truck to a dump truck.). When he showed me how fast the airplanes and cars could go, I said: "like how fast your temper flares up and how much it takes to turn it off." He replied that he very much wanted to go to camp and school but he was afraid of not "being wanted" there because of his behavior. He began to line up the cars and trucks rather obsessively, apparently as a reflection of his desire to get things under control. He also, unlike most boys his age who come into my playroom for the first time, fed a bottle to one of the dolls on top of the toy shelves and a bit later explored the dollhouse corner—where he misplaced the baby figure somewhere else instead of putting it back with the rest of the family.

When I called his mother the next morning on the telephone, she said that she hadn't been surprised by David asking her to leave the playroom (although I had found it quite unusual), because he was so "independent." I shared my idea that perhaps he *had to be* independent. I told her that I had learned from David that he worried that his behavior was going to get him thrown out of camp and out of school and that he wanted to control it. I shared my hypothesis, based on other experiences I had had, that he was so afraid of being sent away that he was compelled to keep testing whether he could *make it* happen.

David's mother stayed with us during the next session. (She has continued to do so ever since and, for many months, we spoke for a while on the telephone some time during the morning following each session). The session began with David, in response to his mother's encouragement, telling me that he had gotten his camp counselor mad at him earlier in the day by throwing her ball over the fence. He later connected this with his recently having gotten his Mom mad at him by throwing his bottle of water over a fence into the "river" (actually a creek.) He could not say anything further about either incident, but, when he noticed that a little, plastic car had lost its wheels, he told me how "sad" (and "mad," I added) he was about having lost the teddy bear he had had "since (he) was a baby." In subsequent sessions, he was to alternate between blaming himself and blaming his mother for its having gotten lost. He (and his Mommy) allowed me to put into words how sad and mad he seemed to be about his having lost "Pookie," his teddy bear from when he was a baby, and how he just couldn't get rid of those "sad and mad" feelings, even though, as Mommy pointed out, he now "had five new teddy bears." David went over to the dollhouse corner, examined the child figures, and wondered about the differences between the ones with solid heads and the ones with "squishy (i.e., hollow) heads. (He was calling attention to their belonging to two different sets of figures.) Then he picked up a little plastic alligator and had it bite his mother's chin, shoulder, and chest, and it bit so hard that it hurt. When she objected, I said "Mommy doesn't want David to get hurt or for Mommy to get hurt." I offered to help the two of them figure out what was behind the painful interaction they were having, so that they could be happy together instead of hurting together. They both accepted the offer. We had drawn up and signed a therapeutic contract.

Early in the treatment, David turned Mommy into an aircraft carrier for the airplanes he zoomed around the playroom. When being covered with little, scratchy, metal airplanes proved to be too uncomfortable for her, he switched to playing the game Battleship with her. They both quickly recognized that he was too young for the game as it is designed to be played. David cleverly devised a novel way to play it. He used the pegs to surround and protect his ships, and he had his Mommy do the same thing. He then used the red and (mostly) white pegs to make a "pattern," and he insisted that his mother make the pattern identical to his *rather than making one of her own*. His mother had difficulty at first recognizing that his need for her to be a haven of safety for his airplanes and his need for them to be *the same* in the patterns they made related in part to his adoptive status (in an open adoption in which somebody he didn't know periodically was sending him pictures or little presents from far away). She said that having adoptive parents who provided a secure, caring, loving family for him should have more than made up for all of that! She thought about what I said to her during our regular talks, however; and she quickly understood what I was getting at when I spoke during the next session about how much I missed a ship that had gotten lost from my Battleship game and how much I missed the driver of the toy jeep, who also had gotten lost (by chance, we found both of them later on) the same way he missed Pookie, his teddy bear from when he was a baby. She sensitively understood and sensitively *helped* David when he went on to wrestle with whether it was he or his Mommy who had been responsible for Pookie getting lost. (When I expressed admiration for her sensitive attunement with David, as indicated by her saying just the right things to him, she was surprised and said, "I thought I'm *not* attuned to him!)

Very soon thereafter, during one of his sessions, David picked up a sheriff's badge he had noticed on one of the shelves. He had difficulty pinning it on, and Mommy helped him do it. When she asked him why he wanted to wear it, he replied: "to catch bad guys." David turned to me and asked, "Do you ever have bad guys in here?" I thought for a moment and then I said: "I've never had bad guys in here, but I have had guys in here who *thought* they were bad guys." He looked thoughtful, so I asked: "Have *you* ever thought you were a bad guy?" (I paused briefly.) "Like when you threw the counsellor's ball over the fence?" David looked away and said: "I *didn't* throw the ball over the fence." Mommy looked surprised. "But you *did*, David!" she declared. "You did do that." "And we still don't know *how come* David did that," I added.

David recruited his mother to join with him in building roads. He had her build one road while he built another one—and then he had her join her road to his. "I can see that it's important to you," I said to David, "for you and your Mommy to work *together* here." She nodded to me understandingly. When he then asked her to play chess with him but quickly made up his own rules after he found himself utterly bewildered by the actual rules, she began to argue with him about his changing the rules (and later about his setting things up so that only he could win), but she quickly caught herself each time and shifted to playing according to *his* rules—and they both seemed to have great fun as they did it. I said that it was good to see them enjoying what they were doing together.

A number of play themes emerged during the next few months. One involved races between two airplanes or between two cars. This seemed to have something to do with the way in which David and his mother emotionally were chasing after each other to connect up and be united even as they banged heads together about which of them would be in charge and in control. (Doesn't this take place, to a greater or lesser extent between *all* children and their parents?) As two strong-willed people, they clashed repeatedly as to which would be the dominant force and which would have to submit. They longed to tenderly melt into one another, but they repeatedly butted heads and pushed each other away. I made periodic, verbal comments about the struggles they were experiencing together around Mommy not wanting David to be behaviorally out of control (and he didn't like being out of control either) at the same time that they vied with each other as to which one of them was the boss, which one was in control.

Another, related theme involved fear of alienation, punishment, and abandonment. Two airplanes oscillated between flying together and either competing against one another or shooting each other down. Two little penguins either huddled together against a common enemy or were separated from each other by hostile forces, who at times threw one into the back of a garbage truck for disposal or locked one of them up in a closet that then was barricaded. The latter segued at times into talking about someone being put in jail or playing at either David or his Mommy being jailed.

David and his mother struggled together to create a common language. Since David was not only bright and verbal but also tall for his age, his Mommy (and his teachers) expected him to understand words which actually were too sophisticated for him. On his part, David tended to guess at the meanings rather than asking for clarification. The word "jail" was one of the words about which there was confusion. After a while, David's mother realized that his conceptualization of jail was not at all the same as that of a grownup. When she asked him what he thought a jail was and why people are put into one, he could only grope in a puzzled way. "It's a building," he said. On another occasion, he said, "It's a room" (as in "Go to your room!" perhaps?). As to why someone might be shut up in one, he said, "So they won't get out." (Was this related to his having been locked in his room to keep him from barging into his parents' room when he was younger? Did he *need* to be locked in to prevent him from being angrily thrown away for bad behavior, or might it have been to guard him from being taken away from his adoptive parents? Can a two and three and four-year-old child understand what it means to be adopted, or even what the word means?) The three of us worked slowly and steadily on this, in the interest of facilitating David and his mother becoming better able to understand each other.

The three of us joined together in looking at David's periodic misbehavior. His behavior had very much improved by now, but there still were periodic episodes of objectionable behavior at home and elsewhere. I was able to help David recognize that his "bad" behavior came from feelings inside him which he didn't yet have the ability to recognize. I also helped his Mommy become clearer about the difference between ordinary boy stuff and socially objectionable acts. She agreed readily to unite with me in helping David put his feelings (especially anxiety and insecurity) into words instead of expressing them in action. David readily agreed that "sad and mad" feelings generated his objectionable behavior. I said, to him at one point, after he made some allusions to it, "and when you're scared." His response was: "I never get scared!" "What?!?" his Mommy said. "How about at night? What about your fear of ghosts!" He not only admitted that she was right, but at a later point in time he even drew them for me—vague, shadowy, shapeless figures with what looked to me like a large mouth.

David began to ask his Mommy to sit with him on the floor instead of on a chair, so that she could help him build things with the wooden blocks. From having them repeatedly build separate roads which then became connected with one another, he progressed to asking her to help him build a fortress, with "two stories," in which his airplanes and her airplanes could be safe from the "bad guys." He continued to do this with her every session for months. He proved to be unable to ever feel safe enough from the "bad guys," and he asked her to ring the fortress with more and more soldiers and cannons for their protection. Mommy, now a more or less accomplished psychological investigator, with my assistance, uncovered a number of significant components of David's fear of the bad guys. It became clear, for example, that it was not always evident who the good guys were and who the bad guys were. Sometimes the danger seemed to come from the good guys themselves.

It also emerged that the most dangerous hostile elements of all were the *dinosaurs*. Mommy reminded David, who was extremely knowledgeable about them, that they existed a long time ago and now were extinct. David, in turn, informed her that it is impossible to be sure that they *won't come back!* I was able to link the dinosaurs with the ghosts that frightened David. They too, as David had told me, were beings that came back from having been dead and gone (like a four-year-old's idea of birth parents?). This led to his introducing into his play an interest in babies and in childbirth (including the idea that baby sharks get born by biting a hole in their mother's belly and swimming out), together with unmistakable references to his having been adopted. When I later referred back to his idea that baby sharks get born by biting a hole in their mother's tummy, he said: "I didn't say that. They come out through their mother's mouth." For the very first (and, so far, only) time, David mentioned that he had two mommies, one who took care of him inside her tummy before he was born and the current one who takes care of him now.

At this point, David had become one with his Mommy to a far greater extent than I had seen in the past, and an age-appropriate, sensual interest in her body crept into his play. He seemed more and more truly and safely in love with her. This is not to say that he is a totally changed person or that sad and mad, anxious and angry eruptions of aggressiveness have totally disappeared (especially in response to loss and the threat of loss), but he and his Mommy have come a long, long way indeed. The three of us still have work to do, but it is true indeed that Rome was not built in a day.

AN EXAMPLE OF A MORE COMPLICATED PARENT-CHILD SITUATION

Eight-year-old Ellen's mother brought her for assistance because she was "acting out" (which made me wonder *what* in the family dynamic she was enacting). She did well at school, and behaved well there, but at home she was tense and on edge, highly emotional, would cry without knowing why she was crying, could not handle even slight disappointments, and could get "violent" toward her parents and her five-year-old sister, throwing things and hitting and kicking them. Her mother felt "terrorized." Ellen refused to speak with her about her meltdowns, but when Mommy told her, "It must be scary to you to be like that," she replied, "That's true!"

Ellen's mother wondered if her condition might be "genetic." Both parents were in psychotherapy and on medication for anxiety and depression. There was "a lot of stress in the household," since both parents worked full time and both were "pretty anxious." Ellen's worrisome behavior got worse after a nanny was hired to spend the days with the girls three months earlier. Ellen's parents handled her "animalistic" meltdowns well at times but not very well at other times, they told me. Mom was at her wit's end, and Dad often got home very late, after a stressful work day, so frazzled that he could have "outbursts" of unhappiness and anger that scared the girls and sometimes frightened Mommy. At times, when Ellen had had a blowup, he would get irate, grab her, and "drag her upstairs to her room." A period of family therapy had helped only "a little bit." Ellen's parents pleaded for assistance not only for Ellen but for them as well.

Ellen's start in life had been far from ideal. Five months before Ellen's mother became pregnant, Ellen's paternal grandmother, who struggled with a bipolar disorder, was hospitalized for a bad back and, when oxycodone for her pain was combined with the Haldol she was on, she lapsed into a coma and almost died. Ellen's mother, an only child, was depressed during the pregnancy and worried constantly about her father to whom she had always been extremely close. Her father was in a nursing home in Florida, suffering from severe cardiac problems and a serious bacterial infection, because of which he was losing his will to live. She could not sleep during the first trimester, and she slept poorly during the rest of her pregnancy. Her father died just two weeks after Ellen was born! She became even more depressed. Neither her mother nor her husband's mother was sympathetic or helpful to her and, in fact, they made life more difficult for her rather than less so. She could hardly be a relaxed, focused, happy mother with Ellen after she was born. Her second pregnancy also was a time of struggling with depression. After Jill was born, it was hard for her to keep up with the demands involved in caring for a new baby, and she could not be available for two-and-a-half-year-old Ellen the way Ellen needed her to be and the way Mommy wanted to be.

I have been working with Ellen together with one of her parents (with her mother more often than with her father) for about three quarters of a year. During the first session, she leaned closely against and into her mother's body. She would not play with the toys, and she said next to nothing. She nodded in agreement when I offered to help her and parents deal with her "sad and mad" feelings and her "hurt and angry" behavior. The second time she came, her mother was not sure whether or not to go into the toy room with Ellen and me. Ellen seemed pleased when I said that unlike other places, where grownups rule, in my office the child is the boss, and if Ellen invites her mother to join with us that would be okay. She signaled to her mother to come in with us, and then she climbed on to her mother's lap and stayed there, burrowing into her Mommy, for the entire session. Mommy wanted us to talk about Ellen's getting out of control at home. I replied that children, and in fact all people, do *not* like being out of control, and I shared a somewhat dramatic experience I once had had that illustrated that.

Ellen's mother deftly followed my lead by shifting to talking about Ellen's little sister, whom I'll call Jill, having gotten out of control that morning, when she didn't get something she wanted. Ellen told me that Jill *put herself* into time out to help her calm down. Mommy periodically asked Ellen to stop sitting on her leg because it was hurting her. Then she thought of asking her to shift to the other leg, and Ellen promptly complied with her request. I asked what the recent Thanksgiving holiday had been like for them. Ellen's mommy replied that it was good—although she and Daddy were exhausted afterward. I went on record as being in favor of the family having good times together. I said that I hoped I'd be able to help them do more of that.

The third time I met Ellen, her daddy came with her. She leaned against him and then snuggled into his lap during the session—lovingly, but also in such a way that now and then she hurt him. He expressed regret that he had been away a lot working recently but was glad to have been able to chaperone Ellen's class's field trip to a bird sanctuary two days earlier. The three of us chatted about the experience. Ellen told me that the barn owl was her favorite bird and that the vulture was "creepy." I repeated the offer I had made to Ellen and her mother to help them have a happier family interaction and less of the sad and mad, angry and unhappy, out of control blowups that were interfering with their all being happy together. Once again, Ellen gladly endorsed this, and Daddy climbed aboard as well.

We have been working together ever since then to achieve that goal. At first, Mommy would call me before each session to tell me about Ellen's latest infraction of the behavioral rules. She listened intently when I suggested a change from reacting with frustration, anger, and fear when Ellen misbehaved to remaining calm and empathizing with what Ellen was feeling that might have triggered the reaction. She told me how her younger sister would annoy Ellen, or vice-versa, and then one of the children would get mad, following which Ellen would explode into a major tantrum. Mommy would get exasperated and Daddy would get angrier and angrier—so that the originally minor dispute would escalate into a very ugly scene. I helped her recognize that Ellen exploded into rages when something made her troubled or anxious. I also observed that a mommy or daddy getting *very angry* can be extremely frightening to children, who then act angrily in order to obtain an illusion of strength. She thought of instances in which Ellen had said things along that very line. I suggested that they might construct a three-color, virtual, emotional traffic light in the house. She liked that metaphor.

During one of our telephone conversations, I observed to Ellen's mother that fighting with parents and being swooped up and carried off by an irate daddy can also be very exciting to a child. That too might be contributing to what was taking place in the household. This was met with a bit of skepticism until five-year-old *Jill* commented to Mommy that *she* could see that Ellen was getting a charge out of Daddy doing that with her. We worked together, during the sessions and in our frequent, brief telephone conversations, on how to tone down the spiraling, agitated excitement that had been swirling repeatedly through the family. We spoke about pausing and thinking about what was happening before springing into punitive action. We spoke about becoming pro-active rather than reactive, and about focusing on and commenting on Ellen's good behavior more than on her bad behavior. Mommy spoke with Daddy about not having so many temper outbursts; and *Ellen* eventually came up with the idea, during one of our sessions, of their agreeing that *both* of them would work on controlling their anger. When her Daddy has joined us in the playroom, Ellen has been very affectionate with him—sitting on his lap, snuggling close to him, reaching into his pockets, and exploring the contents of his wallet. At first, he was somewhat hesitant to do so, but then he relaxed and enjoyed bantering with her as the three of us *talked about* Ellen's behavior and especially about her *feelings*.

A couple of months into the treatment, Ellen began to protest about being singled out as the bad one in the family, by asking why Jill was not coming to see me. After I indicated that she had a very good point, her younger sister did join us for some of our sessions. Jill, just as her father had predicted, made straight for the wooden blocks (and the plastic soldiers). Ellen, who had never before played with any of my toys, joined in with her in parallel building projects. Mommy was impressed with this—and she quickly grasped the significance of it being *Jill* who was the one who demolished *Ellen's* construction with a deftly placed, only *seemingly* errant toe, when I nodded in her direction. In subsequent sessions, when I spoke about the way in which people in a family often arbitrarily become labeled as the "easy one" or the "difficult one," etc., she stated that that was what was taking place in *their* family. She agreed with me that it would be good for everyone if they made some changes in that regard.

In later sessions, Jill began subtly annoying Ellen by reading Dr. Seuss books out loud in the playroom while Ellen, her Mommy, and I conversed. Mommy spoke critically to Jill about what she was doing. Recalling what she had said to me a few weeks earlier about Daddy "modelling" angry behavior to Ellen, I did some modelling. I expressed appreciation of Jill's exhibiting pride in rapidly learning to read, and I not only assisted her with words she couldn't make out but I advised her to "slow down" and figure out what some of the difficult words might be—and I matter-of-factly segued from that into the value of slowing down and thinking about what was presenting a challenge as something that can be useful for controlling a person's behavior. A couple of months later, when I commented to Daddy that Jill was rapidly becoming a good reader, he said "That's because she has a good teacher." *Ellen* had been, calmly and effectively, helping her sister learn to read!

Ellen began to bring pleasantly aromatic magic markers and some coloring books to the playroom with her. I expressed admiration of her good eye for color and of how very well she was able to stay within the lines. The next time I spoke with Mommy on the telephone, I remarked on how well Ellen was able to be in control and stay within the lines while she was coloring, and we renewed our agreement that paying more attention to Ellen's good behavior rather than to her bad behavior might be a very worthwhile experiment. She carried out the experiment both in my playroom and at home. Ellen began to bring in her Rainbow Loom and other craft projects to work on while we spoke (and to garner positive reactions from Mommy and me?).

There was a bit of a breakthrough when Mommy brought up a puzzling occurrence at home in which Ellen had a meltdown for what seemed to be no apparent reason. When the three of us, calmly and uncritically, thought about it together, it became clear that what had precipitated the meltdown was the prospect of beginning to take state-wide proficiency tests the following week. Her teacher had put pressure on the children, stating that they *had to do well on them!* I informed Ellen that the pressure actually was on the teacher, because it was *the school* that was being evaluated rather than the children. The teacher was passing on to the children the pressure *she* was feeling. The children weren't being judged, and Ellen didn't even have to take the tests. She could opt out of them if she preferred. It had been in the newspapers. Mommy immediately joined in with me in empathizing with and attempting to relieve Ellen's anxiety.

This led to a *major* breakthrough. Ellen became able to have a few sessions alone with me, during the week rather than on Saturday. She told me that pressure makes her anxious in general. And she let me know that there were some huge pressures that were frightening her. I learned, for the first time, that through genetic inheritance, like her mother and her mother's mother, she was born with fingers that were not straight but were bent in various directions, with some of them overlapping others. She already had undergone multiple operations on them, and, despite Mommy's assurance that the surgeon, whom they saw periodically, said that there would be no more surgery, she was terrified that he was going to change his mind. She *still* was having problems with her fingers! She was going for occupational therapy to stretch and straighten them out, in order to improve her handwriting. In addition, she had been having frequent strep throats every year, and the pediatrician had said that if she had one more strep throat this year her tonsils would have to be taken out! When Ellen, Mommy and I subsequently spoke together about all of this, it was *very* clear to us that the majority of Ellen's angry outbursts were triggered not only by pressure but, even more so, by Ellen feeling *anxious.*

It also emerged that inability to hide the unusual appearance of her fingers was a source of distress for her. Other children repeatedly asked her about them, looking disturbed and disturbing *her.* We soon became able to link this with another, *major* source of anxious insecurity. Ellen's guidance counselor called Mommy to say that Ellen's teachers were becoming concerned about her. Although she was a smart girl, she was having difficulty concentrating on and doing her work in school because she continually had to keep track of and make contact with a couple of girls with whom she had a vitally important relationship. We subsequently learned that Ellen was *terrified* because her best friend seemed to be turning away from her toward another girl. History was repeating itself.

In the (few) sessions Ellen and I have had alone with each other, and especially in the sessions we have had together with Mommy, we were able to reach back to the interferences, during her first few years after her birth, with the establishment of a firm, solid, secure, *relaxed and reliable* sense of togetherness with her mother. Mommy told me, in Ellen's presence, that, during the brief attempt they had made at doing family therapy, an observation was made that, because Mommy was so sick during her pregnancy with Jill and so overwhelmed with caring for the baby after the birth, it was difficult for her to pay enough attention to Ellen. *It was during her pregnancy with Jill that Ellen's wild outbursts of anger had begun!* Mommy expressed sincere regret about this. We were able, over time, to connect the early interferences with the development of solid, secure bonding between Ellen and her mother with a number of meltdown phenomena that until then had been difficult to understand: an unusual incident in which the angriness spilled over beyond the family confines during a birthday party, involving her best friends, at which Ellen had felt marginalized; a birthday party for her younger sister during which Ellen was incensed at receiving only a few token gifts while Jill was being showered with them; beating up on her little sister after only minor provocations; the hard time she gave to the new nanny who replaced the one who had been with them but then suddenly left for health reasons; and so on. A number of things were beginning to make sense—and we are working on them!

DISCUSSION

The importance of early mother-child interaction has been a major focus of attention for some time now. Sigmund Freud (1940) emphasized that the relationship between a baby and its mother is extremely important and that it serves as the model for all subsequent relationships. What happens early sets the tone for later relationships. Erik Erikson (1959) expanded upon this in his examination of the epigenetic evolution of identity and of relationships with others throughout the life cycle. Freud conceptualized the interaction in terms of the baby becoming attached to the source of its oral nourishment and then extending that attachment to the mother as a whole. Melanie Klein expanded upon this with her ideas about ambivalent, good breast/bad breast and good self/bad self, split images; establishment of self/other internal representations via projective and introjective identification; gratitude for what the mother provides as well as envy of her powers; and oscillation (not only early but throughout life) between what she termed schizoid-paranoid (part object) and depressive (whole object) emotional positions (see Klein, M., (1948); Spillius, E. & O'Shaughnessy, E., 2012; Silverman, M. A., 2014).

W. R. D. Fairbairn (1952) observed that human beings are internally programmed to reach toward others, beginning at or before birth, and are other-directed and relational right from the start (also see Bittles, E. F. & Scharff, D. E., 1994; Clarke, G. S. & Scharff, D. E., 2014). Michael Balint (1949 [1937]), Enid Balint (1949 [1939]), Harry Guntrip (1961, 1969), Edith Jacobson (1964), and others confirmed and elaborated on his observations. Donald Winnicott (1950, 1953, 1958, and 1969), who was a pediatrician before he was a psychoanalyst, made seminal contributions to our understanding of the complex interaction that takes place between mother and baby as they negotiate the passage between mother as developmental facilitator and baby as elaborator of a benign illusion of omnipotent possession of, control over, and ambivalent attachment to its mother as an at first undifferentiated extension of itself. In fortunate circumstances, he emphasized, the child is only very slowly, although never completely, disabused of that illusion.

John Bowlby (1973, 1979) made landmark observations about the powerful impact which early mother-child interaction exerts upon life-long patterns of behavior and life-long ways of perceiving and relating to self and others. His ideas about the importance of secure attachment and the deleterious effects of disturbed attachment have achieved prominence in recent times. At present, we are being inundated with contributions from investigators that assist us in understanding the significance of secure versus insecure attachment in shaping emotional development (see, for example, Ainsworth, M. D.S., et al, 1978; Fonagy, P. & Target, M., 1996; Fonagy, P., Gergely, G., Jurist, E, & Target, M., 2002; Slade, A., 1999; and Stern, D. N., 1985).

Charlie, David, and Ellen are fundamentally sound, constitutionally well-endowed youngsters who have been fortunate enough to have very loving, caring, also fundamentally sound parents who are extremely devoted to them. Each of them, however, has been encumbered by the effects upon them of early and ongoing interferences with the establishment of a sense of safe and secure connection with their mother (and father). The interferences have contributed, furthermore, to a pattern of behavioral expression in which they anxiously fight to obtain possession of her and effect a loving connection with her—which, paradoxically, distresses her and pushes her away! Charlie started out in extra-uterine life as an intense, vigorous youngster who had to fight to get what he needed from his largely depleted and exhausted mother, in competition with his much more placid and less demanding twin sister. He and his mother quickly developed an ongoing relationship in which they interacted with one another by fighting with each other—to the satisfaction of neither of them. Ellen too had to fight to get rid of the little sister who had taken her depressed, worn out, and overwhelmed mother away from her and *force* her mother to be involved with her, even though both of them were relegated by the seismic behavioral eruptions, leading to family tsunamis, to swimming together in a sea of unhappiness and anger. David and his mother started out together in a bonding process that was battered and bruised by the impact of prematurity, nine days in a NICU two thousand miles from home (and the threat of David having to remain there much longer), and the effects of terrible advice from an adoption agency that magnified the degree of relative insecurity generated by an open adoption many fold! Each of these mother-child pairs wanted nothing more than a cheerful, happy, close relationship, but each became mired in fear, unhappiness, and anger together instead.

Working with mother and child together made sense in all three instances, and it proved to be quite effective. This was so partly because with each of the child-and-mommy duos, both members were basically well constructed psychologically, both wanted help, and both were able to make good use of it. Things had happened that compromised the natural bonding process between mother and baby that lies within our brains as a result of millions (if not billions) of years. They only needed the right kind of assistance to get on track. Each child was unhappy with the way things were going and wanted things to change. Each mother was open to learning and adept at implementing what she learned. Each of them was emotionally flexible enough to make fortuitous parenting changes. Each of them quickly became a co- therapist in the treatment process. Each child caught on quickly to the treatment process and made good use of it. Each of the duos also had the support and assistance of a wonderful husband/father. Each time, we jelled rather quickly into an effective team. It is not a treatment process in which all children and parents (or therapists) are able to engage, but when it does work it can lead to important developmental progress, as Arietta Slade(1999) has observed .

This is not to say that this kind of treatment modality is an easy one to carry out. For one thing, neither time nor the developmental process stand still. No one has a time machine. It is not possible to simply reach back and repair damage that took place years ago. Much has happened and has been continuing to happen since the crucial events occurred during and after the child's birth. The impact of those events cannot be addressed immediately or in isolation from all the developmental and other life changes which have been occurring since then in the child, the mother, or the family—and the work cannot be done hastily. A staircase can only be built one step at a time, and there are no short cuts. It takes patience, persistence and perseverance.

The Contributions of Current Neuroscience Investigators

Exciting information has been coming to us in recent times from the neuroscience laboratories. The advances which have been made in imaging techniques, in particular, have enabled those who work in them to learn things about how the nervous system works that would not have been available to them just a little while ago. A number of recent findings are relevant to the topic addressed in this communication. Antonio Damasio (2010) has concluded from his many years of research that the human brain has evolved as an instrument for testing strategies for interacting with our animate and inanimate environment in such a way as to obtain satisfaction of our needs and wants as effectively and safely as possible. It does this by mapping out the results of our interactions with our surround, estimating from past and ongoing experience which strategies are better than others, and then firming up the ones that seem to work best—in such a way that it then becomes difficult to give up employing those strategies and switching to new ones. Behavior at this point becomes difficult to change. He has concluded that our ability to think has evolved out of our ability to feel, and that, at the same time that our thinking exerts control over our feelings and, therefore, over our actions, it also is controlled by our feelings and our urges, since its basic function is that of serving them (Roelke, D., Goldschmidt, H., & Silverman, M. A. (2013). Communication between the most ancient and primitive component of our brain, our brain stem, and our frontal cortex takes place along a two-way street.

Our Self, furthermore, as Damasio understands it to be constructed by the mindbrain, consists of concentric layers. Around our purely somatic "protoself," a somato-psychic "core self" emerges, beginning at birth, *out of our interaction with the environment*. Around that, over time, we elaborate a truly psychological "autobiographical self" which continues to evolve over the course of a lifetime. We truly are complex, bio-psycho-social creatures. We are basically very similar to other animals, although with a remarkable capacity for thinking and for communicating, both within ourselves and together with other people.

Jaak Panksepp (2012) tells us that our brain stem, which we have inherited in part from distant reptilian ancestors and in part from (less) distant mammalian ancestors, contains seven basic emotion-generating and action-generating neurological centers (Fear, Rage, Lust, Care [especially for our young], Play, Panic/Grief [reaction to separation or loss], and Seeking [curiosity]). These centers produce, in conjunction with one another and in conjunction with our neuro-endocrine systems, both self-gratifying behavior and social behavior. Of significance is that he informs us that the "Fear" center and the "Rage" center are very close to one another in the brain stem. When one of them is activated, the other tends to be activated as well. Fear and rage generally operate in unison with one another, in response to the perception of danger. What might this say about the behavior exhibited by Charlie, David, and Emma? All three of them were brought for treatment mainly because they were exhibiting wildly angry behavior that turned out be largely connected with anxiety (i.e., perceived danger). The treatment process that was employed, and which has been very helpful for them, is organized around: (a) facilitating reduction of the intense fear that, because of faulty development of a secure and reliable relationship between them and their mother, the most important other in their lives, their basic needs will not be met when they need them to be met; and (b) facilitating improvement in the ability to use higher order, executive functions, especially the ability to think and to communicate verbally, to tame the frantic, impulsive, knee-jerk explosions of anxious rage that paradoxically irk and push away the very need-fulfilling mother with whom the child is trying to establish contact.

Stephen Porges (2011) has been studying how our tenth cranial nerve, the vagus nerve, operates. The vagus communicates back and forth between our brain and our internal organs in order to regulate their functioning. The connection between vegetative functioning and emotion (our "gut feelings") has long been apparent. His decades of research have led him to the conclusion that what is at work is not a single system but a dual, "polyvagal" system. One part of the vagus is unmyelinated. It originates from the dorsal motor nucleus of the brain stem. By far the older one phylogenetically, it has come down to us from our distant, cold- blooded, reptilian ancestors, who were largely sessile hunters who waited for prey to approach the vicinity rather than chasing after them. It produces, in response to danger, an immediate, reflexive reaction of freezing to avoid the motion detection alertness of a predator or ducking under water (figuratively in humans—holding one's breath and fainting— rather than literally, the way reptiles do) in order to escape.

The second part, which is myelinated, is the mammalian part. It orig- inates not from the dorsal motor nucleus, but from the nucleus ambiguus, whose cells migrated away from the reptilian dorsal motor nucleus millions of years ago. It appears to serve two functions. One is that of shutting down the activity of our internal, digestive system and shifts glucose and oxygen to our musculoskeletal system during vigorous activity. Together with the hormone oxytocin, it also places a "vagal brake" upon the sympathetic nervous and neuro-endocrine system-mediated bursts of vigorous activity that, in our own, warm-blooded predator-like activities, consume such huge amounts of fuel and oxygen that their intensi- ty needs to be modulated and they cannot be allowed to progress too long. The vagal brake, Porges concludes, also plays a vitally important role in promoting human socialization by dampening down the frantic, vigor- ous, agitated excitation that hunger brings and the intense focus on vigorous sucking and chewing that dominate the experience of new- borns, so that calm, attentive, interpersonal, attachment-promoting interaction can take place with the baby's mother in a state of "alert inactivity" (P. H. Wolff, 1966).

The development of the myelinated, mammalian part of our parasym- pathetic, polyvagal system develops later than the unmyelinated, reptilian part, however. It barely matures in time for the baby to be born—and at times it is still developing after birth. (Babies also vary in their activity levels and in their other, biologically determined temperamental givens, as do their mothers.) Newborns who do not yet have mature enough mammalian vagal functioning need to be fortunate enough to have unusually capable, calm, well focused mothers in order to compensate for the immaturity of their own neurological control systems. What might happen if there is a combination of delayed maturation of the mammalian, myelinated vagus in a newborn together with an overwhelmed, anxious, and/or depressed mother? What happened after Charlie was born sounds a good deal like this, and it is very likely that Ellen's early experience was similar. As Sybille Escalona (1963) demonstrated, the fit between the temperamental characteristics of the mother and those of the baby, in interaction with one another, is enormously influential in shaping emotional and behavioral patterns in the child.

When Ellen got to my office on the morning after she had had a huge, angry outburst which had embarrassed her to the point of not wanting to come, I thanked her for coming. I told her: "I'm glad you came, because I already knew you when you were an adorable pussycat. I very much wanted to also meet you when you were the fierce tiger you have to become at times." We were able to talk about what had set her off, about the advantage of being able to be in control of the transformation between pussycat and tiger, and about *the value of having the strength and toughness to become a tiger when it seems necessary.* The last is something which has been addressed with Charlie, David, and *their* mothers as well. After all, being able to fight for what is right and for what you need *is* valuable in the world in which we live, isn't it?

REFERENCES

Ainsworth, M. D. S., Blebar, M., Waters, E., & Wall, S. (1978). *Patterns of Attachment: A Psychological Study of the Strange Situation.* Hillsdale, NJ: Erlbaum.

Balint, E. (1949 [1939]). Love for the mother and mother-love. *Int. J. Psycho-Anal., 30*:251-259.

Balint, M. (1949 [1937]). Early developmental states of the ego. *Int. J. Psycho-Anal., 30*:265- 273.

Bittles, E.F., & Scharff, D. E. (1994). *From Instinct to Self.* Northvale, NJ: Jason Aronson.

Bowlby, J. (1973). *Attachment and Loss: Vol. 2. Separation, Anxiety, and Anger.* New York: Basic Books.

——— (1979). *The Making and Breaking of Affectional Bonds.* London: Tavistock.

Damasio, A. (2010). *Self Comes to Mind: Constructing the Conscious Brain.* New York: Panatheon.

Erikson, E. H. (1959). *Identity and the Life Cycle. Selected Papers. Psychol. Issues,* Vol. I, No.1, New York: Int. Univ. Press.

Escalona, S. K. (1963). Infantile experience and the developmental process. *Psychoanal. Study Child,* 18: 197-244.

Fonagy, P., & Target, M. (1996). Playing with reality: I. Theory of mind and the normal development of psychic reality. *Int. J. Psycho-Anal.,* 77:217-233.

——— P., Gergely, G., Jurist, E., & Target, M. (2002). *Affect Regulation, Mentalization, and the Development of the Self.* New York: Other Press.

Freud, S. (1940 [1938]). An Outline of Psychoanalysis. *Standard Edition,* Vol. 23. Guntrip, H. (1961). *Personality Structure and Human Interaction.* New York: Int. Univ. Press.

——— (1969). *Schizoid Phenomena, Object Relations, and the Self.* New York: Int. Univ. Press.

Jacobson, E. (1964). *The Self and the Object World.* New York: Int. Univ. Press. Klein, M. (1948). *Contributions in Psycho-Analysis 1921-1945.* London: Hogarth.

Panksepp,J. & Biven, L. (2012). *The Archaeology of Mind: Neuroevolutionary Origins of Human Emotions.* New York/London: Norton.

Porges, S. (2011). *The Polyvagal Theory: Neurophysiological Foundations of Human Emotions, Attachment, Communication, and Self-Regulation.* New York: Norton.

Roelke, D., Goldschmidt, H., and Silverman, M. A. (2013). *Sentio ergo cogito:* Damasio on the role of emotion in the evolution of the brain. *Psychoanal. Q.,* 82:193-202.

Silverman, M. A. (2014). When theory meets practice: The value and limitations of the concept of projective identification. *Psychoanal. Q.,* 83:691-717.

Slade, A. (1999). Representation, symbolization, and affect regulation in concomitant treatment of a mother and child: attachment theory and child psychotherapy. *Psychoanal. Inquiry*, 19:797-830.

Spillius, E., & O'Shaughnessy, E., eds. (2012). *Projective Identification: The Fate of a Concept.* London: Routledge.

Stern, D. N. (1985). *The Interpersonal World of the Infant.* New York: Basic Books. Winnicott, D. N. (1950). The theory of the parent-infant relationship. *Int. J. Psycho-Anal.*, 50:711-717.

——— (1953). Transitional objects and transitional phenomena. In: *Playing and Reality.* New York: Basic Books, 1971, pp. 1-25.

——— (1958). The capacity to be alone. In: *The Maturational Processes and the Facilitating Environment.* New York: Int. Univ. Press, pp. 29-36.

——— (1969). The use of an object and relating through identifications. In: *Playing and Reality.* New York: Basic Books.

Wolff, P. H. (1966). *The Causes, Controls, and Organization of Behavior in the Neonate. Psychol. Issues*, Vol. V, No. 1. New York: Int. Univ. Press.

BRIEF BIO.

MARTIN A. SILVERMAN, M.D., is a Training and Supervising Analyst and Supervising Child Analyst at the Institute of Psychoanalytic Education, affiliated with the New York University (NYU) College of Education. He is also a Training and Supervising Analyst at the Center for Psychoanalysis and Psychotherapy of New Jersey. In addition, Dr. Silverman is the Associate Editor and Book Review Editor of *The Psychoanalytic Quarterly*. He has authored over 70 psychoanalytic papers and book chapters and over 80 book reviews. A former Clinical Professor of Psychiatry at the NYU College of Medicine and former President of the Association for Child Psychoanalysis, he was named New Jersey Child Psychiatrist of the Year by the New Jersey Council of Child and Adolescent Psychiatry in 2005.

CHAPTER 10

The Effect on Children when the Attachment to their Mother is Broken: The Developmental Phases of Mourning

Corinne Masur, Psy.D.

The Effect on Children when the Attachment to their Mother is Broken: The Developmental Phases of Mourning

Corinne Masur, Psy.D.

The subject of childhood has been taken up by writers, film makers, psychologists, psychiatrists, sociologists and anthropologists among others. And the popularity of the recent film, "Boyhood" speaks to the general public's fascination with this subject. We were all children once and many of us have children. Our own development and that of the children we raise is a truly miraculous and mysterious process which can only be described in tiny bits and pieces by the most talented amongst us. And no one can be said to have devoted more of his or her professional life to this work than Sylvia Brody. She did what has rarely been done prior to her work or since, by conducting a longitudinal study of mothers in regard to the parenting of their infants and young children. Brody collected 131 mothers in order to study the mother-child relationship and later, with the addition of fathers, the parent-child relationship. It is in part thanks to Sylvia Brody that we now take it as common knowledge that the more adequately mothered a child for the first three years of life, the more adequate the child's development proves to be. Brody followed mothers and their infants from 4 months to age 7. She painstakingly documented mothering patterns and later, parenting styles and their relationship to developmental outcome.

Brody's work laid the foundation for later infant research and research on patterns of attachment. And while my interests overlap with those of Sylvia Brody and her colleagues, I have looked at some of the same questions as they from the opposite point of view: that is, rather than looking at the development of mothering styles and patterns of attachment, I have looked at the effect on children when the attachment to their mothers is broken. I have wondered what the developmental consequences are of the loss of the mother in infancy and early childhood and to what extent the child can recover from such a devastating loss.

If separation occurs between a mother and her child, whether due to death, illness, divorce or other circumstances can the child give up that attachment in order to form other, new attachments in his or her current life? To explore this question, we must start by looking at the original work on understanding the mourning process. Sigmund Freud defined mourning as the struggle which takes place within the bereaved person between the wish for the beloved to continue to exist and the reality testing that proves that she does not. Each memory and hope is reviewed and in so doing the individual gradually divests him or herself of his attachment to the lost loved one. Other psychoanalytic writers have expanded on Freud's description. As Wolfenstein (1966) stated, the lost object is gradually decathected by a process of remembering and reality testing, separating memory from hope. That this is a gradual process serves an important function as Fenichel (1945) and Wolfenstein noted, that is, to prevent the mourner's ego from being intruded upon and overwhelmed by too great a quantity of traumatic material. What occurs in normal mourning, according to Fenichel, is a gradual working through of affect which, if released in full strength, would be overwhelming. Through normal mourning then, the individual comes to realize that the beloved person no longer exists and the attachment to that person is severed.

But when speaking of childhood mourning in particular, the question arises as to whether any child can willingly give up the attachment to the mother. And, to what extent can this bond be given up? As Sigmund Freud said, "man never willingly leaves a libidinal position...even if another is already beckoning". If this is true of adults, it is doubly true for children. And in particular, this is true of the libidinal tie to the mother. This bond is primary, necessary for survival, for nurturance, for the feelings of security and for the progression of growth and optimal development. Much of the literature on mourning in childhood has addressed this question by asking whether young children can mourn.

Nagera (1970) proposed a developmental framework for the mourning process. He, among others, proposed that perception, memory,
affect tolerance, self and object differentiation, understanding of the
concept of death and the establishment of object constancy are all necessary for true mourning to take place. However, rarely, if ever, has the
literature on mourning looked at the way in which children of specific
developmental stages – from birth to adolescence – mourn the loss of
their mothers. Here, the questions of how, whether, and to what extent
children mourn this loss at each of these stages will be examined.

The ability to love has to be learned and practiced. If, in the course of
learning to love, the primary love object is lost—to depression, divorce, or
most ultimately, and irretrievably, to death, the implications for the child
and his ability to love are critical (A. Freud, 1944). The original alliance
between mother and infant is perhaps the most significant of all human
relationships; it is the wellspring for all subsequent attachments and it is the
formative relationship in the course of which the child will develop a sense
of himself (Klaus and Kennel, 1975). If this relationship is interrupted
during the early stages, the effects may be devastating for the young child's
future interpersonal relations and personality development.

What is believed to be essential for mental health is that the infant
should experience a warm, intimate and continuous relationship with
his mother in which both find satisfaction and enjoyment (Bowlby,
1980). When the mother dies, the child is in a unique situation because
of the special nature of his tie to her. The adult distributes his love
among several meaningful relationships— his spouse, parents, siblings,
children, friends, colleagues, etc. The young child, by contrast, invests
almost all of his feelings in his parents. Only in childhood can death
deprive an individual of so much opportunity to love and be loved and
face him with so difficult a task of adaptation (E. Furman, 1974).

Children at different ages and stages of development vary in their ability to adapt to the loss of their mother. As such, there is a developmental
progression in the child's reactions to loss and in his ability to mourn.
And, contrary to previously held theoretical and clinical opinion, by age
four to five years of age, the child CAN begin to mourn if provided with
several crucial elements, that is, with an optimally supportive milieu for

the experiencing of his grief and other affects associated with the loss. The child needs help with the identification and discussion of feelings associated with his loss; he needs help working though these feelings and processes by the supportive adults in his world. The inability to mourn prior to this age and following this age when accompanied by external stressors, the lack of adequate ego support and other factors, such as preexisting developmental challenges or personality factors, lack of socio-economic supports, etc. will also be discussed.

Robert and Erna Furman pioneered the early work on the child's ability to mourn. And while they championed this idea, they were also clear on the fact that "the experience of a parent's death always remains a very troubling part of a child's life" (1974, p. 26). Throughout life, the individual who has lost his mother early in life will experience the reverberations of this loss over and over and he will be presented with opportunities to rework the experience and meaning of this loss.

MOURNING AND MELANCHOLIA AND BEYOND

In order to shed light on childhood bereavement it is important to start with the early conceptualization of bereavement in general. Sigmund Freud provided seminal insights into the grief process in his articles Studies in Hysteria (1893), Mourning and Melancholia (1917), Lectures on Psychoanalysis (1909) and in his letter to the mother of a young soldier who died in combat. He stated, as noted previously, that in mourning, the survivor's memories and hopes are detached from the dead. He stated that both affection and hostility may be felt toward the person who has died but that hostility must be repressed in order for mourning to go forward (Pollack, 1961). Freud describes mourning as the struggle which takes place within the bereaved person between the wish for the beloved person to continue to exist and the reality testing that proves that he does not. Each memory or hope is reviewed, and in so doing, the mourner gradually divests himself of his attachment to the lost loved one. Freud called this "the work of mourning".

In mourning, Freud listed several distinguishing characteristics: a profoundly painful dejection, loss of the capacity to adopt new love objects, a turning away from activities not concerned with the lost loved one and a loss of interest in the outside world. He suggested that a normal period of mourning would be one to two years. Abraham (1924) added to Freud's conceptualization by stating that the mourner may introject the lost object as a way of keeping the beloved with him: "In the normal process of mourning...the person reacts to a real object loss by effecting a temporary introjection of the lost person. (The main purpose of this mechanism) is to preserve the person's relation to the lost object". p. 435. Fenichel (1945), Klein (1935) and Jacobson (1957) weighed in on mourning and along with Sigmund Freud are considered to be the theoreticians most responsible for the current psychoanalytic conceptualization of grief and mourning.

Eric Lindemann (1944) was the first to conduct research on bereavement based on his observations of 101 survivors and relatives of victims of the disastrous Coconut Grove Nightclub fire, patients who had lost a loved one and relatives of members of the armed forces. He identified the following as characteristic of what he referred to as normal grief:

- Somatic or bodily distress.
- Preoccupation with the image of the deceased.
- Guilt related to the deceased and/or the circumstances surrounding the death.
- Hostile reactions.
- The inability to function as one had before the death.
- Taking on characteristics of the deceased.

And he named stages of grief in his adult subjects:

1. Shock and disbelief
2. Acute mourning
3. Resolution

Renee Spitz (1948), in his observations of infants in a nursery and a foundling home, contributed to the understanding of the effects of separation and loss in infancy. He discovered that infants separated from their mothers in the second half of the first year of life, if not provided with adequate nurturance and stimulation, would develop what he called failure to thrive. In these cases, the infants would fail to continue physical and psychological growth, become passive, lose weight and eventually die. Those infants between six and eight months of age with previously good relationships with their mother if separated from them for three months would develop a syndrome which looked similar to depression in adults which he called anaclitic depression (1946). Those infants whose mothers did not return and who were not provided with adequate substitute mothering after five months would develop what he termed, "Hospitalism" in which rapid deterioration in functioning occurred, analytic depression developed, including motor retardation, passivity and failure to continue forward development. By four years of age these children could not sit, talk or walk. If the mother did return, development resumed although Spitz hypothesized that complete recovery was unlikely and scars would inevitably remain.

Later, John Bowlby, an ethologist and psychoanalyst, made a study of the effects of separation and loss resulting in his three volume series on these subjects. One of his most important contributions to the field and one of the most remembered (and argued about) in the current day literature was his delineation of four specific phases of mourning:

1. Numbing – which usually lasts from a few hours to a week and may be interrupted by outbursts of extremely intense distress and/or anger.
2. Yearning and searching for the lost loved one – which may last from months to years.
3. Disorganization and despair.
4. Reorganization – to a greater or lesser degree.

Others have weighed in on the question of whether there are specific stages to the mourning process for children (LeShan, 1988; Wardon, 1991; Grollman, 1991; Goldman 2001 and others). Le Shan (1988) suggested the following: denial, disorganization and integration.

Worden (1991) continued with the idea of a more process oriented description of mourning in childhood in which he stated that there must be an acceptance of the reality of the loss of the loved one (similar to Freud's, "comparing memories and hopes to the reality of the fact that the loved one is no longer there"), experiencing of pain and grief, adjusting to an environment in which the lost loved one is missing, withdrawal of emotional energy for the lost loved one and a new investment in others. Most adherents to the idea that there are stages to the mourning process utilize the caveat that the grief process of any individual child is just that – individual – and that any stages described can be experienced in a variety of orders and intensities and completed to varying degrees.

CHILDHOOD BEREAVEMENT: CAN CHILDREN MOURN?

One of the most fundamental issues in the study of childhood bereavement has been the question regarding whether and to what extent children can mourn. A debate has raged in the literature since the early 1960's regarding this question. There are those who believe that the young child's ego is too weak to accomplish the work of mourning. This argument has focused on the young child's inability to sustain painful affects for a prolonged time, and the immature reality testing of the child. Those on this side of the debate feel that it is not until adolescence that the child has the ego capacities for mourning. Anna Freud said, "mourning, taken in the analytic sense, is the individual's effort to accept a fact in the external world and to effect corresponding changes in the inner world" (p. 58). To accomplish this task requires sophisticated intrapsychic and ego capacities which as Helene Deutsch (1937), Mahler (1961), Fleming and Altschul (1963), Wolfenstein (1966) and others have stated, exist only after the completion of adolescence.

Others, such as Robert Furman (1964, 1968, 1969, 1973), Erna Furman (1974), Lopez and Kiliman (1979), Bowlby (1980), etc. have agreed that even the young child is capable of mourning given adequate support. Bowlby believed that once a child has formed an attachment to the mother figure, which has ordinarily occurred by the first year of life, its rupture leads to separation anxiety and grief and sets in train the process of mourning. When, in 1960, he he first drew attention to the similarities between the responses of young children following the loss of the mother and the response of bereaved adults, he stated that these similarities had not been observed before.

Critical to this debate is the definition given to the term, "mourning". If one adheres to Sigmund Freud's definition, the answer is simple, young children cannot mourn. If one expects the young child to be able to "detach...memories and hopes from the dead" (S. Freud, S. E. 13, p. 65) then the young child cannot accomplish this task. For small children, the lost loved one (especially if it is the mother or the primary attachment object) is never entirely relinquished. Some fantasy of the mother and/or some internalization/identification with the mother continues and at every developmental phase the mother is again evoked and missed anew. Moreover, even Freud admitted that it is debatable as to whether anyone ever entirely decathects from a lost loved one, particularly a mother. Many if not most adults who lose their mothers in adulthood continue to preserve identifications with their mothers, to yearn for her presence at times and to miss various aspects of her in their lives. Have they fully mourned? As Freud said, it is questionable as to whether complete decathexis is a possible or desirable accomplishment by anyone of any age. Erna Furman (1974) stated, "Knowing and understanding that (the) loved one is dead is not the same as accepting it. Clinical examples (have shown) that people of all ages grapple for varying periods of time for different reasons with the task of integrating reality" (p. 51). Thus, whether anyone of any age ever fully decathects a lost loved one remains an open question.

Earlier theorists suggested that the following capacities are necessary for mourning to take place: perception, memory, affect tolerance, object differentiation, reality testing, the establishment of object constancy and a cognitive understanding of death. Until a child possessed all of these, the completion of mourning was considered impossible.

If an expanded, process oriented definition of mourning is utilized however, then it becomes more possible to accept that even the youngest children can experience mourning to some extent. Bowlby (1980), for example, suggested that mourning can be defined as the psychological processes set in motion by the loss of the love object and which commonly lead to the relinquishment of the object. Similarly, Erna Furman (1974) defined mourning as the mental work following the loss of the loved one through death. Furman believed that successful mourning hinged upon a sufficient amount of decathexis from the beloved to allow for the development of other significant relationships with highly cathected and trusted others. There is little doubt that children of any age, from infancy onward can experience affects associated with their experience of the loss; what is in doubt is whether infants and young children can decathect sufficiently from the lost loved one on their own and whether and to what extent they can successfully invest fully in new object relationships varies from child to child and situation to situation.

While both Bowlby and Furman refer to decathexis, they do not consider this the sine-qua-non of mourning. It is the use of an expanded definition of mourning which seems to provide the most useful framework for the exploration of the processes of children's reactions to loss. Rather than perpetuating a tired debate which continues to rage, the definitions of Bowlby and Furman and the understanding of mourning which they illustrate set the stage for specific inquiry into the nature of the mental and affective processes experienced by young children following loss and the determinants of these. The questions thus become, at what age and to what extent does the loss of the mother affect the infant, at what age does the infant perceive loss and in what way does he do so; at what age does the young child begin to understand death from the cognitive standpoint, at what age can children experience some or all of the affects associated with mourning, what ego capacities are necessary to do so and at what age and under what circumstances can the child begin to decathect sufficiently from the lost loved one in order to be able to invest fully or partially in a new object?

THE DEVELOPMENTAL PROGRESSION
OF MOURNING

Many variables effect the child's reaction to loss. The capacity for grief and mourning of any individual child must be seen in the context of his development, including his age, his stage of psychosexual development, his innate predisposition and individual characterologic makeup, his defensive functioning prior to the loss and in response to it, his object relations prior to and following the loss, his attachment style, as well as the availability, nurturing capacity and mental health of the surviving parent, the family atmosphere following the loss, the availability of supports for the child and the family following the loss, the nature of the child's environment, and the plethora of stressors which may accompany the loss.

One of the major difficulties in the discussion of children's mourning has been the tendency of psychoanalytic writers to group all bereaved children together and to make generalizations about their capacities for mourning rather than looking at mourning as a process which follows a developmental sequence similar to the developmental lines proposed by Anna Freud (1965).

Helene Deutch !1937) stated that children resort to narcissistic self protection in the face of overwhelming affect through regression and by the mobilization of defenses or by the absence of affect. While this may be true of some children at some levels of development or for those who are unsupported in their grief and mourning or at the mercy of a great number of environmental stressors, observation and clinical experience indicate that some children can grieve and mourn without having to resort to pathological use of defenses or defensive withdrawal. However, it is important to continue the early work of Deutsch and others by discriminating between these variables. By doing so it may be seen under what conditions and at what stages of development children can begin to experience the affects associated with mourning and to work through these affects.

AT WHAT AGE DOES LOSS FIRST EFFECT THE CHILD?

It can be said that the loss of the mother at any age is a devastating blow. However, this is particularly true if the loss occurs in infancy and childhood when the mother is still so important to the child and his optimal development. The effects of loss will be great at any age but the specific ways the child is affected at the time of the loss and subsequently are related to the stage of development at which the infant or child finds himself. Depending on what skills are being acquired at that age and stage, these are the aspects of the child's development that can be expected to be effected most immediately. When referring to the infant and very young child, recently acquired skills may be lost, physiological homeostasis such as appetite, sleep, and bowel habits may be interfered with; mood and self regulation may change and forward development may slow or cease entirely. Regression or stasis, fussiness, changes in schedule and other expressions of discomfort may be the only ways we can see the infant's profound confusion over the disappearance of his major source of comfort and security. However, the effect upon the infant cannot be underestimated and the entirety of the future impact is impossible to fully determine.

THE NEWBORN

Evidence in the literature suggests that as early as several weeks of age, the infant may respond to separation from or loss of the mother (Bowlby, 1980). However, research has shown that even at birth the infant recognizes his mother's voice, the smell of her breast milk and the appearance of her face (Brazelton, 1974). Thus, the effects of separation from mother even from the moment of birth must be considered.

Newborns who experience complications prior to or during the birth process are often placed in neonatal intensive care. Some can be held by the parents and some are so ill that they cannot. These infants and those who are immediately put up for adoption, those whose mothers are critically ill or who die following delivery, and those who are given over to the care of a full time nanny must, by virtue of the in utero experience of the mother, suffer a major disruption when the person who cares for them is not the same person who carried them – who does not smell or sound or feel the same. But what can the newborn perceive? What does he experience when the familiar mother is not his caretaker? And what is the effect on the infant of this discontinuity of his care?

These are questions which are very difficult to answer given the newborn's inability to clearly communicate his experience and due to the lack of research regarding these infants. However, there are cases in the literature demonstrating distress even in the youngest infants who are separated from their mothers.

We can say that newborns have the capacity for perception on many levels but of the other criterion put forth by Nagera, they are lacking. Perhaps it is fair to say that the youngest of the infants' experience SOME of the affects associated with mourning such as discomfort, dysregulation, and unpleasure without the full ability to experience all the affects associated with loss and the ego capacities to perceive the nature of their loss.

The outcome for newborns who have lost their mothers is, of course, varied. Long term studies are needed to delineate whether particular outcomes are more likely with loss occurring so early in life. And, as Bowlby (1980) noted, how an infant develops following loss will depend in part on the nature of the substitute parenting provided. Consistent, responsive nurturing, of course, is considered the most optimal for the bereaved infant.

THE TWO TO THREE MONTH OLD

Following the initial phase of life during which the infant is largely occupied with establishing his own bodily homeostasis, the infant then begins to coexist with his caretaker/mother in a symbiotic orbit. He does not perceive a separation between himself and the giver of nourishment and comfort. While recent research tells us that infants of this age do perceive external stimuli of all sorts, the baby's basic existence at this point is governed by his requirement for help with his bodily needs and the regulation of his affects. The mother is profoundly affected by the baby's needs and feelings and the baby is profoundly affected by the mother's needs and feelings in a relationship which involves mutual regulation. If the mother should leave the infant during this period, the common belief has been that the infant will manage if an adequate substitute caretaker is found.

For the purposes of this work, however, it is necessary to consider what it must be like for the infant to be in a completely dependent state, reliant on one adult, accustomed to her style of affect regulation, mood and self expression, only to have her disappear and another take over who has entirely different moods and methods. It may be expected that such an infant would experience a period of disorientation, displeasure, and discomfort indicated either by pronounced fussiness and dysregulation of sleeping, eating and digestion or a retreat into an earlier position of increased sleep and decreased interaction.

Again, the infant of this age possesses perception but he does not have affect tolerance, memory, self and object differentiation or the other qualifications for mourning but forth by Nagera. So at this age, also, the infant is capable of experiencing affects associated with mourning which include yearning and searching the environment for the lost mother, and to protest against her absence as well as the discomfort associated with her unavailability.

Spitz (1965) observed that infants who were cared for by their mothers for the first three months of life and then separated from their mothers and provided with bodily care but NOT provided with adequate substitute love and nurturing developed a devastating halt to physical and emotional development or what he termed "Hospitalism" or failure to thrive. This is the most severe type of reaction to the loss of love and nurturance and stimulating human interaction and it is typical only of those infants who are severely deprived in addition to suffering the loss of their primary caregiver.

THE FOUR TO SIX-MONTH OLD

This is the period during which "hatching" (Mahler 1978) occurs. The previously sessile infant suddenly seems to become a person, to be more outwardly directed and to respond more directly to external stimuli and attempts at engagement. What allows this to occur is the familiarity of the mother/caretaker and the child's trust in her ongoing care, presence and regulatory functions and the nascent recognition of differentiation between the baby's self and the mother as "other". Should the mother disappear from the infant's life at this point, of course nothing can be known by the infant of death, but again, the infant can be expected to experience a period of disorientation, dysregulation and discomfort which may result in a retreat from the hatching process. Because the process of differentiation is starting at this age, the loss of the other will be even more noticeable and potentially even more disruptive to the infant than previously.

THE 6 TO 12 MONTH OLD

During this period, the infant is in an accelerated process of bodily and cognitive growth. New skills such as sitting up, crawling, walking and running, along with speaking words and indicating desires through gestures and vocalizations are acquired. Moreover, the infant becomes increasingly aware of the singularity of mother and of her separateness from himself. Stranger anxiety occurs when the baby recognizes the visual differences between mother and other. Meanwhile he is also increasingly independent due to newly acquired motor skills. More fully than previously, the infant recognizes his own separateness from mother. This is a period of great mastery (Mahler, 1978) and joy in which the infant demonstrates a love affair with the world (Greenacre, 1960). Should the mother leave at this point, a daunting blow to the child's growing sense of competence and separateness is dealt and feelings about independence and self efficacy may be affected.

John Bowlby (1980) believed that the attachment to the mother figure, when ruptured at this stage of development, sets in train what he referred to as a process of mourning. When, in 1960, he first drew attention to the similarities between the response of young children following the loss of the mother and the responses of bereaved adults, he stated that these similarities had not been observed or acknowledged before. Bowlby suggested that even the toddler proceeds through various stages following separation, including protest, yearning and searching and ultimately, detachment. Later, he added despair to these stages.

Spitz, as noted previously, observed that it is at six to eight months of life that an infant with a previously good relationship with the mother will develop dramatic symptoms in response to separation from her if it is paired with the lack of provision of adequate substitute mothering. He termed the syndrome which develops "analytic depression" (1965).

THE 1 TO 2-YEAR-OLD

The young toddler is firmly attached to his mother or primary caretaker. He knows who she is – affectively, visually and otherwise. He knows increasingly well that she is separate from him. She is not interchangeable. He relies on her for help in all things including self regulation and safety and he relies on her to be there when he experiments with independence and moves away from her to explore. Having her there to come back to sets the stage for the development of person permanence and object constancy.

Work by The Robertson's in the late 1960's and 1970's amply demonstrates—through film—the effects of separation on the young toddler. Moreover, the work by Ainsworth, Main, Hesse and others, furthered the understanding of the variations in response to separation at this age. This research was performed with toddlers between the ages of 9 and 18 months using the "Strange Situation". In this paradigm, they separated toddlers briefly from their mothers and introduced a stranger to the room in order to observe the reactions of the children to separation and to the introduction of an unfamiliar adult. Given the toddler's overall styles of relatedness and reactions to separation, Ainsworth et al were able to divide children into the following categories: Securely Attached and Insecurely attached with the latter category being further subdivided into Anxious/ambivalent, Avoidant and Disorganized/disoriented. It was found that the Anxious/ambivalent toddlers responded to brief separations with great distress. The Avoidant toddlers reacted with a detached and uncaring affect and the Disorganized/Disoriented toddlers demonstrated a fluctuation in feeling, alternating between extreme distress and complete detachment.

Extrapolating from this work, it can be theorized that attachment style may effect the bereaved toddler's reaction to the more permanent separation from his mother through death. Further research in this area would contribute immeasurably to the study of grief reactions in the one to two-year-old child.

Up to this point in development, mourning as defined by Sigmund Freud, his daughter, Anna, and other early theorists cannot be said to occur. Infants and toddlers are certainly affected by the loss of the mother and affects associated with loss are definitely experienced. Sadness, grief, yearning and searching, anger and profound discomfort can be identified in the young toddler who has lost his mother (see Ainsworth et al. and the Robertson's). Schaffer and Callender (1959) noted that upon separation, it was typical for the two-year-old to cry to excess, to refuse food and to become either more or less active than usual. Heinicke and Westheimer (1965) noted sleep disturbances as well. This is mourning more along the lines of what is described by Bowlby and the Furman's, but not as described by theorists who believe that memory, perception, reality testing, object constancy and a mature understanding of death are necessary for mourning. Research and further study must be pursued to understand better the specific nature of the effects, both short and long term, of separation and loss at this age.

THE 2 – 3-YEAR-OLD

At two to three years of age the toddler needs his mother to care for him physically, to love him, to let him know he is loved and to help him with the tasks he has not yet mastered. Like the younger child, he continues to need his mother in order to successfully attain further autonomy, that is to slowly relinquish his dependence on his mother. At this age he is both emerging from the exclusive, dyadic relationship with his mother and accepting others into his affective life but he is also establishing a reliable internalized image of mother which allows him to be separated from her for increasingly longer periods of time and to have an internalized image of mother, at least for brief periods.

Starting at this age, with intensive intervention, the two to three-year-old can start to experience true mourning as described by both the Freud's and the Furman's. However, without help or with insufficient help, the two to three-year-old is likely to become arrested in one of the initial stages of the mourning process. This occurs not only because he lacks the ego capacities required for mourning but also because of the specific nature of the issues and conflicts normally experienced by the child of this age in combination with his intense need for the continuing presence of his mother. Loss of the mother at this age represents a particularly grievous deprivation. It is not that the toddler is unable to experience sadness or anger associated with loss which interferes in the progression of the mourning process – because he is – but rather his inability to go beyond the anger which is so overwhelming and under so little control at this stage of development. At this age, the child feels powerful and omnipotent and he desires to be independent and autonomous. He is just beginning to master his aggression and as such, when he is angry he is powerfully angry and may feel that he hates the person he is angry with. He is fiercely angry when others, especially mother limit his independence by saying "no". As a result, he may wish at these times that mommy would go away and as such he is at risk for feeling particularly angry with himself if mommy should actually go away through illness or death.

However, at this age there is generally not a realistic concept of death. The two to three-year-old may or may not be familiar with the idea of death and he will not understand that death is permanent. The child of this age is likely to understand death as temporary and as reversible. When someone dies, that person may be fantasized as living on in some other location. At this age, the idea that they can be reunited with the lost loved one is common (Zelig, 1967, Gessell and Ilg, 1946; Anthony, 1972). When bereaved, he needs extensive support and love from those adults who are available and a great deal of help with understanding what has happened. He will require simple answers to his questions and gentle reminders that mommy cannot come back to be with him although she might have wanted to.

CASE EXAMPLE: THE 3 TO 4-YEAR-OLD

The Furman's and their group in Cleveland, felt that it is at this age that, given a sufficiently supportive environment, clear and concrete explanations regarding the meaning of death, and the achievement of the other developmental requirements of mourning, the child can mourn. At this age, the child can be preoccupied with the lost loved one and he does attempt to review his memories of her. It is true that he does this in a way that is qualitatively different from the adult and thus, he must have access to adults who understand and can interpret for him the meaning of his feelings.

It is also true at this age that the child is at the stage of development at which object constancy is normally being developed. He is beginning to modulate his own feelings and tolerate some of his more powerful affects. He can begin to understand the concept of death, with an adult's repeated help. In other words, the evolving developmental acquisitions of the three-year-old are precisely those which are needed to begin a mourning process according to some theorists.

If it is necessary to have a firmly internalized image of the mother in order to perform the work of mourning, the child of this age has generally acquired such an image and while not necessarily functional over long periods of time, such an internalized image can be considered to be present over days and weeks.

However, at three and four, the child is particularly prone to specific distortions regarding the causality and meaning of loss. His egocentricity makes him vulnerable to the feeling that his mother disappeared because of something he did and he is therefore prone to feel responsible, ashamed and later, guilty over her loss. He may feel that he was unlovable and these feelings will be colored by his psycho-sexual stage of development. He may feel that his anality, his messiness, his failures at toilet training repelled the mother and he may also feel that his genital strivings, competitiveness and aggression drove her away.

From a cognitive standpoint, children from three to four are becoming more familiar with the concept of death. They have seen dead bugs and dead animals by the side of the road and they may have heard of the death of adult friends and relatives. Most three and four year olds ask questions about death and some even become worried about what it would mean to have mommy or daddy die. They often look for reassurance from parents that this will not happen for a long long time. At the same time, children of this age are not clear on what happens after death. As at earlier ages, they often believe that the deceased can come back to life. As such, the bereaved child of this age needs a great deal of support from the adults in his environment to answer his questions, to remind him that the deceased cannot come back even if she might have wanted to and to explain and re-explain what has happened. And while it may be explained to him that mommy can no longer breathe or walk or see or hear, he may defensively reverse this explanation in the belief that she is now omniscient – all knowing and all seeing, watching over him at all times. At the same time, the child of this age will be worried about who will continue to take care of him and meet his needs and will need many reminders about this. Moreover, the three to four-year-old does not understand that death can occur due to natural causes; up until approximately the age of eight or nine children often believe that death is always caused by an active agent – a disease, accident or intentional act by another person. Additionally, he may generalize from what he is told about his mother's death thinking that what happened to her will happen to others including himself.

Because he was in the process of establishing a firm internalized image of the mother when she died, it will be helpful to provide photographs for the child to keep and to remind the child of what mommy was like and what things he did and enjoyed with mommy. Adults should not shy away from mentioning mommy, telling stories about her and talking directly to the child about her. This is helpful to the young child who is desperate to know and remember that he was loved by his mother before she died.

CASE EXAMPLE: JACKY

Jacky was almost three and a half when he first presented for evaluation. This was eight months after his mother's suicide. He was an adorable blond boy with blue eyes and a sturdy build. He was at once ready for action and shy, alternating between running around to explore and hiding behind grandmother.

Jacky's father and grandmother were seen together for the first evaluatory session to provide information regarding Jacky's developmental history and to discuss their ideas regarding his current difficulties. Included in the discussion were their own reactions to Jacky's mother's death and their own current feelings.

Mrs. B., Jacky's grandmother, was a tall, attractive, outspoken 62-year-old woman, while Jack, her son, was a handsome 26-year-old man who seemed somewhat cowed in her presence. Together they described the events of the last several years: Jack and Marie were married when Jack was 21 and Marie was 20. After 3 months, Marie became pregnant. Although they had not planned on having a baby "so soon," Jack reported that they were "not unhappy" about the pregnancy. However, while Marie was pregnant, Jack's business began to lose money. Meanwhile, Marie proved that she did not know how to clean house or cook and as a result, Jack took care of most of the household duties while also tending to his failing business.

Jacky was born following a difficult labor. He was not breast fed because Marie found it to be "too much of a hassle." Jacky went everywhere with his young parents resulting in his having no set eating or sleep schedule. When Jacky was 2 years old, Marie became pregnant again. Jack reported that she became increasingly concerned about her appearance, upset that she could no longer fit into her designer jeans. She began to hide knives under her pillow at night and then to stay up all night. Jack was at his wit's end, and while he tried to take her for help at the local mental health center, she would not agree to go.

Jack tried to care for both Marie and Jacky, staying up all night to make sure that Marie did not hurt herself. One night he fell asleep in the early morning and when he woke up he found that Marie had locked herself in the bathroom and had suffocated herself in the bathtub. Jack was not sure what Jacky had seen or heard and he believed that Jacky knew nothing about what had happened. Later that day, he and his parents told Jacky that his mother "had gone to live with God" and that she was "up there," pointing to the sky.

Jack and Jacky moved in with Jack's parents. There Jacky was terrified of the bathtub and of his bed. Jacky's grandmother wondered if Marie might have tried to drown Jacky and whether she might also have beaten him in his bed. Jack did not share these suspicions although he did say that when Marie was afraid of hurting Jacky she sometimes went to sleep with him.

One month after his mother's death, Jacky became ill with the flu and experienced a major deterioration in functioning. He would not take any baths, he did not want his father to leave him for any reason and he clung desperately to his father whenever he attempted to go out.

At the time of the evaluation, Mrs. B reported that Jack was spending long hours at a new job and that he seemed depressed. She stated that she did not know whether to talk to him about Marie's death or about his current feelings. Jack, in a session alone, admitted to feeling angry with Marie's family for not having helped her more and he discussed his own guilt over her death. He felt considerable responsibility for her suicide and he admitted to feeling depressed and uninterested in dating or going out to have fun of any sort.

When it was time for Jacky's first appointment, he began to cry when it was suggested that he go into the playroom with the therapist. When Jacky's father agreed to come along, Jacky willingly took his hand and set off. Once in the play room Jacky immediately went to the doll house. He sat near the therapist on the floor and picked up two female dolls. He called both "mommy" and quickly threw one behind the house. When the therapist asked what happened to the mommy, Jacky replied, "She went up there" pointing to the sky. When the therapist asked, "Where's that?" He said "to the moon!"

Sessions with Jacky continued twice weekly. He played variations of the same game he had started in the first session variously saying that the mommy was on the roof of the house, on the moon or in space. He showed the people in the house going about their business until one day a gorilla came into the house and a fight broke out. When the therapist commented that the people must be very angry to be fighting so hard, Jacky himself began to punch the air. When the therapist asked why he was fighting he said, "I'm mad! I'm mad at God!"

Jacky was a three-year-old who did not understand death. When he was told that Mommy was "up there," he thought that this meant that she was on the roof of the house, on the moon, or in outer space. His understanding of his father's explanation about mommy's whereabouts was very concrete. As such, he believed that mommy continued to live— but elsewhere— in a place where she was not accessible to him. And when he was told that Mommy had gone to live with God, he became angry that God got to have his mommy and he did not. Moreover, Jacky's fears indicated that he may have seen more at the time of his mother's death than his father believed. His fear of the bath tub might well have been linked to the fact that his mother had killed herself in the tub. He might have felt that if he were to sit in the tub that he too would die.

Jacky passionately missed his mother. In her absence, he needed the love and support of his father and yet his father retreated into work. Jacky was angry—angry that God had his mother, angry at his mother for leaving, angry that his mother just sat on the roof and would not come down to him, and angry that his father was not more available to him. He was desperate for the love of a mother and one day, well into treatment he looked at his therapist with love in his eyes and asked her, "are you the mommy on the roof?"

This was a poignant moment for both Jacky and his therapist. It was clear that this young boy both missed his mother and desperately needed a mother substitute to meet his needs for understanding, nurturance, love and attachment. He was actively mourning his mommy, feeling both sad and angry about her absence, trying to understand what death was and attempting to find a new source of love to whom he could become attached.

THE 5 TO 6-YEAR-OLD

The five to six-year old child uses his mother as a secure base from which to explore the world, make friendships and learn new skills and concepts. He also loves his mother dearly and perhaps even romantically. The child of this age will vie with others for her attention and will take special comfort in her ministrations when sick or injured. If the mother of a five or six-year-old should die, his loss is profound. He may retreat from learning, from friends and from exploration of the world. He may regress to babyish behavior and he may show great sadness. Children of this age are capable of tolerating sad feelings for periods of time. They are also beginning to understand that death is a permanent state, making the death of a parent particularly heart breaking. They require loving support from the adults in their lives and, as at earlier ages, simple, direct answers to their many questions and concerns.

Often the issue arises as to whether a child should be allowed to go to his parent's funeral. It is advised that children do go and that they be seated with a loving adult who will be ready and willing to take them outside if they should need a break or become very upset. While previously it was thought best to "protect" young children by keeping them from the funeral, it is important that the child be able to see that others are sad too and that there is a community of people mourning the same loss as they.

LATENCY

The latency aged child (7 – 11) is a more knowledgeable, practical being than he was at earlier ages. He is interested in friends and school, games and learning. If the parent of a latency aged child should die, he will understand what has happened and he will be capable of sadness, anger, yearning and many other affects associated with his loss but he may utilize extensive defensive functioning against the experience and expression of feelings.

Symptoms often develop when a loss has occurred during this stage of development. For example, the child may cease doing homework.

When asked, he may say that he does not know why – but it is common for children of this age to feel that there is "no point" in doing homework if Mommy isn't there to show the work to or to help with the work as she may have done previously.

"Carmen" was a child profiled in a New York Times article about a mother and child and how they coped with the mother's impending death from AIDS. In an interview with Carmen when she was in her early 20's she discussed her wish as an 11-year-old to "forget" her mother's illness. She denied the seriousness of her mother's condition for a period of time and then when it became impossible to ignore, she spent time with another family where she admitted that she would spend hours without thinking about her mother. She tried to find another woman to be her "new mother" but in the end, she realized that her mother simply could not be replaced.

While Carmen is not typical of all latency aged children, her story does illustrate several points: in the absence of support or other adults with whom to process her experience, she utilized strong denial to protect herself from the pain and sadness of acknowledging her mother's condition; she separated herself from her mother for periods of time in order to give herself relief from her feelings of sadness and distress. However, her connection to her mother was so strong by the age of 12, when her mother died, that it was clear to Carmen after a period of wishing and hoping to replace her mother, that this was not possible.

Due to the strength of the defensive functioning in the latency aged child, he is particularly in need of adult help in sustaining the affects associated with loss rather than retreating into defensive denial and isolation of affect. The natural tendency of the latency aged child is to ward off disturbing emotions so as to protect his energy for learning, socialization and the other activities associated with this age.

PREADOLESCENCE AND ADOLESCENCE

From the cognitive standpoint, from 11 or 12 years old and onward, the child has acquired quite a mature concept of death. He knows that death is final, that it can happen due to natural causes or due to accident, illness, murder and the like and he knows that it happens to others and will happen to himself. However, at this point in life, the child will most often deny his own vulnerability and will not be likely to think too often about his own death unless something has occurred to cause anxiety about this subject.

Should the mother of a child of this age die, the child is capable of being practical about the event and he may try to hide his sadness. Defensive maneuvers will often be used to keep the affects associated with loss at bay. Adults are often surprised that children of this age do not show more signs of grief or talk more about the person who has died, however it is not unusual for them to hide their feelings and to avoid the subject as much as possible. At the same time, they may be curious about whether their surviving parent will remarry and if so, when.

The lack of outward signs of feeling, however, does not mean that the child is not grieving. In fact, quite the opposite. Starting in early adolescence, the child is capable of all the affects associated with mourning and of doing the work of mourning given adequate support. Whether he shows it or not, the child of this age will generally experience great sadness, anger, feelings of loneliness and abandonment. Given that the relationship prior to the loss was at least adequate, the child of this age will yearn for his lost parent. While he might wish for a replacement, he will not necessarily accept one easily. Despite his show of independence, the teenager still needs his mother. He relies on her emotionally and actually for the provision of love, support and nurturance and most of all, to be there as he experiments again and again with his autonomous strivings.

Pre-teens and teenagers will often need great encouragement to speak about their feelings and memories; they will also need to know that their needs will continue to be met and that they are still loved by the family members who remain. For those teens who are not provided with adequate support, encouragement to express their affects and to talk about their loss, mourning may be truncated, disrupted or delayed. At this age, mourning particularly comes into conflict with the normal developmental needs for autonomy and independence and as such, the child will often need special attention in order to proceed with the experiencing of affects associated with grief and mourning.

CASE EXAMPLE

T was 14 when her mother died. She was at home, eating dinner, while her mother prepared for a dinner party. When her mother went upstairs to change her clothes, T heard her father shout and then she heard him call 911. She sat frozen downstairs as the ambulance came and she overheard the ambulance attendant apologize to her father saying that there was nothing he could do for T's mother. T continued to sit frozen until she was so tired that she went upstairs to go to sleep. Her father returned from the hospital to find her in bed and he did not talk with her until the next day to tell her the cause of her mother's death.

T did not cry in front of her father. She took over some of her mother's duties around the house and refused to talk in any detail with anyone about her mother. She continued with school and with friends, but in a muted, less animated way than previously. Gradually, T took on more and more responsibilities at home and she acquired a job outside the house as soon as she was able. Outwardly, she appeared to be an extremely mature, self sufficient girl. She did well in school, went off to college and did well there, making friends and enjoying many activities.

The truth, however, which emerged in treatment in her 20's, was that T had been extremely bereft when her mother had died and she had been very frightened of what life would be like without her mother. She suppressed her terror and her sadness and became counter-dependent, insisting on doing for herself all that her mother had done for her and more. Affects associated with mourning were suppressed and only emerged in the presence of the therapist who gently explored T's thoughts and feelings about her mother's death.

LATE ADOLESCENCE AND EARLY ADULTHOOD

Teenagers and young adults, despite their increased autonomy and independence, their ability to function in the world, and their more mature judgement and intellectual capacity, STILL need their mothers. Throughout later adolescence and young adulthood, it is important to them to have a home base in order to be able to leave it and to come back to it. In a way, not unlike that of the two-year-old, in the late teens and early 20's, the individual is experimenting again with separation and individuation. They are forming their identities, their values and beliefs and their confidence in their own abilities. Having a place to roost and a mother who loves them can provide a sense of security while their internal milieu is ever changing.

Losing a mother during this stage of life is disruptive, though in most cases not as disruptive as loss that occurs earlier. Emotions are less threatening at this age than previously and outward signs of grief and mourning are common. The older teenager and young adult CAN experience the affects associated with death, they understand the permanency of death, and they can do the work of mourning—especially if they are provided with support from the surviving parent and other loving adults. However, the death of a parent at this age may be disruptive in terms of their continued development of autonomy and independent pursuits. Without adequate support they may choose to drop out of college and/or to return home. Concerns over the well being of the surviving parent and other siblings may preoccupy the young adult.

CASE EXAMPLE

R was 18 when her father died suddenly. After the funeral, when she was back at college she found herself worried that her mother would be lonely, living in the family house all by herself. R dreamed up ways of having other students go to live in the mother's house while on internships in the city where the mother lived. R felt satisfied that she was finding company for her mother while simultaneously neglecting to examine her own loneliness and feelings of needing additional emotional support. Finally, after the third group of students had moved out, her mother called her at college and told her to PLEASE not send any more students! R's mother said that she was doing just fine on her own and did not want to buy groceries or prepare beds and meals for anyone else anymore!

R's worry about her mother was a clear projection of her own feelings and needs. As an older teenager, she was so busy preserving her independence and autonomy that she had defensively denied her deepest feelings about the loss of her father.

OBSTACLES TO MOURNING

Developmental immaturity is one obstacle to mourning that, as stated, has been discussed at length and with great debate throughout the literature on mourning in childhood. However, there are many other obstacles to mourning in infants and children. Those who are not provided with an adequate substitute caretaker, those who experience many additional external stressors at the time of the loss and those who did not have an adequate relationship with the mother prior to her loss may experience difficulties in the effort to mourn her death. Incomplete mourning, delayed mourning, prolonged mourning or an absence of grief may result.

The lack of an adequate substitute caretaker is one of the most profound obstacles to mourning and to ongoing development which a bereaved child can face. The infant or child who has lost his mother requires love and nurturance for his psychological survival. The provision of a substitute caretaker who is able to maintain the child's routines, to be there to help the infant or child to regulate himself, to provide for his physical needs and to help him feel loved and cared for is absolutely crucial.

The presence of additional stressors can affect the bereaved child's ability to feel his own feelings and to go forward with the mourning process. Children who are forced to move to a new home, who experience the surviving parent as withdrawn, depressed or distraught, those whose economic circumstances become unstable, those who must deal with illness or injuries of their own or of other family members are at risk. For example, an 11-year-old girl was seen in a clinic setting in individual psychotherapy. Her mother had no idea what had happened with her, but suddenly the girl's grades had slipped and she had become withdrawn. In the course of the evaluation, the therapist found out from the girl herself that she had recently moved to a new house. The house she had lived in previously had been the one where she last lived with her father before he had committed suicide. It was also the place where he committed suicide. Over the course of several sessions, the girl was able to talk about the fact that she had never mourned her father's death. When he died she felt she had to become the model child to make her mother happy. She did well in school and helped her mother around the house and with her younger brother. When the family moved, the girl experienced the loss of the home as a reminder of the loss of her father and the mourning she had delayed began to occur and to express itself in her sad mood and in her withdrawal from previously enjoyed activities.

And finally, Bowlby and Robertson (1952) observed that children who did not have an adequate relationship with their mother prior to separation from her did not experience the typical sadness, yearning and searching, regression, etc following her loss. Instead, they adapted to their new situation readily and expressed interest in the adults around them. While this may seem a better response than that experienced by children who are bereft, this behavior suggests poor ability to attach to intimate others and portends poorer attachment availability in the future.

OUTCOMES

The research literature is mixed as to whether early parental death predisposes individuals to clinical depression or physiological illness, while there is a definite causal relationship with other psychopathology such as anxiety disorders, phobias, panic attacks and schizophrenia. As stated previously, complex interactions are thought to occur between the loss experience and variables such as the child's age at the time of the loss, the expression of grief or the lack thereof, the provision of an adequate substitute caretaker or the lack thereof, the occurrence of stressful events following the loss, the relationship with the surviving parent and the mental health of the surviving parent (Stroebe, et al., 2008).

Bifulco, et al., (1987) demonstrated that poor parental care following loss proved to be a strong mediator of the relationship between early parental loss and adult depression. Saler and Skolnick (1992) found that adults who described their surviving parent as neglectful, lacking in affection, over controlling or overprotective reported significantly more experiences of depression (Stroebe, et al., p.22). Kendler, Gardner, and Prescott (2006) found that early parental loss is a pathway to major depression in adult men, but numerous other factors also influence this pathway, such as genetic risk, low parental warmth, neurosis, low educational attainment, drug use and later stressful events. In women, early parental loss was also found to be a pathway to adult depression as well as to decreased educational attainment and poor interpersonal relationships later in life.

More research is needed to understand what the protective factors are in terms of the promotion of positive outcomes for children who have experienced early parental death. As might be expected given the above, a strong relationship with the surviving parent has been shown as protective against depression and deterioration in functioning in one of the few studies that has been performed on this topic (Lueken, 2000). This study also suggests that uncontrollable stress in childhood can, in some cases, given the appropriate external support, result in enhanced adaptive capacities later in life (Stroebe et al., 2001).

These findings in the research literature are congruent with the previously mentioned opinions of Bowlby, E. Furman, R. Furman, and this author. Support for children who have lost a parent early in life is crucial to scaffold and support the expression of affects associated with mourning, to help the child to understand the reality of their loss, to help them to work through the loss and to provide them with the love and support for their ongoing developmental needs.

Further research and clinical reports are needed to continue to answer the questions posed here: to what extent can children who have experienced the early loss of their mother fully mourn? To what extent can these children re-attach to a new love object, and what are the circumstances—internal and external—which allow and encourage these outcomes?

BIBLIOGRAPHY

Abraham, K., 1924. A short study of the development of the libido; viewed in light of mental disorders. In Selected papers on psychoanalysis. London: Hogarth Press.

Ainsworth, M., Blehar, M., Water, E. and Wall, S. 1978. Patterns of Attachment: Hillsdale, NJ, Earlbaum.

Anthony, S.1940. The child's discovery of death. New York: Harcourt Brace.

Anthony, S. 1981. The discovery of death in childhood in childhood and after. Sydney, Australia: Penguin Books.

Bowlby, J., 1980. Attachment and loss: vol. 3. Loss: Sadness and depression. Harmondsworth, England: Penguin Books.

Bowlby, J. 1961. Processes of mourning. International Journal of Psycho-Analysis, 42, 317-340.

Brody, S., Siegel, M. & Rosenblum, A. (1992). The Evolution of Character. Birth to 18 Years: A Longitudinal Study. NY: International University Press.

Brody, S. & Axelrad, S. (1978). Mothers, Fathers, and Children: Explorations in the Formation of Character in the First Seven Years. NY: International Univ Pr

Deutsch, H. 1937. The absence of grief. Psychoanalytic Quarterly, 6, 12–22.

Freud, A., Burlingham, D., 1944. Infants without families. New York: International Univ. Press.

Freud, S. 1917. Mourning and melancholia. Standard Edition 14:237-258.

Furman, E. 1974. A Child's Parent Dies. New Haven: Yale University Press.

Furman, R. A. Death and the young child: some preliminary considerations. Psychoanalytic Study of the Child, 19, 321-333.

Greenacre, P (1960). Considerations regarding the parent-infant relationship. Int. J. Psychoanal. vol. XLI, pp. 571-584.

Grollman, E. 1967. Explaining Death to Children, Boston: Beacon Press.

Jacobson, E. 1957. Denial and repression. Journal of the American Psychoanalytic Association, 5:61-92.

Klein, M. 1953. A contribution to the psychogenesis of manic depressive states. In Love, guilt and reparation and other papers, 1921 – 1946. London: Hogarth.

LeShan, E. 1976. Learning to say goodbye: When a parent dies. New York: MacMillan.

Lindemann, E. 1944. Symptomatology and management of acute grief. American Journal of Psychiatry, 101:141-148.

Lopez, T. and Kliman, G. 1979. Memory, reconstruction and mourning in the analysis of a four-year-old child. Psychoanalytic Study of the Child, 34, 235-271.

Mahler, M., Pine, F. and Bergman, A. 1975. The psychological birth of the human infant. New York: Basic Books.

Masur, C. 1991. The crisis of early maternal loss. Play Therapy with Children in Crisis. pp.164 – 166. New York: Guilford Press.

Masur, C. 2001. Can women mourn their mothers? in Three Faces of Mourning, Akhtar, Salman (Ed). Jason Aaronson.

Masur, C. 1991. Alternative approaches in treating the bereaved child in Young People and Death, John D. Morgan (Ed.): Charles Press.

Nagera, H. (1970). Children's reactions to the death of important objects: A developmental approach. Psychoanalytic Study of the Child, 25, 360-400.

Nagera, H. 1981. The developmental approach to childhood psychopathology. NY: Aaronson

Spitz, R. 1965. The First Year of Life. New York: International Universities Press.

Stroebe, M., Hanson, R. O., Stroebe, W., and Schut, H. (Eds.) 2001. Handbook of bereavement research: Consequences, coping and care. Washington D C.: American Psychological Assoc.

Wolfenstein, M. 1966. How is mourning possible? Psychoanal. Study of the Child, 21, 93-123.

Wolfenstein, M. 1969. Loss, rage and repetition. Psychoanalytic Study of the Child, 24, 432-460.

Worden, J. W. 1991. Grief counseling and grief therapy: a handbook for the mental health practitioner (2nd ed.). New York: Springer Publishing Company.

Bio

CORRINE MASUR, PSY.D., is a clinical psychologist and psychoanalyst who has been in private practice for over thirty years. She maintains offices in Center City, Philadelphia and Exton, PA. Dr. Masur is on the faculty of the Psychoanalytic Center of Philadelphia and is Co-Director of the Parent-Child Center. She is a Co-Founder of the Philadelphia Center for Psychoanalytic Education and the Philadelphia Declaration of Play. She has written on the subjects of early childhood bereavement, the development of trust in childhood, the fear of mortality in adults, and the psychoanalytic theory of development.

CHAPTER 11

An Unexpected Pathway for Interpsychic Exchange: Music in the Analysis of a Young Adult

Rosa Spagnolo, M.D.

An Unexpected Pathway for Interpsychic Exchange: Music in the Analysis of a Young Adult

Rosa Spagnolo, M.D.

We usually consider creativity and art accordingly, as a way to explore and disclose the human mind. D. Winnicott (1953) linked primary creativity with the origins of life in the primitive mother-child relationship. In his opinion (Winnicott, 1953, 1970) the baby creates the object "mother" placing her in a transitional area between me and not me, during the early months of life. The infant uses creativity to conjure an illusion using its omnipotent ability to create and find the object without any adaptation to reality. Musical creativity is different. It is a pre-verbal communication, and is present in the intrauterine life via the sounds and rhythms of the mother's body. Quoting Di Benedetto (1991, p 418): "If we think for a moment about what music consists of, we will find that it contains elements derived from the bodily experience. The fundamental components of music are rhythm, harmony and melody. Rhythm is obviously related to the heart beat; harmony, which acts as an element of cohesion, is somewhat analogous to the experiencing of connective tissue, of a sustaining web. Melody, which consists of rising and falling sounds, could be like air traveling along a sinus and can be regarded as the breathing of music. Music is also a set of sound stimuli, which strike our receptive organs not only acoustically, but also at a tactile level, so that it reproduces the primeval "bath of sounds" (Anzieu 1985), one of the earliest experiences which defines the limits of the body. In such a physical space, representations, let alone thinkable elements, can't yet exist."

Thus the musical receptivity precedes the creation of a transitional space. This means that the power of musical creativity, and above all its powerful communication, is not connected to the transitional phenomena nor to the cognitive process. The neuroscience of affect today outlines that: "Music derives its affective charge directly from dynamic aspects of brain systems that normally control real emotions and which are distinct from, albeit highly interactive with, cognitive processes." (Panksepp & Bernatzky, 2002, p. 135). Throughout the psychoanalytic treatment we spend a lot of time in an affective area (transference/countertransference phenomenon) out of consciousness, with any possibility to take control of what happens inward. Being in contact with our and the patient's inner world would mean living together in a double register wherein, usually, no one loses his subjectivity. Sometimes, with patients who adopt primitive defenses music helps us to restore contact when it seems lost. Music has the ability to dwell in a physical space without belonging to anyone, and this allows everybody to use it in a subjective emotional way. What I'm proposing is to enhance the concept of transitional space. Brody's paper in 1980 showed the limits of Winnicott's statements on illusion and transitional phenomenon, thereby elucidating the concept of interpsychic realm (Bolognini 2004).

It is within this space/psychic extension that S. Bolognini (2004) has placed his studies on the interpsychic dimension which he describes as follows: "The 'interpsychic' is an extended psychic dimension, regarding the joint functioning and reciprocal influences of two minds. The concepts of 'subjectivity' and 'person' can be included in the 'interpsychic'. They can sometimes overlap with each other, and sometimes all three together can overlap, but they do not necessarily coincide" (Bolognini 2004, p. 337).

We could describe the interpsychic not only as a corridor through which to convey information, but also as a transition zone between different psychic dimensions (those marked by subjectivity). Let's consider the example of the collective dimension of the virtual space network, which has assumed the characteristics of a planetary interpsychic extended among millions of people, which do not belong to anyone, but which is co-produced by everyone and influences the individual psyche transforming it continually. This "'wide-band' functioning (The interpsychic), in that it allows the natural, uninterrupted and not dissociated coexistence of

344

mental states in which the object is recognized in its separateness alongside others in which the recognition is less clear" (Bolognini 2004, p.345). Learning more about the features of the interpsychic could provide us with tools for further exploration so that we might be able to access this extended psychic network more easily. In particular, becoming familiar with visiting the area of the interpsychic can be essential with those patients who will not allow the analyst to enter the working chambers of the psyche (the intrapsychic), therefore requiring long halts in the antechamber of the Self waiting for "something to happen".

Starting from these two top issues, the interpsychic (Bolognini 2004, 2011) and music, which: "*Like dreams, serves as a point of entry to affect and the unconscious*" (Nagel J.J., 2008, p.508), we will explore the potential of the latter to stretch along as an interpsychic conduit between the analyst and the patient.

Through the clinical material presented, we will reflect on a young patient's analysis, in which music has given us the opportunity to open an unexpected pathway of exchange between two closed minds unable to communicate. This openness, unexpectedly introduced by rock music,[1] has allowed the transmission of reciprocal information (emotions, affections, traces of memories) capable of restarting those intrapsychic processes that sometimes appeared to be blocked by an excessive recurrence (recursive use) of the same images.

Y., is 20 years old, has black hair and eyes, and he is tall and strong. He finished high school with outstanding grades and now lives at home, isolated, trying to figure out what he wants to do. He spends the day wondering what would make him happy and what the best choice for his future might be. Ever since our first talk he has been repeating to himself, and to

---

[1] "It should also be noted that some rock music, with its often subversive, antiestablishment, counterculture lyrics and performance practices, can play an important role, especially in adolescence and early adulthood (transitional developmental stages that entail the relinquishing of previously held self-object representations), in providing a Kohutian-like mirroring and affirmation of experience, and in serving to lessen feelings of isolation or alienation. Here music contains and assuages overwhelming affects and thus can serve a consoling function similar to that of more conventional mourning music" A. Stein, (2004, p. 795).

me, that he fails to feel convinced of any choice made. His mother, with whom he has lived since his parents separated when he was about 10 years old, has just decided to move to another country, leaving him alone.

In the psychotic temptation, the withdrawal of the ego from external reality and the weakening of reality itself play an important role in the organization of an early stage of psychosis (Freud 1924). When I meet him, he was coming fast down a narrow ridge that leads straight to psychotic withdrawal. I can perceive the possible occurrence of a structural form of psychosis, as described by Monniello (2012): "They are the psychosis without a delusional or hallucinatory episode, at least initially. They are often much more present in the second part, or the end of adolescence, that is, between 16 and 20 years old ... Being on top of the list here the problem of narcissistic withdrawal, autoerotic negativizing and instinctual de-fusion. The aggressive drive unrelated to those erotic ones will attack, in this case especially, ...thought as a whole".

Throughout the first months of therapy he rarely spoke of his parents. His voice was low, monotonous, without any emotional color. He spoke about his few friends and his lack of desire around attending university. He would oscillate continuously between an extremely passive interactive closure and timid attempts at emotional contact with his lonely and suffering core. As soon as contact with his core takes place, Y., who is gifted with a high level of intelligence, spots the source of suffering and deletes it through a crescendo of obsessive thoughts, a sort of: "Undoing what has been done and isolating" (Freud 1926), saying: "*The problem has gone, it no longer exists – solved.*" My words, which he apparently agrees with, follow the same fate, being cleared through this crescendo of obsessive thoughts centered around one idea: "*This is not a problem.*"

Months have gone by and we are close to the summer break. We are exactly at the same point of departure. Then, one day, in the middle of the session, my mobile phone ringtone went off breaking in on our session, as I had left it turned on in the next room. He jumped up in his chair saying, with much emphasis: "*But, they're the Muse, Starlight. But you don't listen to this music, do you?*" "*Well! Sorry, but why not?* "I replied immediately and spontaneously. And he goes on: "*Well, it is just that I believed psychoanalysts were those ancient things that listen to Jethro Tull, or sort of Ian Anderson's flute, or at most Pink Floyd, crying over "wish you were here", but the Muse…no way! Are you telling me that you are going to the concert in July!"* Then I say: *"So, you, what kind of music do you listen to?"* *"Rolling Stones."* Disbelievingly, thinking I had failed to get it right, I add: *"You mean Rolling Stones from the 60/70s?"* *"Yeah! The one and only, the unbeatable ones!"* He replies with a broad smile. As I smile back to him, I add: *"It seems that we have swapped positions! Sorry, but you should listen to Muse, Green Day, Linkin Park whereas I, the old one, should be a fan of Jethro Tull, Bob Dylan, Lou Reed, and enjoy the company of The Rolling Stones, I am the one who belongs to the last century."* He laughs amused, surprised by the ringtone and my reaction. It was the first time I have seen him laughing. He adds: *"I'm going to Mom's for two months, but then I'll be back in July for The Rolling Stones concert, if you're still here, I'll see you."* And so it will be.

The ringtone has been our "cat-flap"[2] and after this brief interaction, his treatment takes a different pace, sometimes slow, sometimes fast and relentless. Together we manage to climb onto the first step towards confidence in the treatment (he no longer asked why analysis) and then towards the sharing of dreams, emotions and affects. However, there will be long dark halts to progress, in which he actively locks all forms of communication in an attempt to contain the suffering that envelops him. Music manages to open, sometimes suddenly and unexpectedly, an interpsychic corridor through which there is a flow to the exchange of thoughts between us. This starts clandestinely somewhere (impossible to know in advance who will start and what the subject of trade will be) and has the power to reboot both the intrapsychic communication and the inter-subjective exchange. V. Zuckerkandl (1973) claims, in several passages, that music dissolves the boundaries between the self and

---

[2] "I would like to pause briefly on this element of the 'cat-flap'. In my opinion, it is a good symbol for a structural (it is part of the door) and functional device (it was specifically designed so that the cat can carry out its function of catching mice inside and outside the house) that is not only intra-psychic, but also Interpsychic. The cat-flap is quite distinct from the door, which allows the passage of people, and from incidental cracks, which allow the passage of mice, clandestine, parasitical guests that harm the community/inter-psychic-relational apparatus" (Bolognini 2004, p.343).

others; thesis taken from Rose in 2004, when he asserts that music can be used as an important indicator of the permeability of psychic boundaries (Dimitrijevic, A. 2008). When this boundary-fading occurs during the session, the therapist must have the analytical skill to make a space for the exchange of information that flows freely, and to prepare to capture the material to make it operative within the analytical process as well as to mobilize new therapeutic resources.

Let's go back to the analysis of our clinical material. The patient began to attend university. He expressed his unresolved reluctance to attend through the performance of exhausting rituals (how to get there, which lectures to attend, what number of pages must be studied) he will mention and describe in detail. I sometimes joke about his obsessive style only to lighten the suffocation I feel during the session. I also try to bypass the resistance to look for new resources, saying, for example, that the best part of going to university is the encounter with that world of varied characters that he describes but, it seems to me, he keeps away from meeting new people. He will defend himself from these invitations, having perceived them as too seductive, so the next time he will attend our meeting with his headphones and the music turned on: "*Sorry, I got hooked on Bauhaus;*" then I will listen to a bit and I comment: "*Wow I can't tell if they are just sad or deeply mourning.*"

He tells me that he would like to talk about this, but he feels ashamed because he feels he is as sick as the singer. I look at him in silence for a long time while the colorful images of a varied university world and this sad music run across my mind. Meanwhile I realize that he is having a minor panic attack (he sweats, he suffers shortness of breath and he asks if the window is open or closed). I look at him intently, and I tell him: "*We are not Peter Murphy wedged between sadness and death, alone in the dark ... we also have other instruments that we know and we can play.*"

Then he calmed down and talked about his panic attacks. On this occasion, while stopping in the interpsychic transition of music listening, we have been able to "fish" lived experiences (and symptoms) of malaise never expressed before.

"Additionally, music can function as a surrogate or auxiliary cry or wail, an externalization of an intolerably overwhelming, incomprehensible, or crushing internal state. It can give voice to feelings otherwise inexpressible, to the vast areas of overwhelming affect for which spoken and written language may be inadequate. Music is in essence speaking for the self that is obliterated or muted by despair, or symbolizing experiences and affects otherwise too intense or overwhelming to express directly" (Stein A., 2004, p. 807).

The close contact with such experiences was still intolerable at that time. Therefore, during the subsequent sessions, he would arrange for a cancellation of affects, undoing what has been done (ungeschehenmachen, Freud 1926). In the patient's words: *"What has been said is not a problem, I am able to control everything by thinking while talking about it that it is all absolutely useless. I'd better put it all under the rug".*

We went on like this until one day he came to his session seemingly alarmed and he complained about not getting any warmth, that our relationship is not a human one. *"There are no hugs or caresses or any sort of contact. It is not an even exchange, there is nothing human."*

I sensed that he was coming into contact with bizarre objects (Bion, 1992), hard, stinging objects which he usually kept away. However, at this point they were breaking into our room, harassing him (he looked like he was suffering) and he added hastily: *"I'd better keep everything hidden under the rug otherwise I might feel like those bits of dust... that are tossed around the room....later it is going to be too tiring for me to put all this back under the rug."*

Very cautiously, I try to put together all these sensations and images (the dust floating in silence) and I realize that he seems to want to show me something of himself (the dust floating) and/or his relationship with Mom or Dad (the human relationship with me), but it seems also that the only thing I can do is pick up the carpet and help him hide everything. He calms down and talks to me about his Mom. Young, beautiful. *"Mom is so changeable, I'm sometimes afraid that you might be the same. She is capable of great closeness, but then she is so hypercritical she will not miss a thing or let you go with it. You cannot say "no" to her or she will dig her heels in and cling to the death. Dad is fluid and evanescent, inconsistent always ready to doubt everything, in constant conflict with her. I carry these two halves inside and sometimes I do not know how to keep them together."*

As he keeps on talking about them I can picture them in my mind, almost seeing them with him, like a little baby lying between them under the rug, almost lifeless, not breathing (the same asphyxiation mutually experienced in our sessions) so that they will not get into conflict, so as to avoid having to choose. I let him talk till the end while I listen in rapt silence. When he is finally leaving I will tell him:

"I have had the impression that today there were many people in here, me, you, Mom, Dad, and even all your stuff out of the carpet and our stuff, the one we are always speaking about. " He smiles and asks for a spare minute to tell me a couple of things: *"A good one and a bad one. The first: Before coming to see you ... I had been listening to the Rolling Stones while dancing and singing along with them I managed to feel my body... the second only, -sad and mourning – is that I sometimes feel like a piece of rotting flesh to which I add some spice so as not to perceive its smell."*

I instantly thought of an excerpt from Di Benedetto's work: "Music is a unique language, different from all other human languages. Unlike other languages, which tend to move from the body to the mind, music prompts our knowledge to shift from the mind to the body, from the symbolic to the sensory, towards a musical matrix with a wide potential and an emotional nature" (Di Benedetto, 1991, p. 424). The investment, product of the body in motion when dancing in an emotional contact with the music, involves various sensory levels forcing the mind to perceive both the inside and outside, which are confusingly intertwined. In my opinion, his tiring, hard and secret work of covering up (spices, perfumes, filters, carpets), allowed him to bear contact with the dead or inanimate parts. These parts also had their stench or sharpness and they burst into the obsessive order he had painstakingly built, making him scared. I realize that unless I managed to hold those elements, now flowing through the interpsychic corridor, they would be back under the rug becoming unavailable for further transformations. We share my concerns of that and he begins to dream.

His dreams are inhabited both by those few people he meets and the sudden irruption of bizarre elements. They are indecipherable and we hold them without rushing to shape them. There is, for instance, his dream of a strange dancing of colors in movement that has anguished him since he was a child: "*It is a dream that comes and goes, I do not know how to describe it but it has been chasing me since I was a child. It lacks images and seems to be made up of both a calm and bustling part, the first part is yellow and I am sailing in it, the second is green / black. It is a form that hits me; as if they were punches that strike me and toss me up and down, but they are not definite forms or real things.*"

He looks around in the room searching for the boundaries between yellow and green. Next he talks about a television series "Walking Dead". I can see that he is quite distressed. I say to him: "*Sometimes even what appears to be just virtual, formless, or unreal, like dreams and music, have the power to evoke emotions and feelings as real and deep as all the things you're telling me today.*"

He will dwell upon describing this feeling of non-recognition. I reckon there is also a lack of recognition of parts of the self that he is still unable to contact. Next session he bears an expression of disgust on his face throughout the entire session, which alternate with an equally bizarre oral tic. They were a strange bodily choreography which matched his discourse. Every corridor has been blocked again and, except for those strange grimaces he made up rhythmically and repeatedly, nothing betrayed an unconscious discourse among parts of the Self. We know the repetition can be sometimes organized on non-symbolized relational tracks. Every analyst is expected to recognize them since they come up within the analytical session in the form of corporeal elements, such as gestures, movements, postures, prosody. So, I remain entangled in those bizarre images until his return. Y. leaves earlier for the summer holidays and reassures me that he will return because there is a concert he has to go to. It is mid-July when he texts me, during his session time, he is being taken to the hospital. He is described as being in a delirious state with panic attacks and will be given some medication. He keeps writing a lot of messages over the course of several hours. He is deeply distressed because his mother does not want to send him back to Italy and everything seems to blur around him. He does not know what to do. Being so far from him, I actually do not know what to say, and after reassuring him not to worry about his panic attacks (which were not an acute psychosis). I write: "*Why don't you stop to think a little about your music*".

I sent him this image

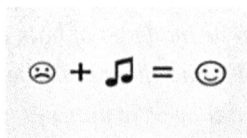

and he sent back this

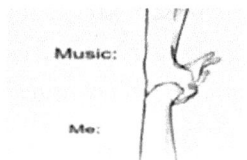

When his holidays were over he returned and said: "H*ow did you manage to know I was thinking of the Rolling Stones? I had to go on living to be able to listen to them again!*"

From then on, we spoke more frankly about his hypochondria and his suicidal thoughts. His incoherently strange and bizarre speech that seemed express his experience of the waves of music could be acknowledged playfully: "Y*ou are lending words to the waves so that they can also become intelligible*"; My theoretical understanding of my intervention was that I was attempting to transform traumatic hallucinatory into symbolic forms which could then be freed from the compulsion to repeat the traumatic experience of the primary relationship. I feel that the original feeble interpsychic channel has now become a corridor built up on a stronger structure through which to travel.

A few months after an episode of derealization and depersonalization, to which we have repeatedly returned, he seems once again lost in his obsessions. I say something about this work of disconnection and isolation of affects from the bond with people and his defensive operation which requires so much energy to keep it going. He becomes confused, gets lost. Later he emerges talking about electronic sound systems in which using the same basic elements the musicians can produce many different effects: "*It is a real sound scaffolding that they manage to build even though they are combining only a few elements,"* he adds while continuing to talk about the structure of the music.

I discover myself thinking of what the psychic space is made of, what kind of scaffolding supports it and whether the so-called scaffolding may be similar to that "Geomag construction" whose structure can be changed by putting on or removing metal spheres and rods. I think that even our psychic space is made up like a "Geomag", adding or subtracting pieces to build the framework that will momentarily support our work. At the end of the session, he says: *"Today we have had a strange session, what did we talk about? Even so, I don't know why, but it seemed very nice."* I answer him (but maybe I am answering myself): *"We found this expression: "sound scaffolding" and we entered an interpsychic space where each of us contributed with a piece of something to build a scaffolding. Music helped us to feel that things can be shared without losing our own subjectivity".*

When he leaves, clearly satisfied, I am completely aware of being the most grateful for this gift: the scaffolding of sounds that will definitely enable us to build new melodies which helps me hold all those bizarre elements that wait for a new transformation.

CONCLUSION

There are a lot of remarkable works regarding music and psychoanalysis such as those by Nagel (2008), Grassi (2014), Stein (2004), Di Benedetto (1991, 2001), Rose (1991, 1993, 2004), to name just a few, which discuss the interaction with each other at different levels: from the pre-symbolic constituent elements of music to music listening. Unfortunately, it would take me too long to go into each theoretical model related to artistic creation. Instead, I would like to highlight that the premise of our work, which is obviously what we have in common, is the analytic listening. I tried to bring it close to music listening. I think that the missing object might be fancied or imagined, but it can't be heard or experienced without any sensory input.

My impression is that the patient's primary relationship was one of marginal cathexis, or non-investment. It probably lacked music or rhythm. For this reason, the patient could not bring the sonorous elements of speech with appropriate tone (monotone) nor any rhythm or music. Patient's living in this music-less internal world experience perceptive elements as bizarre, and this can generate an internal chaos. The analyst should read through, infer sense, and bind these traces to help him to emerge from the cacophonic chaos of his inner world. Through several sound presentations, it was possible to speak about the disharmonic affective identifications provided by his parents. From this moment on the sharing of affective states will go through the most mature expression of the linguistic structuralism of narrative style and the process will also get nourished by the words (words lent to the waves). Once the transit had been opened, by the music listening, it was possible to work on the intrapsychic register by reshuffling the present traces and new transcriptions.

I would like to conclude by returning to the two fundamental initial issues, music and the interpsychic. I am convinced that their interweaving effect has promoted that particular kind of listening together with the patient. Beside other observational vertices which could have been used to describe what was happening inside the analyst's room, such as Bion's reflections on bizarre elements (1992), I would draw a few points of contact between music and psychoanalysis that could instead be of some contribution to further investigations. First of all, melody. Aniruddh D. Patel, in his book "Music, Language and The Brain" (2008, Oxford University Press, London) defines melody by means of two strategic perspectives: on the one hand, it can be seen as sound sequences that contain a lot of affective, syntactic, pragmatic and empathetic information and on the other, it can qualify as melody by virtue of the rich mental patterns it engenders in a listener.

Here comes the clinical reference to the short musical sequence listened to on my cell phone. Its melodic structure, more complex than our own voices, may have promoted the opening of the interpsychic corridor that enabled the start of a kind of communication less related to the repetition of the usual elements (historical narrative of the same tracks).

Secondly let's not forget rhythm. L. Grassi (2014) describes the rhythm at the origin of the life where some basic rhythms combine the visual element, the sound element and other perceptive channels. The rhythm is in the alternation from night and day, sleep and wakefulness, presence and absence. In other words, rhythm accompanies human development throughout life. For this psychoanalytic treatment it has been very important to connect the obsessive rhythm of words beaten in the same way to the chaos of some speechless and shapeless oneiric movement.

Finally, I get back to the interpsychic drawing another potentiality to be explored: "The ability to frequent the interpsychic with an acceptable degree of awareness and technical know-how, to reduce the random nature of analytic developments and open up new access routes to the intrapsychic, therefore requires constant self-analysis, a sense of respect and continuity with the work of those who have gone before us in a century of psychoanalytic research, and 'trustful resignation' in the extraordinary paradoxical nature of our work" (Bolognini 2004, p. 353).

REFERENCES

Bion, W.R. (1992). Cogitations. (Edited by F. Bion). London: Karnac Books.

Bolognini, S. (2004). Intrapsychic-Interpsychic. Int. J. Psycho-Anal., 85:337-358

Bolognini, S. (2011). Secret Passages towards the Unconscious: Styles and Techniques of Exploration. Ital. Psychoanal. Annual, 5:75-87.

Brody, S. (1980). Transitional Objects: Idealization of a Phenomenon. Psychoanalytic Quarterly, 49:561-605

Di Benedetto, A. (1991). Listening to the Pre-Verbal: The Beginning of the Affects; Rivista di Psicoanalisi, 37:400-426

Di Benedetto, A. (2001). Before Words. Psychoanalytical Listening to the Unsaid through the Medium of Art. London, Free Association Books, 2005.

Dimitrijevic, A. (2008). Between Couch and Piano: Psychoanalysis, Music, Art and Neuroscience, by Gilbert J. Rose, Brunner-Routledge, New York, 2004; J. Am. Acad. Psychoanal. Dyn. Psychiatr., 36:763-766

Freud, S. (1924). The Loss of Reality in Neurosis and Psychosis. SE 19

Freud, S. (1926a). Inhibitions, Symptoms and Anxiety. SE 20

Grassi, L. (2014). The dimension of sound and rhythm in psychic structuring and analytic work. The Italian Psychoanal. Annual, 2014

Monniello, G. (2012). Un giorno questa adolescenza ti sarà utile. Soggettualizzazione e principio di realtà. 10° Convegno Nazionale dei gruppi Italiani di Psicoterapia AGIPPsA; Adolescenza e psicoanalisi oggi, Roma, 13-14 ottobre 2012

Nagel, J.J. (2008). Psychoanalytic Perspectives on Music: An Intersection on the Oral and Aural Road. Psychoanalysis Q., 2008, 77: 507-5

Panksepp J., Bernatzky G. (2002). Emotional sounds and the brain: the neuro-affective foundations of musical appreciation. Behavioral Processes 60 (2002) 133 155

Patel, A. D. (2008). Music, Language and the Brain, Oxford University Press, London

Rose, G. J. (1991). Abstract art and emotion: Expressive form and a sense of wholeness. J. Amer. Psychoanal. Assn., 39, 131-156.

Rose, G.J. (1993). On form and feeling in music. In S. Feder & R. Karmel (Eds.), Psychoanalytic explorations in music? Second series.

Rose, G. J. (2004). Between Couch and Piano: Psychoanalysis, Music, Art and Neuroscience. Brunner-Routledge, New York.

Stein, A. (2004). Music, Mourning, and Consolation Journal of the American Psychoanalytic Association, 52:783-811

Winnicott, D.W. (1953). Transitional objects and transitional phenomena. Int. J. Psychoanal., 34:89-97

Winnicott, D.W. (1971). Playing and Reality. London: Tavistock Publications

Zuckerkandl, V. (1973). Sound and Symbol, vol. 2: Man the Musician, trans. Norbert Guterman. Princeton, NJ: Princeton University Press, 1973

BRIEF BIO

ROSA SPAGNOLO, MD, is a Pediatric Neurologist and Child Psychiatrist, A Child and Adolescent Psychotherapist, Psychoanalyst, Full Member of

Italian Psychoanalytical Society (SPI), and an IPA Member.

She currently lives and works in Rome. In the Public Health practice, she works at the Institute Filippo Smaldone, for the Rehabilitation of Deafness, Learning and Speech Disabilities, and Developmental Disorders. She is primarily an expert in the treatment of Cognitive Delays, Autism, and Psychoses in Children; she has been working for over 20 years with newborns with neuro-motor and rare diseases, like Cerebral Palsy, Epilepsy, Severe Sensory Disorders. Dr. Spagnolo is also a Psychotherapist/Psychoanalyst in private practice. She is the treasurer in the board of Psychoanalytic Center of Rome, Editor-in-Chief of local psychoanalytical website and editorial member of SPIweb (national website of the SPI). She is the founder of Italian Psychoanalytic Dialogues. In addition, she is a passionate scholar of neuroscience: mind/brain perception, image and language development, articulated with a psychoanalytic perspective. She is a member of NPSA (The Neuropsychoanalysis Association) and leader of the Italian group of NPSA. She was SIAIS member, Italian Society of Architects and Engineers for Public Health, with whom she collaborated for the development of a shared language between professions. She was the founder, and former scientific secretary of Moreabilities.com, a network between medical doctor and other experts in the field of pediatric rehabilitation. She has collaborated with the Institute of Pediatrics of the University "La Sapienza" of Rome, Division for the diagnosis and treatment of developmental and psychiatric illness. In particular, Dr. Spagnolo has been a member of various working groups on -predictive signs of psychosomatic disorders and early onset of pervasive developmental disorders. She has developed numerous publications, participated in conferences and lectures on topics related to neuropsychiatric developmental disorders and various other psychoanalytical topics. She has also published a novel in 2007 "Chantal" – Maremmi Editore, Firenze -on ethical issues in science.

Correspondence to: Dr. Rosa Spagnolo, Via Buonarroti 30, 00185 Rome, Italy. Tel: +39 339 19 19 525, fax: +39 6 86 00 894 (email address: r.spagnolo@libero.it)

CHAPTER 12

The Emergence of the Speaking Subject: Child Therapy and the Subject of Desire

Michael O'Loughlin, Ph.D.

The Emergence of the Speaking Subject: Child Therapy and the Subject of Desire

Michael O'Loughlin, Ph.D.

I often share with my students an image from the website of the late Stanley Greenspan. In this image Dr. Greenspan can be seen on the floor with a mother and child.1 The intersubjectivity of the interaction between therapist and child leaps from the page. In Dr. Greenspan's obituary in the *New York Times*, Serena Wieder, a colleague, was quoted as saying that "Dr. Greenspan's singular gift in dealing with little children 'was to get that connection, that gleam in the eye.'" The obituary continued: "Of the session with the 22-month-old boy, Dr. Wieder said the child 'was watching Stanley as much as Stanley was watching him — the look, the gleam of anticipation, the two-way back and forth.'" (Corcoran, 2010). I often think of that picture as I find myself on the floor seeking to draw a young child into an intersubjective space where feeling is possible and desire can be experienced. It is no accident that Greenspan named his approach to child work *Floortime.*

In this chapter I hope to explore one central concern of my work in *meeting* children, in relation to elements of my own history. We have reasons for what we do, and although most of the great child analysts who have been formative in my understanding of the work do not dwell on their personal lives, their vivacious work with children leaps off the page and leaves the reader in no doubt as to the embodied and located nature of their passion. I have written in more detail elsewhere of some of the elements of my life story and how the threads of that story have helped shape my professional posture toward working *obliquely* with children. I began my professional life as a teacher of young children. I was an accidental teacher really, since I joined the profession largely because it provided one of the few paths to upward mobility for children who grew up poor in the Ireland of my childhood. Those early encounters provided me with a passion for child work that finds me regularly mimicking Dr. Greenspan, sitting on the floor with children despite the protestations of my aging body. As it happens, I am also an accidental psychoanalyst. It was only when my original full-time academic career soured because of my inability to 'go along to get along' in a very intolerant and oppressive university setting, that I seriously thought about abandoning institutional academic life altogether. At that critical moment, some ten years into my professorial life and some twenty years ago now—a time of intense personal destabilization—I began analytic training and finally activated my psychology license. However, having spent my years as a professor teaching teachers and consulting in schools, I thought it was time I finally grew up. Leaving children behind, I threw myself with relish into working exclusively with adults... except that I found myself indelibly drawn to my adult patients' stories of the origins of psychic experiences, and this soon led me to reading about early experience and eventually to devoting a significant amount of my time to child work—work that is laden in equal parts with unremitting passion and profound difficulty and suffering.

Maud Mannoni reminds us of Freud's conviction, derived from his thoughts about Little Hans, that the "psychoanalysis of children is psychoanalysis in its purest form" (Mannoni, 1970, p. 3). This is, no doubt, because the transparently primal nature of childhood experience, and the evident perplexity of a child whose experience resists symbolization, or for whom struggles with the enmeshments and silent entanglements that come with particular kinds of unstated familial and societal demands and expectations are debilitating. Childhood suffering calls for an analytic relationship in which a commitment to raw honesty and the naming of pain is required to lift the veil of obfuscation that often produces a child's symptoms. While an attitude of respectful frankness should underlie all analytic work, there seems to be a lot more room for shadow-boxing and rhetorical maneuvers such as intellectualization in adult work. In child work honesty and directness are vital. Children are often only too willing to return the favor, as one of my young adolescent patients repeatedly reminded me. In my inexperience I sometimes proffered spurious interpretations about the consequences of the early loss of this child's mother, to which, unfailingly, he responded with a salutary "No shit, Sherlock," accompanied by a sly smile.

RETURN TO MOTHER

I have written elsewhere (e.g., O'Loughlin 2007, 2009, 2010) about the psychic effects of the lengthy hospitalizations that dominated my earliest years. I have long ruminated about the undoubted connection between those recurrent early hospitalizations and lifelong feelings of anxiety and narcissistic vulnerability of the kind that Bion (1961) characterized as *nameless dread*, and that Kristeva (1982) refers to as *inaugural losses.* I was born with a severe gastric condition that required multiple hospitalizations. The periods between hospital stays were characterized by regular bouts of projectile vomiting. This placed me in obvious distress, but also caused tremendous stress for my mother. We had no extra sets of linens, and there was no running water, washer or dryer for laundering soiled linens and clothing. While visiting the local hospital, my parents were often advised to gaze at me through the window in the door of the hospital bedroom as the staff said that I got "too upset" if my parents came in and held me. A saving grace for me was one nurse O'Halloran. She 'adopted' me in the hospital. She dressed me in other children's finery, loved me, and obviously provided a critical mirroring function in the absence of my mother. I experienced arrested development, and ceased to grow. My developmental progression stalled. This, and a distended belly, brought on by starvation, led me to the brink of death. When my father was advised to purchase a coffin, he took matters into his own hands, and moved me to the only other hospital in town, where, in due course, I responded to treatment My mother told me that when she came in to the hospital to pick me up at age two, the taxi driver accompanying her was aghast: He said I looked more like a newborn than a two- year-old.

There is much grist for analysis here. There was my own ongoing struggle to live, bolstered at a critical moment by decisive action on my father's part to insist on more effective medical intervention. There was the persistent worry of my parents about the uncertainty of my life chances, compounded by severe financial austerity, and the need to simultaneously keep in mind and create containing environments for my two toddler siblings. One effect of this parental worry is that I developed a somewhat fragilized posture toward life. In a sense, you might say, I *lived*, but I lacked the robust vitality of my peers. Like the invalid Colin, the tyrannical wheelchair-bound boy with a crippled personality in Frances Hodgson Burnett's *The secret garden* (1909), I was closed off from the world by my fragility. My investment in that same fragility, however, also effectively hemmed me in. In the parlance of the day, I was described as a *delicate* child—one that needed a special diet and special treatment, and from whom wholehearted participation in life could not be expected. The one exception to that was in matters intellectual. Having leapfrogged some developmental stages, I was able to read the local newspaper by age four. The intellectual realm gave me pleasure, and while this was salutary it also served to separate me further from my rough and tumble peers and siblings. Anxiety became my constant companion and no doubt my capacity to lose myself in a book served as a buffer against breakdown of the kind I discuss below. Developing a sympathetic identification with the suffering of the characters in Charles Dickens' novels, particularly those who experienced abject suffering and loss, caused me to develop a lifelong identification with oppression and suffering. To this day, the sight or sound of an ambulance causes feelings of fleeting panic.

I marvel now at the ways in which my mother and I managed to fill the gaps in a relationship where symbiosis was often not possible, and sometimes mirroring, containment and recognition were more than I could expect. My mother had lost her own mother at age six, and she had been raised by an unfeeling and willfully misrecognizing father. What effects could such losses have on her capacity to experience herself as a mother? What possible effects could the potential loss of me, her third child, have on her capacity for mothering me? What effects did her fear of my potential death have on my emerging subjectivity? And what of the sociohistorical circumstances that shaped the psyches of both my parents? For example, what were the effects of Ireland's Great Hunger (cf., O'Loughlin, 2012), that unremitting catastrophe in which over a million famished souls died of starvation or disease, and the survivors—including my parents' grandparents—not only suffered severe privation, but also bore witness to unimaginable suffering? What residue of this intergenerationally transmitted trauma and suffering did my parents inherit and in what way was their worry about me amplified by and suffused in such unspeakable archaic losses? The literature on intergenerational transmission of familial and historical trauma (e.g., Abraham & Torok, 1994; Davoine & Gaudillière, 2004; Emery, 2002; Faimberg, 2005; Fraiberg, Adelson & Shapiro, 1975; Frosh, 2013; Garon, 2004: O'Loughlin, 2013c, 2015; O'Loughlin & Charles, 2015; Pisano, 2012; Schützenberger,1998) leaves me in no doubt as to the psychic significance of such genealogical trauma narratives which persist as archaic embodied remnants or unmetabolized, residue in my own subjective experience.

The difficult-to-mourn losses that are at the root of the earliest formation of my subjectivity (cf. O'Loughlin, 2007) are a constant preoccupation. I have parsed these losses in my analysis and in my writings in order to improve my therapeutic receptivity to suffering. It is only now, though, that I see this as a one-sided narrative. I realize that I have given surprisingly little thought to the positive aspects of my subjective formation. Particularly in view of the adversities I experienced, surely there must have been potent countervailing identifications that allowed me to move forward with living? What could be the source of that vitality, libido, or perhaps remnant of *jouissance* that has animated my being? It is as if, in coming to think of myself as fragile, I failed to acknowledge or explore the sources of resilience that have allowed me to weather adversity and pursue desire. Boris Cyrulnik (2009) notes the importance of never underestimating those fleeting but intense existential moments that infuse our lives with purpose and that buttress us with resilience in the face of the trauma of misrecognition and the narcissistic vulnerability created by a lack of secure containment.

Ruminations about vitality and resilience unexpectedly came into sharp relief for me in recent months as I journeyed back and forth to

Ireland to join my siblings in keeping vigil at my mother's bedside as she passed through her final illness to death. What struck me as we sat with my mother over a lengthy period was the intensity of her psychic presence. As her physical presence declined precipitously, I felt she became increasingly alive for each one of us and the intensity of each of our responses to her fading presence seemed to reflect the ways in which she had infused each of us with our own particular form of vitality, resilience, and life purpose. It was an almost mystical experience in which the realization of our mother's imminent passing evoked in each of us archaic experiences of primal love and desire and an attempt to articulate identifications with the maternal imago and to hold onto that desire. It felt like a sacred moment: a moment when the gift of her maternal essence was suddenly rendered manifest. While I had long paid homage to my mother's desire that I live, and I had recognized that my identifications with her deep interest in books had led me to a scholarly career, it was only now that I really began to reflect on the intensity of her desire for my being. I saw this reflected in my siblings, too, most tangibly in my brother, who remarked more than once on his physical resemblance to our mother. While a final leave-taking is a sad and unspeakable process of relinquishment, I felt that this loss was balanced out by an uncanny communication of some basic element of vitality and urgent desire that bonded us together. We have been scattered across the diaspora, and emotional gaps have developed in our family over the last half century, yet we felt willed to come together in harmony and produced a testimony to my mother that bore witness to some fundamental essence or desire in her being that had infused each of us. In collectively composing the eulogy with my siblings, I had proposed saying that our mother had exhibited "ferocious aspiration" for all of us. My siblings gently vetoed the word 'ferocious', fearing that any potential negative connotation of the term might dilute in any way the goodness of the drive emanating from our mother.

The issue that I wish to address in the remainder of this essay, therefore is the animation of childhood subjectivity, and the therapeutic possibilities in working with children who present with emotional constriction, anxiety, or thwarted desire, through an analytic approach that takes consideration of the maternal contribution and that allows for collateral work with parents—most often with mothers in my experience—to help flesh out the contours of maternal demand and desire, and to explore the possibilities for therapy when the issue of how desire is enacted or communicated is brought explicitly into the room.

THE GENESIS OF EMOTIONS AND THE BEARER OF THE WORD

The ruminations presented above are evidence of my capacity, however rudimentary, to metabolize emotions. This type of narrative retelling is indicative that basic metabolic functions were set in place during my infancy despite the adversities I endured. I will turn now to writers who have done useful archaeological work on the genesis of emotions. While much can be learned about the effects of maternal communication on the development of child emotions from, for example, the writings of Melanie Klein, Daniel Stern and Donald Winnicott, I will focus here on contributions from the French Lacanian tradition—a tradition that in some respects complements those other approaches. Leading theorists in this tradition include Piera Aulagnier (2001), Françoise Dolto (1973, 2013; Hall & Hivernel, 2009), Rosine Lefort (1994), Maude Mannoni, (1970, 1999); and Catherine Mathelin (1999). Aulagnier (2001), for example, offers a theory of early emotional development that illustrates how an infant develops representations of emotions that eventually lead, in good circumstances, to a capacity for metabolization and speakability. Her work is valuable in pointing out how the early foundation of psychosis is laid when mother-infant communication fails and the emotional foundation remains in a primal state, with the child failing to fully enter the symbolic arena. The challenge for the mother is to create a transformative space where the infant can tolerate separateness and the 'I' can come into being, The difficulty, from a Lacanian perspective, is that this requires entry into language, and, in Aulagnier's terminology, this necessitates the infant undergoing the risky business of experiencing through the mother's words the *violence of interpretation*. All maternal speech presents a violent interpretation because as Aulagnier notes, "[b]y linking the register of the desire of the one to the register of the other's need, the aim of violence is assured of victory... to make of the fulfilment of the desire of him [sic] who exerts it what will become the object *demanded* by him [sic] who undergoes it" (p. 13). While entry into the symbolic is violent for all primal infants, Aulagnier points out that if the words offered by the word-bearer are ummetabolizable, as discussed below, that poses a grave risk of the child failing to enter the symbolic and falling into psychosis. Is it possible to create a tone in maternal emotional communication that invites the child to experience separateness and being in ways that are not potentially annihilatory and that do not foreclose symbolization?

Aulagnier proposes that the earliest learning encounters of the infant, occurring in the pre-verbal period, are pictographic. The challenge, Aulagnier suggests, for the child receiving maternal verbal productions, is to construct "a representation of self from the encounter" (p. 11). The mother, through her presence invites an infant into a performative or "speaking space" (p. 71) and invites the child to take up his or her place in a "genealogical destiny" (p. 29) delimited by the discursive and socio-historical expectations inherent in the mother's words. The infant's first representation of self, therefore, is constructed from the mother's discursive representation of the child—a process that began way before the infant's birth, or even conception. The discursive demand is "that the child conform to an image of the child that occupied the cradle long before this body was placed in it" (p. 53). The child's initial introjection of reality, therefore, is of a reality already metabolized and imagined by the mother. Aulagnier refers to this as the prosthetic function of maternal speech (p. 72).

For Aulagnier the phenomenon of specularization, described by Lacan as occurring in the mirror stage of toddlerhood, has a primal precursor in the early pictographic introjections that enable the child to begin a process of self-representation—the construction of the earliest relational schemas (p. 25). Crucially, even at this early stage, Aulagnier claims that the infant is capable of experiencing pleasure from the kind of merger feelings produced by an absorption of the mother's discourse, and conversely, if the mother's words are discordant and cannot be absorbed, feelings of extreme unpleasure are produced. If the process of pictographic representation proceeds fluidly, the stage is set for a transition to thinkable and eventually sayable emotions, and to metabolic processes of the kind referred to by Fonagy et al. (2010) as *mentalization* functions. Aulagnier points out that throughout life humans are likely to experience moments of the "fading of the I" (p. 38) which produce the kinds of catastrophic anxiety or nameless dread that I alluded to in my autobiographical note. What distinguishes the non-psychotic person, Aulagnier notes, is "the possibility that the I retains of retaking possession of one's space and mode of functioning, of forgetting those moments of tribulation, *but only in their deferred action,* treating them as 'foreign bodies', 'passing symptoms', whose cause one will impute to this or that external event" (p. 38). Lacking the requisite foundational capacities, and confronted with a tsunami of anxiety, any person is vulnerable to falling into psychosis.

A significant challenge arises for the young child when the oedipal transition requires the child to shift from the symbiotic of a desire co-constructed with the mother, to a realization that the mother possesses desires for a different Other than the child him- or herself. The child then has to abandon the fantasy of merger "as soon as he [sic] gleans the possibility of the mother's desire for an elsewhere that dislodges him [sic]from his [sic] position as her exclusive object of pleasure" (p. 48). She captures the existential crisis this produces:

> Near the mother there is usually that other subject, to whom she is linked by a privileged relation, whatever it may be, who is usually responsible for the breakdown in mother- child communication, who has something to say and often to shout, about the tears by which the child conveys his [sic] refusal to remain alone, who may give him, though less frequently a *bodily pleasure*, caressing him [sic], whispering in his [sic] ears a series of sounds whose tone transforms into the equivalent of a cradle song, which comes no longer solely from the mother's voice (p. 49).

One final consideration that I will address from Aulagnier's complex theory has to do with the consequences of the nature of the mother's speech. It is important, Aulagnier says, for the mother to possess metabolic capacity and that her speech embody properties of signification. However, in the earliest stage, she notes, while the infant take into itself "an object marked by the reality principle" the child absorbs the object, at this stage, purely as a sense of pleasure (p. 73). Leaving aside the obvious risks in families with pathognomonic characteristics, where, for example boundaries are poor, or where a mother projects excess desire on the infant, there are risks even in more conventional situations. Aulagnier employs the term "shadow side" to describe unconscious desires in the mother, and how mother and infant must collude to maintain barriers of repression around these desires. Aulagnier captures an aspect of the shadow side this way:

It is the discourse of the shadow that allows the mother to ignore the sexual component inherent in her love for her child; it is this discourse therefore that sees to it that what must remain in the repressed does not return. Hence the functional attributes attached to everything in bodily contact that participates in a pleasure whose cause must remain unknown: one rocks a baby because that makes him [sic] go to sleep, and sleep is good; one washes a baby because it is hygienic, and because the law prescribes it; one feeds a baby according to a model of good health etc. Fortunately this does not prevent the presence of fault lines: the kiss given is surplus to requirements or the infant's sex may be touched with pleasure.... What I call the shadow is constituted therefore by a series of statements that testify to the *mother's wishes* for the child. (p. 78).

Aulagnier describes, therefore, a "functional reciprocity" (p. 82) between mother and infant where each serves "as agent of repression for the other" (p. 82) where dangerous desires are neither spoken nor enacted.

Finally, Aulagnier notes that while the violence of interpretation is necessary to induct the child into the symbolic, an excess of violence will lead to a collapse in representational capacity in the child and lead to a refusal of meaning-making, thereby forming the basis of psychosis: "Insanity is the extreme form of the only refusal accessible to the I" (p. 91). This might be illustrated, for example, by a mother who repeatedly says things that are ostensibly positive but uses an angry, depressed, or critical emotional tone which results in a collision between the linguistic and libidinal messages and causes a child to refuse impossible meaning. Similarly, a mother who consciously or unconsciously communicates ambivalent or obfuscating messages about lovableness, and who fails to speak a truth to the child, also risks engendering foreclosure of meaning.

In the introduction to Rosine Lefort's *Birth of the other,* Russell Grigg (1994) notes that, from a Lacanian perspective, infant and child analysis is all about "the subject's emergence, as what Lacan calls a *parlêtre,* speaking being" (1994, p. x). Lefort documents her work over a long period with Nadia, a child of thirteen months, who had experienced nothing but institutional life.

The case study illustrates the complexity for a young child who had lost the expectation of mirroring, and who handled the specular experience Lefort offered with a mixture of apprehension and a gradually increasing receptivity toward a state of experiencing selfhood and accepting being seen. Lefort articulated the goal and tenor of the work thus: "I had to allow her to totter toward me as if toward an arena where her drama could be spoken and heard" (1994, p. 8). This case study offers a carefully observed clinical illustration of the application of the clinical underpinnings of Lacanian child analysis and is quite consistent with the principles articulated by Aulagnier. Nadia had been institutionalized for her entire life and she appeared depressed and withdrawn when Lefort first met her. At the outset, Nadia was functioning in what Lacan refers to as *invidia*. That is to say she could only covet the emotional expression of others whom she observed, but she showed no capacity to desire the breast for herself. As Lefort notes, having failed to inscribe the Real in the Other, through processes such as the pictogram discussed by Aulagnier, Nadia was "reduced by it to completely withdrawing her demand and not being able to maintain her desire except in the gap of the object she had not let go of, or *invidia*" (1994, p. 10). In clinical work that echoes Winnicott's writings, Lefort documents Nadia's very subtly developing capacity to employ transitional objects as a way of mediating contact with the analyst. Lefort describes the transition from *invidia* to the scopic drive, when Nadia could finally experience allowing herself to be the subject of another's gaze. Naturally, her forward progress was impeded by frequent regressions as she became invaded from time to time by the unmodulated anxiety that being in relation with an Other produced. Lefort documented Nadia's first embrace of the Other, and thereby her acknowledgement of her own separateness when she first uttered the signifier "mama":

> First it was the buttons on my white coat; on 4 December she rubbed my breast with her hand—not without anxiety; finally, on 5 December, again leaning against my breast, she grasped my white coat with her hands. At that moment the signifier "mama" emerged from her mouth, putting the seal on the difference between her and me. (p. 38).

Lefort summarized Nadia's core task this way:

> ...she had moved in an instant from the fear of being taken up again by the Other in a relation she has always known in hospital institutions and that would inevitably have returned her again to putting forward her protecting image, to her demand to the Other in the field of the signifier, the very coming into being of the subject. (p. 49)

It is notable that Lefort wrote her clinical notes as an observer at a French clinical facility in 1950, and it was only in the late 1970s, having undergone Lacanian training, that she applied the post-hoc Lacanian commentary discussed in the book. In her initial foray, much like nurse O'Halloran who 'adopted' me, Lefort worked by instinct, and she was driven by a confidence that somehow the animation of Nadine's subjectivity lay in the provision of a relation with a present, persistent, and willfully recognizing Other.

CLINICAL PRACTICE

My first introduction to French Lacanian child practice was clinical rather than theoretical. I began with the work of Maude Mannoni, and then I read the works of Danon- Boileau (2001), Dolto, and Mathelin. In the preface to *The child, his 'illness', and the others*, Mannoni (1970) notes that the difficulty that is produced in a child originates in some kind of half-truth or falsehood, which takes the form of a symptom (p. viii). Drawing on Erikson's work on the importance of social context in the production of symptoms, she states that those social and cultural norms and expectations that are left *unsaid* play a critical role in producing a symptom. Echoing Lacan's (1988) distinction between full speech (*parole pleine*) and empty speech (*parole vide*), Mannoni suggests that it is vital to pay attention to who is speaking: Is the child speaking from a place of desire or merely ventriloquating parental and societal demand and expectation? (p. 20). Attention to the symptom, therefore, is key, "It is not the myths about storks or cabbages that trouble children but the deception of adults who put on an air of *speaking truthfully*" (p. 32). The symptom, Mannoni notes, necessarily constitutes the locus of the mother's anxiety—an anxiety that may have intrapsychic and/or archaic ancestral components. The anxiety and withdrawal that are manifest means that such a child will likely display "echoes of the parents' communication" (p. 103), which, of course, may be a communication spoken loudly only through silence (cf. O'Loughlin, 2010). Mannoni summed up her clinical orientation thus:

> Whatever the child's real state of deficiency or disturbance may be, the analyst endeavors to understand the words that remain petrified in an anxiety encased in a physical disorder. In treatment, the subject's question will replace the demand or anxiety of parents and child, a question that is his [sic] deepest wish, concealed hitherto in a symptom or in a particular type of

relationship with his [sic] surroundings. What will become clear is the manner in which the child bears the imprint not only of the way his birth was awaited but also of what he is going to represent for each parent as a function of their respective past histories... If the child gets the impression that every access is barred to a true word, he [sic] can in some cases search for a possibility of expressing himself in illness. (p. 61)

In the Introduction to Mannoni's *Separation and creativity,* Brenkman, points out how Mannoni's work "foregrounds the ways in which the mother's fantasy and history are inscribed in the emotionally troubled child's symptoms" (Brenkman, 1999, p. xxvii). The challenge, Brenkman states, is to understand a child's struggle "to articulate his or her desire or fear in a language freed from the saturating symbols of the parents' fears and desires" (p. xxvii) and thus to enable the child to achieve full speech. Lacking this capacity, which Mannoni sees as foundational to creativity, the child is in danger of developing a form of speech that serves merely as a hollow echo of the mother's false self (Mannoni, 1999, p. 4). Such a child will be suffused in anxiety. Addressing the issue of serious maternal deficiency, Mannoni notes that in such a blank or dead space there can be no room for imagination and such a child will seek security "by filling in a hole at the fantasmic level, taking on obligations and restrictions that leave him no time to think" (p. 80). In many respects, I became that dutiful and studious child, staving off what Winnicott (1974) called *fear of breakdown* through intellectual activity, and sometimes simply by reordering the items in my mother's food pantry. In an approach complementary to Winnicott's, Mannoni argues against didactic or heavily interpretive work with children, arguing instead for approaching the child "obliquely" (Brenkman, 1999, p, xx ; see also O'Loughlin & Merchant, 2012) or "in a different register" (Mannoni, 1999, p. 138); listening to "the nonsense of desire" (p. 99); and refinding a play space (p. 94) in which the child can begin to claim a space as a thinking, imagining, and speaking subject:

The more painful reality is for the child, the more important is the ability of the parents to dream along with him [sic] of a different world in which the wondrous has its rightful place, its place as the inspiration for the poet and the storyteller in search of the lost language of childhood. (p. 156)

In *The broken piano*, Catherine Mathelin critiques Kleinian infant and child analysis for its exclusively intrapsychic focus, and she contrasts this to the Lacanian position practiced by Dolto and Mannoni in which what is stopped up in the mother is necessarily expressed through the child (1999, p. 2). Mathelin presents a series of case studies that deftly illustrate how a child, caught in a nexus of multiple transferences and interventions may feel overwhelmed and will withdraw. She therefore poses the question of child analysis thus: "Who is demanding what? How, in this labyrinth, can we find the red thread that will finally enable the child to come to occupy the position of subject?" (p. 28). Working with a child named Xénophon, Mathelin describes—and this is reminiscent of the picture of Dr. Greenspan with which I opened this chapter—seeking fleeting moments of contact with the child, and doing as little as possible so as to allow the unconscious to speak through the symptom (p. 87). Elsewhere (O'Loughlin & Merchant, 2012), I have explored Laurent Danon-Boileau's (2001) image of the analyst as a drowsy nanny—or as I prefer, a limp puppet—that can only become aroused or animated by the child's unconscious and who thereby provides the conditions in which the child may be invited to risk entering speech and claiming a space for the I. Mathelin makes liberal use of children's drawings and reminds us to stay close to the child's associations: "It is always the child who instructs" (p. 96). I find this feature of Lacanian work—one that substitutes patient observation of the child; an emphasis on the question; and restrained interpretation—as opposed to the more frequent and insistent depth interpretations that are characteristic of Kleinian work— a good fit with my therapeutic style. The following description of her work with a child called Jeremy summarizes the potential of a Lacanian approach:

Each advance in this child's treatment seemed to be connected, not to interpretations, which were apparently useless, but instead to the staging of what was going on in his interior theater, his extraordinary fantasy life. The same play, each time it was repeated in every session, was no doubt what finally enabled his story to be inscribed and to take on meaning... He staged his story (for it is not the analyst who is the producer of the drama), anchoring himself in the transference session after session so as to be able to write his theory, his own myth. (pp. 140-41)

CLINICAL ILLUSTRATION:
THE DYNAMICS OF DISAPPOINTMENT

Neil came into my office screaming. This five-year-old boy's mom explained that he was having difficulty separating, experienced difficulty in being around his peers, was extremely fearful of leaving her to go to kindergarten, and often spoke in baby talk. When mom left the room Neil crawled behind my chair and screamed loudly. After he quieted down I made some brief commentary about his feeling state which produced more screaming. He occasionally peeked out from behind the chair but the moment he experienced my gaze he resumed screaming. He could not tolerate any words whatsoever. He screamed if I made the briefest remarks about his feelings or invited him to join me in play. This pattern persisted for weeks, and in the ensuing years this regression to an infantile state recurred whenever he was stressed. The only posture left to me was that of the limp puppet: I waited for some animation so that I might reciprocate. As the weeks progressed, Neil continued to hide behind my chair, but gradually he began to peer around the corners of the chair. Seated opposite him on the couch or on the floor, I began to make some free association comments about his state and his presence with me and this yielded his first dialogical response. This response took the form of growling. Sometimes these growls were delivered with an angry snarl that shut down my speech. Other times, much like the delicate interplay of *fort-da*, in response to me growling back playfully he began to smile and laugh at his own growling. Slowly he came out from behind the chair, and after a number of months he could sit on the floor and engage in solitary play with some toys. He made humming noises as he played, and he occasionally asked for my assistance, but he resolutely resisted the kind of dialectical play required, for example, to participate in a two-person board game or a squiggle game. He resisted revealing himself through drawing or painting. However, over time he allowed more contact, and at school he began to achieve social and academic milestones. His confidence developed sufficiently that, at age 6, he began raising his hand in class and volunteering information. Word play, jokes, or anything that challenged the boundaries of conventional language still caused him to flee. He needed clearly delineated borders to address his engulfment anxieties. He also continued to react unpredictably in new social situations, sometimes handling the social demands gracefully, sometimes losing his words and regressing to growls or screams.

Neil's mother came to me with a frank acceptance that she was somewhat enmeshed with her son. She knew it was time to address the issues, and she never missed a session, nor did she ever complain when he screamed for the entire session. She sat with me at the beginning of each session and she and I would engage Neil in dialogue about his week, gradually allowing him to develop some words for his experience, and allowing her to develop a capacity to understand the dynamics of his anxiety. She said that her husband thought child therapy was unnecessary, but she insisted on therapy, recognizing that Neil's actions arose from some primal anxieties, ones that in some measure she shared and co-constructed with him. She knew what Neil needed. She had an intuitive trust in the process, and kept coming through thick and thin until she felt that Neil had completed the necessary separation and until she understood how to reassure him when he regressed. Neil's mother was a gift to the therapy. She was capable of recognizing his lack, and she was intuitively sympathetic to an approach that sought to diminish demand and honor desire. She needed an Other to shift the relationship form a two-person to a three-person dialog, and she used the therapy to accomplish this.

I have had occasion to work with two seven-year old girls who presented at therapy with severe symptoms of oppositionality. Jess was a screamer. When awakened in the morning by her parents she was already in a bad mood. At the slightest provocation she began to scream, and, when she met with me her voice was noticeably husky due to the prolonged screaming. She fought with her parents and siblings continually, and was so narcissistically vulnerable that at the slightest disappointment she decompensated. In session with me, she was charming and personable, and delighted in displaying her artistic talents and in making cards with sweet sentiments to give to her mother. In the family constellation her father was a benevolent but rather passive man, and her mother was very volatile and reactive. This mother had given up her professional position to become a full-time mom after Jess became symptomatic, but her continual presence in the house only served to increase the frequency and intensity of the conflict. In sessions with children I typically have the parent join the session at the beginning to recap events of the week and to articulate they dynamics of the relationship and to add myself as a third to the dynamics. When her mom was present in the room, Jess became petulant, and screamed uncontrollably. After her mom's departure she was typically subdued, but lacked self-soothing capacities, and also lacked a capacity to receive comfort from another. In parent consultation sessions, the mother expressed her profound disappointment in her daughter, and feared she as a mother, was turning into her own harsh and uncontaining mother. However, she was not interested in a therapy referral for herself and abandoned therapy shortly after, seeking instead to find a therapist who could handle oppositional defiant disorder to help with her 'disordered' daughter.

Tara presented with remarkably similar symptoms. Her mother reported that she was continually oppositional. Waking in the morning she would get into a battle over what clothes she would wear, even though she had assisted her mother in picking out her clothes the night before. In restaurants and other public places she provoked her parents and decompensated into screaming and rage whenever they attempted to set boundaries. Like Jess's mom, Tara's mother, too, was profoundly disappointed. While she admitted to angry reactiveness at times, for the most part she internalized her hurt and became both depressed and anxious. In session, Tara presented as a polite, sweet girl. She loved drawing and enjoyed the dialog of squiggle drawing. In collateral work between mother and daughter, when her mom laid out some of her grievances, Tara would immediately collapse in tears and cry profusely. At such times her mother held her, but she confided in me she was unsure if her daughter's tears were merely another form of manipulation. She doubted the authenticity of her daughter's speech. In session Tara, too, put a lot of energy into creating reparative drawings for her mom. This mom requested parent consultation sessions and we explored her parenting style both in terms of its effects on Tara, and in terms of her disappointment that she could not reproduce the good mothering she had experienced as a child. She seemed to have an intuitive understanding that, despite the awfulness of her daughter' rage, it also contained some meaning and she and I worked to develop a collaborative process to seek to understand her daughter's struggle with seeking to claim a position as subject.

Both girls could be seen as resisting ventriloquation through their mother's voices. The only sane solution to such a crisis is the creation of a space where desire can emerge and the child can come to claim a place where speaking from the position of a genuine I becomes possible.

Author note: This article is dedicated to the memory of Ann O'Loughlin (1926-2015).

REFERENCES

Abraham, N. & Torok, M. (1994). *The shell and the kernel.* [Edited, translated and with an Introduction by N. Rand]. Chicago: University of Chicago Press

Aulagnier, P. (2001). *The violence of interpretation: From pictogram to statement.* A. Sheridan (Trans.). London: Brunner Routledge.

Bion, W. (1961). *Experiences in groups.* London: Tavistock/ Routledge.Brenkman, J. (1970). Preface. In M. Mannoni, *The child, his 'illness', and the others.* London: Karnac.

Burnett, F. H. (1909). *The Secret Garden.* London, England: F. H. Burnett.

Corcoran, D. (2010). Obituary: Stanley I. Greenspan, Developer of 'Floor Time' Teaching, Dies at 68. Retrieved from http://www.nytimes.com /2010/05/05/us/05greenspan.html, May 4, 2015.

Cyrulnik, B. (2009). *The whispering of ghosts.* New York: Other Press

Danon-Boileau, L. (2001). *The silent child: Bringing language to children who cannot speak.* London: Oxford University Press.

Davoine, F. & Gaudillière, J. (2004). *History beyond trauma.* New York: Other Press.

Dolto, F. (2013). *Psychoanalysis and Paediatrics: Key Psychoanalytic Concepts with Sixteen Clinical Observations of Children.* F. Hivernel & F. Sinclair (Trans.). London: Karnac.

Dolto, F. (1973). *Dominique: analysis of an adolescent.* I. Kats (Trans.). New York: E. P. Dutton.

Emery, E. (2002). The ghost in the mother: Strange attractors and impossible mourning. *Psychoanalytic Review,* 89, (2): 169-194.

Faimberg, H. (2005). *The telescoping of generations: Listening to the narcissistic links between generations.* London: Institute of Psychoanalysis & Routledge.

Fraiberg, S., Adelson, E. & Shapiro, V. (1975). Ghosts in the nursery. *Journal of the American Academy of Child Psychiatry,* 14, 387–421

Fonagy, Peter, Gergely, G., Jurist, E. & Target, M. (2010). *Affect Regulation, mentalization, and the development of the self.* New York: Other Press.

Frosh, S. (2013). *Hauntings: psychoanalysis and ghostly transmissions.* London: Palgrave. Garon, J. (2004). Skeletons in the closet. *International Forum of Psychoanalysis,* 13, 84-92.

Grigg, R. (1994). Foreword. In R. Lefort, (with R. Lefort).*The birth of the other.* Urbana, IL: University of Illinois Press.

Hall, G. & Hivernel, F. (Eds). (2009). *Theory and practise in child Psychoanalysis: An introduction to Françoise Dolto's Work.* London: Karnac.

Kristeva, J. (1982). *Powers of horror: Essays on abjection.* New York: Columbia University Press.

Lacan, J. (1988). *The seminar of Jacques Lacan. Book I. Freud's papers on technique.* J.-A. Miller (Ed.) J. Forrester (Trans). New York: Norton

Lefort, R. (with R. Lefort). (1994). *The birth of the other.* Urbana, IL: University of Illinois Press. Mannoni, M. (1999). *Separation and creativity: Refinding the lost language of childhood.* New York: Other Press.

Mannoni, M. (1970). *The child, his 'illness', and the others*. London: Karnac.

Mathelin, C. (1999). *The broken piano: Lacanian psychotherapy with children*. New York: Other Press.

O'Loughlin, M. (Ed.). (2015). *The Ethics of Remembering and the Conse-quences of Forgetting: Trauma, History and Memory*. Lanham, MD: Rowman & Littlefield.

O'Loughlin, M. (Ed.) (2013a). Introduction. In O'Loughlin, M. (Ed.). *Psychodynamic Perspectives on Working with Children, Families and Schools*. Lanham, MD: Jason Aronson.

O'Loughlin, M. (2013b). The uses of psychoanalysis. In O'Loughlin, M. (Ed.). *The uses of Psychoanalysis in Working with Children's Emotion-al Lives*. Lanham, MD: Jason Aronson.

O'Loughlin, M. (2013c). Reclaiming genealogy, memory and history: The psychodynamic potential for reparative therapy in contempo-rary South Africa. In C. Smith, G. Lobban, & M. O'Loughlin (Eds.). *Psychodynamic psychotherapy in Contemporary South Africa: Con-texts, theories, practices*. Johannesburg, SA: Wits University Press.

O'Loughlin, M. (2012). Trauma trails from Ireland's Great Hunger: A psycho-analytic inquiry. In Willock, B., Curtis, R. & Bohm, L. (Eds.). *Loneliness and Longing: Conscious & Unconscious Aspects*. New York: Routledge

O'Loughlin, M. (2010). Ghostly presences in children's lives: Toward a psychoanalysis of the social. In O'Loughlin, M. & Johnson, R. (Eds.). *Imagining children otherwise: Theoretical and critical perspectives on childhood subjectivity*. New York: Peter Lang Publishing. [Reprinted in O'Loughlin, M. (Ed.). *Psychodynamic Perspectives on Working with Children, Families and Schools*. Lanham, MD: Jason Aronson.]

O'Loughlin, M. (2009). Being otherwise, teaching otherwise: The decolo-nizing potential of the displacement, loss, and "homelessness" of migrant experiences. In D. Caracciolo, & A. Mungai. (Eds.). *In the spirit of ubuntu: Stories of teaching and research*. Rotterdam: Sense Publishers.

O'Loughlin, M. (2007). On losses that are not easily mourned. In L. Bohm, R. Curtis, & B. Willock (Eds.). *Psychoanalysts' Reflections on Deaths and Endings: Finality, Transformations, New Beginnings*. New York: Routledge

O'Loughlin, M. (2006). On knowing and desiring children: The signifi-cance of the unthought known. In G. Boldt & P. Salvio (Eds.). *Love's return: Psychoanalytic essays on childhood teaching and learning*. New York: Routledge.

O'Loughlin, M. & Charles, M. (Eds.). (2015). *Fragments of trauma and the social production of suffering: Trauma, History and Memory*. Lan-ham, MD: Rowman & Littlefield.

O'Loughlin, M. & Merchant, A. (2012). Working obliquely with chil-dren. *Journal of Infant, Child & Adolescent Psychotherapy, 11,* 149-159.

Pisano, N. (2012). *Granddaughters of the Holocaust: Never forgetting what they didn't experience*. Boston: Academic Studies Press.

Rustin, M., Rhode, M., Dubinsky, H. & Dubinsky, A. (1997). *Psychotic states in children*. London: Karnac.

Schützenberger, A.A. (1998). *The ancestor syndrome: Transgenerational psychology and the hidden links in the family tree*. London and New York: Routledge Books.

Winnicott, D.W. (1971). *Playing and reality*. London: Routledge.

Winnicott, D.W. (1960). The theory of the parent-infant relationship. *International Journal of Psychoanalysis, 41,* 585-95.

Winnicott, D.W. (1958). Primary maternal preoccupation..In *Through paediatrics to psycho- analysis*. London: Tavistock..

BIO

MICHAEL O'LOUGHLIN PH.D., is Professor in the School of Education and Clinical and Research Supervisor in the Ph.D. program in Clinical Psychol-ogy at Adelphi University. He is co-chair of the *Association for the Psychoanalysis of Culture & Society*. He published *The Subject of Childhood* in 2009, and edited *Imagining Children Otherwise: Theoretical and Critical Perspectives on Childhood Subjectivity* with Richard Johnson, in 2010. He is co-editor with Cora Smith and Glenys Lobban of *Psychodynamic Psycho-therapy in Contemporary South Africa: Contexts, Theories, and Application ,* 2013, and also edited two books in 2013 on children's emotions: *The Uses of Psychoanalysis in Working with Children's Emotional Lives and Psychody-*

namic Perspectives on Working with Children, Families and Schools. He is the Editor of, *The Ethics of Remembering and the Consequences of Forgetting: Essays on Trauma, History and Memory*, and co-Editor with Marilyn Charles of *Fragments of Trauma and the Social Production of Suffering: Trauma, History and Memory,* both published in 2015. He has a private practice for psychotherapy and psychoanalysis on Long Island, N. He may also be reached at his website: **michaeloloughlinphd.com**.

CHAPTER 13

Sophistry and ADHD: The Dual Myths of Organicity and Biochemical Imbalance and the Ensuing Medication Tidal Wave

Burton Norman Seitler, Ph.D.

Sophistry and ADHD: The Dual Myths of Organicity and Biochemical Imbalance and the Ensuing Medication Tidal Wave

Burton Norman Seitler, Ph.D.

In a time of universal deceit, telling the truth is a revolutionary act
—George Orwell

When I was about eight or nine years old, I recall having a teasing *tête a tête* with my father in which he issued a somewhat mischievously conceived, but as it turned out, clever challenge to me. He told me that he could demonstrate that I was not here. Oedipal rivalry implications aside, my father said that through the simple use of logic alone, he would be able to do this. I was young, wide-eyed and curious, so I eagerly dared him to prove to me that I was not here. His demonstration was fairly simple, to the point, and short. He asked me the following questions: "Are you in Chicago?" My reply was even shorter. "No," I answered. "Are you in San Francisco?" Again, my answer was "No." He continued, "Are you in Winnipeg?" I answered, "No." He named several other locations, but each time, my answer was an unequivocal, "No." Finally, he said, "Well, if you are not in any of those places, you must be somewhere else, is that correct?" "Sure," said I. Armed with little more than a twinkle in his eyes and a mischievous grin, my father then summed up his argument by concluding, "Well, if you are somewhere else, you cannot be here!"

Taken at face value, this was merely light-hearted banter between a father and his son. Of course my father and I both knew the truth about my whereabouts (which was New York City). It goes without saying that even though I was not in any of the places that he named, this simply meant that I was somewhere other than in those places, not somewhere other than where I actually was. In other words, being somewhere else did not negate where my real location was. Nor did our mutual understanding of the truth about my whereabouts negate our being able to suspend our spatial orientation temporarily and allow us to mutually delight in this display of verbal chicanery.

However, on a deeper level, this miniscule vignette represents a veritable demonstration of how manipulation of terminology that *seems* to be logical on the surface can produce a quasi-conclusion that *appears* to make sense, at least superficially, but which has no factual basis in reality. This is a prime example of what is meant by the term, *sophistry*. By that, I am referring to the use of reasoning and/or argumentation that is inherently false, and which is designed to subtly or otherwise, deceive.

Historically, the term, Sophistry, comes from a group of particularly eloquent individuals, called the Sophists, who touted themselves as logicians, and who ardently privileged winning over everything else. This often meant disrespect, disregard for, or distortion of the facts. Logic was utilized as a central part of their argumentation in order to achieve their desired ends.

In opposition to these tactics, Isocrates wrote a treatise entitled, *Against the Sophists*, indicating that anyone who deals in generalizations about the proper way to conduct one's life or attempts to promulgate absolutes, regarding what constitutes virtue, for example, gravely misleads the public into believing that important issues and questions can be reduced to simplistic, one-size-fits-all principles and procedures. He believed that there was no specific "science" which is capable of spelling out all of the conditions necessary for insuring a good life filled with happiness and success, and he showed contempt for the Sophists who argued that this could be taught. In his *Antidosis*, he wrote:

> If all who are engaged in the profession of education were willing to state the facts instead of making greater promises than they can possibly fulfill, they would not be in such bad repute with the lay-public (In, *Classical Rhetoric*, trans. George Norlin, 1980, p. 72).

He characterized the scruples of such individuals as indicative of a kind of "cloud morality," which he maintained was not based on lived experience, and not grounded on earth. He added the following:

Indeed, who can fail to abhor, yes to condemn, those teachers, in the first place, who devote themselves to disputation, since they pretend to search for truth, but straightway at the beginning of their professions attempt to deceive us with lies? (p. 72).

Subsequently, Aristotle declared that sophistry was wisdom in appearance only. Centuries later, D.C. Schindler (2008) distinguished genuine philosophical inquiry from sophistry by observing that:

Sophistry is indifferent to content, and that this indifference prevents it from integrating what it knows into a well-ordered meaningful whole...because to do so would require a genuine knowledge of the good (p. 261).

THREE GENERAL METHODS OF *KNOWING*: AUTOCRATIC, SOCRATIC, AND SCIENTIFIC

This begs the following questions: what is truth, and how does one go about the business of seeking it out? At first, the central means of obtaining a semblance of 'truth" was handed down by *the powers that be*, whose main means of transmitting the canon of the day was by virtue of what I call the Method of Authority. Under this "method," information was derived from the word of the Authority, such as, the High Priest, the Church, the King, the Elder, and so on. Not infrequently, this method was autocratic.

Another method of seeking truth came from the work of Socrates. This refers to what has become known as the Method of Inquiry, in which the quest was as important, or perhaps more important than the answers or conclusions, if any, that might be obtained. However, this method left many matters unsettled and open for debate. Into the void of debate, the autocratic power—intertwined with the authoritarian voice—made itself heard and demanded obedience. The authoritarian diktats usually generated grave risks should they not be heeded, no matter how ridiculous their conclusions and proclamations may have been. Hence, declarations that the earth was flat, or the universe revolved around the earth needed to be respected and strictly obeyed, lest one incur the wrath of the authorities. Mere philosophical inquiry, open debate, or divergent thinking did not dare refute opinions coming from on high, without the threat (and/or actuality) of dire consequences. One of the few ways available could come through the development of carefully gathered, systematic, keen observations and measurements. From this, the next approach—the Scientific Method—and the formal study of the sciences were born. Although, as it happens, even the development of science itself, was not impervious to being influenced, or obstructed by those in power, as evidenced by what happened to Galileo and other "dissenters," many of whom met with a gruesome fate.

Science, and the scientific method emanated out of the need to establish uniform standardized methods of observation for the purpose of obtaining a sense or measure of predictability, consistency, and stability designed to assist us in understanding our environment, as opposed to having it dictated to us by those in power. But it also developed as a means of departing from, and even challenging long-held (sometimes superstitious) beliefs and/or dogma.

Good science attempts to tally the tolls it carefully accumulates and measures. But what if a fake coin is somehow inserted into the computational system's collection device? What happens to the data, to the calculations and resulting conclusions to be drawn? As we know, in any syllogism, if we start with a faulty premise, or if the accumulated data are skewed, as in the above example, we arrive at a faulty conclusion. What has come to be known as, "Attention Deficit Hyperactive Disorder" (ADHD) is a prime illustration of this.

ADHD is a perfect illustration of a controversial diagnostic categorical misnomer. It has long been fraught with misinformation, misunderstanding, and mistakes, but has caught on nonetheless, and persisted, especially once it was officially engraved in the Diagnostic Statistical Manual (DSM), the Holy Bible of psychiatry. Practically from the start, even before it was ever formally studied, ADHD was regarded as a neurobiological disorder. Even though no biological basis had been uncovered at that time or since then, once ADHD was enshrined in the sanctum sanctorum of the holy *Diagnostic Scriptural Mystifier* (the DSM), it became accepted as a real disease entity, necessitating a biological cure. Yet no genetic or biological marker, lesion, bacterium, chemical imbalance has ever been found that has withstood the test of time to support the widespread conjectures of a biological causality connection. As Justman recently wrote (2015):

> The tangled history and mutating specifications of the disorder alternately known as ADD or ADHD make it clear that the disorder (call it ADHD) is not a specific entity given in nature but a construct, and by the same token, its prevalence is highly subject to interpretation (p. 138).

Nevertheless, as a result of being given the premature imprimatur of disease status, millions of children, and subsequently adults who were given this questionable and unsubstantiated diagnosis were prescribed powerful stimulant drugs. Currently, some of the original proponents of ADHD, who were instrumental in it being accepted as a real diagnostic condition cannot run fast or far enough away from their association with it. They too, although quite belatedly, have come to recognize its questionable status which includes, but is not limited to its complete lack of empirical, verifiable validity.

Up to now, a reductionistic biological approach has been taken regarding ADHD. And, based on the extant belief that ADHD had a neurobiochemical origin, an increasing number of children, especially boys, who had been diagnosed with ADHD, have been treated with stimulant medications. However, many are now beginning to question whether ADHD can justifiably be classified and thus treated as a disease (Baughman, 2006; 1993; Furman, 2005, 2002; Rosemond & Ravenel, 2008; Seitler, 2011; Seitler, 2008; Seitler, 2006a; Seitler, 2006b; Kaye, 1994).

A methodical review of the literature shows that the symptoms of ADHD listed in the DSM IV, of inattentiveness, forgetfulness, hyperactivity and impulsivity, are not unique to ADHD. In fact, most of us have exhibited one or more of the previous symptoms in our lives. According to Hallowell and Ratey (1994), Mozart might have been diagnosed today as ADHD, based on the following behaviors that he exhibited. He was said to have been:

> impatient, impulsive, distractible, energetic, emotionally needy, creative, innovative, irreverent, and a maverick (p. 43).

Therefore, the terminology and description add nothing definitive that distinguishes ADHD from other behaviors. Moreover, no neuro-psychological test results or physiological pathology have uniformly been found for ADHD (Rosemond & Ravenel, 2008; Furman, 2005). Also, no structural or functional neuroimaging studies have ever consistently identified a unique etiology for ADHD (Jackson, 2006; Furman, 2002; Weinberg, & Brumback, 1992;). Rather than relinquish the ADHD category, it was now said to be "co-morbid" with other diagnostic entities, such as conduct, oppositional, and mood disorders, and even learning disabilities (Kaye, 1994; Weinberg & Brumback, 1992). Earlier, Henker and Whalen (1989) commented on the broadly written generalities subsumed in the criteria for these "disorders," saying:

> ...the criteria for these disorders are written in such a way that a child with ADHD could and often does receive one of the other two diagnoses at the time. In fact, the overlap between ADHD and the other externalizing disorders is so high—over 50%—that many have questioned the utility of making distinctions among them (p. 216).

Joseph Glenmullen, a psychiatrist at Harvard Medical School, went even further in asserting, "We do not yet have proof either of the cause or the physiology for any psychiatric diagnosis. In every instance where such an imbalance was thought to have been found, it was later proven false" (2002).

In this regard, Flaherty, et al. (2005), on behalf of the American Psychiatric Association, boldly asserted that the current state of neuroimaging does not warrant using such technology for diagnosing psychiatric disorders. Keith Connors (1998) said as much in a paper he presented to the National Institute of Health (NIH) Consensus Development Conference: Diagnosis and Treatment of Attention Deficit Hyperactivity Disorder. In reviewing neuroimaging studies, he stated,

> The embarrassment of riches from neuroimaging studies reflects a poor understanding of any specificity for the neural basis of ADHD. The high levels of comorbidity of ADHD with oppositional, conduct, and mood disorders also call into question the specificity of the definition of the disease and whether current criteria are sufficient to allow further understanding of the neurobiology of the syndrome (p. 23).

Commenting on data from the Centers for Disease Control, which showed that diagnoses for ADHD were given to 15 percent of high school-age youths and that the incidence of children receiving stimulant medication for ADHD had dramatically risen from 600,000 in 1990, to over 3.5 million, Connors, in a New York Times interview on 12/14/13, referred to this as "a national disaster of dangerous proportion." He added, "The numbers make it look like an epidemic. Well, it's not. It's preposterous." In a subsequent interview, Connors uttered an even more powerful disclaimer stating, "This is a concoction to justify the giving out of medication at unprecedented and unjustifiable levels."

According to Craig Newnes (2009), in Great Britain, less than 5000 children were diagnosed as ADHD prior to the 1990s. In 2003, more than 200,000 children were now labeled with this condition (p. 161). To put this in perspective, the sales of stimulant medication for this so-called ADHD entity have quintupled just from 2002 to 2012. So widespread has the connection between stimulants and their presumed attention-enhancing attributes become that the use of stimulants by university students (believing that their test scores would be dramatically enhanced) has skyrocketed. Watson, Arcona, and Antonuccio (2015) assert, "There is no evidence that stimulant medications used for ADHD increase intellectual functioning or scholarly contributions" and point out that:

compelling new evidence indicates that ADHD drug treatment is associated with deterioration in academic and social-emotional functioning (p. 10).

And yet, no genetic markers for ADHD have been identified. Even the definition of ADHD has been fuzzy, thus making studying "it" an empirically murky endeavor, chock full of difficulty. To date, most empirical studies have heavily relied on the Conners Rating Scales, which themselves have questionable validity. Although supporters of the Connors Scales claim that it has high inter-rater reliability, research only notes "high face validity" (Connors, 1998; Goldman, et al., 1998), which is essentially how a test *looks* but not how well it answers two essential questions which constitute the essence of validity: (1) *Does it test what it claims it tests?* And thus, (2) *Does it measure what it claims to measure?* Ultimately, when all is said and done, having "face validity" is really no better than having no validity at all.

Even results of the Conners Revised Rating Scale, as well as teacher or parent "ratings" of school children have been highly discrepant. Additionally, studies have shown that Scales like the Connors, the ADHD Rating scale; the Brown and the Wender Utah are "Significantly easy to fake" (Jachimowicz and Geiselman, 2004). What this means is that an objective basis for the diagnosis of ADHD has been severely undermined by the use of subjective informant data derived from the above scales or from interview material.

On top of that, the use of stimulant medication has been a disaster in its ability to make any differential behavioral distinctions that distinguished children diagnosed as "ADHD" from other children that were not so diagnosed.

In a brilliant presentation at the Australian Association for Research in Education, Graham (2005) invoked the reasoning of Foucault and asserted that when children are called ADHD it is for exclusionary reasons in which such children "are placed in a field of exteriority" (Foucault, 1972, p. 139). She indicated that attaching the label ADHD to students simultaneously accomplishes several self-serving aims:

(1) it is a means of legitimizing the existence of "behavior- disordered" students as a separate class of infra-humans,

(2) it is a means of legitimizing the diagnostic nomenclature of ADHD, and

(3) it is a means of legitimizing the ensuing exertion of control over "them."

Specifically, she maintains:

>...the constitutive effects of psychopathologizing the pedagogical discourse imbued with the positivity of psychological power works to speak into existence the "behaviorally disordered" child as a recognizable object of scrutiny (p. 12).

Adding to this, Justman (2015) makes an interesting connection between the employment of stereotypes and the invocation of the ADHD diagnosis. He maintains:

>...like a stereotype, the diagnosis is highly connotative, distorts interpretation, replicates itself, and marks its objects. A diagnosis that a symptom of *fidgeting* or *tapping* [his italics] comes perilously close to a caricature that plays up physical variations, and a diagnosis expansive enough to acquire millions of new cases from DSM-III to DSM-5 contains more than a seed of exaggeration. Moreover, the very process of adding one symptom to another until they add up to a diagnosis plays to a kind of logic of association (p. 137).

On top of that, proponents of the neurobiological model for the etiology of ADHD have been unsuccessful in their attempts to explain the huge differences in incidence of ADHD between girls and boys (Arnold, 1996; Gaub & Carlson, 1997).

My own work (2011, 2008a, 2008b, 2007, 2006a, 2006b) suggests that the gender differences that we see in the incidence of ADHD in boys as opposed to girls may be cultural manifestations having to do with the manner in which boys and girls are differentially permitted or able to express certain kinds of feelings, particularly sadness or depression. In our culture, it is quite acceptable for girls to cry. However, for boys we seem to have a completely different standard. Boys who cry or show tender feelings of one sort or another are often ridiculed, dismissed, or even bullied.

In short, the chant that has reverberated over a span of more than four decades, namely, that *ADHD* (or any of the multiplicity of terms that have preceded it) *is a neurobiochemical disease*, is simply not supported by a close analysis of the evidence. This is worthy of consideration because a serious consequence of holding to a strictly neurobiochemical substrate for ADHD is that it almost inescapably results in an organic solution to this purported, but not supported, "disease," one that almost invariably results in the use of stimulant medications like Ritalin, Adderall, Straterra, and so on.

While these medications might be able to *subdue* a child's excessive activity level in the short term, when viewed over a substantial period of time they no longer are effective (Rosemond & Ravenel, 2008). Sadly, what is more, children, and their parents typically do not recognize that feelings are what underlie overt behavior; nor do they know what to do when their feelings are consciously experienced. As a result, learning how to regulate or modulate affect may not occur, or may be severely compromised (Schore, 1991). This frequently results in a lifetime of dependence on drug regimens or *chemical cocktails*, rather than on their children's own learning capacities and inner resources. As if that is not bad enough, medications have been shown to have serious after-effects (Baughman, 2006, 1993; Jackson, 2009, 2005; Breggin & Breggin, 1995; Barkley, et al., 1990).

AFTER-EFFECTS—ARE NOT MERELY SIDE-EFFECTS

I use the term *after-effects* instead of *side-effects* because *side-effects* imply that the effects of the prescribed drugs are either rare or minimal. Research is now telling us a different, much more somber story about the after-effects of stimulants (Jackson, 2009, 2005; Lambert, 2005; Lambert, 1998; Lambert & Hartsough, 1998; Raine, et al. 2010; Raine, 2009). The Raine study longitudinally followed Australian children who were receiving stimulant medication for 8 years. Among their findings, a few significant and alarming results stand out:

- The existence of long-term cardiovascular damage; significantly increased diastolic blood pressure, as compared to matched children who did not receive medication.
- School failure was seen. Despite the long-held, and as it turns out, *mis*belief that children concentrate and achieve better when on a stimulant, they have a 10.5 times greater chance of being identified by a teacher as performing below grade level.
- What is more, the study shows that inattention and hyperactivity slightly *worsened* over the long-term, contrary to what the public, as well as professionals in the field, have been told up until now. Drug advocates have made an argument that the above results occurred because the medicated children had more severe forms of ADHD. However, when the children were first being included in the Raine study, the medicated group and non-medicated group were compared with each other on developmental, behavioral, and health measures, producing **no** significant differences between the two groups at the outset. This spikes the "severity of the disorder" argument.
- Other longitudinal research (Lambert, 2005; Lambert & Hartsough, 1998) has noted that children, who are on stimulants over the course of time, have a significantly greater chance of becoming addicted to other stimulants, ranging from cigarettes to cocaine.

COMBINATION OF PSYCHOTHERAPY AND MEDICATION FOR ADHD?

There was a time, not all that long ago, when the idea of using medications *and* psychotherapy for working with patients who had been characterized by the term Attention Deficit Hyperactive Disorder (ADHD) was considered to be the *moderate* position. After all, it was reasoned, that if psychotherapy was effective and not harmful—and if medications had efficacy and did not do any damage, it would make sense to utilize both options together. Moreover, in doing so, the whole messy debate regarding whether or not ADHD had a "neurobiochemical" origin could be straddled by clinicians whose main aim was to focus on, and help those under their care and not have to be concerned with the on-going theoretical quarrel over ADHDs etiology. In fact, one of the initial "casualties" emerging out of the emphasis on the almost exclusive treatment of ADHD with medications was talk therapy, particularly uncovering treatments, like psychoanalysis or psychodynamic psychotherapy. This may explain, to a very large degree why there has been a relative dearth of published psychoanalytic or psychodynamic research or case studies in this area. However, in the last ten years, an ever-increasing body of researchers and clinicians have come to understand that medications were neither as benign as had previously been declared, nor as efficacious in treating this "ADHD condition" as had previously been claimed.

Anthony Roth and Peter Fonagy (2006) carried out one such piece of psychoanalytic research on ADHD. This study was conducted to determine the efficacy of the psychoanalysis of 35 children diagnosed as ADHD. After one year, 67 % of the children remaining in psychoanalysis no longer could be diagnosed as exhibiting signs of ADHD.

My own work with children spans over 40 years and includes many youngsters who were described as hyperkinetic, hyperactive, or what we now refer to as ADHD. During that period of time, I began to question the neurobiochemical ideas that were beginning to take hold. My experiences with children who were diagnosed as exhibiting ADHD lead me to different conclusions. Elsewhere, I have described those experiences in greater detail (Seitler, 2011, 2008a, 2008b, 2007, 2006a, 2006b).

THE CASE OF RAYMOND S.

The following is a case study of a young boy, who I have called "Raymond," who was diagnosed by the family pediatrician as "hyperactive," and who subsequently received psychotherapy treatment with me. I offer it here as a representative case illustrating that psychotherapy, in this instance, psychoanalytically oriented psychotherapy, can provide both a parsimonious, yet not reductionistic, explanation for what has been called "Attention Deficit Hyperactivity Disorder" (in addition to a long list of other preceding names), as well as a safe, effective, long lasting treatment of children on whom we have conferred the term, ADHD.

Raymond was brought in to see me by his parents, Mr. and Mrs. S., when he was 6 years old. Prior to their visit with me, Raymond's parents had to take him out of pre-school due to a series of ongoing misbehaviors, such as— pushing children out of his way, impulsively shouting out in class, repeatedly interrupting classroom activities (often, but not always, by calling for his mother), and not obeying the instructions of his teacher or other adults who were in charge. When Raymond's parents enrolled him in Kindergarten, his behavior was similarly marked by agitation, unrest, and his inability to contain his impulses. So pervasive was his misconduct that it had a negative influence on caretakers and other important figures in his life and on the ways in which they interacted with him.

When I saw Mr. and Mrs. S., they said that they did not know what to do. They indicated that Raymond, their only child, was out of control and that they felt helpless and frustrated. They were also embarrassed, and believed that others looked down on them in the upwardly mobile neighborhood that they worked so hard and were finally able to afford to move into. What appeared to be their great awareness and hyper-concern about "what the neighbors would say" unquestionably compounded their initial apprehensions.

Despite their description of Raymond being highly impatient, with a very limited frustration tolerance and an exceedingly high activity level, they were totally opposed to his being on any kind of medication. They were very emphatic about their antipathy toward the use of any kind of psychoactive medications, particularly stimulants, and asked if I would work with Raymond without drugs. I agreed to work with Raymond and indicated that I thought that it would be helpful if they also received ancillary counseling as part of the process.

Mr. and Mrs. S. were observed to be a bright, articulate, and hard-working couple in their late thirties, who moved from New York City to a fairly well to do suburban area. They were socially conscious and indicated that were attempting to "fit in" to their new, upscale neighborhood by taking an active interest in, and working hard for their community.

Mr. S. was an electrical engineer. His wife was part owner of a small neighborhood restaurant, which demanded a great deal of her time, energy, and focus. At the end of the day, she was often physically spent and emotionally wrung out. And, although she loved her husband and Raymond, her attention was sometimes diverted by the exigencies of work. She was high strung and given to emotional expressiveness, while Mr. S. often tended to retreat to the safe confines of his inner ideation. At first glance, she seemed to be "dramatic," and he appeared to be excessively reserved and perhaps, even a bit "inhibited." Mrs. S. was lively and filled with verve. She broke away from her traditional, strict, Mediterranean family roots to marry Mr. S., whose heritage was Eastern European, with its emphasis on obedience, conformity, and achievement. He seemed to be low-keyed, mild-mannered and thoughtful, but not necessarily in touch with his feelings, while she seemed to be much more aware of and responsive to her inner feelings, but less able to contain them.

However, their work schedules and the heavy demands that they imposed on themselves by moving into a more expensive neighborhood than they had been in before placed considerable stress on both of them. Thus, when Raymond arrived, their family system was now threatened with becoming overtaxed and was susceptible to and in danger of being toppled. As long as they were able to operate together as a unit, they seemed to compliment each other quite nicely and were able to weather most storms. Mr. S. was able to remain calm, cool, and collected in times of stress, while Mrs. S. was able to be assertive, to take charge, and be decisive when action was needed.

Although Mr. S. often deferred to his wife when it came to decision-making, he had a number of respect-worthy ideas of his own. Unfortunately, he rarely voiced them. Nevertheless, they both recognized the centrality of their son's problems, along with their own issues, and were very cooperative, dedicated, and committed to therapy, so much so that both sought out and got involved in treatment for themselves, as time and their schedules permitted. Mr. and Mrs. S. came together once per month, as an adjunct to Raymond's therapy. In addition, Mr. S. came for group psychotherapy once a week, and Mrs. S. sought out individual therapy for herself on a once a week basis.

A developmental history was gathered over several sessions. For the most part, Raymond's developmental milestones did not seem to be out of the ordinary. If anything, he achieved most of his physical and cognitive landmarks considerably earlier than expected. However, he occasionally experienced nightmares and would shriek in the middle of the night, awakening his already overburdened and on-edge mother. Usually, at such moments, she was unable to soothe Raymond and, probably because her own exhausted state left her with limited emotional resources, she became frustrated with his screaming and often screamed back, in what appears to have been an impotent rage on her part. In the latter respect, Sylvia Brody (2009) sensitively observed:

> ...excessive or unprovoked punishment wounds the nascent ego of the child. Such blows may be felt only vaguely, yet they can affect the quality of the child's self-regard. Excessive or hasty punishment is likely to arouse confusion in the child as to whether he or she has done something wrong or is an unworthy person (p. 207).

In some of our monthly sessions, we discussed this and found effective ways in which Mrs. S. could learn to calm herself down and in turn, soothe Raymond. She was assiduous in implementing any suggestions that came out of our meetings, and when she put those suggestions into practice, a very curious thing happened. She discovered that more than once in a while they actually worked. Raymond was now able to return to sleep, and so was she. Of course after that happened, it should come as no surprise that Mrs. S. would then become an ardent devotee of psychotherapy.

PREPARING THE CHILD FOR PSYCHOTHERAPY

I have always felt that it is usually a good idea for a child to be prepped for coming to see "this strange doctor." So, before seeing Raymond, his parents and I discussed what they would tell him in order to help him get ready to come to see me. I have said elsewhere (2011) that there is a significant downside of not doing so:

> When a child is not told why he is being taken somewhere, the potential for all kinds of fantasies to occur (some of which are not necessarily calming) may increase.

Admittedly, fantasies are an integral, and an indisputably fundamental facet of growing up. However, in some cases where the thoughts lend themselves to a misperception of reality, it might be prudent to further the cause of "reality" by simply explaining to the youngster the reason for the visit. The reason ought to be predicated upon, and consistent with the reasons the parents sought treatment for the child in the first place. That is, when the parents let their child know that they are concerned that he gets into "trouble" (I recommend spelling out exactly what is meant in simple language in a concerned, kind, and compassionate tone of voice), the stage is set for the beginning of his/her learning cause and effect in a compassionate context. Simultaneous with this, structure and constancy is subtly introduced in terms of setting up an appointment, with the same person, in the same place, each time.

When I see the child for the first time, I routinely follow up with the child and ask if s/he knows the reason for coming to see me, if s/he knows who I am, and what it is that I do (all of the things that I previously had discussed with the parents). Even a child as young as Raymond was when he first came to see me (6 years-old), can understand a global description given by his parents like, "we're taking you to Dr. Seitler who likes to help children who sometimes have problems in school." So long as the child is aware of the difficulties s/he is having in school (or elsewhere) it is much easier for the child to apprehend the rationale behind the parents' concern and his visit to the doctor. It gives him a chance to orient him/herself or build a "handle" onto which he can hold. In the latter regard, if it is at all possible, it is important that the child be helped to recognize that his being brought in to see "the doctor" is not a punishment, but an attempt to help him deal more effectively with what is bothering him.

HOPE: A WEAPON, WHICH WORKS WONDERS WHEN WIELDED WISELY

Mr. and Mrs. S. took their "job" very seriously and were quite conscientious about properly carrying out their task of prepping Raymond for his first visit with me. They sat down with Raymond and explained to him that they were worried about him— because they could see from the way he behaved that something was upsetting him. They followed this by telling him that they had found someone with whom he could talk that would try to help him with whatever was upsetting him. Almost immediately after their conversation with Raymond, they called me to let me know that they had spoken with him and that everything was in place for me to meet and begin therapy with him. They added, that since their conversation, "he (Raymond) has been behaving like an angel." Sometimes the mere hope that things will get better helps improve things at least for a while, allowing for the real work to begin.

INITIAL MEETING WITH RAYMOND

Raymond came into my office accompanied by his mother, who introduced him to me. She assured Raymond that she would be in the waiting room until Raymond 's first meeting with me was over. Hesitantly, she then ushered him into my office. Raymond was a handsome-looking six-year old, who sported a full, thick head of shiny, auburn hair and a broad toothy grin. He appeared to be enthusiastic and at the same time wary about this novel situation into which he was entering. When Raymond came into my office, he looked up and down and back and forth, apparently in an effort to orient himself to this new circumstance, place, and person. He immediately told me that he wanted to make sure that his mother had remained and asked if he could leave the door open just a crack. Even before I could answer, he rapidly opened the door, stuck his head out, and checked to see if his mother was still in the waiting room. Even though Raymond saw that she was in the waiting room as promised, he still seemed to be somewhat restless throughout the session.

For much of our beginning relationship, Raymond needed to keep the door between my office and the waiting room slightly ajar, apparently to be certain that his mother would not disappear on him. While *his* separation anxieties were obvious, it became clear that they were also shared by his *mother*, who often insinuated herself into many of our sessions. On those occasions—which occurred mainly in the beginning phase of Raymond's overall treatment—I accommodated their mutual attachment needs and in fact, incorporated them into the therapy by making Mrs. S. into an instrumental part of the treatment interaction. During the times when she was present, I paid very close attention to what Raymond was like in relation to his mother, to me, and to both his mother and me. What he was doing, or saying, his facial appearance, what his posture was, or any clues that might help me understand what was going on inside of Raymond, all became grist for the mill. It invariably seemed as if Raymond's "connection," as it were, to his mother was somewhat ambivalent. On one hand, he clearly feared losing her, while on the other, it seemed as if he made every attempt he could to "break from her." While it is understandable why his basic needs for love, nurturing, food, shelter, clothing and protection required him to depend on his mother, it remained to be seen, as we proceeded, why he had what seemed like an equally intense need to disentangle himself from her.

Mrs. S. had positive attitudes about psychotherapy, which she seemed to convey to her son non-verbally. Ultimately, her trust for me transferred to Raymond and acted as a transitional object. As she grew more and more secure that her son would be safe being with me without her physical presence in the consulting room, she seemed to relax sufficiently and to feel comfortable enough to be able to separate from Raymond in our sessions. With my encouragement and assistance, she slowly weaned herself from attending the sessions. Correspondingly, over time, and as we began to understand what was underneath Raymond's overt behavior, the manifestations of Raymond's separation anxiety lessened. After approximately three months, Mrs. S. was generally able to entrust her son's safety to me and to remain in the waiting room. However, there still were occasions when she felt an urgent need to enter the session. Usually, this was when something untoward occurred that she wanted me to know about. At such moments, it was not sufficient for Mrs. S. to merely call me on the phone; she needed to speak with me in person.

As an interesting aside, it is worth noting that as much as Mrs. S. had rebelled against and seemingly broken away from her traditional upbringing, in many ways, she was still a captive of a childhood that emphasized close family ties, and particularly intensive involvement with one's children. Given those cultural circumstances—combined with whatever intrapsychic events that were operating in Mrs. S.—it was not surprising, nor unusual for her to have made herself part of the treatment process. But it was not so much her wish to be helpful that was noteworthy; her motivation was a desirable quality, as much as the intensity of her insistence along with the existence and degree of her incursions that were problematic.

This illuminates Raymond and his mother's interactional and dynamic symbiotic enmeshment and behavioral reactivity to and with each other. Quite possibly, this was a remake of his mother's own family constellation, in which someone was perceived as the good object. In this case, it seemed to be me, or, at least Mrs. S.'s idealized version of me. I was the one who was given the role of a "favored Uncle" and who was granted the privileged and idealized position of reverence, respect, and authority. And, if it was so that I was the Uncle (or some other good object), then I became the one who wore the mantle of *the adult.* Accordingly, she may have unconsciously experienced herself as a child in relation to me, and so, if Raymond had been perceived by his mother as a transferential object associated with an important authority figure from her childhood, then she—via the process of transferential regression—unconsciously becomes the child in relation to her son as well, or, more properly, the object that he represented to her. Under those circumstances, where would that leave Raymond? To briefly reiterate, Raymond thus becomes the embodiment of a negative transferential figure of Mrs. S. when she was but a child.

MORE ABOUT RAYMOND

Although Raymond was constantly in motion, he was never intentionally malicious. Rather, he was often cheerful, gregarious, exuberant, and, of course, a very animated youngster. Just as Raymond was unable to sit still in class for stretches at a time, he also was motorically active and unable to remain in one place in our early sessions (i.e., moving from the chair, to the sofa, to the armchair, and then back again). Even when seated, his legs were constantly flailing about. His difficulty staying in one place was even seen when using some of the games in my office that he selected to play with me. Instead, he would get up, walk around the room, and either change where he sat, or return to his original spot. I quietly took note of this, but, reasoning that many people have probably called this "restless" behavior to his attention on innumerable previous occasions (probably in unkind or critical ways), I decided not to comment on this at first. I could always return to it if it recurred on a regular basis, but at a later time, when rapport was fully established and the therapeutic alliance was solidly in place.

Right at the outset, Raymond was given the time-honored three options that I typically offer to children. I told him that (1) we could talk, (2) we could play games, or (3) we could talk and play games. Much like many children with whom I have worked, he elected to talk and play games. "Talk therapy" is helpful for children, as well as adults, but children sometimes struggle with identifying and then naming what it is they are feeling. For them, playing is a powerful, but non-threatening means of dealing with—and safely expressing—their inner and outer emotional worlds.

Nemiroff and Annunziata (1990) understood this quite well when they stated, "sometimes kids play their feelings better than talk about them" (p. 29). Winnicott (1971) built conceptual bridges between the infant's early objects (the mother and the breast) and transitional phenomena (i.e., those things that are somehow related to and/or stand in place of the primary objects). Included in this are the infant's internal responses to these objects and subsequent behavior, which involves playing with objects. In that sense, the very act of playing, all by itself, becomes a transitional activity.

For Winnicott, play is not a trivial matter, but an essential process by which the very action of the child learning to play enables mental life to proceed. Shakespeare also highlighted the importance of play. In, *As You Like It*, he affirmed how we are all players engaged in some form of play, plays, or playing, famously remarking:

> All the world's a stage. And all the men and women merely players; They have their exits and entrances. And one man in his time plays many parts (Act II, Scene VII).

TO PLAY OR NOT TO PLAY

Raymond was uncertain what to play with, and wound up going from item to item, quickly scanning each one before moving on to the next. Finally, he decided to play the "Candy Land™" game. We played this for a short while. When it no longer held his attention, he moved on to a different game. At first, he stayed with most games for only a short while, moving from one to the next with alacrity.

Although I typically provide children with a great deal of latitude, there is one thing that I uniformly insist on, albeit in a low-keyed manner. The way I work with each child is for both of us to play one game at a time. It is perfectly acceptable for the child to decide to discontinue a game at any time and for any reason. Nonetheless, before we move on to another game, my rule is that we close down and put away whatever we were working on. So, at those moments when Raymond started on another game, I would ask him if he was done with the one that was before us. If he said he was done, I would ask him to help put away that game, toy, and so on. Almost without exception, practically every child with whom I have ever worked has followed this regimen.

This is not simply an arbitrarily imposed condition for playing with the materials in the office; it is a subtle, yet integral part of the treatment. It helps the child develop and internalize a sense of structure; one built on uniform, unambiguous instructions, expectations, sameness, consistency, constancy, and boundary limits. As such, it helps children who either see or internally feel the world as chaotic develop a beginning sense of organization, efficacy, and security.

After the child assists in putting the games etc… away, I am openly grateful and consistently express my appreciation for their helpfulness in the clean up process. For those children who are so extremely chaotic that they are completely overwhelmed by the very prospect of *putting things back in order*, a different tactic must be employed. Fortunately, this was not the case with Raymond.

"NEXT TIME"

Once in a while, a child will be so caught up in the game that s/he does not want the "inconvenience" of stopping when the session ends. When that occurs, I commiserate with the child by expressing the desire aloud, as follows: "This is so much fun, I wish we could do this forever." Then I add, "It's a good thing that we will be able to do this again next time." The idea of a "next time" organically builds in a means by which the child can develop the ability to delay gratification, as well the capacity for hope. As we have learned from the developmental psychological work of Sylvia Brody and Sidney Axelrad (1978), excessive indulgence— much like over-protectiveness, is frequently related to parental compensation for self-reproach—and often results in the failure to nourish the child's capacity to postpone and tolerate frustration, which may be very much akin to the parent's own inability to delay gratification.

Eventually, Raymond became more engrossed in some of the games for longer periods of time. Even so, he could be easily distracted by noises from the street or just random sounds. Whenever he heard even a minute, ambient hum, his reaction was almost catastrophic. "What was that!" he would declare. Fortunately, when I gave him an answer that made sense to him, such as, "that sounded like a train to me; there's one that comes to this town at this time every day," he was able to calm down. In fact, at subsequent sessions, when the "train sound" recurred, he was able to announce, "That's the train, right?" He thus asked for, received, was able to internalize reassurance, and ultimately, was able to settle himself down. By virtue of "knowing" more about his environment, he was able to feel safe.

A REVEALING RIDDLE

Raymond had no problem however, finding ways to amuse himself. He was a very eager youngster, filled with verve and what seemed like very strong needs for interpersonal connection. So, when he lost interest in playing games, he merely talked, or became silly. Sometimes, he made up jokes. For example, he delighted himself with the following witty (and quite telling) riddle that he made up himself and which he returned to often over the course of therapy: "*What did the lonely boy eat?* Answer: *soul (sole) food.*" This is but one example of how bright and exceptionally creative Raymond was; yet so very isolated and lonely. All Raymond wanted to do was join in social activities and play with other children. However, perhaps because he was too rough with them in his exuberance, after awhile, they tended to avoid him. Time and again, whenever he experienced rejection, his feelings were hurt, he felt sad, became frustrated, and then aggressive. This began a cycle of what I call his *intense sociability sequence*, whereby after practically forcing his way into group situations he was repeatedly greeted with reproach. Understandably, this did not always go over very well, leaving him feeling rejected yet again. In an obvious bid for recognition, he then acted the "class clown;" made goofy faces, and so on. This was usually met with further rebuke, which in turn, led to more impulsive activity on his part. On and on went the sequence. Each time, resulting in rebuff and his feeling dejected.

Compounding this, Raymond's ensuing impulsive behavior was then seen as disruptive by his classmates and teacher alike, often prompting his teacher (or other authority figures) to remind him to "control himself," or failing that, to punish him by removing him from interactions with other kids. It seemed as if everyone told him what *not* to do, but not what he *could do* with his feelings. Merely curbing his inner feelings was as inadequate a solution as it was an impossible task. Simply put, it neither addressed nor resolved the underlying problem. As Brody (2009) insightfully reminded us:

> A child's early discontents that are unrelieved may propel the young child to erect close-to-consciousness defenses such as

avoiding, externalization, restriction, and some degrees of denial (p. 15).

She later added:

Naturally, when the poor tolerance of frustration and related be-haviors and affects are relieved in good time, development can proceed to an advancing of the child's capacity to develop an ob-serving ego. Then he or she can see the need to settle partially internalized conflicts with mother and father, and to reduce fears of losing parental love (p. 24).

WHEN DREYFUS ROARED

Raymond had been in treatment for slightly over a year when he came into the session more agitated than I had seen him in a long time. He seemed to be overwrought with fear. Despite this, he tried to let me know as best as he could in words, what had happened to create such inner turmoil. His words came at me almost as rapidly as a hockey puck heading straight for the goalie. I tried hard to field what he was saying, but what he said came so fast that it did not make sense at first. But, as I allowed myself to listen with even hovering attention without trying to apprehend anything, it all started to come together. As opposed to translating what Raymond was telling me by using my cognitive facul-ties, I allowed my thoughts and feelings to wander wherever they might in order to get an experience-near intuitive "sense" of what Raymond was experiencing and trying to communicate. Instead of the words getting in the way, I saw them as the mere conveyance by which I could form inner images which then might help me on a gut level more than my intellect ever could hope to achieve, to fully appreciate and subse-quently understand Raymond's inner experience.

He said, "I had a dream, a very very very bad dream. It was so bad that it scared me and I woke up and was afraid to go back to sleep. I said, it sounds like a nightmare. Nightmare's can be very scary." I asked, "Would you like to tell me about it, perhaps I can help? "It it it was very scary. I'm afraid," he stammered. "I know something about scary dreams, especially nightmares. Would it scare you if you talk about it with me here?"

Although he was quite shaken, Raymond agreed to tell me his dream. He spoke of a lion, named Dreyfus, "All of a sudden," said Raymond, "this great big lion appeared out of nowhere. He was roaring so loud that I thought the whole house was going to break apart and fall down. Then, I saw something else. I'm not sure what to call it. It looked like a big animal, kinda like a deer with horns, but much much bigger, and dark. The two were face-to-face. Then Dreyfus roared real loud and the other animal just put its head down. I thought the two of them were gonna fight and that it would be terrible, but the other animal put its head down and slowly toddled away" (did he mean toddled or trotted, or both, I wondered to myself?). "Then only Dreyfus was left and I felt like—what will save me— if Dreyfus sees me all by myself? I was so scared, but I could not cry out because Dreyfus would hear me. Then I woke up."

When I asked him to tell me more about what he was going through, he said, "I feel scared and sad." As with the clever "riddle" that Raymond had devised, once again the mythic theme reappears, of being alone with his feelings; this time laden with the prospect of imminent danger emanating out of the potential for aggression. In his dream, Raymond depicts himself as all alone and left to his own resources. He was frozen with terror and depressed.

In this dream, we see an imagistic representation of the nucleus of Raymond's symptom constellation, which stands as a coherent explanation of his so-called ADHD. Without interpreting the whole dream, which would go beyond the space available for this chapter, let me provide a brief overview. In the dream, Raymond is frozen and unable to take flight, whereas in real life taking flight is precisely what he does in the face of things that upset him. In short, the dream architecture builds on a combination of his feelings of agitation and depression, which emerges behaviorally in waking life as excessive motoric discharge of Raymond's impulses.

Rather than specifically working to curb his impulses, they needed to be understood and respected as necessary coping devices for his survival (flawed as they may have been). The object was not to take away Raymond's voice (i.e., his ability to cry out for help) or his ability to run away from perceived (or misperceived) danger. On the contrary, by encouraging Raymond to tell me his dream—in the safety of the consultation room—his feelings of inner agitation and sadness could be expressed, heard, worked through, and ultimately relieved. As part of the working through process, the aim was to help Raymond develop an observing ego, by which he could notice what he felt, and how he usually acted in reaction to those feelings, so that he could develop insight into, and subsequently modify his behavioral reactivity.

As time went on, Raymond's inner feelings slowly began to emerge and make themselves known verbally instead of motorically. Raymond increasingly improved his ability to move from action to conversation. As he became more and more aware of his inner turmoil, he became much more comfortable with, and adept at talking about his feelings, eventually learning to transform his reactions from action into observations, reflections, and conversation.

I REFUSE TO CRY

Flashing forward to one of our later sessions, Raymond revealed to me that he recalled crying a great deal as a young child, which is consistent with his mother and fathers' reports. He said, "I used to cry a lot, but now I never cry!" What struck me about this disclosure was the manner in which Raymond related this to me. Instead of figuratively "puffing up his chest" and proudly boasting of his achievement, his tone of voice seemed almost like a defiant refusal. When I asked him about never crying anymore, he vigorously insisted, "I will never cry again!" I asked him "how come?" What he said in reply greatly surprised me. "If I cried, and nobody cared I just wouldn't know what to do. I would feel all by myself like nobody loved me and I would be scared to death." "Just like in that dream you once told me, about Dreyfus?" Raymond looked up at me, almost quizzically, as if taken aback by the fact that someone had paid serious attention to him, to his words, and had regarded them as valuable and remembered them, and what is more, actually understood what he was saying, what he probably had been unable to say ever before. He teared up momentarily, but quickly wiped the moisture away from his eyes... "I guess you're not used to being listened to, except when you're angry or screaming, huh? His answer said it all. He replied, "nobody *ever* heard me if I wasn't mad! Then they heard me a lot, but I would be in big trouble. Great." "How *great* was it?" "Not very," came his reply. "First I would get scolded. Then punished. Then I would have to listen to a really long lecture about how I was upsetting the family and how much they sacrificed for me, and blah blah blah, you know." "I'm guessing that didn't make you feel all that terrific about yourself either." "I felt crummy." "I bet." "I mean, they would be fighting constantly, and that's okay, but if *I* make a commotion, it's the end of the world!" "Just doesn't seem fair does it," I said. "No, I hate it!" At the end of the session, I asked Raymond how he was feeling now? He said, "I feel much better now, thank you." "No thanks necessary. Your feelings are very important. I'm glad we have this chance to talk with each other, and that talking helps."

DOC, ARE YOU THERE?

Once, a session I normally have just before Raymond's ran about 10 minutes overtime. Raymond told me that when his session was supposed to start, I was nowhere in sight, he pressed his ear to my door. However, (because my office is sound-proofed), he heard only silence. He concluded that I was not there and that I had abandoned him. When I *finally* stepped out and brought Raymond into my office, he was not relieved. On the contrary, he was both sad and furious with me. "Why did you leave me, he loudly bellowed?" I knew that when Raymond felt furious, it was because he was filled with fear. In response to him, I neither retaliated nor recoiled. Rather, I sat with him until his emotional storm subsided. And when he had calmed down, I asked him if he wanted to talk about it? If he said "no," I was prepared to accept that he was not up to it just yet, and I would have reassured him that "it's sometimes difficult to talk about painful things and that we will talk when he was able to."

Fortuitously, he had accumulated enough ego strength (or desperation) to discuss his feelings. He did not seem to hold anything back. He verbally pummeled me with his anger about having been deserted by me, and how I was the one person who he always counted on, and now I too had let him down! Possibly for the first time in his life he was able to express his feelings openly, particularly his anger, without the fear (and actuality) of retaliation. Instead, his anger was validated and listened to respectfully, without defensiveness or turning the blame back on him, as had so often been the case in his life. I said, "how scary it must have been for you when you didn't hear any sound coming out of my office. No wonder you thought I was not there. Anyone would have come to that conclusion. I can see why you were so upset and disappointed. It was very important for you to see me. After finally learning to trust me, I was nowhere to be found. How could I leave you like that? What's wrong with me?"

At our next session, Raymond seemed a bit fearful for some reason. I asked him about it, but he was hesitant about responding. I wondered aloud if his unease was at all related to our previous session. He paused for a second, apparently unsure if he should reveal what he was feeling and thinking. I followed up by asking if he was worried? "He said, "yes," but did not continue. I reviewed the last session and said, "You were very angry with me. Is it possible that you are worried that I might get back at you?" "He said, a little bit." As we talked more and more about this, he disclosed that most people get mad at him very easily to begin with, and if he ever dared to *speak the truth to power*, so to speak, then he would dearly have to pay for it—either in the form of reproach, rebuke, or rejection. This was a terribly high price for any human being to pay, particularly a sensitive, vulnerable youngster. "How do you feel now that you told me this?" I asked. "I feel much better. I guess I should have known you wouldn't yell at me. You never have." I answered, I'm glad you told me. When two people are able to talk with each other about feelings, and listen to each other the way we do, there's usually a much better chance to work things out."

Ultimately, it came down to having patience and being able to work collaboratively with each other. Raymond and I had many conversations about the feelings he might have had on a number of occasions that were associated with waiting, having to postpone gratification, tolerate frustration, or endure suspense. My intent was to create an atmosphere for Raymond to feel safe and comfortable enough to be able to freely express his feelings or thoughts. He continued to learn how to speak up for himself in a manner that did not escalate the level of anger or precipitate a subsequent retaliation.

What was an interesting aftermath of this conversation is that at no point did Raymond act "wild," "out of control," "hyperactive" or even a little bit "agitated," all the descriptions that had been assigned to him prior to therapy. Instead, he was able to focus, think clearly, and formulate and describe what he was feeling inside, all in a reasonable, and even touching manner.

Before he was able to learn the *fine art of mutual, back and forth communication*, he had made himself known in a very loud, passionate, and unreserved manner. Now Raymond was starting to substitute speaking for acting, and in particular, speaking about his feelings. Instead of suppressing his inner urges, the emphasis on my part was to help him sublimate his energy into activities that would be meaningful, as well as enjoyable for Raymond. I felt that the more inter-relational dialogue we had, the better it would be for Raymond to be able to transform his action-orientation into a medium involving verbal exchange.

OVER TIME

The good news is that when a child is able to receive and remain in psychotherapy, we are blessed with having an opportunity to effect positive growth. Over time, and with hard work, the possibility increases decidedly for us to be able to form a relational connection, which then will enable us to collaboratively work at discerning whatever patterns might emerge and allow us to figure them out together. It is when this occurs, that significant changes often take place.

We invested considerable time and energy in our work together. And, it was over time that Raymond eventually discovered that my office was not the only place where he could get a fair hearing and that I was not the only person in the world who would be interested in or care about him. Where before, his social and emotional worlds had become severely constricted, now they were noticeably expanding. As Raymond learned to delay gratification, tolerate frustration, and modulate his impulses, he became less "needy" and less desperate about making—and keeping—friends and less intense in his relating to his friends. Raymond's gregarious, but not overdone, newly developed "nature" was now becoming a valuable asset to him, where before, the intensity and extent of his enthusiasm substantially contributed to his undoing.

ADHD's NEUROBIOCHEMICAL ETIOLOGY: "*IT AIN'T NECESSARILY SO*"

Before the term "Attention Deficit Hyperactive Disorder" (ADHD) was invented, a number of names preceded it, such as "minimal brain damage," "minimal brain dysfunction," "minimal cerebral dysfunction," "minimal cerebral insult," "hyperkinesis," until the present time and current nomenclature of ADHD became in vogue (Seitler, 2008b, 2006a). All these different designations beg the question: if the creators of the DSMs and ICDs got it right the first time, why was there such a need for so many revisions?

As Gershwin wrote, in Porgy and Bess (1935):

It ain't necessarily so
It ain't necessarily so
The t'ings dat yo' li'ble
To read in de Bible,
It ain't necessarily so.

In this case, the holy bibles are the multiple versions of the DSMs and ICDs, and the words of their prophets, who have repeatedly preached that ADHD has a neurobiochemical etiological origin. This raises a dilemma, one that is somewhat reminiscent of sophistry, both in terms of the illogical manner in which their claims are proffered as well as the veracity of their assertions.

416

For those who contend that ADHD has a neurological basis, the reasoning goes as follows: Although we see no hard neurological signs, ADHD *must be* neurological in origin because the behavior that it produces is behavior that is associated with neurological impairment, and thus, it could not be otherwise. Moreover, the behavior that we see in ADHD children had to have its origin in a child's faulty neurological makeup; otherwise it would not take place. This verbal slight of hand is an example of the logical fallacy of *circular reasoning*. If my father had said it, there would have been a twinkle in his eyes and it would have been a tongue-in-cheek statement.

Those in the biochemical camp claim that ADHD is the result of a biochemical imbalance. They rest their speculations on the fact that children labeled as ADHD "respond" to stimulant drugs. What they fail to explain, much less acknowledge, is the fact that non-ADHD children and adults respond similarly to stimulant drugs.

Unlike my father, the proponents of the neurological and the biochemical propositions are dead serious and absolutistic about their physical emphasis and reductionistic stance, even though there is no consistent evidence—that has withstood the test of time or replication—to support their conjectures. And, it is mainly because their position stresses the physical that they are married to a physiological solution, namely, the prescribing and administration of drugs.

The case of Raymond is not the only child that I have treated over several decades that has been labeled as ADHD (or any of the preceding labels that were once used). Like the others, he was treated successfully by means of psychodynamic psychotherapy, all without the use of medication.

As the case of Raymond readily reveals, a neurobiochemical substrate for ADHD is not a necessary explanation and thus is less relevant than we have been told. Moreover, what is significant is that medication was not essential in this case or any of the other cases that I have treated, that psychoanalytically informed psychotherapy can be successful in effecting change with youngsters labeled as ADHD, and, ultimately, it is the relationship that seems to be paramount in producing the conditions for nurturing transformative growth. Something that I wrote before, best summarizes my findings:

Practically all of the ADHD kids with whom I have worked have harbored a hidden inner sadness, which came out as hyperactivity. It is my view that the hyperactivity stemmed from sad feelings that were "bottled up" inside and which inexorably were expressed by the "court of last resort," the body—in the form of agitation and excessive motoric activity. (2011, p. 128).

And it is neither an accident nor is it a coincidence that soon after the sadness was gently revealed and carefully and patiently worked through, symptoms of Raymond's so-called ADHD faded away.

As an act of faith and courage (perhaps borne of desperation) on Raymond's part, I was granted the right of entry to Raymond's inner feelings of terror and depression. Along with such a privilege, comes the responsibility to handle such feelings delicately and with respect. Raymond needed (as all children do) to be treated as an individual rather than a diagnostic "entity." In addition, treating the feelings of a human being must be custom-fitted to each child's unique specifications. Therefore, formulaic manualized treatment approaches or medications will not effectively or safely be able to do more than suppress symptoms over time—if that. One (treatment) size cannot fit each individual's unique makeup and needs.

CONCLUDING STATEMENT

Summing up, it is important to ask what was instrumental in making Raymond's treatment successful? Again, I maintain that it was our relationship that made it work, our hard-earned trust and faith in each other (and in the process) that it would all turn out all right, along with painstaking, patient forbearance and working through Raymond's feelings of abandonment, sadness, and fear.

Ultimately, successful psychoanalytically oriented psychotherapy with Raymond renders the dual myths of organicity and biochemical imbalance causalities to be interesting, but irrelevant explanations and raises serious questions about whether stimulants are effective or even a safe modality for treating those children whose behavior is troublesome for adults.

REFERENCES

Arnold, L.E. (1996). Sex differences in ADHD: conference summary. J. Abnorm. Psychol. vol. 24, pp. 555-569.

Barkley, R. (1990). Fischer, M., Edelbrock, C., & Smallish, L. The adolescent outcomes of hyperactive children diagnosed by research criteria. I: An 8-year old prospective follow-up study. J. Am. Acad. Child Adol. Psychiat. vol. 29, pp. 546-557.

Baughman, F. (2006). The ADHD Fraud: How Psychiatry Makes Patients of Normal Children. Bloomington, IN: Trafford Publishers.

Baughman, F. (1993). Treatment of attention deficit disorder. JAMA, 269, p. 2368.

Breggin, P. & Breggin, G. (1995). The hazards of treating "Attention deficit/hyperactivity disorder" with methylphenidate (Ritalin). J. Coll. Student Psychother. vol. 10 (2), pp. 55-72.

Brody, S. (2009). Beginning to Grow: Five Studies. New York: International Psychoanalytic Books.

Brody, S. and Axelrad, S. (1978). Mothers, Fathers and Children. New York: International Universities Press.

Connors, K. (1998, Nov. 16-18). Overview of Attention Deficit Hyperactivity Disorder. NIH Consensus Development Conference: Diagnosis and Treatment of Attention Deficit Hyperactivity Disorder. Bethesda, MD, pp. 21-24.

Flaherty, L.T., Arroyo, W., Chatoor, I., Edwards, R.D., Ferguson, Y.B., et al. (2005). Brain Imagining and Child and Adolescent Psychiatry with Special Emphasis on SPECT. Retrieved on July 9, 2005, from: http://www.psych.org/psych_pract/clin_issues/populations/children/SPECT.pdf.

Foucault, M. (1972). The Archeology of Knowledge. [trans. A.M. Sheridan] New York: Pantheon Publishers Press.

Fraser, N. (1997). Justice Interruptus: Critical Reflections on the "Postsocialist" Condition. London: Routledge.

Furman, L. (2005). What is attention-deficit hyperactivity disorder (ADHD)? J. Child Neurol., 20, (12), pp. 994-1003.

Furman, L. (2002). Attention deficit/hyperactivity disorder: An alternative viewpoint. J. Int. Child Adol Psychiat, vol. 2, pp. 125-144.

Gaub, M. and Carlson, C.L. (1997). Gender differences in ADHD: a meta-analysis and critical review. J. Amer. Acad. Of Child and Adolescent Psychiat., 36, pp. 1036-1045.

Gershwin, G.and Gershwin, I. (1935). *It Ain't Necessarily So*, From the American Opera, Porgy and Bess. Music by George Gerwhin, Lyrics by Ira Gershwin.

Glenmullen, J. (2002). Prozac Backlash: Overcoming the Dangers of Prozac, Zoloft, Paxil, and Other Antidepressants with Safe, Effective Alternatives. NY: Touchstone Books.

Goldman, L.S., Generl, M., Bezman, R. and Slanetz, P. (1998). Diagnosis and treatment of attention deficit/hyperactivity disorder in children and adolescents. Council on Scientific Affairs, American Medical Association, JAMA, 279, pp. 1100-1107.

Graham, L J. (2005). Discourse analysis and the critical use of Foucault. Paper presented to the Australian Association. for Research in Education. Sydney.

Hallowell, E.M. and Ratey, J.J. (1994). Driven to Distraction: Recognizing and Coping with Attention Deficit Disorder from Childhood Through Adulthood. NY: Touchstone.

Henker, B. and Whalen, C. (1989). Hyperactivity and attention deficits. American Psychologist, vol 44, pp. 216-223.

Iosocrates (1980). Against the Sophists. In, George Narlin [Ed]. Cambridge, MA: Harvard University Press

Jachimowicz, G. & Geiselman, R. E. (2004). Comparison of ease of falsification of attention deficit hyperactivity disorder diagnosis using standard behavioral rating scales. Cognitive Science Online. vol. 2, pp. 6-20.

Jackson, G. (2009). Drug Induced Dementia: The Perfect Crime. Bloomington, IN: AuthorHouse Press.

Jackson, G. (2005). Rethinking Psychiatric Drugs: A Guide for Informed Consent. Bloomington, IN: AuthorHouse Press.

Jackson, G. (2006). A curious consensus: "Brain scans prove disease?" Ethical Human Psychology and Psychiatry, vol. 8 Number1, pp. 55-60.

Justman, S. (2015). Ethical Human Psychology and Psychiatry, vol. 17, number 2, pp. 135—144.

Kaye, S. (1994). The place of depression in dysfunctional learning. Psychoanal. Psychol., vol. 11, number 2, pp. 265-274.

Lambert, N. M. (2005). The contribution of childhood ADHD, conduct problems, and stimulant treatment to adolescent and adult tobacco and psychoactive substance abuse. Ethical Human Psychology and Psychiatry. vol. 7, number 3, pp. 197-221.

Lambert, N. M. (1998). Stimulant treatment as a risk factor for nicotine use and substance abuse. Overview of Attention Deficit Hyperactivity Disorder. NIH Consensus Development Conference: Diagnosis and Treatment of Attention Deficit Hyperactivity Disorder. Bethesda, MD, pp. 191-200.

Lambert, N.M. & Hartsough, C. (1998). Prospective study of tobacco smoking and substance dependence among samples of ADHD and non-ADHD subjects. J. Learn Disabil. (6), pp. 533-44.

Nemiroff, M.A. and Annunziata, J, (1990). A Child's First Book About Play Therapy. Washington, D.C.: American Psychological Association Publications.

Newnes, C. (2009). Clinical psychology and attention deficit hyperactivity disorder. In, S. Timimi and J. Leo [Eds.], Rethinking ADHD: From Brain to Culture (pp. 160-168). Basingstoke, UK: Palgrave MacMillan Publishers.

Raine, W. (2009, September). Western Australia Ministerial Implementation Committee for Attention Deficit Hyperactivity Disorder, Raine Attention Deficit Hyperactivity Disorder Study, Perth, Australia: Telethon Institute for Child Health Research.

Raine, W.(2010, January). Attention Deficit Hyperactivity Disorder Study: Draft—long-term outcomes associated with stimulant medication in the treatment of ADHD in children. Perth, Australia: Telethon Institute for Child Health Research.

Roth, A. and Fonagy, P. (2006). Who Works for Whom? A Critical Review of Psychotherapy Research (Second Edition). New York City: Guilford Publications.

Rosemond, J. K. and Ravenel, D. (2008). The Diseasing of America's Children: Exposing the ADHD Fiasco and Empowering Parents to Take Back Control. Nashville, TN: Thomas Nelson Publishers.

Schindler, D.C. (2008). Plato's Critique of Impure Reason: On Goodness and Truth in the Republic. Washington, DC: Catholic University of America Press.

Schore, D. (1991). Early superego development: The emergence of shame and narcissistic affect regulation in the practicing period. Psychoanalysis and Contemporary Thought, 14, (3), pp. 188-250.

Seitler, B.N. (2011). Is ADHD a real neurological disorder or collection of psychosocial symptomatic behaviors? Implications for treatment in the case of Randall E. J. Infant Child Adolescent. Psychotherapy, vol. 10, pp. 116-129.

Seitler, B.N. (2008a, October 10). Successful treatment of an adolescent without medication, ECT, or psychosurgery. Paper presented at the International Center for the Study of Psychiatry and Psychology conference, in Tampa, FL.

Seitler, B.N. (2008b). Successful child psychotherapy of ADHD: An agitated Depression explanation. Amer. J. of Psychoanal., vol. 68, pp. 276-294.

Seitler, B.N. (2007, July 7). An alternative explanation of ADD/ADHD involving agitated depression and an illustration of successful psychotherapy without using medication; paper presented to the Society for the Exploration of Psychotherapy Integration (SEPI) conference, in Lisbon, Portugal.

Seitler, B.N. (2006a). On the implications and consequences of a neurobiochemical etiology of ADHD. Ethical Human Psychology and Psychiatry, vol. 8, number 3, pp. 229-240.

Seitler, B.N. (2006b, January 29). Attention Deficit Hyperactive Disorder: Its neurobiological aetiology put to question. Presentation to the Philadelphia Society of Psychoanalytic Psychologists.

Shakespeare, W. (1848). As You Like It. Act II, scene VII. In, Shakespeare's Seven Age of Man. Van Voorst.

Watson, G.L., Arcona, A.P., and Antonuccio, D. (2015). The ADHD drug abuse on American college campuses. Ethical Human Psychology and Psychiatry. vol 17, number 1, pp. 5-21.

Weinberg, W.A., & Brumback, W. (1992). The myth of attention deficit-hyperactivity disorder: Symptoms resulting from multiple causes. J. Child Neuro. vol. 7, pp. 431-435.

Winnicott, D.O. (1971). Playing and Reality. London: Tavistock Publications.

BIOS

BURTON N. SEITLER, PH.D., is a Clinical Psychologist/Psychoanalyst in private practice. He is the Founder and Editor-in-Chief of the new journal named, J.A.S.P.E.R., which stands for the Journal for the Advancement of Scientific Psychoanalytic Empirical Research, published by International Psychoanalytic Books. For over 20 years, he was the Executive Director of the former Counseling And Psychotherapy Services center in Ridgewood and Oakland, NJ and the former Director of the Child Adolescent Psychotherapy Studies program of the New Jersey Institute for Training in Psychoanalysis (NJI). He currently serves as a Supervising Training Analyst and member of the faculty of NJI. In addition, Dr. Seitler is on the Editorial Board of the journal, Ethical Human Psychology and Psychiatry, and is on the Board of Directors of the International Society for Ethical Psychology and Psychiatry. Also, he is a Research Associate of the Psychohistory Forum. He has presented and published papers locally, as well as internationally, on psychosis, paranoia, ADHD, resilience, myopia, soma-psyche, the DSM, ethnic humor, and a number of other topics.

Burton Seitler and Kim Kleinman are the Co-Editors of this volume. Burton Seitler's bio appears above. Kim Kleinman's bio follows:

KIMBERLY S. KLEINMAN, LSCW, is an IPA Supervising and Training child/adolescent and adult psychoanalyst. She is the former chair of the child and adolescent program at the Psychoanalytic Training Institute of the Contemporary Freudian Society. She has been appointed as visiting faculty at the Wuhan Hospital for Psychotherapy in China, and is on the board and faculty of the Harlem Family Institute. Ms. Kleinman has a private practice in Manhattan and Riverdale. She has used her psychoanalytic skills in special education programs in the New York City public schools, pediatric offices, as director of a clinic for Transgender teens and young adults at St. Luke's Roosevelt Hospital, making home visits to new mothers, and helping children with fears about dental treatment. She has worked as part of a team to publish research concerning mother toddler interaction using video microanalysis. In addition, she speaks Spanish and is currently learning Chinese.